Lecture Notes in Computer Science 15344

Founding Editors

Gerhard Goos
Juris Hartmanis

AF168382

The series Lecture Notes in Computer Science (LNCS), including its subseries Lecture Notes in Artificial Intelligence (LNAI) and Lecture Notes in Bioinformatics (LNBI), has established itself as a medium for the publication of new developments in computer science and information technology research, teaching, and education.

LNCS enjoys close cooperation with the computer science R & D community, the series counts many renowned academics among its volume editors and paper authors, and collaborates with prestigious societies. Its mission is to serve this international community by providing an invaluable service, mainly focused on the publication of conference and workshop proceedings and postproceedings. LNCS commenced publication in 1973.

Albert Meroño Peñuela · Oscar Corcho ·
Paul Groth · Elena Simperl · Valentina Tamma ·
Andrea Giovanni Nuzzolese ·
Maria Poveda-Villalón · Marta Sabou ·
Valentina Presutti · Irene Celino ·
Artem Revenko · Joe Raad · Bruno Sartini ·
Pasquale Lisena
Editors

The Semantic Web: ESWC 2024 Satellite Events

Hersonissos, Crete, Greece, May 26–30, 2024
Proceedings, Part I

 Springer

Editors
Albert Meroño Peñuela (ID)
King's College London
London, UK

Oscar Corcho (ID)
Universidad Politécnica de Madrid
Madrid, Spain

Paul Groth (ID)
University of Amsterdam
Amsterdam, Noord-Holland, The Netherlands

Elena Simperl (ID)
King's College London
London, UK

Valentina Tamma (ID)
University of Liverpool
Liverpool, UK

Andrea Giovanni Nuzzolese (ID)
National Research Council
Bologna, Italy

Maria Poveda-Villalón (ID)
Universidad Politécnica de Madrid
Madrid, Spain

Marta Sabou (ID)
Vienna University of Economics
and Business
Vienna, Austria

Valentina Presutti (ID)
University of Bologna
Bologna, Italy

Irene Celino (ID)
Cefriel - Politecnico Di Milano
Milan, Italy

Artem Revenko (ID)
Semantic Web Company
Vienna, Austria

Joe Raad (ID)
University of Paris-Saclay
Gif-sur-Yvette, France

Bruno Sartini (ID)
Ludwig-Maximilians-Universität München
Munich, Germany

Pasquale Lisena (ID)
EURECOM
Biot, France

ISSN 0302-9743   ISSN 1611-3349 (electronic)
Lecture Notes in Computer Science
ISBN 978-3-031-78951-9   ISBN 978-3-031-78952-6 (eBook)
https://doi.org/10.1007/978-3-031-78952-6

Preface

This volume contains the satellite proceedings of the 21st edition of the European Semantic Web Conference (ESWC 2024). ESWC is a major venue for discussing the latest in scientific results and innovations related to the semantic web, knowledge graphs, and web data. This year we aimed at acknowledging recent developments in AI with a special tagline, "Fabrics of Knowledge: Knowledge Graphs and Generative AI". The satellite events are an important aspect of facilitating the main conference discussion as well as fundamental questions about how we acquire, represent, use, and interact with knowledge in the advent of Generative AI and large language models.

To reflect this year's special topic, the satellite events of ESWC 2024 featured a Special Track on Large Language Models for Knowledge Engineering, in addition to the poster and demo session, the PhD symposium, the industry track, project networking, and workshops and tutorials. Due to scheduling, the papers from these events are published as post-proceedings.

The Special Track on Large Language Models for Knowledge Engineering provided a venue for scientific discussion and community building for early work on this exciting new area of research. The track had 52 submissions, demonstrating the importance of research in this direction, of which 10 were accepted. In addition to the accepted papers, the track had a community discussion session that synthesised and mapped directions forward in this area.

The poster and demo track received 51 submissions of which 17 posters and 20 demos were accepted. All submissions received 2 to 3 reviews. Posters and demos highlight new research trajectories and ideas within the community and allow for discussions of the latest results. Here, we see topics such as ontologies, knowledge graph, multi-modality, domain application, methods for dealing with data sources, and advances in semantic technologies and machine learning.

The PhD symposium is an important venue for doctoral students to present and receive feedback on their research. In total, 18 submissions were received, of which 14 papers were accepted. Both the review and guidance processes were intensive and tailored to helping the students to improve their research plans. This included 3 reviews for each paper as well as peer review by the students themselves. Additionally, all papers were guided by mentors who are senior members of the community. Importantly, senior members of the community attended each presentation to give in-depth feedback. The symposium also featured a social event for students only aimed at facilitating networking among new community members.

The industry track featured papers that discuss the adoption and usage of semantic technologies within organisations. Importantly, papers must have a co-author with a non-academic affiliation. We received 10 submissions of which 7 were accepted. All papers received between 3 and 6 reviews. The industry track featured papers from a wide variety of organisations including Siemens, DATEV, Munich Airport, Dun & Bradstreet,

Beamery, AddQual, and PANTOPIX. Topics included scalability of semantic technologies in real-world cases, the application of knowledge graphs to product management systems and value chains, FAIR and dataset management, and combining knowledge graphs with large language models for ontology modelling, knowledge extraction, and rule optimisation. The accepted papers cover concrete scenarios from a broad range of industries and markets, including manufacturing, industrial IoT, transportation, product data, sales and supply chain, smart building, and human resources.

ESWC 2024 featured a record-breaking selection of 16 workshops and 2 tutorials covering topics ranging from knowledge graph construction to deep learning with knowledge graphs. Workshops and tutorial highlights were summarised in a main conference presentation, describing their outcomes to the entire community, and highlighting the impact of generative AI and large language models in their contributions. Later in this volume you will find a selection of the best papers from the workshops, which have been extended and fast-tracked to be hosted in the ESWC satellite proceedings.

While not formally part of the proceedings, ESWC has a history of providing network opportunities for projects and in particular EU projects. We would like to thank Cassia Trojahn and Sabrina Kirrane for organising this part of the program for this year.

April 2024

Albert Meroño Peñuela
Oscar Corcho
Paul Groth
Elena Simperl
Valentina Tamma
Andrea Giovanni Nuzzolese
Maria Poveda-Villalón
Marta Sabou
Valentina Presutti
Irene Celino
Artem Revenko
Joe Raad
Bruno Sartini
Pasquale Lisena

Organization

General Chair

Albert Meroño Peñuela   King's College London, UK

Research Track Program Chairs

Anastasia Dimou   KU Leuven, Belgium
Raphaël Troncy   EURECOM, France

Resource Track Program Chairs

Mehwish Alam   Télécom Paris, Institut Polytechnique de Paris, France
Heiko Paulheim   University of Mannheim, Germany

In-Use Track Program Chairs

Olaf Hartig   Linköpings Universitet, Sweden
Maribel Acosta   Ruhr University Bochum, Germany

Special Track on Large Language Models for Knowledge Engineering

Oscar Corcho   Universidad Politécnica de Madrid, Spain
Paul Groth   University of Amsterdam, Netherlands
Elena Simperl   King's College London, UK
Valentina Tamma   University of Liverpool, UK

Workshops and Tutorials Chairs

Joe Raad   Paris-Saclay University, France
Bruno Sartini   Ludwig-Maximilians University of Munich,
                                     Germany

Poster and Demo Chairs

Andrea Nuzzolese   ISTC-CNR, Italy
María Poveda-Villalón   Universidad Politécnica de Madrid, Spain

PhD Symposium Chairs

Marta Sabou   Vienna University of Economics and Business,
                                     Austria
Valentina Presutti   University of Bologna, Italy

Industry Track Program Chairs

Irene Celino   Cefriel, Italy
Artem Revenko   Semantic Web Company GmbH, Austria

Sponsorship

Nitisha Jain   King's College London, UK
Jan-Christoph Kalo   University of Amsterdam, Netherlands

Project Networking

Cassia Trojahn   IRIT, France
Sabrina Kirrane   WU Vienna, Austria

Web and Publicity

Stefano De Giorgis	University of Bologna, Italy
Tabea Tietz	FIZ Karlsruhe, Germany

Proceedings and Conference Metadata

Pasquale Lisena	EURECOM, France

Program Committee

Nora Abdelmageed	Friedrich-Schiller-Universität Jena, Germany
Ghadeer Abuoda	Aalborg University, Denmark
Maribel Acosta	TU Munich, Germany
Shqiponja Ahmetaj	TU Wien, Austria
Aljbin Ahmeti	Semantic Web Company GmbH and TU Wien, Austria
Mehwish Alam	Télécom Paris, France
Céline Alec	Université de Caen-Normandie, France
Vladimir Alexiev	Ontotext Corp., Bulgaria
Panos Alexopoulos	Textkernel B.V., Netherlands
Alsayed Algergawy	University of Jena, Germany
Reham Alharbi	University of Liverpool, UK
Bradley Allen	University of Amsterdam, Netherlands
Doerthe Arndt	TU Dresden, Germany
Natanael Arndt	eccenca GmbH, Germany
Luigi Asprino	University of Bologna, Italy
Ghislain Auguste Atemezing	ERA, France
Maurizio Atzori	University of Cagliari, Italy
Sören Auer	TIB Leibniz Information Center for Science and Technology, Germany and University of Hannover, Germany
Carlos Badenes-Olmedo	Universidad Politécnica de Madrid, Spain
Booma Sowkarthiga Balasubramani	University of Illinois at Chicago, USA
Konstantina Bereta	National and Kapodistrian University of Athens, Greece
Abraham Bernstein	University of Zurich, Switzerland
Russa Biswas	Hasso Plattner Institute, Germany
Christian Bizer	University of Mannheim, Germany

Jennifer D'Souza	TIB Leibniz Information Centre for Science and Technology University Library, Germany
Enrico Daga	Open University, UK
Jérôme David	Inria, France
Jacopo de Berardinis	King's College London, UK
Victor de Boer	Vrije Universiteit Amsterdam, Netherlands
Stefano De Giorgis	Alma Mater University of Bologna, Italy
Ben De Meester	Ghent University, Belgium
Daniele Dell'Aglio	Aalborg University, Denmark
Gianluca Demartini	University of Queensland, Australia
Elena Demidova	University of Bonn, Germany
Kathrin Dentler	Triply, Netherlands
Danilo Dessì	GESIS – Leibniz Institute for the Social Sciences, Germany
Gayo Diallo	University of Bordeaux, France
Stefan Dietze	GESIS – Leibniz Institute for the Social Sciences, Germany
Dimitar Dimitrov	GESIS – Leibniz Institute for the Social Sciences, Germany
Anastasia Dimou	KU Leuven, Belgium
Christian Dirschl	Wolters Kluwer Germany, Germany
Daniil Dobriy	Vienna University of Economics and Business, Austria
Milan Dojchinovski	Czech Technical University in Prague, Czech Republic
Ivan Donadello	Free University of Bozen-Bolzano, Italy
Mauro Dragoni	Fondazione Bruno Kessler, Italy
Kai Eckert	Mannheim University of Applied Sciences, Germany
Vasilis Efthymiou	Harokopio University of Athens, Greece
Shusaku Egami	National Institute of Advanced Industrial Science and Technology, Japan
Fajar J. Ekaputra	Vienna University of Economics and Business (WU), Austria
Vadim Ermolayev	Ukrainian Catholic University, Ukraine
Paola Espinoza Arias	Universidad Politécnica de Madrid, Spain
Lorena Etcheverry	Universidad de la República, Uruguay
Pavlos Fafalios	Technical University of Crete and FORTH-ICS, Greece
Alessandro Faraotti	IBM, Italy
Catherine Faron	Université Côte d'Azur, France
Anna Fensel	Wageningen University and Research, Netherlands

Veronika Heimsbakk	Capgemini, Norway
Nicolas Heist	University of Mannheim, Germany
Lars Heling	Stardog Union, Germany
Nathalie Hernandez	IRIT, France
Daniel Herzig	metaphacts GmbH, Germany
Ryohei Hisano	ETH Zurich, Switzerland
Pascal Hitzler	Kansas State University, USA
Rinke Hoekstra	Elsevier, Netherlands
Aidan Hogan	Universidad de Chile, Chile
Andreas Hotho	University of Würzburg, Germany
Wei Hu	Nanjing University, China
Thomas Hubauer	Siemens AG Corporate Technology, Germany
Andreea Iana	University of Mannheim, Germany
Luis Ibanez-Gonzalez	University of Southampton, UK
Ana Iglesias-Molina	Universidad Politécnica de Madrid, Spain
Filip Ilievski	Vrije Universiteit Amsterdam, Netherlands
Antoine Isaac	Europeana & Vrije Universiteit Amsterdam, Netherlands
Hajira Jabeen	GESIS – Leibniz Institute for the Social Sciences, Germany
Nitisha Jain	King's College London, UK
Mustafa Jarrar	Birzeit University, Palestine
Ernesto Jimenez-Ruiz	City, University of London, UK
Milos Jovanovik	Ss. Cyril and Methodius University in Skopje, N. Macedonia
Simon Jupp	Elsevier, Netherlands
Jan-Christoph Kalo	University of Amsterdam, Netherlands
Eduard Kamburjan	University of Oslo, Norway
Maulik R. Kamdar	Optum Health, USA
Katariina Kari	Inter IKEA Systems B.V., Finland
Tomi Kauppinen	Aalto University, Finland
Mayank Kejriwal	University of Southern California, USA
Natthawut Kertkeidkachorn	Japan Advanced Institute of Science and Technology, Japan
Ali Khalili	Deloitte, Netherlands
Sabrina Kirrane	Vienna University of Economics and Business, Austria
Tomas Kliegr	Prague University of Economics and Business, Czech Republic
Matthias Klusch	DFKI, Germany
Haridimos Kondylakis	Institute of Computer Science, FORTH, Greece
George Konstantinidis	University of Southampton, UK

Stasinos Konstantopoulos	NCSR Demokritos, Greece
Roman Kontchakov	Birkbeck, University of London, UK
Manolis Koubarakis	National and Kapodistrian University of Athens, Greece
Kozaki Kouji	Osaka Electro-Communication University, Japan
Maria Koutraki	Leibniz Universität Hannover, Germany
Anelia Kurteva	TU Delft, Netherlands
Tobias Käfer	Karlsruhe Institute of Technology, Germany
Birgitta König-Ries	Friedrich Schiller University of Jena, Germany
Jose Emilio Labra Gayo	Universidad de Oviedo, Spain
Frederique Laforest	INSA Lyon, France
Sarasi Lalithsena	IBM Watson, USA
Andre Lamurias	NOVA School of Science and Technology, Portugal
Davide Lanti	Free University of Bozen-Bolzano, Italy
Danh Le Phuoc	TU Berlin, Germany
Maxime Lefrançois	École des Mines de Saint-Étienne, France
Huanyu Li	Linköping University, Sweden
Sven Lieber	Royal Library of Belgium (KBR), Belgium
Stephan Linzbach	GESIS – Leibniz Institute for the Social Sciences, Germany
Anna-Sofia Lippolis	University of Bologna and ISTC-CNR, Italy
Pasquale Lisena	EURECOM, France
Wenqiang Liu	Xi'an Jiaotong University, China
Giorgia Lodi	Istituto di Scienze e Tecnologie della Cognizione (CNR), Italy
Vanessa Lopez	IBM, Ireland
Pierre Maillot	Inria, France
Maria Maleshkova	Helmut-Schmidt-Universität/Universität der Bundeswehr Hamburg, Germany
Maria Vanina Martinez	IIIA-CSIC, Spain
Miguel A. Martinez-Prieto	University of Valladolid, Spain
Jose L. Martinez-Rodriguez	Autonomous University of Tamaulipas, Mexico
Patricia Martín-Chozas	Universidad Politécnica de Madrid, Spain
Edgard Marx	Leipzig University of Applied Sciences (HTWK), Germany
Philipp Mayr	GESIS – Leibniz Institute for the Social Sciences, Germany
Jamie McCusker	Rensselaer Polytechnic Institute, USA
Lionel Medini	CNRS, France
Albert Meroño-Peñuela	King's College London, UK
Franck Michel	Université Côte d'Azur, CNRS, I3S, France
Nandana Mihindukulasooriya	IBM Research AI, USA

Cogan Shimizu   Wright State University, USA
Pavel Shvaiko   Informatica Trentina, Italy
Lucia Siciliani   University of Bari, Italy
Leslie Sikos   Edith Cowan University, Australia
Gerardo Simari   Universidad Nacional del Sur and CONICET,
                              Argentina
Elena Simperl   King's College London, UK
Hala Skaf-Molli   University of Nantes, France
Blerina Spahiu   University of Milano-Bicocca, Italy
Marc Spaniol   Université de Caen-Normandie, France
Kavitha Srinivas   IBM, USA
Steffen Staab   University of Stuttgart, Germany
Bram Steenwinckel   Ghent University, Belgium
Kostas Stefanidis   Tampere University, Finland
Nadine Steinmetz   University of Applied Sciences Erfurt, Germany
Armando Stellato   University of Rome Tor Vergata, Italy
Simon Steyskal   Siemens AG Österreich, Austria
Lise Stork   Vrije Universiteit Amsterdam, Netherlands
Umberto Straccia   ISTI-CNR, Italy
Chang Sun   Maastricht University, Netherlands
Zequn Sun   Nanjing University, China
Vojtěch Svátek   Prague University of Economics and Business,
                              Czech Republic
Ruben Taelman   Ghent University, Belgium
Yousouf Taghzouti   École des Mines de Saint-Étienne, France
Valentina Tamma   University of Liverpool, UK
Olivier Teste   IRIT, France
Krishnaprasad Thirunarayan Wright State University, USA
Elodie Thiéblin   Logilab, France
Ilaria Tiddi   Vrije Universiteit Amsterdam, Netherlands
Tabea Tietz   FIZ Karlsruhe, Germany
Konstantin Todorov   University of Montpellier, France
Ioan Toma   STI Innsbruck, Austria
Riccardo Tommasini   INSA Lyon, France
Sebastian Tramp   eccenca GmbH, Germany
Trung-Kien Tran   Bosch Center for Artificial Intelligence, Germany
Cassia Trojahn   IRIT, France
Raphaël Troncy   EURECOM, France
Yannis Tzitzikas   University of Crete and FORTH-ICS, Greece
Jürgen Umbrich   Vienna University of Economy and Business
                              (WU), Austria
Ricardo Usbeck   Leuphana University Lüneburg, Germany

Marieke van Erp	KNAW Humanities Cluster, Netherlands
Frank Van Harmelen	Vrije Universiteit Amsterdam, Netherlands
Miel Vander Sande	Meemoo, Belgium
Guillermo Vega-Gorgojo	Universidad de Valladolid, Spain
Ruben Verborgh	Ghent University, Belgium
Maria-Esther Vidal	TIB, Germany
Serena Villata	CNRS, France
Fabio Vitali	University of Bologna, Italy
Domagoj Vrgoc	Pontificia Universidad Católica de Chile, Chile
Kewen Wang	Griffith University, Australia
Ruijie Wang	University of Zurich, Switzerland
Xander Wilcke	Vrije Universiteit Amsterdam, Netherlands
Honghan Wu	King's College London, UK
Zhe Wu	eBay, USA
Josiane Xavier Parreira	Siemens AG Österreich, Austria
Guohui Xiao	University of Bergen, Norway
Nadia Yacoubi Ayadi	Université Claude Bernard Lyon1, France
Fouad Zablith	American University of Beirut, Lebanon
Hamada Zahera	Paderborn University, Germany
Ondřej Zamazal	Prague University of Economics and Business, Czech Republic
Xiaowang Zhang	Tianjin University, China
Ziqi Zhang	Accessible Intelligence, UK
Yihang Zhao	King's College London, UK
Antoine Zimmermann	École des Mines de Saint-Étienne, France
Sara Zuppiroli	ISTC-CNR, Italy
Hanna Ćwiek-Kupczyńska	University of Luxembourg, Luxembourg
Kārlis Čerāns	University of Latvia, Latvia

Additional Reviewers

Akaichi, Ines
Antakli, Andre
Babaei Giglou, Hamed
Bruns, Oleksandra
Cardellino, Cristian
Cintra, Paul
D'Adda, Fabio
Djeddi, Warith Eddine
Efthymiou, Vasilis
Fanourakis, Nikolaos
Fischer, Elisabeth

Gaur, Manas
Gautam, Nikita
Gui, Zhou
Inizan, Olivier
Kommineni, Vamsi Krishna
Lippolis, Anna Sofia
Mahdavinejad, Mohammad Saeid
Martín Chozas, Patricia
Montiel-Ponsoda, Elena
Morales Tirado, Alba Catalina
Nayyeri, Mojtaba

Olivier, Inizan
Omeliyanenko, Janna
Ondraszek, Sarah Rebecca
Patkos, Theodore
Peng, Yiwen
Pons, Gerard
Qu, Yuanwei
Ragazzi, Luca
Raoufi, Ensiyeh
Ratta, Marco
Ringwald, Célian

Saki Norouzi, Sanaz
Samuel, Sheeba
Schlör, Daniel
Schraudner, Daniel
Shao, Chen
Soulard, Thibaut
van der Weijden, Daniel
Viviurka Do Carmo, Paulo Ricardo
Xiong, Bo
Yumusak, Semih
Zuppiroli, Sara

Sponsors

Platinum Sponsors

VideoLectures.NET is an award-winning free and open access educational video lectures repository. The lectures are given by distinguished scholars and scientists at the most important and prominent events like conferences, summer schools, workshops and science promotional events from many fields of Science. The portal is aimed at promoting science, exchanging ideas and fostering knowledge sharing by providing high quality didactic contents not only to the scientific community but also to the general public. All lectures, accompanying documents, information and links are systematically selected and classified through the editorial process taking into account also users' comments.

Gold Sponsors

Ontotext is a global leader in enterprise knowledge graph technology and semantic database engines. Ontotext employs big knowledge graphs to enable unified data access and cognitive analytics via text mining and integration of data across multiple sources. Ontotext™ engine and Ontotext Platform power business critical systems in the biggest banks, media, market intelligence agencies, car and aerospace manufacturers. Ontotext technology and solutions are spread wide across the value chain of the most knowledge intensive enterprises in financial services, publishing, healthcare, pharma, manufacturing and public sectors. Leveraging AI and cognitive technologies, Ontotext helps enterprises get competitive advantage, by connecting the dots of their proprietary knowledge and putting in the context of global intelligence.

Silver Sponsors

Springer is part of Springer Nature, a leading global research, educational and professional publisher, home to an array of respected and trusted brands providing quality content through a range of innovative products and services. Springer Nature is the world's largest academic book publisher, publisher of the world's most influential journals and a pioneer in the field of open research. The company numbers almost 13,000 staff in over 50 countries and has a turnover of approximately €1.5 billion. Springer Nature was formed in 2015 through the merger of Nature Publishing Group, Palgrave Macmillan, Macmillan Education and Springer Science+Business Media.

Founded over 350 years ago, the **University of Innsbruck** today is the most important research and educational institution in western Austria, offering a wide range of programmes across all disciplines. Located in the heart of the Alps, it offers 28,000 students and 5,500 employees the best conditions.

Bronze Sponsors

metaphacts is a German software company that empowers customers to drive knowledge democratization and decision intelligence using knowledge graphs. Built entirely on open standards and technologies, our product metaphactory delivers a low-code, FAIR

Data platform that supports collaborative knowledge modeling and knowledge generation and enables on-demand citizen access to consumable, contextual and actionable knowledge. metaphacts serves customers in areas such as life sciences and pharma, engineering and manufacturing, finance and insurance, retail, cultural heritage, and more. For more information about metaphacts and its products and solutions please visit www. metaphacts.com.

eccenca Corporate Memory is cutting-edge Knowledge Graph technology. It digitally captures the expertise of knowledge workers so that it can be accessed and processed by machines. The fusion of human knowledge with large amounts of data, coupled with the computing power of machines, results in powerful artificial intelligence that enables companies to execute existing processes as well as innovation projects of all kinds at high speed and low cost. And it creates an impressive competitive advantage.

Through eccenca.my you can register and create a eccenca Corporate Memory Community Edition Sandbox for evaluation. Join pioneers like BOSCH, SIEMENS, Astra Zeneca and many other global market leaders – our world-class team of Linked Data Experts is ready when you are.

Contents – Part I

Industry

Posters and Demos

Contents – Part II

Extended Best Papers from the Workshops

Special Track on Large Language Models for Knowledge Engineering

The Role of Generative AI in Competency Question Retrofitting

Reham Alharbi(✉)📵, Valentina Tamma📵, Floriana Grasso📵,
and Terry R. Payne📵

University of Liverpool, Liverpool, UK
{R.Alharbi,V.Tamma,Floriana,T.R.Payne}@Liverpool.ac.uk

Abstract. Competency Questions (CQs) are essential in ontology engineering; they express an ontology's functional requirements as natural language questions, offer crucial insights into an ontology's scope and are pivotal for various tasks, e.g. ontology reuse, testing, requirement specification, and pattern definition. Despite their importance, the practice of publishing CQs alongside ontological artefacts is not commonly adopted. We propose an approach based on Generative AI, specifically Large Language Models (LLMs) for retrofitting CQs from existing ontologies and we study how the control parameters in two LLMs (i.e. `gpt-3.5-turbo` and `gpt-4`) affect their performance and investigate the interplay between prompts and configuration for retrofitting viable CQs.

Keywords: Competency Questions · Large Language Models · Ontology Engineering Methodologies

1 Introduction

Competency Questions (CQs) [9] are natural language questions characterising the scope of knowledge represented by an ontology. They model the functional requirements that an ontology or ontology-based information system should satisfy to achieve its intended purpose.

Within the early stages of ontology development, they can be used to suggest possible concepts and relationships the ontology should model [15,20,21,23,25], and can also be used in subsequent phases to verify and validate the knowledge encapsulated in the ontology [5,10]. However, as it is not always possible to obtain the original CQs when working with many existing ontologies, the `RETROFIT-CQs` approach was proposed [1] to automatically generate candidate CQs from ontology triples by leveraging Large Language Models (LLMs). This work represented a significant shift towards a hybrid model of knowledge representation, merging explicit and parametric knowledge [4,18]. Although an initial analysis (conducted across various ontologies from the CORAL repository [8]) confirmed that CQs could not only be generated, but that they also closely matched the intended design CQs; a number of research questions remained regarding the nuances of LLMs, particularly regarding the research question:

© The Author(s), under exclusive license to Springer Nature Switzerland AG 2025
A. Meroño Peñuela et al. (Eds.): ESWC 2024, LNCS 15344, pp. 3–13, 2025.
https://doi.org/10.1007/978-3-031-78952-6_1

To what extent do the control parameters, such as creativity settings and the specificity of prompts, affect the performance of RETROFIT-CQs? This question is addressed by evaluating two hypotheses: that additional context specified in the LLM prompt will enhance model comprehension and response accuracy; and that more robust and reliable CQs can be obtained by reducing the creativity parameter (i.e. *temperature*) of the LLMs, as defined in GPT API documentation.[1]

We investigate these hypotheses by examining the resulting efficacy of our RETROFIT-CQs approach. In particular, the parameters' effect on the stochasticity of LLM-generated text was analysed, by evaluating its default and deterministic settings, together with the influence that different prompts (i.e. the natural language texts used for communicating with LLMs) has on the resulting CQs. We run a comparative analysis of the generated CQs against those found in existing benchmarks, e.g. CORAL [8] and the CQs dataset in [26]. The study confirms the first hypothesis; that the addition of context within the prompts can result in a more precise and coherent LLM response. However, contrary to our expectations, the second hypothesis was not supported. Our findings suggest that the overall performance of the LLMs, when used by our RETROFIT-CQs approach, is robust and replicable, exhibiting only marginal stochasticity when changing the control parameters (including changes to the creativity parameter, prompt, and even choice of LLM).

The paper is structured as follows: the use of LLMs is briefly discussed in Sect. 2, before detailing the methodology used (including a brief outline of the RETROFIT-CQs approach) in Sect. 3. The results are presented in Sect. 4, and we summarise our conclusions and outline future research directions in Sect. 5.

2 Background

Large Language Models (LLMs) have shown promise for a plethora of tasks, including the automatic generation of natural language questions [14]. Autoregressive LLMs such as those in the GPT family [16] are deep learning models trained on vast data corpora, and are used to predict the next word in a sequence based on the previous context. Through their use, a new text generation paradigm has emerged whereby a 'prompt' guides the generation of various outputs [14]. These prompts, consisting of strings prepended to the input context, incorporate control elements (such as keywords) to guide the text generation [13]. Initial research has already investigated the significant impact of different prompt designs on the performance and outputs of LLMs [24], effectively laying the groundwork for the field of prompt engineering [13]. Despite the impressive capability that LLMs have to produce syntactically correct and complex natural language, ensuring that this output is meaningful and accurate remains a challenge [3]. A more nuanced view suggests that LLMs, when combined with traditional symbolic approaches, can play a vital role in knowledge engineering workflows, leading to a new era in knowledge representation that

---

[1] https://platform.openai.com/docs/api-reference/chat/create.

merges explicit and parametric knowledge [2,3]. The effectiveness of these methods must be validated by addressing LLM-related challenges such as expressivity vs decidability [18], thoroughly evaluating approaches that incorporate LLM components [4], and tackling issues stemming from insufficient information about LLMs, including their reliability and replicability [12].

3   Experimental Setup

The RETROFIT-CQs approach [1] we propose generates candidate CQs by utilising a pipeline that consists of three phases: (i) extract triples from the ontology to represent its statements; (ii) generate an LLM prompt by integrating the triples into a template that also includes contextual cues; and (iii) filter the resulting questions generated by the LLM to remove duplicates and irrelevant questions. In this study, we investigate the impact on the quality of the candidate CQs by investigating the role of various zero-shot prompts and the influence that different creativity parameter settings have on CQ generation, by comparing deterministic and default values. This directly relates to the two hypotheses identified in Sect. 1:

- *Hypothesis 1: Prompting an LLM with more contextual information results in the generation of more concise and coherent responses.*
  This hypothesis stems from the premise that additional relevant information could enhance the model's understanding and response accuracy.
- *Hypothesis 2: Employing the default value of the creativity parameter 'temperature' in an LLM tends to produce responses that are more varied and less focused, in contrast to using a deterministic value which is expected to yield factual responses more closely aligned with the original text.*

In this study we focus on two OpenAI GPT models: gpt-3.5-turbo-0613 and gpt-4-0613[2], that are extensively used as Language-Models-as-a-Service (LMaaS) [12]. We focus on these models because they expose little information to the user, and because we wanted to investigate their stochastic behaviour. A further study with a wider range of LLMs is currently in preparation.

  We compare the CQs generated by our approach against a benchmark comprising two existing CQ repositories: CORAL [8] and the dataset in [26]. Four ontologies were selected from the CQ benchmark based on three criteria: (i) the ontologies were produced by different developers; (ii) they represent various domains; and (iii) each had a significant number of published CQs. The selected ontologies are: (1) 'Video Game' [19]; (2) 'African Wildlife' [11] (3) 'Dem@care' [8]; and (4) 'VICINITY Core' [8]. The characteristics of each of these ontologies (i.e. number of both design CQs and triples) are stated in Table 1.

  For each of these ontologies, we generate CQs using the different prompts and the two GPT models. These prompts allow us to examine the impact of transitioning from general to granular when generating candidate CQs; and to

---

[2] https://platform.openai.com/docs/models/overview.

understand how LLMs can achieve the highest accuracy in the targeted task. Furthermore, we investigate the effect on the accuracy of the generated CQs of injecting more context to the prompt. In a previous study [1] we discussed how LLMs can generate *'narrative questions'*, i.e. questions that can elicit expansive, descriptive responses [7], often representing subjective views. For example, the CQs that `gpt-4` generates for the triple *'Achievement, isAchievementInGame, Game'* with Prompt 1 include *"Can you recall an achievement in a game that you found extremely satisfying to unlock"*, that is not a suitable CQ. The injection of *context* limits the generation of such questions and ensures that the candidate CQs remain focused on defining the ontology's scope and providing context in terms of *how, where, when, why, who* [23]. We define three prompt templates, each providing increasingly richer context:

Table 1. Number (percent) of unmatched Design CQs for each prompt and LLM, comparing deterministic (CP=0.0) and default (CP=0.7) values.

	Prompt	Unmatched CQs (#) %			
		gpt-3.5-turbo		gpt-4	
		CP=0.0	CP=0.7	CP=0.0	CP=0.7
Video Game	P1	(5) 7.57%	(3) 4.54%	(1) 1.51%	(1) 1.51%
Design CQs: 66	P2	(5) 7.57%	(8) 12.12%	(3) 4.54%	(1) 1.51%
# of Triples: 57	P3	(2) 3.03%	(2) 3.03%	(1) 1.51%	(1) 1.51%
African Wildlife	P1	(2) 14.28%	(1) 7.14%	(2) 14.28%	(4) 28.57%
Design CQs: 14	P2	(2) 14.28%	(2) 14.28%	(2) 14.28%	(2) 14.28%
# of Triples: 26	P3	(1) 7.14%	(1) 7.14%	(2) 14.28%	(2) 14.28%
Dem@care	P1	(11) 10.28%	(7) 6.54%	(7) 6.54%	(7) 6.54%
Design CQs: 107	P2	(10) 9.34%	(9) 8.41%	(4) 3.73%	(9) 8.41%
# of Triples: 146	P3	(3) 2.80%	(3) 2.80%	(2) 1.86%	(5) 4.67%
VICINITY Core	P1	(5) 8.77%	(3) 5.26%	(4) 7.01%	(2) 3.50%
Design CQs: 57	P2	(4) 7.01%	(1) 1.75%	(2) 3.50%	(2) 3.50%
# of Triples: 226	P3	(1) 1.75%	(1) 1.75%	(1) 1.75%	(1) 1.75%

P1 *General Competency Questions*: this instructs an LLM to generate competency questions for a given statement: *["Based on <statement>, generate a list of competency questions" avoid using narrative questions + statement]*.

P2 *Definitions of Competency Questions:* this prompt explicitly includes the definition of a CQ: *["Based on the <statement>, generate a list of competency question. Definition of competency questions: the questions that outline the scope of an ontology and provide an idea about the knowledge that needs to be entailed in the ontology." avoid using narrative questions + statement]*.

P3 *Use of a Role with Definitions of Competency Questions*: this contextualises the prompt by specifying the role of "Ontology Engineer", implying a more methodological approach to question formulation that focuses on the structural aspects of the ontology development, with the aim of explicitly generating CQs by including the definition of CQs: *["As an ontology engineer, generate a list of competency questions based on the <statement>. Definition of competency questions: the questions that outline the scope of ontology and provide an idea about the knowledge that needs to be entailed in the ontology" avoid using narrative questions + statement]*.

One of the documented limitations of the GPT models is their stochastic nature [12]. We investigate the diversity of text generated by the LLMs by adjusting the creativity (CP) or *temperature* parameter, whose value is in the range $[0, 2]$. We explore two CP settings: (i) a *deterministic* value of 0.0, which eliminates stochasticity and focuses on the consistent generation of text; and (ii) the *default value*, that allows the generation of more diverse and creative responses.[3]

As identical prompts can produce varied responses depending on the setting of the creativity parameter, in this study, we explore how the creativity parameter's default and deterministic settings impact prompt performance.

4   Results

The evaluation contrasted the performance of our `RETROFIT-CQs` approach using two LLMs (`gpt-3.5-turbo` and `gpt-4`) for the three prompt templates described in Sect. 3 across statements extracted from the four ontologies. The results[4] for two control parameters – determininstic (CP=0.0) and default (CP=0.7) – are discussed below. Table 1 presents the number of *design CQs* (i.e. the original CQs provided for each ontology in the benchmark datasets) for which no corresponding CQs were generated by the evaluated approach.

Tables 2 and 3 report the number of CQs generated for the deterministic and default control parameter settings and for each prompt template respectively, and present: (i) number of generated questions (No. Q.); (ii) filtered questions in the final output (No. Candidate CQs); (iii) number of validated candidate CQs against existing CQs (No. of Validated CQs); i.e. those CQs that appear in the benchmark dataset; and (iv) Performance Metrics (i.e. Precision, Recall & F1 score). In validating the candidate CQs, we use `SBERT` [22] to assess the similarity between CQs while mitigating the effect of paraphrasing, or the use of different morphological structures (e.g. plurals) on the similarity assessment. If *No. of Validated CQs* denotes the number of CQs that are assessed as having similar meaning by `SBERT` (true positives), and if `No. Unmatched CQs` corresponds to the number of questions in the benchmark that do not match any of the generated CQs (true negatives), then $Precision = \frac{No.\ of\ Validated\ CQs}{No.\ Q}$ and $Recall = \frac{No.\ of\ Validated\ CQs}{No.\ of\ Validated\ CQs + No.\ Unmatched\ CQs}$.

---

[3] The default setting, as of December 2023, was 0.7 but has since been adjusted to 1.0.

[4] https://github.com/SemTech23/RETROFIT-CQs_GPT.

Table 2. Summary for each prompt with deterministic creativity value (CP=0.0).

	Prompt	LLMs	No. Q.	Number of CQs		Performance		
				Candidate	Validated	Prec.	Rec.	F1
Video Game	P1	gpt-3.5-turbo	555	555	251	0.452	0.980	0.619
		gpt-4	776	591	482	0.816	0.998	0.898
	P2	gpt-3.5-turbo	570	569	399	0.701	0.988	0.820
		gpt-4	1033	810	639	0.789	0.995	0.880
	P3	gpt-3.5-turbo	570	565	434	0.844	0.995	0.914
		gpt-4	1197	911	759	0.833	0.999	0.908
African Wildlife	P1	gpt-3.5-turbo	215	213	136	0.638	0.986	0.775
		gpt-4	496	373	156	0.418	0.987	0.588
	P2	gpt-3.5-turbo	260	258	151	0.585	0.987	0.735
		gpt-4	423	357	186	0.521	0.989	0.683
	P3	gpt-3.5-turbo	270	256	185	0.723	0.995	0.837
		gpt-4	255	174	94	0.540	0.979	0.696
Dem@care	P1	gpt-3.5-turbo	1360	1339	474	0.354	0.977	0.520
		gpt-4	2039	1660	512	0.308	0.987	0.470
	P2	gpt-3.5-turbo	1435	1418	403	0.284	0.976	0.440
		gpt-4	2574	2042	633	0.310	0.994	0.473
	P3	gpt-3.5-turbo	1461	1386	622	0.449	0.995	0.619
		gpt-4	2850	2129	656	0.308	0.997	0.471
VICINITY Core	P1	gpt-3.5-turbo	2179	2119	501	0.236	0.990	0.382
		gpt-4	4320	3428	1122	0.327	0.996	0.493
	P2	gpt-3.5-turbo	2219	2150	547	0.254	0.993	0.405
		gpt-4	4549	3505	1333	0.380	0.999	0.550
	P3	gpt-3.5-turbo	2249	2115	947	0.448	0.999	0.618
		gpt-4	4958	3863	1485	0.384	0.999	0.555

The results show that neither changing the creativity parameter nor changing the specificity of the prompts has a significantly adverse effect on the number of valid CQs generated, based on the high recall scores observed in both Tables 2 and 3. Our approach consistently achieves a recall of 0.96 or higher for all prompts, regardless of the creativity parameter settings. Thus, the majority of the design CQs catalogued in the benchmark are matched (Table 1), supporting the claim that viable CQs can be generated. However, the precision varies and is influenced by both the prompt's specificity and the creativity parameter. Notably, for all four ontologies, the highest precision is achieved using Prompt 3, where we defined the role of the ontology developer and the definition of CQs. The lowest overall precision was recorded for prompt P1 in VICINITY Core (with gpt-3.5-turbo), where CQs were requested without additional clarification. This prompt lacked contextual information and used the deterministic value (CP=0.7), although a low precision was also observed with CP=0.0 using P1 for both the VICINITY Core and Dem@care data sets. As a result, several

Table 3. Summary for each prompt with default creativity value (CP=0.7).

	Prompt	LLMs	No. Q.	Number of CQs		Performance		
				Candidate	Validated	Prec.	Rec.	F1
Video Game	P1	gpt-3.5-turbo	543	543	348	0.641	0.991	0.779
		gpt-4	1249	1205	963	0.799	0.999	0.888
	P2	gpt-3.5-turbo	567	567	365	0.644	0.979	0.777
		gpt-4	1084	1061	852	0.803	0.999	0.890
	P3	gpt-3.5-turbo	570	565	429	0.759	0.995	0.861
		gpt-4	797	765	628	0.821	0.998	0.901
African Wildlife	P1	gpt-3.5-turbo	206	205	128	0.624	0.992	0.766
		gpt-4	274	266	128	0.481	0.970	0.643
	P2	gpt-3.5-turbo	260	259	141	0.544	0.986	0.701
		gpt-4	441	437	173	0.396	0.989	0.565
	P3	gpt-3.5-turbo	265	262	198	0.756	0.995	0.859
		gpt-4	517	459	229	0.499	0.991	0.664
Dem@care	P1	gpt-3.5-turbo	1329	1319	452	0.343	0.985	0.508
		gpt-4	2134	2101	552	0.263	0.987	0.415
	P2	gpt-3.5-turbo	1428	1406	423	0.301	0.979	0.460
		gpt-4	2681	2628	780	0.297	0.989	0.457
	P3	gpt-3.5-turbo	1475	1459	616	0.422	0.995	0.593
		gpt-4	2929	2811	863	0.307	0.994	0.469
VICINITY Core	P1	gpt-3.5-turbo	2177	2160	573	0.265	0.995	0.419
		gpt-4	4444	4276	1430	0.334	0.999	0.501
	P2	gpt-3.5-turbo	2202	2199	596	0.271	0.998	0.426
		gpt-4	4824	4695	1723	0.367	0.999	0.537
	P3	gpt-3.5-turbo	2265	2230	947	0.425	0.999	0.596
		gpt-4	4975	4787	1887	0.623	0.999	0.767

design CQs were not matched (see the "Unmatched CQs %" column in Table 1), and other irrelevant CQs were generated.

When considering the specificity of the prompt, P3 overall achieved higher precision scores than either P1 or P2 for both creative parameters considered. This can be illustrated using the Video Game ontology. Table 4 presents the candidate CQs for the triple *'Achievement isAchievementInGame Game'* corresponding to each prompt, with the Design CQs relating to this triple. Even when CP=0.0, P1 (which only provided context) elicited narrative questions [7]. In contrast, the inclusion of both the role of ontology engineer and the definition of CQs in P3 resulted in CQs that align more closely with the non-narrative directive [23]. These questions are designed to collect objective information on the classification and properties of achievements within games (thus aligning with the requirements of ontology engineering). This explains the high precision score obtained using P3, as the majority of generated CQs match those in the dataset, compared to P1's three matching CQs.

Table 4. Candidate CQs Generated for the Video Game Ontology Triple *'Achievement isAchievementInGame Game'* with CP=0.0. Green CQs match both Design CQs (at the bottom of the Table), the ones in blue match only the first (blue) Design CQ; likewise the ones in red match the second design CQs.

	Candidate CQs
gpt-3 P3	What are the different types of achievements that can be earned in a game?
	How is an achievement defined within the context of a game?
	What criteria must be met in order for a player to earn an achievement in a game?
	Can achievements be earned in any type of game, or are they specific to certain genres or platforms?
	How are achievements tracked and recorded within a game?
	Are there any limitations or restrictions on the number of achievements that can be earned in a game?
	Can achievements be earned by individual players or are they only awarded to teams or groups?
	Are there any rewards or benefits associated with earning achievements in a game?
	Can achievements be earned retroactively, or must they be earned during a specific time-frame?
	How are achievements displayed or showcased within a game?
gpt-3 P1	Can you provide examples of specific achievements you have earned within the game?
	How do you track and measure your achievements in the game?
	Have you ever faced any challenges or obstacles while trying to achieve a specific goal within the game? How did you overcome them?
	Can you describe a time when you felt particularly proud of an achievement you earned in the game?
	Have you ever collaborated with other players to achieve a specific in-game accomplishment? How did you contribute to the team effort?
	Can you explain the process you follow to unlock new achievements within the game?
	Can you provide an example of a time when you had to demonstrate a specific skill or strategy in order to achieve an in-game accomplishment?

Design CQ: What are the types of achievements in this game?
Design CQ: What are the types of achievements a game can have?

An oft-stated concern regarding the use of LLMs is that their performance is not replicable, as the results of repeated prompts can vary. Therefore, we also examined the overlap in the resulting CQs; i.e. verifying that the same CQs were generated despite changes to the prompt, 'temperature value' and LLM used. Our results demonstrate that: (i) there is only a marginal difference in the recall value between Tables 2 and 3 when varying the creativity parameter, suggesting this value has a marginal effect on the viability of the resulting CQs; and (ii) there is a consistency in the CQs generated by different prompts when one looks at the overlap (Table 5) of the generated CQs, regardless of the LLM used. For example, the overlap of candidate CQs for the Dem@care ontology, across all prompts is 88.91% and 88.70% respectively for `gpt-3.5-turbo` and `gpt-4` when CP=0.0 (conversely, 87.36% and 93.97% for CP=0.7). It was noted, however, that even when CP=0.0, there was a slight variance in the resulting CQs over repeated prompts, thus supporting the claim that both `gpt-3.5-turbo` and `gpt-4` are non-deterministic at the lowest 'temperature' setting [6,17].

Table 5. Summary of the overlap in candidate CQs for each ontology, including the total number of Candidate CQs (# Candidate CQs), the total number of overlapping CQs, and their percentage (# Overlapping CQs (%)).

Ontology	Category	all P in GPT3		all P in GPT4		all P in all LLMs	
		0.0	0.7	0.0	0.7	0.0	0.7
Video Game	# Candidate CQs	1638	1675	2312	3031	3950	4706
	# Overlapping CQs (%)	1402 (85.59%)	1382 (82.51%)	2087 (90.27%)	2827 (**93.27%**)	3538 (89.57%)	4274 (**90.82%**)
African Wildlife	# Candidate CQs	727	726	904	1162	1631	1888
	# Overlapping CQs (%)	693 (95.32%)	681 (93.80%)	884 (**97.79%**)	1100 (94.66%)	1578 (96.75%)	1861 (**98.57%**)
Dem@care	# Candidate CQs	4143	4184	5832	7540	9975	11724
	# Overlapping CQs (%)	3725 (88.91%)	3655 (87.36%)	5173 (88.70%)	7085 (**93.97%**)	8906 (89.28%)	10826 (**92.34%**)
VICINITY Core	# Candidate CQs	6384	6589	10796	13758	17180	20347
	# Overlapping CQs (%)	5590 (87.56%)	5574 (84.60%)	9507 (88.06%)	12414 (**90.23%**)	15254 (88.79%)	18262 (**89.75%**)

5 Conclusions

This paper offers significant insights into the application of LLMs in ontology engineering, in particular for the retrofitting of competency questions from published ontologies. We conducted a study to assess how well LLMs can capture the scope of an ontology. Our analysis confirms that the use of explicit knowledge (ontology triples) paired with specific prompts is effective in generating valid CQs and that these results are independent of the creativity parameter settings: in particular, contextual information is effective in enhancing the precision and coherence of LLM responses, while just using the default creativity setting of the models used produces focused responses, therefore mitigating against the inherent non determinism of these models. In this study we focus on GPT models, and an extended study is currently in preparation to incorporate more LLMs.

References

1. Alharbi, R., et al.: An experiment in retrofitting competency questions for existing ontologies. In: Proceedings of the 39th ACM/SIGAPP Symposium On Applied Computing (to appear) (2024)
2. AlKhamissi, B., et al.: A review on language models as knowledge bases. CoRR (2022). https://doi.org/10.48550/ARXIV.2204.06031
3. Allen, B.P., et al.: Identifying and consolidating knowledge engineering requirements. CoRR (2023). https://doi.org/10.48550/ARXIV.2306.15124
4. Allen, B.P., et al.: Knowledge engineering using large language models. Trans. Graph Data Knowl. **1**(1), 3:1–3:19 (2023)
5. Bezerra, C., Freitas, F.: Verifying description logic ontologies based on competency questions and unit testing. In: Proceedings of the IX Seminar on Ontology Research and I Doctoral and Masters Consortium on Ontologies, vol. 1908, pp. 159–164 (2017)

6. Chann, S.: Non-determinism in GPT-4 is caused by sparse MOE (2023). https://152334h.github.io/blog/non-determinism-in-gpt-4/. Accessed 20 Jan 2024
7. Clandinin, D.: Handbook of Narrative Inquiry: Mapping a Methodology. SAGE Publications, Inc, Thousand Oaks, California (2007). https://doi.org/10.4135/9781452226552
8. Fernández-Izquierdo, A., Poveda-Villalón, M., García-Castro, R.: CORAL: a corpus of ontological requirements annotated with Lexico-Syntactic patterns. In: Hitzler, P. (ed.) ESWC 2019. LNCS, vol. 11503, pp. 443–458. Springer, Cham (2019). https://doi.org/10.1007/978-3-030-21348-0_29
9. Grüninger, M., Fox, M.S.: The role of competency questions in enterprise engineering, pp. 22–31. Springer US (1995). https://doi.org/10.1007/978-0-387-34847-6_3
10. Keet, C.M., Ławrynowicz, A.: Test-driven development of ontologies. In: Sack, H., Blomqvist, E., d'Aquin, M., Ghidini, C., Ponzetto, S.P., Lange, C. (eds.) ESWC 2016. LNCS, vol. 9678, pp. 642–657. Springer, Cham (2016). https://doi.org/10.1007/978-3-319-34129-3_39
11. Keet, C.M.: The African wildlife ontology tutorial ontologies. J. Biomedical Semant. **11** (2019). https://api.semanticscholar.org/CorpusID:219981977
12. La Malfa, E., et al.: Language models as a service: overview of a new paradigm and its challenges. CoRR abs/2309.16573 (2023)
13. Liu, P., et al.: Pre-train, prompt, and predict: a systematic survey of prompting methods in natural language processing. ACM Comput. Surv. **55**(9) (2023)
14. Mulla, N., Gharpure, P.: Automatic question generation: a review of methodologies, datasets, evaluation metrics, and applications. Progress Artif. Intell. **12**(1), 1–32 (2023)
15. Noy, N., et al.: Ontology development 101: a guide to creating your first ontology. Tech. rep., Stanford knowledge systems laboratory technical report KSL-01-05 (2001)
16. Ouyang, L., et al.: Training language models to follow instructions with human feedback. In: Proceedings of the Advances in Neural Information Processing Systems, NeurIPS 2022, vol. 35, pp. 27730–27744 (2022)
17. Ouyang, S., et al.: LLM is like a box of chocolates: the non-determinism of ChatGPT in code generation. arXiv (2023)
18. Pan, J.Z., et al.: Large language models and knowledge graphs: opportunities and challenges. Trans. Graph Data Knowl. **1**(1), 2:1–2:38 (2023)
19. Parkkila, J., et al.: An ontology for videogame interoperability. Multimedia Tools Appl. **76**(4), 4981–5000 (2017)
20. Poveda-Villalón, M., et al.: LOT: an industrial oriented ontology engineering framework. Eng. Appl. Artif. Intell. **111**, 104755 (2022)
21. Presutti, V., et al.: Extreme design with content ontology design patterns. In: Proceedings of the 2009 International Conference on Ontology Patterns, vol. 516, pp. 83–97 (2009)
22. Reimers, N., Gurevych, I.: Sentence-BERT: sentence embeddings using Siamese BERT-networks. In: Proceedings of the 2019 Conference on Empirical Methods in Natural Language Proceedings and the 9th International Joint Conference on Natural Language Proceedings (EMNLP-IJCNLP), pp. 3982–3992 (2019)
23. Sequeda, J.F., Briggs, W.J., Miranker, D.P., Heideman, W.P.: A pay-as-you-go methodology to design and build enterprise knowledge graphs from relational databases. In: Ghidini, C., et al. (eds.) ISWC 2019. LNCS, vol. 11779, pp. 526–545. Springer, Cham (2019). https://doi.org/10.1007/978-3-030-30796-7_32

24. Shin, T., et al.: AutoPrompt: eliciting knowledge from language models with automatically generated prompts. In: Proceedings of the 2020 Conference on Empirical Methods in Natural Language Processing (EMNLP), pp. 4222–4235. Association for Computational Linguistics (2020)
25. Suárez-Figueroa, M.C., et al.: The neon methodology framework: a scenario-based methodology for ontology development. Appl. Ontol. **10**(2), 107–145 (2015)
26. Wiśniewski, D., et al.: Analysis of ontology competency questions and their formalizations in SPARQL-OWL. J. Web Semant. **59**, 100534 (2019)

Evaluating Class Membership Relations in Knowledge Graphs Using Large Language Models

Bradley P. Allen[(✉)] and Paul T. Groth

University of Amsterdam, Amsterdam, The Netherlands
{b.p.allen,p.t.groth}@uva.nl

Abstract. A backbone of knowledge graphs are their class membership relations, which assign entities to a given class. As part of the knowledge engineering process, we propose a new method for evaluating the quality of these relations by processing descriptions of a given entity and class using a zero-shot chain-of-thought classifier that uses a natural language intensional definition of a class. We evaluate the method using two publicly available knowledge graphs, Wikidata and CaLiGraph, and 7 large language models. Using the gpt-4-0125-preview large language model, the method's classification performance achieves a macro-averaged F1-score of 0.830 on data from Wikidata and 0.893 on data from CaLiGraph. Moreover, a manual analysis of the classification errors shows that 40.9% of errors were due to the knowledge graphs, with 16.0% due to missing relations and 24.9% due to incorrectly asserted relations. These results show how large language models can assist knowledge engineers in the process of knowledge graph refinement. The code and data are available on Github (https://github.com/bradleypallen/evaluating-kg-class-memberships-using-llms).

Keywords: Knowledge engineering · large language models · knowledge graph refinement · natural language generation

1 Introduction

Knowledge graphs (KGs) have become a key technology in many applications in industry and academia [20]. This has brought attention to the area of KG refinement [28], for which a main goal is ensuring that the knowledge captured in KGs is as complete and correct as possible. This is a challenge, given that large-scale KGs composed of contributions from multiple sources of knowledge often contain incomplete, misaligned, and inaccurate information [29,31]. At the same time, as part of the knowledge engineering process, direct manual evaluation of KG quality by human reviewers to detect and remediate these problems is expensive [18,37].

The recent emergence of large language models (LLMs) has inspired work towards understanding how LLMs can applied to knowledge graph construction.

© The Author(s), under exclusive license to Springer Nature Switzerland AG 2025
A. Meroño Peñuela et al. (Eds.): ESWC 2024, LNCS 15344, pp. 14–24, 2025.
https://doi.org/10.1007/978-3-031-78952-6_2

To date, much of this work has centered on the use of LLMs for knowledge graph completion [38] and the evaluation of provenance [5] and correctness [32] in a knowledge graph. In this paper, we describe work on using LLMs to evaluate *class membership relations* in a KG. Class membership relations are important because they are a principal way in which knowledge graphs represent classification schemes. Classification schemes are a major consideration in many knowledge engineering efforts, often with significant implications for social policy and scientific consensus [9].

We present an approach to evaluate class membership relations by using an LLM to define a zero-shot chain-of-thought (CoT) [23,36] classifier that takes natural language descriptions of an entity and a class in a given KG, and predicts whether or not the entity is an instance of the class, providing a natural language rationale for the prediction. The motivation for this approach is to leverage an LLM's capabilities for natural language processing to allow knowledge engineers to use intensional knowledge expressed in natural language by domain experts directly, as opposed to having to first transform it into a symbolic knowledge representation, and apply it to determining if that knowledge is accurately reflected in a given knowledge graph.

2   Related Work

Using LLMs for Knowledge Engineering Tasks. Beyond uses for KG refinement, LLMs are beginning to be applied to other tasks in the engineering of knowledge graphs. In [4], two scenarios for the use of LLMs in knowledge engineering are described: creating hybrid neurosymbolic knowledge systems and enabling knowledge engineering in natural language. Pan et al. [27] describe three categories of LLM/KG hybrids: KG-enhanced LLMs, LLM-augmented KGs, and synergized LLMs + KGs. Specific examples of LLM augmentation of KGs include the use of LLMs for KG completion [3,38] and for ontology engineering [26]. We view our work as an example of an LLM-augmented KG approach that performs knowledge engineering using intensional knowledge expressed in natural language to develop classifiers; classification is a well-known instance of an analytic knowledge task as defined in the CommonKADS taxonomy of knowledge-intensive task types [30].

KG Refinement. Knowledge graph refinement is defined by Paulheim [28] as the process of improving an existing KG by adding missing knowledge or identifying and removing errors. KG refinement has been implemented using manual, statistical, rule-based and hybrid methods [18,37]. Interactive solutions to aid human reviewers have been developed, including tools for crowdsourcing KG quality assessment [24], fact-checking triples using textual evidence [32], ontology repair using description logic reasoners [25], and sampling techniques to better focus manual reviewers' attention [13]. Our work builds on these results by creating classifiers that can be used to alert a knowledge engineer to misalignments between natural language definitions of a class and elements of the class's extension in a given KG.

Automated Fact Checking. A recent survey [14] provides a useful overview of the large amount of methods for fact checking. The work most related to ours is that of Atanasova et al. [7] on justification production using language models of the BERT family. That work focuses on the fact checking applied to claims expressed as natural language statements; in contrast, our methods admit of the combination of both serialized RDF statements and natural language descriptions as input for both justification production and verdict prediction.

3   Preliminaries

To precisely specify the integration between KGs and LLMs in our experiments, we now introduce a formalization of a neurosymbolic workflow [12] for entity classification.

Language Models. Let $\mathcal{T}$ be the set of sequences of tokens $T_i = t_1, t_2, \ldots, t_n$ such that t_i is a token in a predefined vocabulary V. Given a *corpus* $\mathcal{C} \subseteq \mathcal{T}$, a *language model* $\mathcal{L}_{\mathcal{C}}$ is a probabilistic model trained on a sample of $\mathcal{C}$ that defines a distribution over sequences of tokens.

$$\mathcal{L}_{\mathcal{C}}(T_i) = p(t_1, t_2, \ldots, t_n) \tag{1}$$

is an estimate of the probability of a sequence T_i, given a corpus $\mathcal{C}$. A *prompt* $P = (T, F)$ is a pair of a sequence of tokens T and an set of *free* tokens $F \subseteq \{f_1, f_2, \ldots, f_n\}$. A *substitution* θ with respect to a prompt P is a set of pairs (f_i, T_i) such that $f_i \in F$ and $T_i \in \mathcal{T}$. An *instantiation* $\mathtt{instantiate}(P, \theta)$ is a prompt P' such that $\forall (f_i, T_i) \in \theta$ every occurrence of f_i in P is replaced with f_i. Given a prompt P, the goal of a language model $\mathcal{L}_{\mathcal{C}}$ is to generate a sequence of tokens that maximizes the conditional probability under $\mathcal{L}_{\mathcal{C}}$.

$$T_{\mathrm{out}} = \arg\max_{T} \mathcal{L}_{\mathcal{C}}(T|P) \tag{2}$$

is the output sequence generated by the language model, conditioned on P.

Knowledge Graphs. Following [6], we use the RDF data model to describe knowledge graphs. Let I be an infinite set of IRIs (Internationalized Resource Identifiers [11]), B be an infinite set of blank nodes [19], and L an infinite set of literals [8]. A *knowledge graph* G is a set of *triples* $\{(s, p, o) \mid s \in S, p \in P, o \in O\}$, where $S \subset I \cup B$ is the set of *subjects* in G, $P \subset I$ is the set of *properties* in G, and $O \subset I \cup B \cup L$ is the set of *objects* in G. Let $\mathtt{instanceOf}, \mathtt{subClassOf}, \mathtt{label} \in P$ denote an instance-of relation, a subclass-of relation, and a label property in G, respectively. A *class* $c \in I \cup B$ is an entity that represents a set of entities sharing common properties and relationships in G. Let

$$\mathtt{ext}(c) = \bigcup_{i \in \mathbb{N}} \mathtt{ext}_i(c) \tag{3}$$

be the *extension* of a class c, where

$$\mathtt{ext}_0(c) = \{e \mid \exists (e, \mathtt{instanceOf}, c) \in G\} \tag{4}$$

$$\text{ext}_{i+1}(c) = \text{ext}_i(c) \cup \{e \mid e \in \text{ext}(c') \wedge \exists (c', \text{subClassOf}, c) \in G\} \tag{5}$$

Zero-Shot Chain-of-Thought Entity Classifiers. Given the definitions above, we now proceed to show how to construct classifiers that prompt LLMs with intensional definitions of classes in natural language to classify entities in a knowledge graph. For any entity $e \in I \cup B$, let $Ge = \{(s, p, o) \in G \mid s = e \vee o = e\}$ be the *neighborhood* of e. Let $T_{label(e)} = \{o \mid \exists (e, \text{label}, o) \in G\}$. A *serialization* T_G of a knowledge graph G is a sequence of tokens T that represents the triples in G using a structured formal language (e.g. RDF). For any entity $e \in E$, let T_{Ge} be the serialization of Ge. A *verbalization* T_e of an entity e is a sequence of tokens T that represents a description of e in natural language. Given an language model $\mathcal{L}_\mathcal{C}$, we define a function classify as follows:

$$(T_R, T_\mathbb{B}) = \text{classify}(c, e) \tag{6}$$

where T_R is a sequence of tokens that represents a rationale for a classification decision, and $T_\mathbb{B} \in \{\text{positive}, \text{negative}\}$ are tokens that represent classification decisions, i.e., whether or not $e \in \text{ext}(c)$, respectively. We instantiate T_R and $T_\mathbb{B}$ as follows:

$$T_R = \arg\max_T \mathcal{L}_\mathcal{C}(T \mid \text{instantiate}(P_{rationale\_generation}, \theta_0)) \tag{7}$$

$$T_\mathbb{B} = \arg\max_T \mathcal{L}_\mathcal{C}(T \mid \text{instantiate}(P_{answer\_generation}, \theta_1)) \tag{8}$$

$$\theta_0 = \{(\{\text{label}\}, T_{label(c)}), (\{\text{definition}\}, T_c), \\ (\{\text{entity}\}, T_{label(e)}), (\{\text{description}\}, T_e)\} \tag{9}$$

$$\theta_1 = \theta_0 \cup \{(\{\text{rationale}\}, T_{R_c})\} \tag{10}$$

given two prompt templates $P_{rationale\_generation}$ and $P_{answer\_generation}$. The specific prompt templates used in the experiments were manually authored and iteratively refined between June 2023 and October 2023. Figure 1 shows an example of such a classifier instantiated for a class and entity in the CaLiGraph KG.

4 Experiments

To understand the potential of classifiers built using the above approach for the problem of KG refinement, we conducted experiments to explore two research questions:

Q_1: **Can the classifiers exhibit good alignment with KGs?** Much of the work on LLM/KG synergy to date is predicated on the idea that KGs, as curated sources of knowledge, can be used to address gaps in the knowledge obtainable from LLMs, or mitigate the problem of hallucination by grounding LLMs. This makes assumptions about the degree of alignment between LLMs and KGs, hence this question aims to measure this alignment.

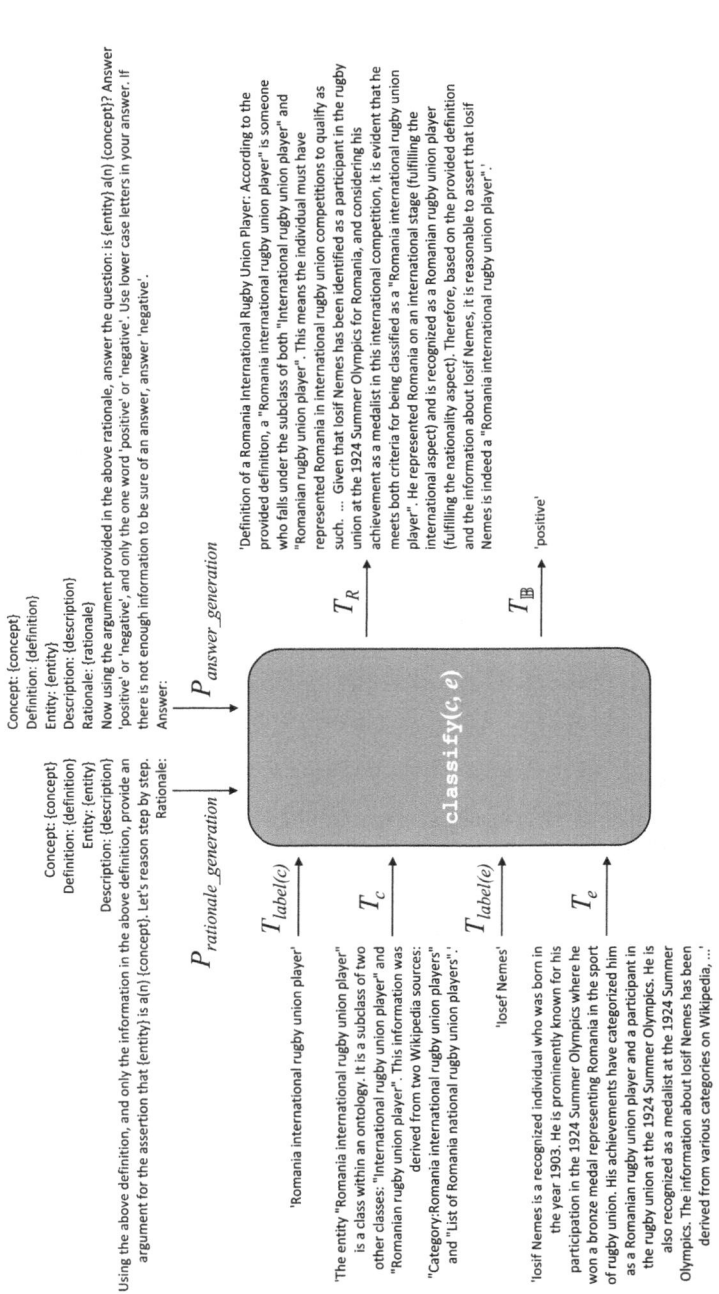

Fig. 1. A zero-shot chain-of-thought classifier applied to the class clgo:Romania_international_rugby_union_player and the entity clgr:Iosif_Nemes from the CaLiGraph knowledge graph [15].

Q_2: **Can the classifiers detect missing or incorrect relations?** Our main goal is to generate classifications based on intensional class definitions in with natural language rationales to help guide human reviewers to areas where KGs may be incomplete or incorrect. Any such approach must demonstrate the ability to do so across multiple knowledge graphs and classes.

The experiments to address these questions were implemented as follows:

Knowledge Graphs. Two publicly available knowledge graphs were used to construct evaluation datasets: Wikidata [34] and CaLiGraph [15–17]. The two KGs represent distinct approaches to KG construction. Wikidata is the result of the crowd-sourced contribution of factual statements by thousands of human contributors and automated processes working independently, yielding relatively diverse approaches to modeling concepts and entities, and is loosely coupled with and derived from information in Wikipedia. CaLiGraph is the result of the automated extraction of terminology and assertions from Wikipedia and DBPedia pages, and as such is more consistent in how it models concepts and entities than is Wikidata.

Data Sets. We randomly sampled 20 classes from Wikidata and 19 from CaLi-Graph using SPARQL queries, including their super-classes. For each, 20 entities were selected as positive examples, and up to 20 entities from the set difference of the extensions of the class and one of its superclasses as negative examples (in some of the sampled classes the cardinality of the set difference was less than 20).

Language Models. We evaluated seven large language models accessible using services provided by OpenAI and Hugging Face: OpenAI's gpt-4-0125-preview and gpt-3.5-turbo, Google's gemma-7b-it and gemma-2b-it, Mistral AI's Mixtral-8x7B-Instruct-v0.1 and Mistral-7B-Instruct-v0.2, and Meta's Llama-2-70b-chat-hf. For all experiments, temperatures were set to a value of 0.1.

Classifiers. We use the definitions provided above to instantiate a classifier for each class in the datasets. For each class c and entity e, we obtained natural language descriptions to use as T_c and T_e arguments for the classifier. For Wikidata, we retrieved natural language summaries of the class or entity from its associated Wikipedia page. For CaLiGraph, we used gpt-4-1106-preview to generate RDF verbalizations to serve as T_c and T_e, given inputs of T_{G_c} and T_{G_e} obtained as the TSV serialization of the triples returned from SPARQL DESCRIBE queries for c and e with LIMIT = 20.

Evaluation Procedure. Experimental runs were then conducted by applying classifiers to each class/entity pair for a given class in each of the two knowledge graphs, generating for each class a confusion matrix based on the resulting set of classifications, from which performance metrics are computed. Algorithm 1 describes this procedure in pseudo-code. Evaluations whose statistics are reported below were conducted during the period from 24 February 2024 to 27 February 2024. Costs incurred through calls to language model APIs during this period totalled around $225 USD.

input : a pair of classes c, d from $G \mid (c, \mathtt{subClassOf}, d) \in G$
output: a confusion matrix M

$(TP, FP, TN, FN) \leftarrow (0, 0, 0, 0);$
$E^+ \leftarrow$ a sample from $\mathtt{ext}(c);$
$E^- \leftarrow$ a sample from $\mathtt{ext}(d) \setminus \mathtt{ext}(c);$
foreach $e \in E^+$ **do**
$\quad | \quad (T_R, T_\mathbb{B}) \leftarrow \mathtt{classify}(c, e);$
$\quad | \quad$ **if** $T_\mathbb{B} = positive$ **then** $TP \leftarrow TP + 1;$
$\quad | \quad$ **else** $FP \leftarrow FP + 1;$

end
foreach $e \in E^-$ **do**
$\quad | \quad (T_R, T_\mathbb{B}) \leftarrow \mathtt{classify}(c, e);$
$\quad | \quad$ **if** $T_\mathbb{B} = negative$ **then** $TN \leftarrow TN + 1;$
$\quad | \quad$ **else** $FN \leftarrow FN + 1;$

end
$M \leftarrow [[TP, FP], [FN, TN]];$

Algorithm 1: Evaluation procedure

5   Findings

We summarize below the finding obtained from our evaluations. Detailed results can be found in our aforementioned Github repository.

Classifier performance (assuming the KG as ground truth) of the seven closed- and open-source LLMs is shown in Table 1. The performance as shown supports the following finding: **classifiers can exhibit good alignment with KGs** (Q_1). As evidenced by Cohen's κ values, one LLM was in moderate agreement with Wikidata, and four were in moderate agreement with CaLiGraph.

Table 2 shows the results of an error analysis of the evaluation results for the highest-performing classifier (using gpt-4-0125-preview). It was conducted by having one of the authors manually annotate each classification error with their own classification decision, based on the information in the provided descriptions. This human judgment was then compared with that of the KG and classifier using the pairwise Cohen's κ value as a measure of inter-annotator agreement. In cases where Wikidata and the classifier using gpt-4-0125-preview disagreed, the human showed fair agreement with Wikidata and no agreement with the classifier, and for examples where CaLiGraph and the given classifier disagreed, the human showed slight agreement with the classifier and no agreement with CaLiGraph.

In addition, the annotator assigned each error to one of five causes: missing data in the entity description that comprised the LLM's ability to classify the entity, a missing class membership relation in the KG between the given entity and class (an example of which is shown in Fig. 1), an incorrectly asserted class membership relation in the KG between the given entity and class, and an error on the part of the LLM, through either hallucination or misinterpretation of

Table 1. Classifier performance by LLM.

KG	LLM	ACC	AUC	F1	κ
Wikidata	gpt-4-0125-preview	**0.830**	**0.830**	**0.823**	**0.660**
	gemma-7b-it	0.726	0.727	0.705	0.454
	Mixtral-8x7B-Instruct-v0.1	0.697	0.696	0.654	0.393
	Mistral-7B-Instruct-v0.2	0.671	0.671	0.620	0.342
	gemma-2b-it	0.674	0.670	0.629	0.330
	gpt-3.5-turbo	0.627	0.627	0.547	0.255
	Llama-2-70b-chat-hf	0.631	0.616	0.569	0.239
CaLiGraph	gpt-4-0125-preview	**0.900**	**0.893**	**0.889**	**0.788**
	Mixtral-8x7B-Instruct-v0.1	0.893	0.884	0.874	0.767
	gpt-3.5-turbo	0.842	0.833	0.815	0.665
	Mistral-7B-Instruct-v0.2	0.812	0.803	0.779	0.605
	gemma-7b-it	0.783	0.774	0.750	0.547
	Llama-2-70b-chat-hf	0.637	0.625	0.558	0.252
	gemma-2b-it	0.563	0.543	0.422	0.090

the class definition or entity description. We assert that these results support another finding: **classifiers can detect missing or incorrect relations** in KGs (Q_2). The error analysis showed that in instances where the classifier using gpt-4-0125-preview was in disagreement with the KG, 40.9% of errors were due to the knowledge graphs, with 16.0% due to missing relations and 24.9% due to incorrect relations. 29.1% of the errors could be ascribed to missing or insufficient data in the entity description, which may have had a negative impact on classifier performance. This is attributed primarily to one of two reasons: for CaLiGraph, RDF verbalizations missed relevant information about entities due to the omission of relevant triples in the set produced by the SPARQL DESCRIBE queries; and for Wikidata, some entities had descriptions that were simply the label assigned to the entity. We plan to address these shortcomings in future versions of the evaluation datasets. These results suggest that, *pâce* efforts focused on using KGs to mitigate knowledge gaps and hallucinations in LLMs, LLMs may have a corresponding role to play in mitigating knowledge gaps and errors in KGs.

Table 2. Summary of the analysis of classification errors by gpt-4-0125-preview.

KG	N	FP	FN	human-KG κ	human-LLM κ	missing data	missing relation	incorrect relation	incorrect reasoning
Wikidata	136	46	90	**0.243**	−0.241	34 (25.0%)	15 (11.0%)	33 (24.3%)	54 (39.7%)
CaLiGraph	77	27	50	−0.295	**0.198**	28 (36.4%)	19 (24.7%)	20 (26.0%)	10 (13.0%)
	213	73	140			62 (29.1%)	34 (16.0%)	53 (24.9%)	64 (30.0%)

6   Discussion

Contributions. The principal contributions of this work are 1) a formal approach to the design of a neurosymbolic knowledge engineering workflow integrating KGs and LLMs, and 2) experimental evidence that this method can assist knowledge engineers in addressing the correctness and completeness of KGs, potentially reducing the effort involved in knowledge acquisition and elicitation. **Limitations.** Challenges with the use of LLMs include the cost of API calls to proprietary LLMs and the speed of processing tasks with such resource-intensive systems. Our results show the potential for open source, locally deployed LLMs to address the first problem; we expect that sampling approaches, frequently used in other approaches to KG refinement in large-scale KGs, can help address the second. The human evaluation for error analysis could be improved through the use of crowd-sourcing to expand the number of reviewers (allowing much larger sets of rationales and classification decisions to be evaluated), by evaluating the true positives and true negatives produced by the classifier, and by evaluating the soundness of rationales and faithfulness of classification to the given rationales. The potential impact of one or more of the LLMs having processed the Wikidata and CaLiGraph data during pre-training was not considered in the analysis. The question of whether the use of gpt-4-1106-preview to generate RDF verbalizations in the CaLiGraph experiments approach to verbalization introduced bias relative to the other LLMs is yet to be addressed. Finally, this work is limited to the evaluation of class membership relations in a KG, and evaluated against KGs that are domain-general and either crowdsourced (Wikidata) or automatically generated from crowdsourced content (CaLiGraph). To support use against KG refinement challenges faced by domain-specific KGs, such as those developed for life sciences applications [10], this needs to be generalized to support the definition of classifiers based on intensional definitions of predicates in natural language.
Future Work. We have in this work taken a minimalist approach to the prompt engineering of classifiers, restricting ourselves to a zero-shot chain-of-thought approach. Expanding this to include using temperature sampling [1] for self-consistency [35] and uncertainty estimation [21], mitigating hallucination in rationale generation [22], and addressing faithfulness in rationale generation [2,33] are three other areas for future work, in addition to work on addressing the limitations described above by expanding the number and types of relations considered, and evaluating our approach against domain-specific KGs.

Acknowledgements. This work is partially funded by the Dutch Research Council (NWO) through grant MVI.19.032. The authors wish to thank Filip Ilievski, Jan-Christoph Kalo, Xue Li, Fina Polat, Thivyan Thanapalasingam, and Lise Stork for discussions and suggestions that have been invaluable in refining this work. We would also like to thank the anonymous reviewers for their insightful comments and suggestions, which have been invaluable in refining our work.

References

1. Ackley, D.H., Hinton, G.E., Sejnowski, T.J.: A learning algorithm for Boltzmann machines. Cogn. Sci. **9**(1), 147–169 (1985). https://doi.org/10.7551/mitpress/4943.003.0039, http://dx.doi.org/10.7551/mitpress/4943.003.0039

2. Agarwal, C., Tanneru, S.H., Lakkaraju, H.: Faithfulness vs. Plausibility: on the (un) reliability of explanations from large language models. arXiv preprint arXiv:2402.04614 (2024)

3. Alivanistos, D., Santamaría, S.B., Cochez, M., Kalo, J.C., van Krieken, E., Thanapalasingam, T.: Prompting as probing: using language models for knowledge base construction. arXiv preprint arXiv:2208.11057 (2022)

4. Allen, B.P., Stork, L., Groth, P.: Knowledge engineering using large language models. Trans. Graph Data Knowl. **1**(1), 3:1–3:19 (2023). https://doi.org/10.4230/TGDK.1.1.3, https://drops.dagstuhl.de/entities/document/10.4230/TGDK.1.1.3

5. Amaral, G., Rodrigues, O., Simperl, E.: ProVe: a pipeline for automated provenance verification of knowledge graphs against textual sources. arXiv preprint arXiv:2210.14846 (2022)

6. Angles, R., Thakkar, H., Tomaszuk, D.: Mapping RDF databases to property graph databases. IEEE Access **8**, 86091–86110 (2020)

7. Atanasova, P., Simonsen, J.G., Lioma, C., Augenstein, I.: Generating fact checking explanations. arXiv preprint arXiv:2004.05773 (2020)

8. Beek, W., Ilievski, F., Debattista, J., Schlobach, S., Wielemaker, J.: Literally Better: analyzing and improving the quality of literals. Semant. Web **9**(1), 131–150 (2018)

9. Bowker, G.C., Star, S.L.: Sorting things out: Classification and its consequences. MIT Press (2000)

10. Chen, J., et al.: Knowledge graphs for the life sciences: recent developments, challenges and opportunities. Trans. Graph Data Knowl. **1**(1), 5:1–5:33 (2023). https://doi.org/10.4230/TGDK.1.1.5, https://drops.dagstuhl.de/entities/document/10.4230/TGDK.1.1.5

11. Dürst, M., Suignard, M.: Internationalized Resource Identifiers (IRIS). Tech. rep., RFC Editor (2005)

12. Ekaputra, F.J., et al.: Describing and organizing semantic web and machine learning systems in the SWEMLS-KG. In: European Semantic Web Conference, pp. 372–389. Springer (2023). https://doi.org/10.1007/978-3-031-33455-9_22

13. Gao, J., Li, X., Xu, Y.E., Sisman, B., Dong, X.L., Yang, J.: Efficient knowledge graph accuracy evaluation. arXiv preprint arXiv:1907.09657 (2019)

14. Guo, Z., Schlichtkrull, M., Vlachos, A.: A survey on automated fact-checking. Trans. Assoc. Comput. Linguist. **10**, 178–206 (2022)

15. Heist, N., Paulheim, H.: The Caligraph ontology as a challenge for owl reasoners. arXiv preprint arXiv:2110.05028 (2021)

16. Heist, N., Paulheim, H.: Information extraction from co-occurring similar entities. In: Proceedings of the Web Conference 2021, pp. 3999–4009 (2021)

17. Heist, N., Paulheim, H.: Transformer-based subject entity detection in Wikipedia listings. arXiv preprint arXiv:2210.01482 (2022)

18. Hofer, M., Obraczka, D., Saeedi, A., Köpcke, H., Rahm, E.: Construction of knowledge graphs: state and challenges. arXiv preprint arXiv:2302.11509 (2023)

19. Hogan, A., Arenas, M., Mallea, A., Polleres, A.: Everything you always wanted to know about blank nodes. J. Web Semant. **27**, 42–69 (2014)

20. Hogan, A., et al.: Knowledge graphs. ACM Comput. Surv. **54**(4) (2021). https://doi.org/10.1145/3447772
21. Huang, Y., Song, J., Wang, Z., Chen, H., Ma, L.: Look before you leap: an exploratory study of uncertainty measurement for large language models. arXiv preprint arXiv:2307.10236 (2023)
22. Ji, Z.: Survey of hallucination in natural language generation. ACM Comput. Surv. **55**(12), 1–38 (2023)
23. Kojima, T., Gu, S.S., Reid, M., Matsuo, Y., Iwasawa, Y.: Large language models are zero-shot reasoners. Adv. Neural. Inf. Process. Syst. **35**, 22199–22213 (2022)
24. Kontokostas, D., Zaveri, A., Auer, S., Lehmann, J.: TripleCheckMate: a tool for crowdsourcing the quality assessment of linked data. In: Klinov, P., Mouromtsev, D. (eds.) KESW 2013. CCIS, vol. 394, pp. 265–272. Springer, Heidelberg (2013). https://doi.org/10.1007/978-3-642-41360-5_22
25. Lambrix, P.: Completing and debugging ontologies: state of the art and challenges in repairing ontologies. ACM J. Data Inf. Qual. (2023)
26. Mateiu, P., Groza, A.: Ontology engineering with large language models. arXiv preprint arXiv:2307.16699 (2023)
27. Pan, S., Luo, L., Wang, Y., Chen, C., Wang, J., Wu, X.: Unifying large language models and knowledge graphs: a roadmap. arXiv preprint arXiv:2306.08302 (2023)
28. Paulheim, H.: Knowledge graph refinement: a survey of approaches and evaluation methods. Semant. Web **8**(3), 489–508 (2017)
29. Piscopo, A., Simperl, E.: What we talk about when we talk about Wikidata quality: a literature survey. In: Proceedings of the 15th International Symposium on Open Collaboration, pp. 1–11 (2019)
30. Schreiber, A.T., et al.: Knowledge engineering and management: the CommonKADS methodology. MIT Press (2000)
31. Shenoy, K., Ilievski, F., Garijo, D., Schwabe, D., Szekely, P.: A study of the quality of Wikidata. J. Web Semant. **72**, 100679 (2022)
32. Syed, Z.H., Röder, M., Ngonga Ngomo, A.C.: FactCheck: validating RDF triples using textual evidence. In: Proceedings of the 27th ACM International Conference on Information and Knowledge Management, pp. 1599–1602 (2018)
33. Turpin, M., Michael, J., Perez, E., Bowman, S.R.: Language models don't always say what they think: unfaithful explanations in chain-of-thought prompting. arXiv preprint arXiv:2305.04388 (2023)
34. Vrandečić, D., Krötzsch, M.: Wikidata: a free collaborative knowledgebase. Commun. ACM **57**(10), 78–85 (2014)
35. Wang, X., et al.: Self-consistency improves chain of thought reasoning in language models. arXiv preprint arXiv:2203.11171 (2022)
36. Wei, J., et al.: Chain-of-thought prompting elicits reasoning in large language models. Adv. Neural. Inf. Process. Syst. **35**, 24824–24837 (2022)
37. Xue, B., Zou, L.: Knowledge graph quality management: a comprehensive survey. IEEE Trans. Knowl. Data Eng. (2022)
38. Zhang, B., Reklos, I., Jain, N., Peñuela, A.M., Simperl, E.: Using Large Language Models for Knowledge Engineering (LLMKE): a case study on Wikidata. arXiv preprint arXiv:2309.08491 (2023)

LLMs4OM: Matching Ontologies with Large Language Models

Hamed Babaei Giglou(✉)⬤, Jennifer D'Souza⬤, Felix Engel⬤,
and Sören Auer⬤

TIB Leibniz Information Centre for Science and Technology, Hannover, Germany
{hamed.babaei,jennifer.dsouza,felix.engel,auer}@tib.eu

Abstract. Ontology Matching (OM), is a critical task in knowledge integration, where aligning heterogeneous ontologies facilitates data interoperability and knowledge sharing. Traditional OM systems often rely on expert knowledge or predictive models, with limited exploration of the potential of Large Language Models (LLMs). We present the LLMs4OM framework, a novel approach to evaluate the effectiveness of LLMs in OM tasks. This framework utilizes two modules for retrieval and matching, respectively, enhanced by zero-shot prompting across three ontology representations: concept, concept-parent, and concept-children. Through comprehensive evaluations using 20 OM datasets from various domains, we demonstrate that LLMs, under the LLMs4OM framework, can match and even surpass the performance of traditional OM systems, particularly in complex matching scenarios. Our results highlight the potential of LLMs to significantly contribute to the field of OM.

Keywords: Ontology Matching · Ontology Alignment · Large Language Models · Retrieval Augmented Generation · Zero-Shot Testing

1 Introduction

In the dynamic field of information and data management, ensuring the interoperability and integration of varied knowledge systems is critical. Ontologies play a key role in achieving semantic interoperability by providing a structured, understandable framework for both humans and machines [31,44]. However, the proliferation of new ontologies presents challenges in aligning them for seamless communication across different systems [34,51]. Ontology matching (OM) emerges as a vital solution, automating the discovery of correspondences across ontologies [10]. The emergence of Large Language Models (LLMs) in natural language processing has revolutionized the traditional boundaries between human and machine understanding of language, making LLMs highly relevant for OM tasks. Despite initial efforts to apply LLMs to OM [21,30], the rapid development of these models calls for an in-depth exploration of their potential in OM, which this study aims to provide, emphasizing the importance of OM and the promising capabilities of LLMs in addressing its challenges.

ⓒ The Author(s), under exclusive license to Springer Nature Switzerland AG 2025
A. Meroño Peñuela et al. (Eds.): ESWC 2024, LNCS 15344, pp. 25–35, 2025.
https://doi.org/10.1007/978-3-031-78952-6_3

To pursue this objective, we present the LLMs4OM framework, which assesses diverse LLMs across various tracks introduced within the Ontology Alignment Evaluation Initiative (OAEI) [40]. OM aims to map concepts between source $C_{source} \in O_{source}$ and target $C_{target} \in O_{target}$ ontologies. Formally, the task is to identify for any $C_s \in C_{source}$, possible $C_t \in C_{target}$ that $(C_s, C_t, S_{C_s \equiv C_t})$, where $S \in [0, 1]$ represents the likelihood of equivalence $C_s \equiv C_t$ [11].

An initial study using ChatGPT-4 [30], demonstrated the OM task via a conversational, naive approach, where ontologies O_{source} and O_{target} were fully inputted into the LLM to solicit matchings. This approach, however, highlighted two primary drawbacks: i) the limited context length LLMs can process, which may be exceeded by larger ontologies, and ii) the increased likelihood of erroneous or "hallucinated" responses due to the volume of information provided. To address these, LLMs4OM employs a dual-module strategy based on Retrieval-Augmented Generation (RAG) [26]: first, using retrieval model for candidate selection for a given query C_{source} from a knowledge base of C_{target}, and then LLM-based matching, in a second module, for finer accuracy. This approach mitigates the limitations of direct LLM prompting by optimizing for the specific challenges of OM, demonstrating a strategic advancement in leveraging LLMs for OM. In our study using the LLMs4OM framework, we conduct extensive evaluations, beginning with the RAG module where we explore four retrieval methods: TFIDF [38], sentence-BERT [37], SPECTER2 [42], and OpenAI text-embedding-ada [33]. Subsequently, within the LLM module, we pair these retrieval techniques with seven state-of-the-art LLMs: LLaMA-2 [46], GPT-3.5 [32], Mistral [22], Vicuna [52], MPT [45], Falcon [2], and Mamba [16], to assess their combined effectiveness. Furthermore, detailed large-scale experiments are framed based on three main research questions (**RQs**). **RQ1**: What impact do the three concept representations (concept, concept-parent, concept-children), respectively have on improving matching efficacy? **RQ2**: For the RAG module, which retriever performs best per track? (*RQ2.1*) Additionally, how does recall vary in the retrieval module across our different retrieval techniques employed? (*RQ2.2*) **RQ3**: Which LLM performs best per track? (*RQ3.1*) Furthermore, how does the performance of various LLMs differ across the three concept representations for the OM tracks? (*RQ3.2*).

This study presents and empirical evaluation of LLMs across six tracks of the OAEI campaign, covering 20 datasets. The primary contributions of this paper are threefold: 1) Introduction of the LLMs4OM, an end-to-end framework that utilizes LLMs for OM; 2) A thorough empirical evaluation of seven state-of-the-art domain-independent LLMs and four retrieval models for their suitability to the various OM tasks; and 3) The source code implementation of the LLMs4OM framework released in here https://github.com/HamedBabaei/LLMs4OM.

2   Related Work

Ontology matching, a well-explored research area, has seen diverse methodologies, from traditional techniques [1,13,23,39,41] to recent transformer-based methods [4,9,14,15,18,19,21,30,35,43,47,48], each contributing to advancements in the field. Despite the proven effectiveness of conventional approaches, this work focuses on classifying ontology matching systems, especially those utilizing transformers [49], into three categories based on their research goals: unsupervised learning, supervised learning, and LLM-based approaches.

Unsupervised learning methods in OM often use embeddings for similarity assessments. Techniques such as TTEXTO [35], PropMatch [43], AMD [47], and Matcha [14] primarily leverage BERT [7] variants (e.g., RoBERTa [28], sentence-BERT) to generate ontology embeddings for these calculations. Additionally, some methods combine transformer models with multiple representations: TEXTO integrates GloVe [36] with BERT, AMD pairs knowledge graph embeddings with BERT, GraphMatcher [9] combines universal sentence encoder [5] with graph learning techniques, and PropMatch uses sentence-BERT with TFIDF for enhanced matching accuracy. Supervised OM methods predominantly fine-tune transformer models. Truveta Mapper [4] utilizes ByT5 [50] on the Bio-ML track, employing a sequence-to-sequence approach. LaKERMap [48] focuses on domain-specific tuning with Bio-ClinicalBERT [3]. SORBETmatcher [15] combines BERT with random walks and regression loss for ontology embeddings. Matcha-DL [14] uses sentence-BERT in a semi-supervised setup with a dense network for candidate ranking. BERTMap [18] integrates unsupervised and semi-supervised strategies by initially fine-tuning BERT on ontology texts, and then refining mappings based on ontology structure.

Research on larger parameter models [19,21,30] reveals significant strategies for ontology matching (OM). [30] leverages prompt templates with LLMs to input source and target ontologies, showcasing OM potential. OLaLa [21] utilizes LLaMA-2 models and BERT retrievers to extract top-k matches from target ontologies for LLM prompts, refining final alignments with a precision matcher and filters. LLMap [19] investigates Flan-T5 [6] and GPT-3.5's zero-shot capabilities, focusing on concept labels and structural contexts.

3   LLMs4OM Methodological Framework

The LLMs4OM framework offers a RAG approach within various LLMs for OM. LLMs4OM uses O_{source} as query $Q(O_{source})$ to retrieve possible matches for any $C_s \in C_{source}$ from $C_{target} \in O_{target}$. Where, C_{target} is stored in the knowledge base $KB(O_{target})$. Later, C_s and obtained $C_t \in C_{target}$ are used to query the LLM to check whether the (C_s, C_t) pair is a match. As shown in Fig. 1, the framework comprises four main steps: 1) Concept representation, 2) Retriever model, 3) LLM, and 4) Post-processing.

1) Concept representation. Within this module, we process the ontologies, to extract the child, parent, and concept-specific representations of ontology elements. These representations will be utilized to generate three distinct input representations: i) Concept (C), a foundational representation that encapsulates the core characteristics of a standalone concept within the ontology, ii) Concept-Parent (CP), extending beyond individual concepts, this representation

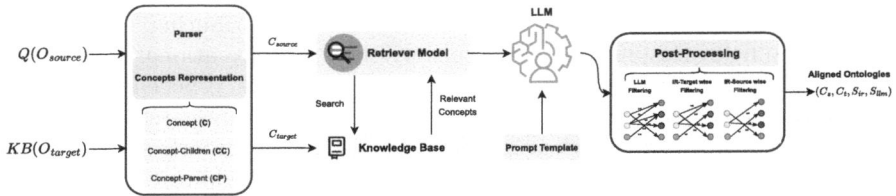

Fig. 1. Overview on LLMs4OM as an end-to-end framework for OM.

establishes the hierarchical relationships by incorporating information about the parent concepts, and iii) Concept-Children (CC) complementing the CP representation which focuses on the descendants of a given concept. These variant representations ensure a comprehensive understanding of ontologies, capturing both individual concepts and their hierarchical relationships, thus supporting the complete nature of ontologies. Subsequently, minor preprocessing is carried out to acquire clean textual data by converting representations to lowercase and removing punctuation.

2) Retriever model. First, an embedding extractor model operates by extracting embeddings for $C_{target} \in O_{target}$ and forming an embedding knowledge base for all C_{target}. Next, for a given $C_s \in C_{source}$, using the embedding extractor model, a C_s embedding is generated to calculate cosine similarity across all C_{target}, to identify top_k most similar candidates for alignments. The retrieval model will result in a $\{(C_s, C_{t_1}), ..., (C_s, C_{t_k})\}$ pairs with similarity score of S_{ir} per pair. For other input representations, C can be substituted with CC to include children or with CP to integrate the parent of C within the representations for the retrieval model.

3) LLM. Using obtained $\{(C_s, C_{t_1}), ..., (C_s, C_{t_k})\}$ pairs from the retrieval model, each pair is verbalized as text and replaced in the prompt template to input LLMs. Subsequently, employing the LLM prompting technique [27], inputs are categorized into "yes" and "no" classes using label words such as yes/true/right for the "yes" class and no/false/wrong for the "no" class. Later, the confidence score of S_{llm} is derived from the probabilities assigned to the "yes" and "no" classes label words corresponding to the obtained pairs. The following prompt template is designed to use C, CC, or CP representation of ontology concepts.

Classify if two concepts refer to the same real-world entity or not (answer only yes or no).\n### First concept:\n{C_s}\n[Parents|Children]: {$CP|CC$}\n### Second concept:\n{C_t}\n [Parents|Children]: {$CP|CC$}\n### Answer:

Where in the template {C_s} and {C_t} are placeholders for pair concepts. The notation *"[Parents|Children]: {$CP|CC$}"* offers flexibility in representing ontology concepts, allowing for the inclusion of either parent or children concepts via CP and CC representations.

4) Post-processing. After obtaining the retrieval model similarity score of S_{ir} and LLM's confidence scores of S_{llm} for "yes" and "no" classes, we conducted hybrid post-processing to obtain final pairs that match among $(C_s, C_{t_1}), ..., (C_s, C_{t_k}))$. The hybrid post-processing involves three steps:

1. *Confidence-driven filtering by LLM*: First, predicted pairs with the "no" class are disregarded. Then, pairs with $S_{llm} > 0.7$ for the "yes" class are retained.
2. *The high precision matcher*: This step applies to the retrieval model similarity score using $S_{ir} > 0.9$. The resulting output consists of exact matches.
3. *Cardinality-based filtering*: Implemented to ensure uniqueness in matches per C_{source} or C_{target} concept. This step resolves any potential ambiguity arising from multiple pairs with identical source or target concepts, although such cases are not present in the ground truth data.

This yields $(C_s, C_t, S_{ir}, S_{llm})$ as the set matching between concepts.

4   LLMs4OM Ontology Matching Evaluations

This section delves into empirically validating LLMs4OM by employing precision, recall, and F1-score metrics. Experimental datasets, models, and results are presented in the following.

Evaluation Datasets OAEI Tracks and Tasks. We selected six tracks from the OAEI campaign, covering diverse domains, and utilized three setups, i.e. concept, concept-children, and concept-parent, for our experiment. These configurations aim to identify the most effective ontology representation for OM, particularly focusing on the equivalence matching problem. The chosen tracks includes: ANATOMY) Anatomy [8] (Mouse-Human), BIODIV) Biodiversity and Ecology [24] (8 tasks), PHENOTYPE) Disease and Phenotype [17] (DOID-ORDO and HP-MP), COMMONKG) Common Knowledge Graphs [12] (Nell-DBpedia and YAGO-Wikidata), BIO-ML) Biomedical Machine Learning [20] (5 tasks), and MSE) Material Sciences and Engineering [29] (MI-EMMO and MI-MatOnto) OAEI tracks which resulted in 20 tasks/datasets.

Evaluation Models Retrievers and LLMs. As already introduced earlier, in this work, this study evaluates 7 state-of-the-art LLMs across 4 retriever models using the LLMs4OM framework. We assess retrieval models including TFIDF [38], sentence-BERT [37], SPECTER2 [42], and OpenAI text-embedding-ada [33]. Afterward, we combine these with LLMs (number of parameters written in parenthesis) such as LLaMA-2 (7B) [46], GPT-3.5 (174B) [32], Mistral (7B) [22], Vicuna (7B) [52], MPT (7B) [45], Falcon (7B) [2], and Mamba (2.8B) [16] to measure their effectiveness for OM.

LLMs4OM Results. For each track, retriever models with $top_k = 5$ are evaluated across proposed concept representations and results are reported in Fig. 2. The assessment includes 7 LLMs with C, CC, and CP input representations, along with retrievers like *text-embedding-ada* and *sentence-BERT*, detailed in Table 1. Approximately 50 runs per dataset were conducted, providing foundational results for further analysis (the complete results are indicated in supplementary material). We focus on zero-shot evaluations of LLMs and retrieval models in addressing our research questions.

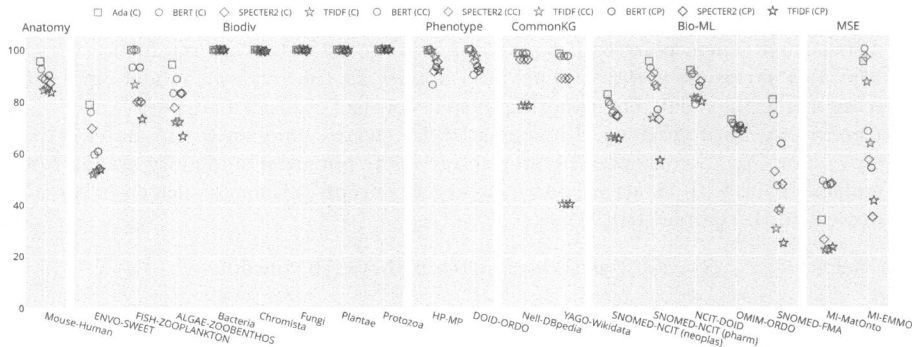

Fig. 2. Comparing retrieval models using recall and $top_k = 5$.

RQ1: What impact do the three concept representations, respectively have on improving matching efficacy? We address this question by analyzing the findings presented in Fig. 2, demonstrating the superiority of the C representation across all 20 tasks for retrieval models using the proposed method. Additionally, in Table 1, we find C excelling in 6 tasks, while CP outperforms in 9 tasks. Notably, based on observation of results in Fig. 2, SNOMED-FMA tasks from BIO-ML show high sensitivity to input representation. Furthermore, the inclusion of information about concepts, i.e. parents or children, shifts representations towards other concepts within the ontology. However, such information proves to be valuable for LLMs in enhancing their understanding of concepts, as evidenced in the results.

RQ2.1. [Retrieval module] Which retriever performs best per track? Given the results in Fig. 2, we analyze this question. Across tracks ANATOMY, BIODIV, PHENOTYPE, COMMONKG, and BIO-ML, OpenAI *text-embedding-ada* consistently outperforms. However, in MSE track tasks, *sentence-BERT* emerges as the standout performer. Specifically, for the challenging MI-MatOnto task, *sentence-BERT* achieves a 49% recall. Combining top retrievers, *text-embedding-ada* and *sentence-BERT*, with LLMs, as shown in Table 1, highlights *sentence-BERT*'s suitability for PHENOTYPE and MSE tracks, while *text-embedding-ada* excels in the remaining 4 tracks. These findings underscore the importance of selecting appropriate retrievers tailored to specific task requirements in LLMs4OM.

RQ2.2: [Retrieval module] How does recall vary in the retrieval module across our different retrieval techniques employed? We investigate this question by comparing retriever models across different values of $top_k \in [5, 10, 20]$. On average, for $top_k = 5$, the retrieval models achieve a recall of 82.09%, increasing to 84.66% for $top_k = 10$, and further to 86.82% for $top_k = 20$. Specifically, given the results in Fig. 2, when considering $top_k = 5$, the *text-embedding-ada* retriever achieves a recall of 90.88%, followed by *sentence-BERT* with 86.09%, *SPECTER2* with 82.10%, and *TFIDF* with 75.15%, highlighting the superior performance of *text-embedding-ada* and *sentence-BERT*. However, it's important to note that higher values of top_k lead to increased time complexity and longer waiting times. Consequently, we may opt to sacrifice a 4% average recall with $top_k = 20$ in exchange for reduced waiting times using $top_k = 5$.

RQ3.1: [LLM module] Which LLM performs best per track? We examine this question given the results in Table 1. The **Best Model** column in the table showcases

Table 1. Zero-shot performance comparison across 20 tasks with 7 LLMs, 3 concept representations (C, CP, CC), and 2 retriever models. Bold indicates LLM4OM outperforming OAEI 2023 OM systems. "OAEI" column shows the top F1-scores from OAEI.

Track	Tasks	Prec	Rec	F1	Best Model	OAEI
ANATOMY	Mouse-Human	90.82	87.46	89.11	GPT-3.5(C)+Ada	94.10
BIODIV	ENVO-SWEET	59.00	51.67	55.09	Mistral(C)+Ada	71.40
	FISH-ZOOPLANKTON	100	80.00	88.88	LLaMA-2(C)+Ada	92.80
	ALGAE-ZOOBENTHOS	100	38.88	**56.00**	Mistral(C)+Ada	50.00
	TAXR-NCBI(Bacteria)	67.96	99.42	**80.74**	GPT-3.5(CP)+Ada	74.80
	TAXR-NCBI(Chromista)	69.87	98.07	**81.61**	GPT-3.5(CP)+Ada	77.30
	TAXR-NCBI(Fungi)	86.97	99.08	**99.63**	GPT-3.5(CP)+Ada	89.10
	TAXR-NCBI(Plantae)	82.59	96.34	**88.94**	GPT-3.5(CP)+Ada	86.60
	TAXR-NCBI(Protozoa)	86.06	98.59	**91.90**	GPT-3.5(CP)+Ada	85.70
PHENOTYPE	DOID-ORDO	85.79	94.26	**89.83**	Mistral(CP)+BERT	75.50
	HP-MP	76.67	95.40	**85.01**	Mistral(CP)+BERT	81.80
COMMONKG	Nell-DBpedia	100	89.14	94.26	GPT-3.5(C)+Ada	96.00
	YAGO-Wikidata	100	85.52	92.19	LLaMA-2(C)+Ada	94.00
BIO-ML	NCIT-DOID (disease)	86.19	80.06	83.01	GPT-3.5(C)+Ada	90.80
	OMIM-ORDO (disease)	71.80	57.96	64.14	GPT-3.5(CC)+Ada	71.50
	SNOMED-FMA(body)	21.12	32.60	25.64	GPT-3.5(CP)+Ada	78.50
	SNOMED-NCIT(neoplas)	46.96	52.96	49.47	GPT-3.5(CP)+Ada	77.10
	SNOMED-NCIT(pharm)	81.84	58.19	68.02	GPT-3.5(CC)+Ada	75.20
MSE	MI-EMMO	96.66	92.06	**94.30**	LLaMA-2(CC)+BERT	91.80
	MI-MatOnto	89.70	20.19	32.97	MPT(C)+BERT	33.90

the top-performing models, starting with GPT-3.5, followed by Mistral-7B, LLaMA-2-7B, and finally MPT-7B among the 7 LLMs. The summary of best model results concerning OM systems proposed in OAEI 2023 [40] using F1-score are as follows: for MI-EMMO LLaMA-2-7B 94.30% > Matcha 91.8% [14], for HP-MP Mistral-7B 85.01% > LogMap 81.8% [23], for DOID-ORDO Mistral-7B 89.93% > AML 75.5% [13], for ALGAE-ZOOBENTHOS Mistral-7B 56.00% > OLaLa 50.0% [21], for TAXR-NCBI(Bacteria) GPT-3.5 80.74% > LogMapLt 77.3% [23], for TAXR-NCBI(Fungi) GPT-3.5 99.63% > OLaLa 89.9% [21], for TAXR-NCBI(Plantae) GPT-3.5 88.94% > OLaLa 86.6% [21], and for TAXR-NCBI(Protozoa) GPT-3.5 91.90% > OLaLa 85.7% [21].

RQ3.2: [LLM module] How does the performance of various LLMs differ across the three concept representations for the OM tracks? Using results from Table 1, we find LLMs perform better with additional contexts like parents or children, as seen in tasks across BIODIV, PHENOTYPE, and BIO-ML tracks. In BIODIV, CP consistently boosts LLM performance, especially in TAXR-NCBI tasks. Similarly, PHENOTYPE tasks show improved results with CP representations, notably in DOID-ORDO (89.83%) and HP-MP (85.01%). However, BIO-ML tasks exhibit mixed outcomes; some like NCIT-DOID perform well (83.01%) with C representation, while others like SNOMED-FMA (25.64%) struggle even with CP representation. In MSE, tasks vary greatly; for example, MI-EMMO achieves 94.30% success with LLaMA-2-7B and CC representation. This highlights the importance of selecting the right model architecture and contextual representation for each task. Overall, this analysis stresses the significance of context in LLMs across diverse domains, emphasizing the need for tailored approaches based on task specifics.

5   Discussion

Benefits of using our RAG technique for OM. Integrating retrieval with LLMs yields benefits. Querying LLM with all pairs initially led to impractical $O(n^2)$ time complexity, particularly with larger datasets. However, integrating retrieval reduces complexity to linear $O(kn)$, enabling faster processing while preserving LLM-generated confidence scores. Additionally, providing all ontologies at once to the model, as seen in [30], results in mixed outputs, posing challenges in computing matching scores and increasing the risk of high hallucination, especially with larger ontologies.

Low performance on the Bio-ML track. LLMs4OM showed low performance compared to traditional methods across the BIO-ML track tasks. Analyzing their performance with two retrievers, we found an average F1-score of 53% with *text-embedding-ada* and around 44% with *sentence-BERT*. Despite strong retriever performance in candidate retrieval (see Fig. 2), LLMs' overall performance remains low. There is a general under-performance on this track when LLM solutions have been used, and given the low performance, we tested domain-specific LLM i.e. BioMistral-7B [25] and we obtained the following results (* refers to the best model result from Table 1). NCIT-ORDO 69.04% < 83.01%*, OMIM-ORDO 57.84% < 64.14%*, SNOMED-FMA 33.98% > 25.64%*, SNOMED-NCIT(neoplas) 46.24% > 49.47%*, and SNOMED-NCIT(pharm) 62.00% < 68.02%*. The low performance on all the tasks even with domain-specific LLM, showed a need for a different approach for the BIO-ML track.

6   Conclusion

The proposed LLMs4OM framework highlights the efficacy of LLMs in OM, specifically in aligning diverse ontologies for knowledge engineering. By rigorously evaluating 20 tasks spanning different domains, our framework shows that LLMs, when combined with retriever models and guided by zero-shot prompting while utilizing C, CP, and CC representations, can surpass traditional OM systems in complex matching scenarios. These findings underscore the significant potential of LLMs in OM, paving the way for further exploration.

Acknowledgments. We thank *Nenad Krdzavac* for valuable insights on a previous draft of this paper. This work was supported by the German BMBF project SCINEXT (ID 01lS22070), the European Research Council for ScienceGRAPH (GA ID: 819536), and German DFG for NFDI4DataScience (no. 460234259).

References

1. Algergawy, A., Babalou, S., Klan, F., König-Ries, B.: Ontology modularization with OAPT. J. Data Semant. **9**(2), 53–83 (2020). https://doi.org/10.1007/s13740-020-00114-7, https://doi.org/10.1007/s13740-020-00114-7
2. Almazrouei, E., et al.: The falcon series of open language models (2023)
3. Alsentzer, E., et al.: Publicly available clinical BERT embeddings. In: Proceedings of the 2nd Clinical Natural Language Processing Workshop, pp. 72–78. Association for Computational Linguistics, Minneapolis, Minnesota, USA (2019). https://doi.org/10.18653/v1/W19-1909, https://www.aclweb.org/anthology/W19-1909
4. Amir, M., et al.: Truveta Mapper: a zero-shot ontology alignment framework (2023)

5. Cer, D., et al.: Universal sentence encoder (2018)
6. Chung, H.W., et al.: Scaling instruction-finetuned language models (2022)
7. Devlin, J., Chang, M.W., Lee, K., Toutanova, K.: BERT: pre-training of deep bidirectional transformers for language understanding (2019)
8. Dragisic, Z., Ivanova, V., Li, H., Lambrix, P.: Experiences from the anatomy track in the ontology alignment evaluation initiative. J. Biomed. Semant. **8**(1), 56 (2017). https://doi.org/10.1186/s13326-017-0166-5
9. Efeoglu, S.: GraphMatcher: a graph representation learning approach for ontology matching. In: OM@ISWC. CEUR Workshop Proceedings, vol. 3324, pp. 174–180. CEUR-WS.org (2022)
10. Euzenat, J., Shvaiko, P.: Ontology Matching. Springer Publishing Company, Incorporated, 2nd edn. (2013). https://doi.org/10.1007/978-3-642-38721-0
11. Euzenat, J., Meilicke, C., Stuckenschmidt, H., Shvaiko, P., Trojahn, C.: Ontology alignment evaluation initiative: six years of experience. J. Data Semant. **15**, 158–192 (2011). https://doi.org/10.1007/978-3-642-22630-4_6
12. Fallatah, O., Zhang, Z., Hopfgartner, F.: A gold standard dataset for large knowledge graphs matching (2020). https://eprints.whiterose.ac.uk/173366/, 2020 for this paper by its authors. Use permitted under Creative Commons License Attribution 4.0 International (http://creativecommons.org/licenses/by/4.0)
13. Faria, D., Pesquita, C., Santos, E., Palmonari, M., Cruz, I.F., Couto, F.M.: The AgreementMakerLight ontology matching system. In: Meersman, R., et al. (eds.) OTM 2013. LNCS, vol. 8185, pp. 527–541. Springer, Heidelberg (2013). https://doi.org/10.1007/978-3-642-41030-7_38
14. Faria, D., Silva, M.C., Cotovio, P., Ferraz, L., Balbi, L., Pesquita, C.: Results for Matcha and Matcha-DL in OAEI 2023. In: OM@ISWC. CEUR Workshop Proceedings, vol. 3591, pp. 164–169. CEUR-WS.org (2023)
15. Gosselin, F., Zouaq, A.: SORBET: a Siamese network for ontology embeddings using a distance-based regression loss and BERT. In: Payne, T.R., et al. (eds.) The Semantic Web - ISWC 2023, pp. 561–578. Springer Nature Switzerland, Cham (2023)
16. Gu, A., Dao, T.: Mamba: Linear-time sequence modeling with selective state spaces. arXiv preprint arXiv:2312.00752 (2023)
17. Harrow, I., et al.: Matching disease and phenotype ontologies in the ontology alignment evaluation initiative. J. Biomed. Semant. **8**(1), 55 (2017). https://doi.org/10.1186/s13326-017-0162-9, https://doi.org/10.1186/s13326-017-0162-9
18. He, Y., Chen, J., Antonyrajah, D., Horrocks, I.: BERTMap: A BERT-based ontology alignment system (2022)
19. He, Y., Chen, J., Dong, H., Horrocks, I.: Exploring large language models for ontology alignment (2023)
20. He, Y., Chen, J., Dong, H., Jiménez-Ruiz, E., Hadian, A., Horrocks, I.: Machine learning-friendly biomedical datasets for equivalence and subsumption ontology matching. In: Sattler, U., et al. (eds.) The Semantic Web - ISWC 2022, pp. 575–591. Springer International Publishing, Cham (2022). https://doi.org/10.1007/978-3-031-19433-7_33
21. Hertling, S., Paulheim, H.: OLaLa: ontology matching with large language models. In: Proceedings of the 12th Knowledge Capture Conference 2023, pp. 131–139. K-CAP '23, Association for Computing Machinery, New York, NY, USA (2023). https://doi.org/10.1145/3587259.3627571
22. Jiang, A.Q., et al.: Mistral 7B (2023)

23. Jiménez-Ruiz, E., Cuenca Grau, B.: LogMap: logic-based and scalable ontology matching. In: Aroyo, L., et al. (eds.) ISWC 2011. LNCS, vol. 7031, pp. 273–288. Springer, Heidelberg (2011). https://doi.org/10.1007/978-3-642-25073-6_18

24. Karam, N., Khiat, A., Algergawy, A., Sattler, M., Weiland, C., Schmidt, M.: Matching biodiversity and ecology ontologies: challenges and evaluation results. Knowl. Eng. Rev. **35**, e9 (2020). https://doi.org/10.1017/S0269888920000132, https://doi.org/10.1017/S0269888920000132

25. Labrak, Y., Bazoge, A., Morin, E., Gourraud, P.A., Rouvier, M., Dufour, R.: BioMistral: a collection of open-source pretrained large language models for medical domains (2024)

26. Lewis, P., et al.: Retrieval-augmented generation for knowledge-intensive NLP tasks (2021)

27. Liu, P., Yuan, W., Fu, J., Jiang, Z., Hayashi, H., Neubig, G.: Pre-train, prompt, and predict: a systematic survey of prompting methods in natural language processing (2021)

28. Liu, Y., et al.: RoBERTa: a robustly optimized BERT pretraining approach (2019)

29. Nas, E., Huschka, M.: MSE Benchmark. https://github.com/EngyNasr/MSE-Benchmark (2023)

30. Norouzi, S.S., Mahdavinejad, M.S., Hitzler, P.: Conversational ontology alignment with ChatGPT. In: OM@ISWC. CEUR Workshop Proceedings, vol. 3591, pp. 61–66. CEUR-WS.org (2023)

31. Noy, N., Mcguinness, D.: Ontology development 101: a guide to creating your first ontology. Knowl. Syst. Lab. **32** (2001)

32. OpenAI: ChatGPT. https://openai.com/chat-gpt/ (2023). Accessed 5 May 2023

33. OpenAI: new and improved embedding model (2023). https://openai.com/blog/new-and-improved-embedding-model. Retrieved 15 Dec 2022

34. Osman, I., Ben Yahia, S., Diallo, G.: Ontology integration: approaches and challenging issues. Inf. Fus. **71**, 38–63 (2021). https://doi.org/10.1016/j.inffus.2021.01.007

35. Peng, Y., Alam, M., Bonald, T.: Ontology matching using textual class descriptions. In: OM@ISWC. CEUR Workshop Proceedings, vol. 3591, pp. 67–72. CEUR-WS.org (2023)

36. Pennington, J., Socher, R., Manning, C.: GloVe: global vectors for word representation. In: Moschitti, A., Pang, B., Daelemans, W. (eds.) Proceedings of the 2014 Conference on Empirical Methods in Natural Language Processing (EMNLP), pp. 1532–1543. Association for Computational Linguistics, Doha, Qatar (2014). https://doi.org/10.3115/v1/D14-1162, https://aclanthology.org/D14-1162

37. Reimers, N., Gurevych, I.: Sentence-BERT: Sentence embeddings using Siamese BERT-networks (2019)

38. Sammut, C., Webb, G.I. (eds.): TF–IDF, pp. 986–987. Springer US, Boston, MA (2010). https://doi.org/10.1007/978-0-387-30164-8_832

39. Sharma, A., Jain, S.: LSMatch and LSMatch-multilingual results for OAEI 2023. In: OM@ISWC. CEUR Workshop Proceedings, vol. 3591, pp. 159–163. CEUR-WS.org (2023)

40. Shvaiko, P., Euzenat, J., Jiménez-Ruiz, E., Hassanzadeh, O., Trojahn, C. (eds.): Proceedings of the 18th International Workshop on Ontology Matching co-located with the 22nd International Semantic Web Conference (ISWC 2023), Athens, Greece, November 7, 2023, CEUR Workshop Proceedings, vol. 3591. CEUR-WS.org (2023)

41. da Silva, J., Revoredo, K., Baião, F., Lima, C.: ALIN results for OAEI 2023. In: OM@ISWC. CEUR Workshop Proceedings, vol. 3591, pp. 140–145. CEUR-WS.org (2023)

42. Singh, A., D'Arcy, M., Cohan, A., Downey, D., Feldman, S.: SciRepEval: a multi-format benchmark for scientific document representations. ArXiv abs/2211.13308 (2022)

43. Sousa, G., Lima, R., Trojahn, C.: Combining word and sentence embeddings with alignment extension for property matching. In: OM@ISWC. CEUR Workshop Proceedings, vol. 3591, pp. 91–96. CEUR-WS.org (2023)

44. Stephan, G., Pascal, H., Andreas, A.: Knowledge Representation and Ontologies, pp. 51–105. Springer, Berlin, Heidelberg (2007). https://doi.org/10.1007/3-540-70894-4_3

45. Team, M.N.: Introducing MPT-7B: a new standard for open-source, commercially usable LLMs (2023). www.mosaicml.com/blog/mpt-7b. Accessed 05 May 2023

46. Touvron, H., at el.: Llama 2: open foundation and fine-tuned chat models (2023)

47. Wang, Z.: AMD results for OAEI 2023. In: OM@ISWC. CEUR Workshop Proceedings, vol. 3591, pp. 146–153. CEUR-WS.org (2023)

48. Wang, Z.: Contextualized structural self-supervised learning for ontology matching (2023)

49. Wolf, T., et al.: HuggingFace's transformers: state-of-the-art natural language processing (2020)

50. Xue, L., et al.: ByT5: towards a token-free future with pre-trained byte-to-byte models (2022)

51. Zhang, X., Zhao, C., Wang, X.: A survey on knowledge representation in materials science and engineering: an ontological perspective. Computers in Industry **73**, 8–22 (2015). https://doi.org/10.1016/j.compind.2015.07.005

52. Zheng, L., et al.: Judging LLM-as-a-judge with MT-bench and chatbot arena (2023)

NeOn-GPT: A Large Language Model-Powered Pipeline for Ontology Learning

Nadeen Fathallah[1]([✉]), Arunav Das[2], Stefano De Giorgis[3], Andrea Poltronieri[4], Peter Haase[5], and Liubov Kovriguina[5]

[1] Analytic Computing, Institute for Artificial Intelligence, University of Stuttgart, Stuttgart, Germany
nadeen.fathallah@ki.uni-stuttgart.de
[2] King's College London, London, UK
[3] Institute of Cognitive Sciences and Technologies - National Research Council (ISTC-CNR), University of Bologna, Bologna, Italy
[4] Department of Computer Science and Engineering, University of Bologna, Bologna, Italy
[5] metaphacts GmbH, Walldorf, Germany

Abstract. We address the task of ontology learning by combining the structured NeOn methodology framework with Large Language Models (LLMs) for translating natural language domain descriptions into Turtle syntax ontologies. The main contribution of the paper is a prompt pipeline tailored for domain-agnostic modeling, exemplified through the application to a domain-specific case study: the wine ontology. The resulting pipeline is used to develop NeOn-GPT, a workflow for automatic ontology modeling, and its proof of concept implementation, integrated on top of the metaphactory platform. NeOn-GPT leverages the systematic approach of the NeOn methodology and LLMs' generative capabilities to facilitate a more efficient ontology development process. We evaluate the proposed approach by conducting comprehensive evaluations using the Stanford wine ontology as the gold standard. The obtained results show, that LLMs are not fully equipped to perform procedural tasks required for ontology development, and lack the reasoning skills and domain expertise needed. Overall, LLMs require integration with the workflow or trajectory tools for continuous knowledge engineering tasks. Nevertheless, LLMs can significantly alleviate the time and expertise needed. Our code base is publicly available for research and development purposes, accessible at: https://github.com/andreamust/NEON-GPT.

Keywords: Ontology Modelling · Large Language Models · NeOn Methodology

Conceptualization: N.F., A.D, S.D.G, A.P, P.H; **Investigation:** N.F., A.D, S.D.G, A.P, P.H; **Methodology:** S.D.G, A.P, P.H; **Software:** N.F, A.D, S.D.G, A.P; **Validation:** N.F, A.D; **Visualization:** N.F, A.D; **Writing - original draft:** N.F., A.D; **Writing - review & editing:** N.F, A.D, S.D.G., L.K.

A. Meroño Peñuela et al. (Eds.): ESWC 2024, LNCS 15344, pp. 36–50, 2025.
https://doi.org/10.1007/978-3-031-78952-6_4

1   Introduction

LLMs have revolutionized the landscape of both artificial intelligence research and our daily life [14,29], showing unparalleled capabilities in language understanding, generation, and interpretation. Despite their advancements, LLMs face critical challenges including a lack of real-world grounding [18], issues with hallucinations and information processing [13], and insufficient fact-checking mechanisms [27]. These limitations underscore the necessity for continued research to enhance LLM reliability and utility, particularly in knowledge-intensive applications. This work uses LLMs for ontology learning [17], using semi-automatic techniques to produce initial drafts of domain-specific ontologies from natural language descriptions, formalized in Turtle syntax. To improve ontology learning efficiency and reliability, we adapt the NeOn methodology [11,31] as a guiding framework for generative LLMs [34] to address the previously mentioned LLMs limitations.

Our contributions can be summarized as follows:

- Prompt pipeline implementation based on the principles of the NeOn methodology, to facilitate ontology learning for domain-specific ontologies.
- Development of the NeOn-GPT workflow, an automated workflow for ontology generation. NeOn-GPT uses the NeOn methodology to guide LLMs through structured ontology-building phases, including concept refinement and axiom elaboration, with features for validation and soundness checks.
- In-depth evaluation of our approach, with the wine ontology as a use case.

The paper is structured as follows: Sect. 2, an overview of the existing literature. Sections 3 and 4 present our approach, the NeOn-GPT workflow, and the integration on top of the metaphactory platform. Section 5 is dedicated to the experiments and in Sect. 6, the results obtained from applying our methodology. Finally, Sect. 7 offers a conclusion and future research endeavors.

2   Related Work

Relevant work to this contribution includes ontology learning from text, LLMs for conceptual modeling, and the NeOn methodology for ontology development.

Ontology Learning from Text is the task of automatically extracting and generating the components of an ontology from textual data [17]. An early approach [12], utilizes lexico-syntactic patterns for ontology learning, enabling the automated extraction of hierarchical relationships from large text collections and enhancing existing lexical databases like WordNet. [2] uses corpus analysis for ontology construction, extracting relevant concepts and relationships from the linguistic and domain-specific terminology in text corpora. [17] elaborates on integrating Natural Language Processing (NLP) and Semantic Web applications in ontology learning, utilizing NLP techniques to extract concept hierarchies and relationships from unstructured web content to automate the creation of semantic web annotations. [6] proposes Text2Onto framework for data-driven ontology learning, utilizes probabilistic algorithms, association rule mining, and clustering techniques for extracting concepts, relationships, and categorizing entities within ontologies from textual data. These works inspire our use of an established ontology development framework to guide LLMs, demonstrating the effectiveness of structured rule-based methods and NLP methods in extracting and organizing knowledge from text.

LLMs for Conceptual Modelling. The fusion of LLMs with conceptual modeling practices represents a novel approach to understanding and organizing knowledge. Early experiments like the LAMA benchmark [24] evaluate LMs' understanding of factual and commonsense knowledge through 'cloze' prompts, where the model's task is to accurately complete sentences missing words that represent subject-relation-object triples. This showcases LMs' ability to interpret and utilize structured knowledge required for conceptual modeling. Further experiments use ChatGPT for generating entity-relationship diagrams to illustrate LLMs' capability to translate natural language descriptions into structured conceptual models, leveraging structured prompts and a zero-shot learning approach [7]. [32] uses LLMs to visualize data interconnections by introducing GraphGPT, prompting LLMs to transform textual information into the corresponding knowledge graphs (KGs). [4] proposes a method for KG generation where LLMs are prompted in a bottom-up approach to create an element hierarchy and subsequently identify possible relationships between elements. These works are relevant to our work, demonstrating LLMs' capability to interpret and structure domain-specific knowledge into conceptual models.

NeOn Methodology for Ontology Development [11,31] is designed to facilitate ontology development through a comprehensive, scenario-based framework. It enables flexibility with alternative development paths and delivers a structured approach through detailed guidelines for processes and activities associated with ontology development. Contrasted with Agile methodologies like the eXtreme Design (XD) [26], NeOn emphasizes detailed planning over Agile's rapid, minimal design approach [30]. This makes NeOn well-suited for projects that require deep conceptualization and systematic methodology, especially in collaborative and iterative ontology development. NeOn offers a generic framework that aligns with software engineering principles for a broad array of ontology development projects, this sets NeOn apart from more specialized methodologies such as SAMOD [23] and RapidOWL [1].

We follow three distinct phases from the NeOn methodology: (i) specification of ontology requirements—defining purpose, scope, and target group; (ii) ontology conceptualization—establishing class hierarchy and structuring concepts; and (iii) ontology implementation in a specific formalism (e.g., Turtle syntax [3]).

3 Methodology

3.1 NeOn-GPT Workflow

Our proposed approach capitalizes on LLMs' ability to interpret and generate natural language to understand domain descriptions and convert them to their corresponding ontologies. We use the NeOn methodology framework, known for

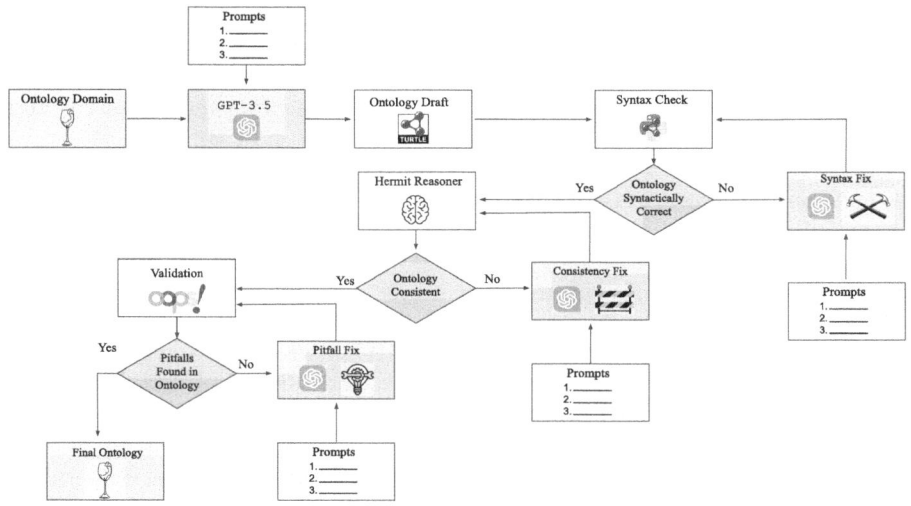

Fig. 1. NeOn-GPT Ontology Engineering Pipeline

its structure and iterative approach to guide ontology development through distinct phases: requirement specification, ontology conceptualization, and ontology implementation, to ensure that the generated ontology is not only logically sound but also aligned with domain requirements. We convert the NeOn methodology framework to a series of prompts to an LLM, specifically GPT-3.5. This synergy is encapsulated in our workflow (NeOn-GPT) illustrated in Fig. 1.

Step 1 - Ontology draft generation: We are following the NeOn Methodology Framework for ontology development, with a particular focus on the 'Specification of ontology requirements' section. This section includes: (i) providing a generic domain description, (ii) specification of the ontology purpose, (iii) defining the scope, (iv) identifying the requirements of the ontology, and (v) generating example competency questions (CQs). We translate this framework and domain description into structured prompts for an LLM, GPT-3.5 [36]. To enhance prompt quality, we use prompt engineering techniques, such as Chain-of-Thought (CoT) [37] and Role-play prompting [28]. CoT prompts guide GPT-3.5 through a series of logical steps to a final output clarifying LLMs' reasoning process, while Role-play LLMs to adopt specific perspectives or personas (e.g., "Experienced Knowledge Engineer"), resulting in more contextually relevant responses. This approach is detailed in Fig. 2a. We further prompt GPT-3.5 to generate CQs as brief queries that help clarify and assess the knowledge representation within the ontology (see Fig. 2b).

Following this, ontology conceptualization, and conceptual modeling in the NeOn methodology involves entity and relationship extraction. Through few-shot prompting [35], we prompt GPT-3.5 to extract entities and relationships from the generated CQs and generate a conceptual model of the ontology in the form of subject-relation-object triples (see Fig. 3). Few-shot prompting involves the construction of prompts that describe the task, accompanied by a set of examples from the domain enabling the LLM to generate contextually relevant outputs. In the context of the wine ontology, examples of entities include `Wine` and `GrapeVariety`. Examples of properties of the `Wine` entity include `Color` and `SugarLevel`. The domain range for the property `Color` of the `Wine` entity is: (`Red, White, Rosé`). The relationship between `Wine` and `GrapeVariety` entities is: `Wine hasGrapeVariety GrapeVariety`.

Lastly, for ontology implementation, we prompt GPT-3.5 to use the generated triples to implement a full ontology serialized in Turtle syntax. Following this, we apply formal modeling to accurately capture the domain's complexities and relationships in the ontology, ensuring it is logically sound and capable of supporting advanced reasoning. This entails prompting GPT-3.5 to include object properties: inverse, reflexivity, transitivity, symmetry, and functional. The prompt is constructed such that object properties are added when meaningful while ensuring the ontology remains consistent. An example of the generated triples is shown in Fig. 4. To enhance ontology usability and readability, we prompt GPT-3.5 to enrich entities and relationships with natural language descriptions and add essential metadata such as IRI, labels, and versions (see Fig. 5). To ground the ontology in real-world data and facilitate knowledge discovery, we use few-shot prompting to populate the ontology with real-world instances (see Fig. 6).

Step 2 - Syntax validation: our workflow illustrated in Fig. 1 verifies that the generated ontology draft is syntactically correct using the RDFLib python package [16]. RDFLib detects syntax errors and error messages are used to prompt GPT-3.5 for error correction (example in Fig. 7).

Step 3 - Consistency check: after examining the resulting ontology, it became apparent that introducing domain complexity, also resulted in the introduction of some inconsistencies. To remedy this, we use the HermiT reasoner API [9] to ensure that the resulting ontology is logically sound and free from inconsistencies. The inconsistency error messages generated by the HermiT reasoner are used as prompts to GPT-3.5 for inconsistency resolution, as shown in Fig. 8.

Step 4 - Pitfall resolution: our workflow uses OOPS API [25] for pitfall scanning to validate the generated ontology, common pitfalls include circular axioms and missing disjointness. OOPS API categorizes common pitfalls into three categories: Critical, Important, and Minor. GPT-3.5 showed proficiency in addressing Critical and Important pitfalls but failed to address Minor pitfalls and maintain a consistent and coherent ontology. Validation results from OOPS API are used as prompts for GPT-3.5 for pitfall resolution, as shown in Fig. 9.

The visualization of the final wine ontology structure generated by NeOn-GPT is illustrated in Fig. 10c.

4   NeOn-GPT Integration on Top of Metaphactory

An important aspect of facilitating ontology development with LLMs is providing the ontology designer with sufficient guidance for the chosen methodology while ensuring that the output of each step is valid and consistent to qualify as the input for the subsequent step. This poses a challenge in the context of LLMs, as they struggle with procedural tasks, producing hallucinated and fragmented results, or missing the steps of the process.

To address this challenge, we have integrated the NeOn-GPT prompt pipeline on top of the metaphactory platform [10] as an app. To guide the user consistently through the NeOn methodology, we leveraged the Workflow Ontology in metaphactory, designed for representing interactive workflows. This ontology outlines workflows at both conceptual and instance levels, associating each workflow step with specific instructions, templates, and artifacts (see Fig. 12). The implementation step is detailed in Fig. 13. Through this structured approach, the metaphactory platform ensures a smooth transition from one workflow step to the next, enhancing user guidance for automated ontology development.

5   Experiments

In our experiments, we use the wine ontology to validate the NeOn-GPT workflow, showcasing its practical utility in ontology learning. The wine ontology [22] is a structured framework that organizes wine attributes and relationships, from grape varieties to taste profiles and production methods, enhancing information systems for wine knowledge management, retrieval, and recommendations.

To identify a suitable LLM for our task, we used GPT-3.5 [36], Llama [8], and PaLm [5] through zero-shot prompting experiments. GPT-3.5 generated syntactically sound and non-redundant ontologies, outperforming Llama and PaLm, thus chosen for developing NeOn-GPT workflow. In our experiments, we prompt LLMs to generate ontologies in Turtle syntax [3] after initial experiments with OWL syntax [19] generated ontologies with syntactical errors. We conducted three experiments to evaluate our approach:(i) Zero-shot Prompting [15], prompt GPT-3.5 with wine domain natural language description to generate the wine ontology in Turtle syntax, (ii) Ontology Development Guide Prompts, parse the Stanford guide to create ontologies [22], to a series of structured prompts for GPT3.5 to generate the wine ontology in Turtle syntax, and (iii) NeOn-GPT Workflow (Our approach).

6   Results

We employed the Protégé Stanford University Wine Ontology [22] as the gold standard ontology for benchmarking our resulting ontologies. Comparing the Zero-Shot Prompting Ontology, Ontology Development Guide Ontology, and NeOn-GPT Ontology against gold standard ontology, illustrated in Fig. 10, revealed that both the Zero-Shot Prompting and Ontology Development Guide ontologies exhibited a flat hierarchy, lacked conceptual structure, and contained syntactical errors and redundant terms. Given NeOn-GPT's wine ontology's superior capacity to capture domain complexity while remaining logically sound and consistent compared to its counterparts, we conduct in-depth evaluations to compare NeOn-GPT's wine ontology to the gold standard wine ontology, illustrated in Table 1. These evaluations encompass both structural assessment and pre-inference and post-inference assessment.

Table 1. Ontology Metrics Comparison - gold standard wine ontology and NeOn-GPT wine ontology [source: OntoMetrics [33], Protégé [20]].

Metric	Gold standard wine ontology	NeOn-GPT wine ontology
Axioms	911	387
Logical axioms count	657	139
Asserted Class count	77	39
Object property count	13	24
Data property count	1	12
Properties count	14	36
Individual count	161	25

6.1   Structural Assessment

Involves schema and hierarchical comparisons. Results from the schema comparison illustrated in Table 1, can be summarized as:

– NeOn-GPT wine ontology exhibits approximately half the asserted classes found in gold standard wine ontology, suggesting a narrower scope of conceptual richness.
– NeOn-GPT wine ontology has approximately twice the object properties compared to gold standard wine ontology, suggesting better identification of salient features within the wine domain.
– NeOn-GPT wine ontology has twelve times the number of data properties compared to gold standard wine ontology, pointing to greater depth in class membership assignment.
– Although NeOn-GPT wine ontology has higher counts of object and data properties than the gold standard wine ontology, it features significantly fewer axioms. Reflecting that LLMs struggle to establish subject-relation-object triples. This can be attributed to LLMs generative capabilities that rely on statistical correlations and vector search methods, not on deductive reasoning or formal logic.
– NeOn-GPT wine ontology contains only one-sixth the number of individuals present in gold standard wine ontology, reflecting its stronger emphasis on identification rather than instance enumeration.

Results from hierarchical comparison illustrated in Fig. 10 and Table 1, can be summarised as:

– Class distribution: NeOn-GPT wine ontology differs notably from gold standard wine ontology, featuring a total of 39 classes, 36 classes without and 3 with sub-classes, compared to gold standard wine ontology with a total of 77 classes, 67 without and 10 with sub-classes.
– Class depth: NeOn-GPT wine ontology hierarchy has levels L0-L2 (Thing -> Wine -> Red Wine) versus gold standard wine ontology's L0-L3 more granular hierarchy (Thing -> Potable Liquid -> Bordeaux -> Sauterness).

6.2   Pre-Inference and Post-Inference Steps Assessment

Highlights the changes introduced by reasoning in both ontologies.

Pre-inference steps, NeOn-GPT's wine ontology allows instances of "WhiteWine" and "RedWine" to inherit from the "Wine" class due to their subsumption relationship. Conversely, the gold standard wine ontology uses class equivalence with color property restrictions, preventing "WhiteWine" and "RedWine" instances from inheriting "Wine" class memberships.

Post-inference steps, the gold standard wine ontology expands "Wine" instances, after including entities: "WhiteWine", "RedWine", and "RoseWine". NeOn-GPT wine ontology only adds "BurgundyRegion" to "Wine", showing limited classification properties by classifying based on basic concepts like geographical regions. Using the example of "CabernetSauvignon", the gold standard wine ontology infers it as "DryRedWine" through class equivalence and restrictions, in contrast, NeOn-GPT wine ontology accurately, yet simplistically, infers it just as a "GrapeVariety" (see Fig. 11), reveals the limited depth of concept definition in the NeOn-GPT wine ontology for wine classification.

7   Conclusion and Future Work

We present a novel approach to ontology learning using LLMs and the NeOn Methodology Framework. Results from our experiments are presented in Sects. 5 and 6. Our results suggest that effective prompt engineering techniques alongside established ontology development methodologies can significantly influence LLMs' output to generate more consistent ontologies. However, experiments conducted in this study indicate that the inherent statistical representation of knowledge within LLMs can not be directly converted to a formal representation for a domain-specific ontology creation with the same expressivity as the gold standard ontology for that domain. These limitations appear to stem from - class expressions and property restrictions. Class expressions in LLM-generated ontology are generally limited to subsumption type and lack conjunction, and disjunction expression types. This can limit their ability to create complex classes from simple class definitions during the inference step. Similarly, property restriction types are primarily limited to "HasValue" restrictions, the absence of cardinality, existential, and universal restrictions may limit the scope of class membership inferences during the reasoning step. Our experiments demonstrate LLMs can potentially be integrated into semi-automatic pipelines for generating base ontologies for enhancement through human-assisted knowledge. Recent studies with LLMs suggest they will eventually support Knowledge Engineering [21,34].

Future research work could explore augmenting our NeOn-GPT workflow with KG link prediction techniques to improve the expressivity and chain of reasoning for improving class expressions and property restrictions. Another path involves closely combining LLMs with workflows to create a system, acting as a copilot to support and guide users to build ontologies more effectively. Another approach, using pre-trained LLMs designed for code generation (e.g., Codex,

Code LlamA) or fine-tuning pre-trained LLMs to produce valid and consistent ontologies could also enhance outcomes.

Appendix A: Figures

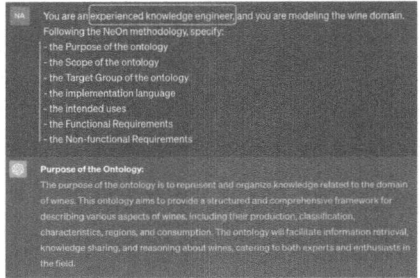

(a) Using Chain-of-Thought prompting to prompt ChatGPT to specify the wine ontology requirements following the NeOn Methodology Framework.

(b) Prompting ChatGPT to generate competency questions for the wine ontology.

Fig. 2. Step - 1 Ontology draft generation: specification of ontology requirements, prompting ChatGPT to specify the wine ontology requirements following the NeOn methodology framework.

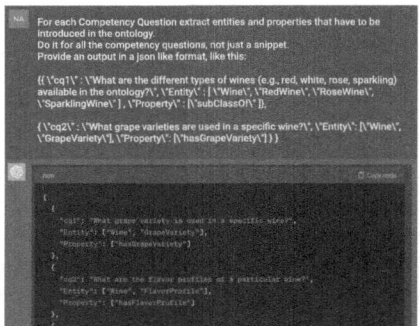

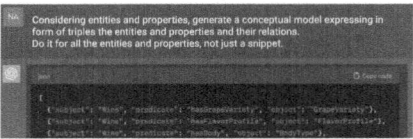

(a) Using Few-shot prompt- ing to prompt ChatGPT to extract entities and properties.

(b) Prompting ChatGPT to generate the corresponding triples to the extracted entities and properties.

Fig. 3. Step - 1 Ontology draft generation: prompting ChatGPT to create a conceptual model of the wine ontology based on the generated competency questions in Fig. 2b.

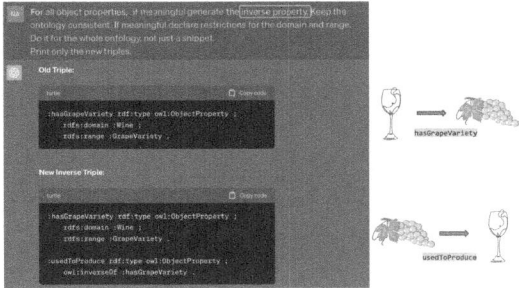

Fig. 4. Step - 1 Ontology draft generation: illustration of prompting ChatGPT to extend the generated wine ontology with inverse object properties: `"usedToProduce"` inverse to the existing `"hasGrapeVariety"` property.

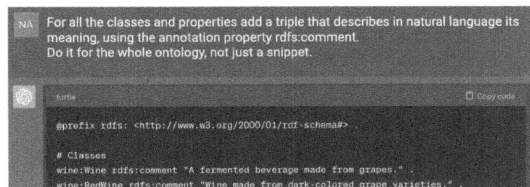

Fig. 5. Step - 1 Ontology draft generation: prompting ChatGPT to generate natural language descriptions for entities and properties in the wine ontology.

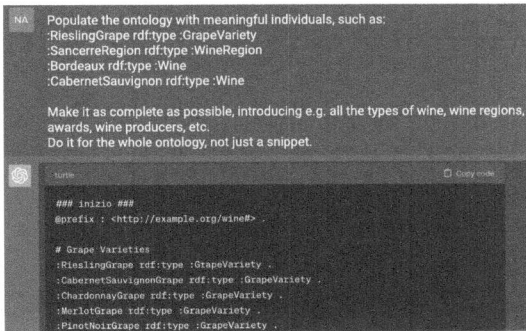

Fig. 6. Step - 1 Ontology draft generation: using Few-shot prompting to prompt Chat-GPT to populate the wine ontology with real world instances.

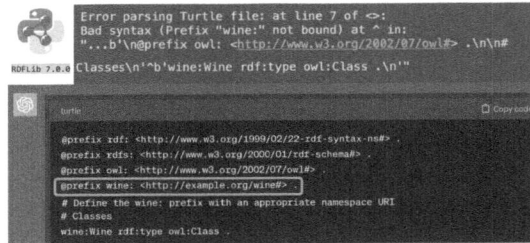

Fig. 7. Step - 2 Syntax validation: example of using errors produced by RDFLib to prompt ChatGPT to fix syntax errors, declaring undefined prefix **"Wine"**.

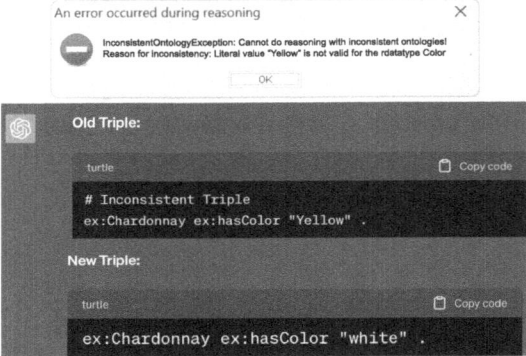

Fig. 8. Step - 3 Consistency check: illustration of an inconsistency in the wine ontology detected by HermiT Reasoner, incorrect assignment of **"Yellow"** as a wine color. ChatGPT identified **"White"** as the valid color using the HermiT reasoner error as a prompt, aligning with the domain range: **(Red, White, Rosé)**. (Color figure online)

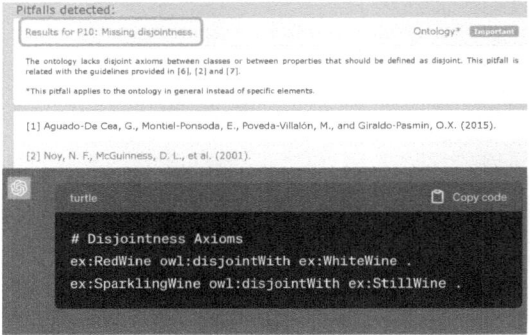

Fig. 9. Step - 4 Pitfall resolution: illustration of a pitfall detected by OOPS API where the wine ontology lacked disjointness. Prompting ChatGPT using the pitfall description from OOPS API as a prompt, ChatGPT introduced the necessary disjointness axioms such as **"RedWine"** is disjoint with **"WhiteWine"**.

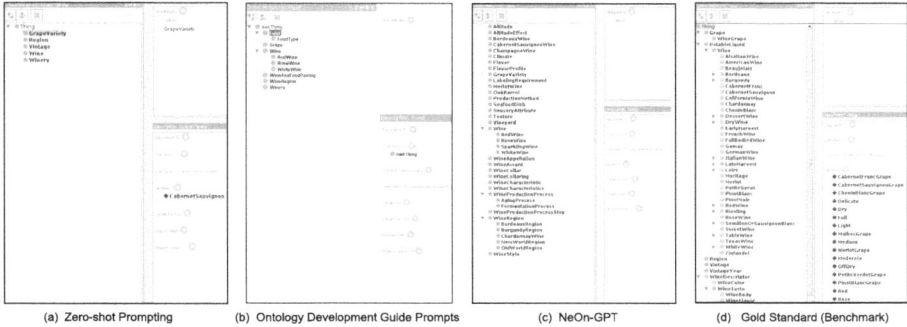

(a) Zero-shot Prompting   (b) Ontology Development Guide Prompts   (c) NeOn-GPT   (d) Gold Standard (Benchmark)

Fig. 10. Comparative overview of the wine ontology structures.

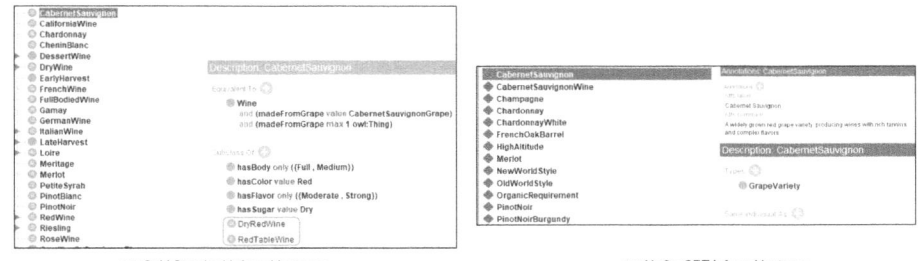

(a) Gold Standard Inferred Instance   (b) NeOn-GPT Inferred Instance

Fig. 11. Ontological inferences of `"CabernetSauvignon"`.

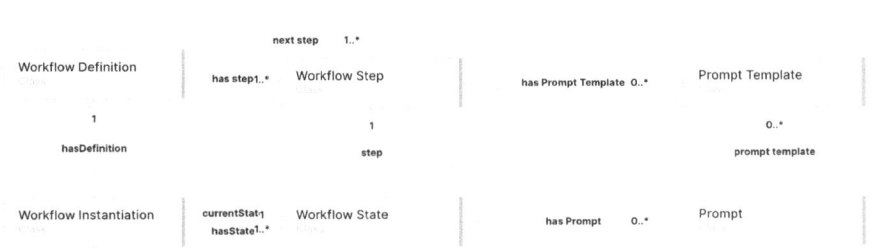

Fig. 12. Workflow Ontology in metaphactory. *Workflow Definition* and *Workflow Instantiation* are distinguished. A workflow is defined by a sequence of *Workflow steps*, where each step has one or more *Prompt Templates*. A workflow instance is a sequence of *Workflow states*, where each state has one or more *prompts*.

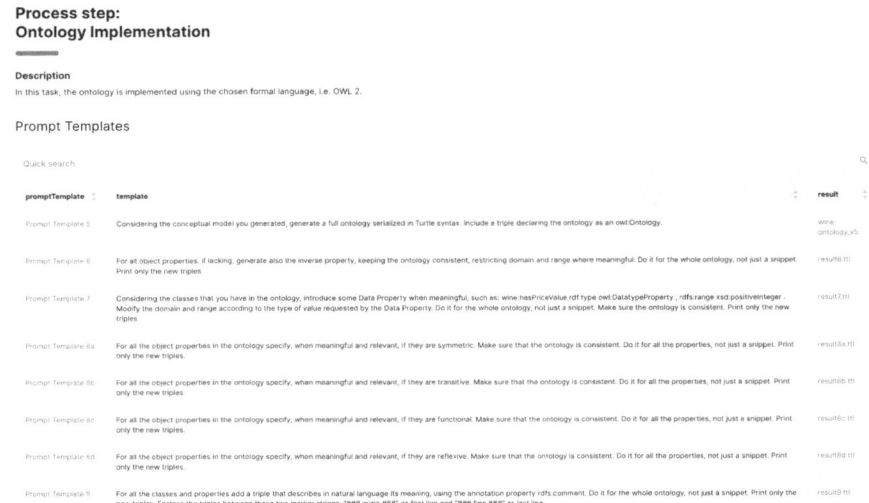

Fig. 13. NeOn-GPT Integration on top of metaphactory: Ontology Implementation Step.

References

1. Auer, S.: The RapidOWL methodology–towards agile knowledge engineering. In: 15th IEEE International Workshops on Enabling Technologies: Infrastructures for Collaborative Enterprises (WETICE 2006), 26-28 June 2006, Manchester, United Kingdom, pp. 352–357. IEEE Computer Society (2006). https://doi.org/10.1109/WETICE.2006.67, https://doi.org/10.1109/WETICE.2006.67
2. Aussenac-Gilles, N., Biebow, B., Szulman, S.: Revisiting ontology design: a methodology based on corpus analysis. In: Dieng, R., Corby, O. (eds.) Knowledge Acquisition, Modeling and Management, 12th International Conference, EKAW 2000, Juan-les-Pins, France, October 2-6, 2000, Proceedings. Lecture Notes in Computer Science, vol. 1937, pp. 172–188. Springer (2000). https://doi.org/10.1007/3-540-39967-4_13
3. Beckett, D., Berners-Lee, T., Prud'hommeaux, E., Carothers, G.: RDF 1.1 Turtle. World Wide Web Consortium, pp. 18–31 (2014)
4. Bikeyev, A.: Synthetic ontologies: a hypothesis. Available at SSRN 4373537 (2023)
5. Chowdhery, A., et al.: PaLM: scaling language modeling with pathways. J. Mach. Learn. Res. (JMLR) **24**, 240:1–240:113 (2023). http://jmlr.org/papers/v24/22-1144.html
6. Cimiano, P., Völker, J.: Text2Onto. In: Montoyo, A., Muñoz, R., Métais, E. (eds.) NLDB 2005. LNCS, vol. 3513, pp. 227–238. Springer, Heidelberg (2005). https://doi.org/10.1007/11428817_21
7. Fill, H., Fettke, P., Köpke, J.: Conceptual modeling and large language models: impressions from first experiments with ChatGPT. Enterprise Modelling and

Information Systems Architectures International Journal of Conceptual Modelling (EMISAJ) **18**, 3 (2023). https://doi.org/10.18417/EMISA.18.3, https://doi.org/10.18417/emisa.18.3

8. Gao, P., et al.: LLaMA-adapter V2: parameter-efficient visual instruction model. arXiv preprint arXiv:2304.15010 (2023)

9. Glimm, B., Horrocks, I., Motik, B., Stoilos, G., Wang, Z.: HermiT: an OWL 2 reasoner. J. Autom. Reason. **53**, 245–269 (2014)

10. Haase, P., Herzig, D.M., Kozlov, A., Nikolov, A., Trame, J.: metaphactory: a platform for knowledge graph management. Seman. Web **10**(6), 1109–1125 (2019). https://doi.org/10.3233/SW-190360

11. Haase, P., Lewen, H., Studer, R., Tran, D.T., Erdmann, M., d'Aquin, M., Motta, E.: The neon ontology engineering toolkit. World Wide Web J. (WWW) (2008)

12. Hearst, M.: Automated discovery of WordNet relations. WordNet an electronic lexical database (1998)

13. Ji, Z., Yu, T., Xu, Y., Lee, N., Ishii, E., Fung, P.: Towards mitigating LLM hallucination via self reflection. In: Bouamor, H., Pino, J., Bali, K. (eds.) Findings of the Association for Computational Linguistics: EMNLP 2023, Singapore, December 6-10, 2023, pp. 1827–1843. Association for Computational Linguistics (2023). https://aclanthology.org/2023.findings-emnlp.123

14. Joshi, I., Budhiraja, R., Akolekar, H.D., Challa, J.S., Kumar, D.: It's not like Jarvis, but it's pretty close! - examining ChatGPT's usage among undergraduate students in computer science. CoRR abs/2311.09651 (2023). https://doi.org/10.48550/ARXIV.2311.09651

15. Kojima, T., Gu, S.S., Reid, M., Matsuo, Y., Iwasawa, Y.: Large language models are zero-shot reasoners. In: Koyejo, S., Mohamed, S., Agarwal, A., Belgrave, D., Cho, K., Oh, A. (eds.) Advances in Neural Information Processing Systems 35: Annual Conference on Neural Information Processing Systems 2022, NeurIPS 2022, New Orleans, LA, USA, November 28 - December 9, 2022 (2022). http://papers.nips.cc/paper_files/paper/2022/hash/8bb0d291acd4acf06ef112099c16f326-Abstract-Conference.html

16. Krech, D., et al.: RDFLib (2023). https://doi.org/10.5281/zenodo.6845245, https://github.com/RDFLib/rdflib

17. Maedche, A., Staab, S.: Ontology learning for the semantic web. IEEE Intell. Syst. **16**(2), 72–79 (2001). https://doi.org/10.1109/5254.920602

18. Marcus, G.: Sora's surreal physics. https://garymarcus.substack.com/p/soras-surreal-physics (2024). Accessed 27 Feb 2024

19. McGuinness, D.L., Van Harmelen, F., et al.: OWL web ontology language overview. World Wide Web Consortium recommendation **10**(10), 2004 (2004)

20. Musen, M.A.: The protégé project: a look back and a look forward. AI Matters **1**(4), 4–12 (2015)

21. Neuhaus, F.: Ontologies in the era of large language models - a perspective. Appl. Ontol. **18**(4), 399–407 (2023). https://doi.org/10.3233/AO-230072

22. Noy, N.F., McGuinness, D.L., et al.: Ontology development 101: a guide to creating your first ontology (2001)

23. Peroni, S.: A simplified agile methodology for ontology development. In: Dragoni, M., Poveda-Villalón, M., Jiménez-Ruiz, E. (eds.) OWL: - Experiences and Directions - Reasoner Evaluation - 13th International Workshop, OWLED 2016, and 5th International Workshop, ORE 2016, Bologna, Italy, November 20, 2016, Revised Selected Papers. Lecture Notes in Computer Science, vol. 10161, pp. 55–69. Springer (2016). https://doi.org/10.1007/978-3-319-54627-8_5

24. Petroni, F., et al.: Language models as knowledge bases? In: Inui, K., Jiang, J., Ng, V., Wan, X. (eds.) Proceedings of the 2019 Conference on Empirical Methods in Natural Language Processing and the 9th International Joint Conference on Natural Language Processing, EMNLP-IJCNLP 2019, Hong Kong, China, November 3–7, 2019, pp. 2463–2473. Association for Computational Linguistics (2019). https://doi.org/10.18653/V1/D19-1250

25. Poveda-Villalón, M., Gómez-Pérez, A., Suárez-Figueroa, M.C.: Oops! (ontology pitfall scanner!): an on-line tool for ontology evaluation. Int. J. Seman. Web Inf. Syst. (IJSWIS) **10**(2), 7–34 (2014). https://doi.org/10.4018/IJSWIS.2014040102

26. Presutti, V., Daga, E., Gangemi, A., Blomqvist, E.: extreme design with content ontology design patterns. In: Blomqvist, E., Sandkuhl, K., Scharffe, F., Svátek, V. (eds.) Proceedings of the Workshop on Ontology Patterns (WOP 2009), collocated with the 8th International Semantic Web Conference (ISWC-2009), Washington D.C., USA, 25 October, 2009. CEUR Workshop Proceedings, vol. 516. CEUR-WS.org (2009). https://ceur-ws.org/Vol-516/pap21.pdf

27. Quelle, D., Bovet, A.: The perils & promises of fact-checking with large language models. CoRR abs/2310.13549 (2023). https://doi.org/10.48550/arXiv.2310.13549

28. Shanahan, M., McDonell, K., Reynolds, L.: Role play with large language models. Nature **623**(7987), 493–498 (2023). https://doi.org/10.1038/S41586-023-06647-8

29. Smith, M., Zorpette, G., Choi, C.Q., Boyd, J.: Generative AI slims down for a portable world: > consumer tech aims LLMs everywhere-with laptops as the beachhead. IEEE Spectrum **61**(2), 5–13 (2024)

30. Spoladore, D., Pessot, E., Trombetta, A.: A novel agile ontology engineering methodology for supporting organizations in collaborative ontology development. Comput. Industry **151**, 103979 (2023). https://doi.org/10.1016/J.COMPIND.2023.103979

31. Suárez-Figueroa, M.C., Gómez-Pérez, A., Fernández-López, M.: The neon methodology framework: a scenario-based methodology for ontology development. Appl. Ontol. **10**(2), 107–145 (2015). https://doi.org/10.3233/AO-150145

32. Tang, J., et al.: GraphGPT: graph instruction tuning for large language models. CoRR abs/2310.13023 (2023). https://doi.org/10.48550/ARXIV.2310.13023

33. Tello, A.L., Gómez-Pérez, A.: ONTOMETRIC: a method to choose the appropriate ontology. J. Database Manage. (JDM) **15**(2), 1–18 (2004). https://doi.org/10.4018/JDM.2004040101

34. Wei, J., et al.: Emergent abilities of large language models. Trans. Mach. Learn. Res. (TMLR) **2022** (2022). https://openreview.net/forum?id=yzkSU5zdwD

35. Wei, J., et al.: Chain-of-thought prompting elicits reasoning in large language models. In: Koyejo, S., Mohamed, S., Agarwal, A., Belgrave, D., Cho, K., Oh, A. (eds.) Advances in Neural Information Processing Systems 35: Annual Conference on Neural Information Processing Systems 2022, NeurIPS 2022, New Orleans, LA, USA, November 28 - December 9, 2022 (2022). http://papers.nips.cc/paper_files/paper/2022/hash/9d5609613524ecf4f15af0f7b31abca4-Abstract-Conference.html

36. Ye, J., et al.: A comprehensive capability analysis of GPT-3 and GPT-3.5 series models. CoRR abs/2303.10420 (2023). https://doi.org/10.48550/ARXIV.2303.10420

37. Zhou, Y., et al.: Large language models are human-level prompt engineers. In: The Eleventh International Conference on Learning Representations, ICLR 2023, Kigali, Rwanda, May 1–5, 2023. OpenReview.net (2023). https://openreview.net/pdf?id=92gvk82DE-

Assessing the Evolution of LLM Capabilities for Knowledge Graph Engineering in 2023

Johannes Frey[1]([✉]) [ID], Lars-Peter Meyer[1] [ID], Felix Brei[1] [ID],
Sabine Gründer-Fahrer[1] [ID], and Michael Martin[1,2] [ID]

[1] InfAI/Leipzig University, Leipzig, Germany
frey@informatik.uni-leipzig.de, lpmeyer@infai.org ,
[2] Chemnitz University of Technology, Chemnitz, Germany
https://infai.org , https://tu-chemnitz.de/

Abstract. In this article, we evaluate the evolution of LLM capabilities w.r.t. the RDF Turtle and SPARQL language as foundational skills to assist with various KGE tasks. We measure the LLM response quality using 6 LLM-KG-Bench tasks for a total of 15 LLM versions available over the course of 2023, covering 5 different "major version" LLM classes (GPT-3.5 Turbo, GPT-4, Claude 1.x, Claude 2.x, and Claude Instant 1.x).

Keywords: LLM benchmarking · knowledge graph engineering · RDF · large language models · evolution of llms

1 Introduction

Combining the power of large language models (LLMs) and knowledge graphs (KGs) [8,15,16] to improve both LLM response quality, but also automation of the creation or processing of KGs via LLM-assistants, received huge attention 2023. In order to assist with KG engineering (KGE), it is crucial that LLMs can access, understand, and manipulate KGs but also artifacts that are involved in their construction within various KGE processes. RDF Turtle is a widely adopted language for representing KGs and KGE artifacts (RML mappings, SHACL shapes, SPARQL BGPs, Ontologies, etc.) and could serve in combination with SPARQL as a general low-level KG(E) interface to be leveraged by LLMs. While there exist works that employ or study LLMs for KGC/KGE tasks, investigating the performance of LLMs w.r.t. such low-level interfaces and basic graph comprehension, still remains under-explored, albeit a studies showed [4,13] that syntactical issues hinder the usefulness of semantically meaningful responses. This study compared leading GPT4all models to leading commercial models w.r.t. how well they speak Turtle. However, the obtained results only represent a snapshot from July 2023, LLMs rapidly evolved over the course of 2023 and studies reported that the performance of newer LLM versions can decrease [3,9] for selected workloads, raising the question whether this also affects KGE

A. Meroño Peñuela et al. (Eds.): ESWC 2024, LNCS 15344, pp. 51–60, 2025.
https://doi.org/10.1007/978-3-031-78952-6_5

workloads. In this paper, we focus on closing this gap by assessing the evolution in Turtle and SPARQL query generation skills of the commercial models from that study, for all versions that were accessible at the end of December 2023. Our work encompasses the following novelties and contributions:

- We present the first comprehensive, quantitative, and qualitative examination of the evolution of Turtle and SPARQL language skills for all Claude and GPT-3.5T/GPT-4 releases (until Dec 2023). We assess 15 versions and provide evidence that the performance of specific successors decreased for a subset of RDF-KGE tasks.
- We published a reusable time capsule dataset [6], capturing experiment replay data enabling further in-depth investigations (e.g. custom scores). Given the (ongoing) discontinuation of old(er) OpenAI models, this resource is a valuable asset, since it also enables future LLM efforts to be compared with a state-of-the-art-2023-baseline independent of model availability.
- We released an evolved version [11] of the LLM-KG-Bench framework [12] with updated prompts (enhanced clarity), a novel SPARQL task, a feature to rerun (modified) evaluations on captured model responses (e.g. using the time capsule), and support for instantiation-based tasks.
- We performed a replication experiment of findings in [4], thereby verifying and reinforcing the original research outcomes and the soundness of the benchmark setup and tasks.

2   Related Work

Recent studies have started to explore the use of LLMs in the context of various KGE tasks. For instance, [22] investigated the performance of LLMs on typical KG construction (KGC) tasks, namely entity, relation, and event extraction as well as link prediction, on eight benchmark datasets. Similarly, [18] showed that current LLMs can be used to streamline the process of automatic creation of KGs from raw texts as well as for automatic ontology creation. In [7,20], LLMs have been used for automatic Knowledge Base construction, completion or correction. Utilizing instruction training on LLMs was motivated and showcased by [10] for RDF(S) triple generation from text, performing further RDF(s) reasoning and constraint verification as well as in [2] for KG-specific SPARQL generation. Many of those works emphasize the need of deeper investigation and more systematic test scenarios. Therefore, the development of new benchmarking frameworks and generators currently is a topic of high relevance. The Open LLM Leaderboard [1], aims to evaluate the impressive performance claims of LLMs using the 7 Key Benchmarks from the *Eleuther AI Language Model Evaluation Harness* [17]. A highly promising approach within a sub-discipline of LLM-driven KGC is highlighted in Text2KGBench [14] and measured using a benchmark developed for that purpose.

A hardly-researched aspect of benchmarking LLMs is the evolution and shift of model performance over time [21]. LLM services have been observed to substantially change within a relatively short amount of time, forcing users to continuously adapt prompts, settings or even model choices as to keep the performance to their respective downstream applications stable. This is especially challenging because, it is currently not transparent how exactly LLMs like GPT-3.5 or GPT-4 are updated and how model behavior will be affected for its different, multi-faceted capabilities [3]. In consequence, there is the need for empiric studies, which try to systematically assess skills of LLMs for different perspectives of KGE. At the time being, though, the task of systematically evaluating model performance states itself a real challenge, as standard approaches and procedure, like regression testing, need to be substantially re-examined in the context of LLMs, e.g. due to different correctness notions, prompting brittleness, and non-determinism [9].

3   Assessment Setup

We performed 6 tasks via LLM-KG-Bench 1.2 [11], that assess individual skills of LLMs to read, understand, analyze, and create KGs using Turtle or SPARQL. The tasks are executed in two different manners, T1, T2, T5 and T6 are executed as *static* tasks (fixed problem size) 20 times per model, while T3 and T4 are *scalable* in problem size and are executed 20 times per combination of size and model for 8 different sizes.

Additionally, for the original tasks from [4] we performed a replication study using the same model versions. Due to the randomness with the default temperature, there is a slight variation but the results remain in the same interval (see [5]).

Task T1 - Find Connection in a Turtle Org Graph checks basic understanding for the RDF-KG data model and Turtle reading skills, and asks to find the shortest connection from *:Anne* to *:Bob* in a small organizational graph. For reasons of brevity, we refer the reader to the task fact sheets[1] or [4] for the input documents and prompts. F1 score is measured for the list of IRIs mentioned in the model response with regard to the list of IRIs representing the nodes of the shortest path.

Task T2 - Find Syntax Errors in Turtle Org Graph is based on the same file from T1 but has a period missing and a semicolon in another line was removed. We prompt to correct the error without altering the formatting. Correcting the errors demonstrates the LLM's knowledge of Turtle grammar while also showing its ability to transform it into a proper form without altering existing facts and adhering strictly to the task requirements like answering with just the corrected turtle document and keeping the original formatting. F1 is calculated for the parsable, normalized triples, comparing the LLM's answer with the perfect answer.

Task T3 - Create Example Person Graph requests to generate a KG using the FOAF vocabulary with n (ranging from 10 to 80 with step size 10) persons who each have between 2 and 5 friends. The task is motivated by the idea of

---

[1] https://github.com/AKSW/LLM-KG-Bench/tree/main/LlmKgBench/bench/.

using LLMs to generate test, training, or example data of various sizes for KGE steps, but also assesses Turtle writing and RDF-KG modeling skills (rdf:type, etc.). Although multiple scores were evaluated, we report a relaxed normalized score person_relative_error, which is 0 iff number of foaf:Person matches n, > 0 if there are more, < 0 if there are less persons than n.

Task T4 - Count Friends in Person Graph asks to name the IRI of the person with most incoming foaf:knows edges, given a simple KG with n persons (6, 16,..., 76). Each person is known by two other persons, but one designated foaf:Person is known by three additional persons (one for size 6), resulting in 5 (resp. 3 for size 6) incoming links instead of 2. This task tests for graph comprehension (direction of edges) and processing skills by aggregating link counts for various KG sizes. F1 is reported w.r.t. the expected person IRI.

Task T5 - Create KG from Factsheet assesses the LLM's fact extraction and advanced RDF modeling abilities, by requesting to generate a Turtle file that captures a subset of information from a 3D printer spec PDF plaintext excerpt.

The prompt is designed to be very specific and unambiguous on how the data should be represented, but also challenges knowledge about ontologies. We evaluate F1 measure, comparing the set of parsable normalized triples to the reference document.

Task T6 - Wikidata SPARQL query generation tests SPARQL syntax formulation skills as basic strategy to extract information from a (larger) KG. Leveraging LC-Quad [19], we provide a natural text input query, along with a mapping for all IRIs, that occur in the reference SPARQL query, to their English labels. We calculate F1 by comparing the result values with values of the reference query.

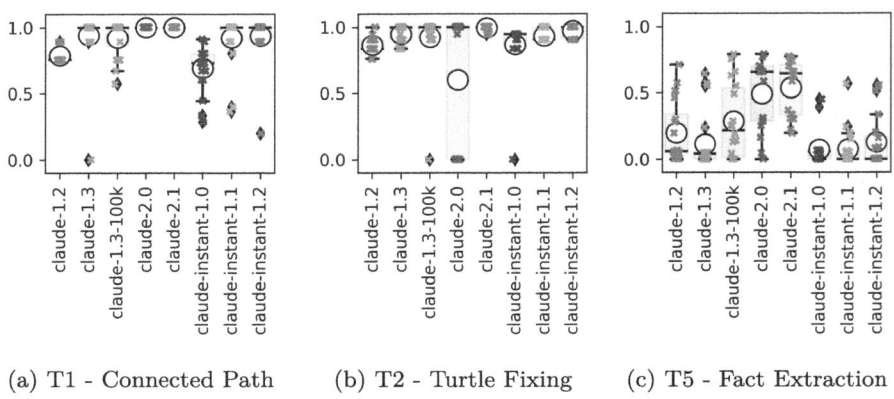

(a) T1 - Connected Path   (b) T2 - Turtle Fixing   (c) T5 - Fact Extraction

Fig. 1. Claude Evolution for Static Tasks: Distribution of F1 scores

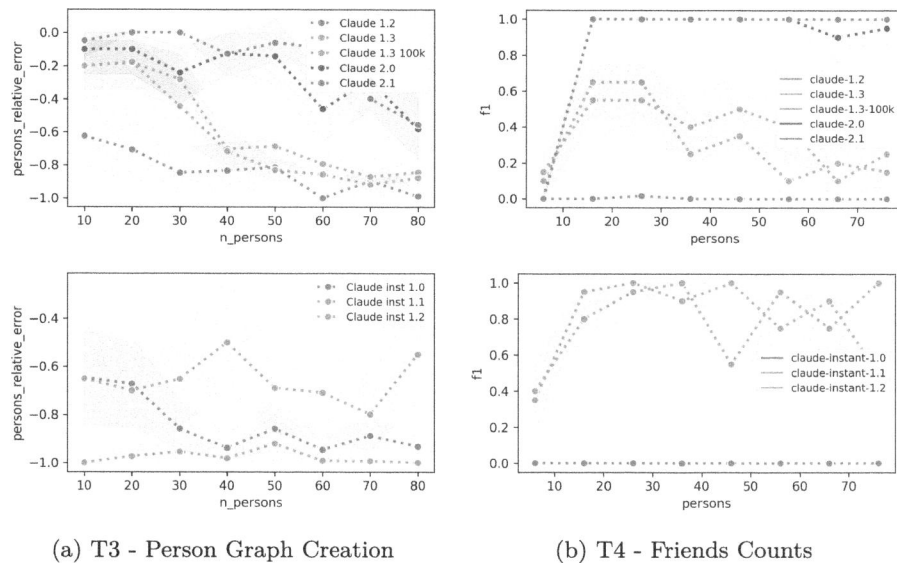

(a) T3 - Person Graph Creation   (b) T4 - Friends Counts

Fig. 2. Claude Evolution for Scalable Tasks: Mean of task metric - 95% CI

4   Claude Models Evolution

For **T1**, Fig. 1a shows that Claude 2.0 and 2.1 reply consistently with accurate answers. All Claude 1.x versions give a few incorrect answers. Claude 1.3 performs better than Claude 1.2 but both miss expected nodes in the answer. This effect can also be observed for the Instant versions, but additionally, nodes are reported twice in the answer. There is a light trend of performance improvement for every model evolution.

As can be seen in Fig. 1b for **T2**, Claude models improved over time within the three model lines Claude Instant 1.x, Claude 1.x and Claude 2.x. However, while Claude 2.1 performs best (although sometimes syntax errors remain), Claude 2.0 performs worst. Several ratings of 0 for F1 were caused by too much modifications to the original formatting and structure.

Claude 1.2, as well as all Instant versions struggle with **T3** for all graph sizes (see Fig. 2a). However, for the 2.x versions, the performance is significantly more stable with increased graph size. Claude 2.1 delivers the best answers and the correct amount of persons for sizes 20 and 30. The larger context size of Claude 1.3 100k did not help improve the quality of the results. There is a clear tendency for improvement for all non-Instant Claude version iterations. However, Claude inst. 1.1 performed slightly worse than its predecessor.

Considering **T4**, all versions seem to be challenged by the size of 6 persons as indicated in Fig. 2b. In this tricky case, only 2 persons (instead of 4) are different compared to the other persons. The models often respond with the incorrect person having the most outgoing instead of ingoing edges. Claude 1.2

is struggling over all sizes and in all iterations to name the correct Person. Similarly, it proposes one of the 3 persons that have one more outgoing link to the designated target person (that has the most friends) in almost every iteration. Both Claude 1.3 versions also have this confusion but only in around half of the cases, with a slight tendency of doing this error more often with increased person size. For Claude 2.1, this confusion does not happen for all larger sizes and for Claude 2.0 only in 2 instances. As shown in Fig. 2b(lower), Claude Instant 1.0 performs similar to Claude 1.2. Claude Instant 1.2 gives a slight performance improvement, by being more reliable and consistent and having less confusion. In general, we observed in Task 4, that every new version brought an improvement. When comparing the Instant versions to the full Claude version it is noteworthy that the Instant versions seem to adhere more strictly to the output format request.

For **T5**, Fig. 1c shows that Claude 1.2 is on median and average slightly better than its direct successor (which produces invalid Turtle in almost half of the cases that leads to zero triples using our recovery parsing heuristic), but worse than Claude 1.3–100k. All Instant versions struggle to produce valid Turtle, leading to very few Triples that can be extracted (approx. half of all the instances lead to zero recovered triples). There is a slight improvement between every Instant version: if triples can be recovered, the number of triples extracted increases with every version step. The Claude 2.x versions do not make severe syntactical errors that render entire documents as unusable. Unfortunately, the trend that was discovered in [4], that Claude 2.0 severely violates the output constraints by giving explanations or titles in the first lines ("here is your RDF:") also materialized in version 2.1.

The Claude LLMs seem to have severe problems with **T6**. While most of the time syntactically valid SPARQL is produced, the execution just returns empty result sets. This is caused by semantic errors. Most often we have seen Claude mixing up Wikidata IRIs or using them in a wrong fashion. There has been only one instance with a correct result. In favor of readability, we refrain from showing a plot for this task.

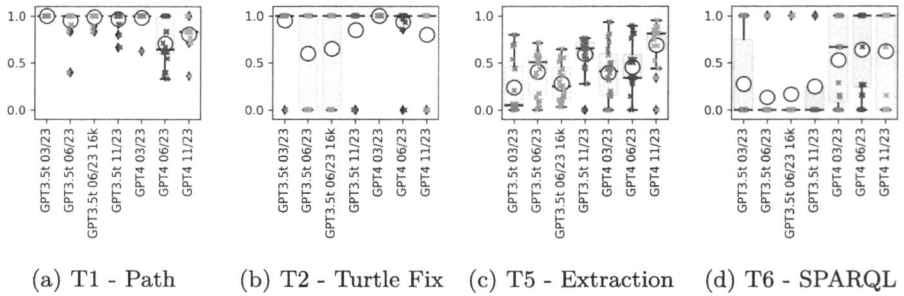

(a) T1 - Path   (b) T2 - Turtle Fix   (c) T5 - Extraction   (d) T6 - SPARQL

Fig. 3. GPT-3.5 and GPT-4 evolution for Static Tasks: Distribution of F1 scores

5   GPT-3.5 and GPT-4 Models Evolution

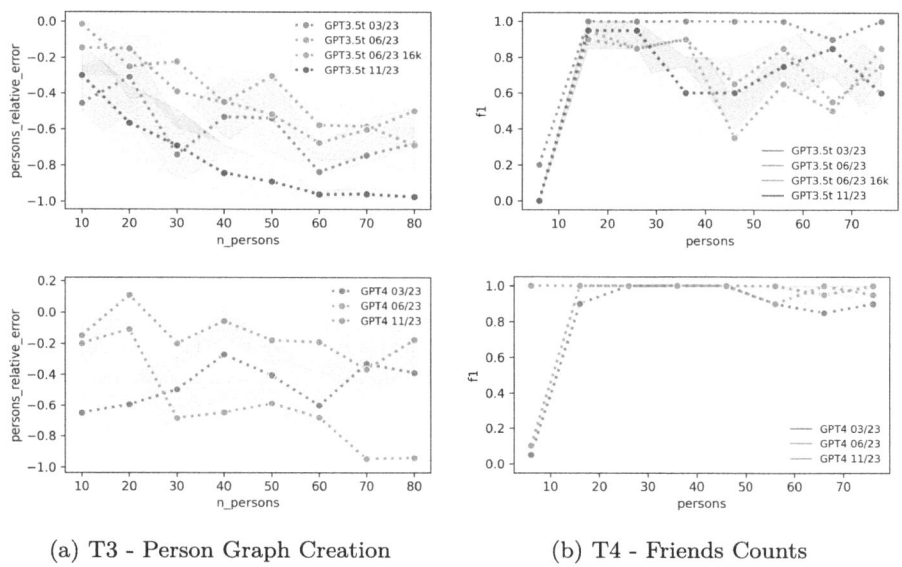

(a) T3 - Person Graph Creation   (b) T4 - Friends Counts

Fig. 4. GPT-3.5/4 Evolution for Scalable Tasks: Mean of task metric - 95% CI

As indicated by Fig. 3a, GPT versions from March 2023 seem to tackle **T1** very well (only one mistake by GPT-4). This shows that the effect of a decreased performance for newer model versions, which has been reported in several online posting as well as in [9], also affects KGE workloads. For later versions we experienced problems like additional or missing list entries. There is a very clear performance drop for GPT-4 6/23, which unfortunately has not been resolved entirely for the November version.

T2 reveals a similar pattern, that the performance for the March versions is the best (see Fig. 3b). We discovered two main error classes: performing no fix but stating no error would exist, or changing the turtle formatting too much. For GPT 3.5 typically the first class could be observed. This seems to happen especially with the 6/23 versions from GPT 3.5 (4k and 16k). In contrast, GPT 4 seems to ignore the instruction to keep the original layout. In certain instances, it modifies the turtle format so drastically that the evaluation code fails to retrieve the turtle snippet from the response, resulting in a penalty of 0 values for F1.

As shown in Fig. 4a for **T3**, except for the March releases, all models perform relatively well for the smallest graph size and we see a decrease in answer quality as the size of the output increases. This trend is not significant for the March versions. Interestingly, the latest version of GPT-3.5 demonstrates the poorest performance among all models, opposed to the latest GPT-4 version showing the best performance. While GPT-4 6/23 exhibits a decline in performance relative to its predecessor like in T1 and T2, the situation is reversed for GPT-3.5.

For **T4** we found w.r.t. GPT-3.5 (see 4b, upper), that version 3/23 is the only one that in some iterations is able to name the correct person in the tricky case of the smallest size, but it also very clearly outperforms all newer versions for the remaining sizes. Only for the size of 66 persons there are two erroneous responses where it chooses the first person. Picking Person-1 (which has no special characteristic other than its position at the beginning of the file) seems to be the most common error for all newer GPT-3.5 versions. While there is a tendency that the 16k version performs worse compared to the default (4k) version of 6/23 for the tested sizes, there is no clear ranking between the remaining versions, given the confidence interval and interleaving mean curves. In contrast, our observations of the GPT-4 versions presented a reverse scenario (see Fig. 4b, lower). The novel November version reports only one incorrect person in the entire test, showing an almost perfect performance. It is the only version tested, that dealt correctly with the tricky case. Version 6/23 made an error, in 3 instances (Person 1 as answer), while the majority of incorrect answers of the March version (that performs worse) are due to the incoming vs. outgoing edges confusion.

In **T5** we can see a clear improvement trend from old versions to new versions for both GPT-3.5 and GPT-4 versions (see Fig. 3c). The version of 6/23 that supports a 16k context window, has a slightly worse performance than the version with default context size (4k). The pattern observed for Claude, that it does not respond with the plain turtle, was also experienced for the GPT versions. While the GPT-3.5 versions correctly reply with the plain turtle, the GPT-4 versions sometimes wrap the answer in Markdown code blocks. However, starting for the November version of GPT-4 this is consistent for all runs and in a unified format.

T6 seems to be quite difficult for GPT-3.5 and GPT-4 as can be seen in Fig. 3d. SPARQL queries produced by all GPT-3.5 versions often produce no result, but roughly every fourth answer is perfect. The GPT-4 versions have a better probability and create partial correct results as well.

6 Conclusion and Future Work

From the perspective of basic skills for KGE, the latest cutting-edge versions (GPT-4T 11/23, Claude 2.1) demonstrated for the majority of tasks improved capabilities over all their predecessors. However, we provided evidence that the phenomenon which has been reported in blogs and literature, that for specific tasks the performance degraded over the course of 2023 also applies for selected KGE workloads (especially for the GPT March/June evolution). One troubling reason is, that the newer models, although explicitly requested, do not consistently respond in the specified output format (e.g. plain Turtle) but include short explanations or markdown ticks. This impedes interfacing these models from code and requires complex and failure tolerant extraction and parsing routines. Since we observed very different behavior, this additionally hinders a plug-and-play integration of various LLM (versions) into tools. Therefore, we see as a next step to define multi-shot tests that are stricter, however provide feedback to the models (e.g. parsing errors). Moreover, it could be of interest to assess the performance using N-Triples (allowing easier data extraction from partially inconsistent responses), or JSON-LD (popular for websites employing schema.org) and adding other KGE task (e.g. RML, SHACL, more SPARQL tasks).

Acknowledgments. This work was partially supported by grants from the German Federal Ministry for Economic Affairs and Climate Action (BMWK) to the KISS project (01MK22001A) and CoyPu project (01MK21007A) as well as from the German Federal Ministry of Education and Research (BMBF) to the project StahlDigital (13XP5116B).

References

1. Beeching, E., et al: Open LLM leaderboard (2023). https://huggingface.co/spaces/HuggingFaceH4/open_llm_leaderboard
2. Brei, F., Frey, J., Meyer, L.P.: Leveraging small language models for Text2SPARQL tasks to improve the resilience of AI assistance. In: Holze, J., Tramp, S., Martin, M., Auer, S., Usbeck, R., Krdzavac, N. (eds.) Proceedings of the Third International Workshop on Linked Data-driven Resilience Research 2024 (D2R2 2024) (2024). https://ceur-ws.org/Vol-3707/D2R224_paper_5.pdf
3. Chen, L., Zaharia, M., Zou, J.: How is ChatGPT's behavior changing over time?. Harvard Data Sci. Rev. **6**, 2 (2023). https://doi.org/10.1162/99608f92.5317da47
4. Frey, J., Meyer, L., Arndt, N., Brei, F., Bulert, K.: Benchmarking the abilities of large language models for RDF knowledge graph creation and comprehension: how well do LLMs speak turtle? In: Alam, M., Cochez, M. (eds.) Proceedings of the Workshop on Deep Learning for Knowledge Graphs (DL4KG 2023) co-located with the 21th International Semantic Web Conference (ISWC 2023), Athens, 6–10 November 2023. CEUR Workshop Proceedings, vol. 3559. CEUR-WS.org (2023). https://ceur-ws.org/Vol-3559/paper-3.pdf
5. Frey, J., Meyer, L.P., Brei, F., Gründer-Fahrer, S., Martin, M.: LLM-KG-bench-results: 2024 ESWC LLM evolution 2023 results (2024). https://github.com/AKSW/LLM-KG-Bench-Results/blob/main/2024-ESWC_LLM-Evo-2023/Readme.md
6. Frey, J., Meyer, L.P., Brei, F., Gründer-Fahrer, S., Martin, M.: LLM-KG skills evolution time capsule 2023 for Claude & ChatGPT - results and log of LLM-KG-Bench runs (2024). https://doi.org/10.5281/zenodo.10572907
7. Hofer, M., Frey, J., Rahm, E.: Towards self-configuring knowledge graph construction pipelines using LLMs - a case study with RML. In: Chaves-Fraga, D., Dimou, A., Iglesias-Molina, A., Serles, U., Van Assche, D. (eds.) Proceedings of the 5th International Workshop on Knowledge Graph Construction co-located with 21th Extended Semantic Web Conference (ESWC 2024), Hersonissos, Greece, May 27, 2024, vol. 3718 (2024). https://ceur-ws.org/Vol-3718/paper6.pdf
8. Hu, X., Tian, Y., Nagato, K., Nakao, M., Liu, A.: Opportunities and challenges of ChatGPT for design knowledge management (2023). https://doi.org/10.48550/ARXIV.2304.02796
9. Ma, W., Yang, C., Kästner, C.: (Why) Is My Prompt Getting Worse? Rethinking Regression Testing for Evolving LLM APIs. In: Proceedings of the IEEE/ACM 3rd International Conference on AI Engineering - Software Engineering for AI, pp. 166–171. ACM, New York (2024). https://doi.org/10.1145/3644815.3644950. Lisbon, Portugal, CAIN '24

10. Martin, A.: Challenges requiring the combination of machine learning and knowledge engineering (2023). https://ceur-ws.org/Vol-3433/preface.pdf
11. Meyer, L.P., Frey, J., Arndt, N., Junghanns, K., Brei, F., Stadler, C.: AKSW/LLM-KG-bench: 1.2.0 (2023). https://doi.org/10.5281/zenodo.10302307
12. Meyer, L., et al.: Developing a scalable benchmark for assessing large language models in knowledge graph engineering. In: Keshan, N., Neumaier, S., Gentile, A.L., Vahdati, S. (eds.) Proceedings of the Posters and Demo Track of the 19th International Conference on Semantic Systems Co-located with 19th International Conference on Semantic Systems (SEMANTiCS 2023), Leipzing, Germany, 20–22 September 2023. CEUR Workshop Proceedings, vol. 3526. CEUR-WS.org (2023). https://ceur-ws.org/Vol-3526/paper-04.pdf
13. Meyer, L.P., et al.: LLM-assisted knowledge graph engineering: experiments with ChatGPT. In: Zinke-Wehlmann, C., Friedrich, J. (eds.) First Working Conference on Artificial Intelligence Development for a Resilient and Sustainable Tomorrow (AITomorrow) 2023, pp. 103–115 (2024). https://doi.org/10.1007/978-3-658-43705-3_8
14. Mihindukulasooriya, N., Tiwari, S., Enguix, C.F., Lata, K.: Text2KGBench: A Benchmark for Ontology-Driven Knowledge Graph Generation from Text. In: Payne, T.R., et al. (eds.) The Semantic Web – ISWC 2023, pp. 247–265. Springer, Switzerland (2023). https://doi.org/10.1007/978-3-031-47243-5_14
15. Pan, J.Z., et al.: Large language models and knowledge graphs: opportunities and challenges (2023). https://doi.org/10.4230/TGDK.1.1.2
16. Pan, S., Luo, L., Wang, Y., Chen, C., Wang, J., Wu, X.: Unifying large language models and knowledge graphs: a roadmap. IEEE Trans. Knowl. Data Eng. **36**, 3580–3599 (2023). https://doi.org/10.1109/tkde.2024.3352100
17. Sutawika, L., et al.: Eleutherai/LM-evaluation-harness: v0.4.1 (2024). https://doi.org/10.5281/zenodo.10600400
18. Trajanoska, M., Stojanov, R., Trajanov, D.: Enhancing knowledge graph construction using large language models (2023). http://arxiv.org/abs/2305.04676, arXiv:2305.04676 [cs]
19. Trivedi, P., Maheshwari, G., Dubey, M., Lehmann, J.: LC-QuAD: a corpus for complex question answering over knowledge graphs. In: d'Amato, C., et al. (eds.) ISWC 2017. LNCS, vol. 10588, pp. 210–218. Springer, Cham (2017). https://doi.org/10.1007/978-3-319-68204-4_22
20. Zhang, B., Reklos, I., Jain, N., Meroño-Peñuela, A., Simperl, E.: Using large language models for knowledge engineering (LLMKE): a case study on Wikidata. In: Razniewski, S., Kalo, J.-C., Singhania, S., Pan, J.Z. (eds.) Joint proceedings of the 1st workshop on Knowledge Base Construction from Pre-Trained Language Models (KBC-LM) and the 2nd challenge on Language Models for Knowledge Base Construction (LM-KBC) co-located with the 22nd International Semantic Web Conference (ISWC 2023), Athens, Greece, November 6, 2023, vol. 3577 (2023). https://ceur-ws.org/Vol-3577/paper8.pdf
21. Zheng, S., et al.: GPT-Fathom: Benchmarking large language models to decipher the evolutionary path towards GPT-4 and beyond. In: Findings of the Association for Computational Linguistics: NAACL 2024, pp. 1363–1382. Association for Computational Linguistics (2024)
22. Zhu, Y., et al.: LLMs for knowledge graph construction and reasoning: recent capabilities and future opportunities (2024). https://arxiv.org/abs/2305.13168, https://doi.org/10.48550/arXiv.2305.13168

Column Property Annotation Using Large Language Models

Keti Korini[(✉)] and Christian Bizer

Data and Web Science Group, University of Mannheim, Mannheim, Germany
{kkorini,christian.bizer}@uni-mannheim.de

Abstract. Column property annotation (CPA), also known as column relationship prediction, is the task of predicting the semantic relationship between two columns in a table given a set of candidate relationships. CPA annotations are used in downstream tasks such as data search, data integration, or knowledge graph enrichment. This paper explores the usage of generative large language models (LLMs) for the CPA task. We experiment with different zero-shot prompts for the CPA task which we evaluate using GPT-3.5, GPT-4, and the open-source model SOLAR. We find GPT-3.5 to be quite sensitive to variations of the prompt, while GPT-4 reaches a high performance independent of the variation of the prompt. We further explore the scenario where training data for the CPA task is available and can be used for selecting demonstrations or fine-tuning the model. We show that a fine-tuned GPT-3.5 model outperforms a RoBERTa model that was fine-tuned on the same data by 11% in F1. Comparing in-context learning via demonstrations and fine-tuning shows that the fine-tuned GPT-3.5 performs 9% F1 better than the same model given demonstrations. The fine-tuned GPT-3.5 model also outperforms zero-shot GPT-4 by around 2% F1 for the dataset on which is was fine-tuned, while not generalizing to tasks that require a different vocabulary.

Keywords: Table Annotation · Large Language Models · Column Property Annotation

1 Introduction

Table annotation is the task of annotating elements of a table using terms from a pre-defined vocabulary in order to discover their semantics [14]. It consists of several sub-tasks that aim at discovering the semantics of different elements of the table. Two of the sub-tasks are column property annotation (CPA) which focuses on discovering the semantic relationship between two columns, and column type annotation (CTA) which aims at discovering the semantic type of entities contained in a column. Figure 1 shows an example of both tasks. The example table describes books, the names of which are contained in the first column and some of their attributes are contained in the other three columns. The goal of a CTA system is to discover the types of each column separately, for

A. Meroño Peñuela et al. (Eds.): ESWC 2024, LNCS 15344, pp. 61–70, 2025.
https://doi.org/10.1007/978-3-031-78952-6_6

example the last column contains dates therefore the CTA label assigned to this column by the system would be *Date*. The goal of a CPA system is to annotate the relationships of the columns with the first column of the table, also referred to as the subject column [21]. As the last column contains the dates when the books listed in the first column were published, a CPA system would annotate this relationship with the label *datePublished*.

BookName	BookFormatType	Language	Date
A Handbook for Morning Time	Paperback	English	01-01-2016
The Intentional Brain	Hardcover	English	15-06-2016
The Comeback	Hardcover	English	03-08-2020

inLanguage

datePublished

Fig. 1. Example of CTA and CPA annotations. CTA labels are shown above the table columns, while CPA labels are shown below the table.

Early statistical approaches [12,21] use a maximum likelihood or maximize joint probabilities to assign CTA and CPA labels to columns or pair of columns. Later systems [7,15,16] use a knowledge base (KB) such as DBpedia [1] to first match the entities in columns to entities in the KB and consider the KB class of the entity as its column type while considering the KB properties of the entities as potential CPA labels. Cannaviccio et al. [2] use a combination of language modeling and using a KB. Recent approaches often rely on pre-trained language model (PLM) such as BERT [4]. The approaches fall into two groups: methods that learn tabular embeddings such as TURL [3] where the authors propose an architecture that learns cell representations which can be used for predicting CTA and CPA labels, or works that fine-tune PLMs such as DODUO [19] which experiments with table serialization and a multi-task learning architecture for CTA and CPA. With the advancements in generative large language models (LLMs) [17,20,24], such as GPT-3.5, GPT-4, LLaMa, Gemini, and Mixtral, research has started to explore prompt designs for table tasks as well as fine-tuning these models on table tasks: [9] compares prompt designs for the CTA task. In Chorus [8], different table tasks are explored, including CTA. The authors test adding instructions to their prompts and introduce the concept of *anchoring* for mapping the answers of the model to the original label space. ArcheType [5] fine-tunes a LLaMa-7B model on the CTA task and compares its results to two PLM baselines. Table-GPT [11] fine-tunes the *text-davinci-002* GPT-3.5 model using a combination of unsupervised table tasks such as row/column filtering, row/column sorting as well as supervised table tasks such as schema matching and entity matching. They show that their fine-tuned model generalizes to other unseen tasks. In our work, we also fine-tune a GPT-3.5

model, *gpt-3.5-0613*, on the CTA and CPA task separately as well as their combination to test if fine-tuning on both tasks provides a better generalization ability than fine-tuning on the tasks separately. In TableLlama [23] a LLaMa-7B model is fine-tuned on six table tasks, two of which are CTA and CPA. [23] does not experiment with zero-shot prompts for the CTA task nor does it fine-tune the LLM exclusively for CPA. This paper fills these gaps. The contributions of the paper are:

1. We are the first to compose prompt designs for the CPA task in a zero-shot and few-shot setting while existing work only explores fine-tuning LLMs for the CPA task amongst other tasks.
2. Using different zero- and few-shot prompts, we analyze the performance and prompt sensitivity of GPT-3.5, GPT-4, and SOLAR-70B for the CPA task.
3. Existing research has only fine-tuned for the CPA task as one task amongst others in a multi-task learning setting. In contrast, we explore the effect of fine-tuning *gpt-3.5-turbo-0613* exclusively for the CPA task and explore how the fine-tuned model generalizes to other datasets and to the CTA task.

2   Experimental Setup

This section introduces our experimental setup. We make the code and data available on GitHub[1] so that all our experiments can be replicated.

Datasets. We use two datasets for the experiments on the CPA task. The first dataset is SOTAB V2 CPA [10] which consists of tables whose topics range across 17 domains, including books, products, local businesses etc. Its test set consists of 595 tables with 2,340 columns annotated using 108 schema.org[2] terms which are manually verified. The second dataset is the T2Dv2 CPA dataset. The dataset was originally published by Ritze et al. [18] and we use the manually verified version[3], the test set of which consists of 80 tables from domains such as animals, book, country etc. labeled using 48 terms from DBpedia.

Additionally, for the fine-tuning experiments we use two more datasets for the evaluation of the CTA task. SOTAB V2 CTA [10] consists of tables with topics ranging over 17 domains including movies, music albums, events etc. Its test set consists of 609 tables where 1851 columns are labeled using 82 schema.org terms and the annotation is manually verified. Lastly, we build the T2Dv2 CTA dataset by using T2Dv2 CPA's tables where we map the DBpedia properties to DBpedia classes to generate the CTA labels. Statistics about all datasets can be found in Table 1. For training in our experiments, we do not use the original large training sets for SOTAB V2 CTA and CPA, but we use down-sampled train sets to explore the scenario where less training data is available.

---

[1] https://github.com/wbsg-uni-mannheim/TabAnnGPT.
[2] https://schema.org/.
[3] https://webdatacommons.org/structureddata/smb/.

Table 1. Statistics of datasets used.

Dataset	Original Train		Sampled Train		Test		Labels
	Tables	Columns	Tables	Columns	Tables	Columns	
SOTAB V2 CTA	44,769	116,887	1199	1640	609	1,851	82
T2Dv2 CTA	74	146	-	-	71	145	16
SOTAB V2 CPA	29,158	109,994	1264	2160	565	2,340	108
T2Dv2 CPA	81	170	-	-	82	166	48

Language Models. The LLMs that we test in the zero and few-shot scenario are two of OpenAI's GPT models[4], *gpt-3.5-turbo-0125* and *gpt-4-0125-preview* and one open-source model SOLAR-70B[5], which is a LLaMa-2-70B [20] fine-tuned model. In our experiments, we will refer to these models as GPT-3.5, GPT-4 and SOLAR respectively. For our fine-tuning experiments, we fine-tune *gpt-3.5-turbo-0613*. To build our prompt templates and to access OpenAI's models we use the *Langchain*[6] library, while for using the open-source model we use the *Huggingface transformers*[7] library. In order to make our experiments reproducible, we set the temperature of the models to 0. We use one NVIDIA A100 provided by *bwHPC*[8] to run the SOLAR experiments.

Evaluation Setup. We use a multi-class classification setup and report Micro-F1 as evaluation metric due to the imbalance of the different classes. We consider answers that do not directly mention terms from the label set as errors and do not try to map such OOV (out of vocabulary) answers to the label set.

3 Comparison of Zero-Shot Prompts

This section compares the performance of different zero-shot prompts for the CPA task. We distinguish three main parts in the prompts: task description, instructions, and classification sentence. The task description part aims at describing the CPA task to the model. In the instructions part we aim at writing some simple instructions that can help the model follow the CPA tasks' steps and inform the model of a preferred format for generating its answer. In the last part, we test how classification words can influence the answer of the model. Two example prompts are shown in Fig. 2. The prompt on the left contains as its first message a formulation of the task part where we only *describe* the CPA task without mentioning the name of the task. It is followed by a five-step *instructions* part which informs the model that the input is a table and the answer should be returned in a required format. In the classification message we ask the model to

---

[4] https://platform.openai.com/docs/models.
[5] https://huggingface.co/upstage/SOLAR-0-70b-16bit.
[6] https://www.langchain.com/.
[7] https://github.com/huggingface/transformers.
[8] https://www.bwhpc.de/cluster.php.

classify the table columns and pass the first five rows of a table in a markdown format. If in the first five rows some values are missing, we fill the cells using values from the rest of the rows. The prompt on the right contains in the first message a task formulation where the *cpa* task is mentioned and explained. It is followed by a second message that contains *less instructions* than the prompt on the left, where we have removed the first two steps. Finally in its last message we test the keyword *annotate* to ask the model to return the labels for the CPA task. For the last message, we also test the words *determine* and classification of *relationships*.

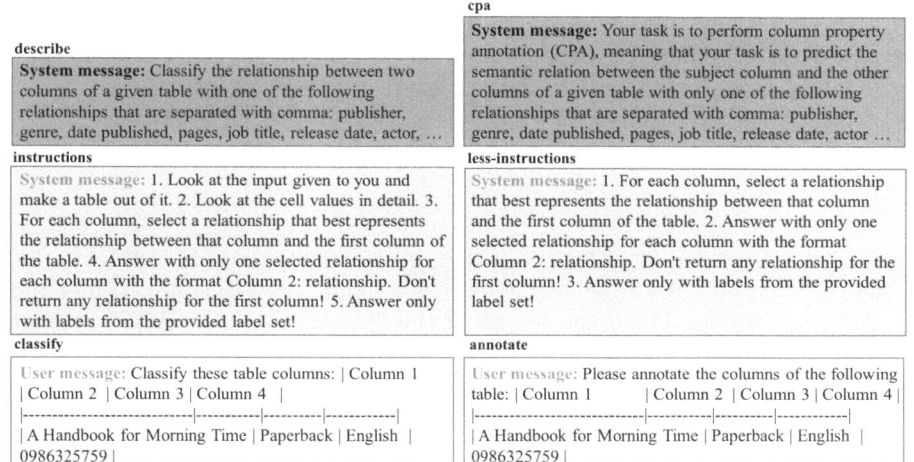

Fig. 2. Example of two CPA prompts showcasing the prompt building blocks.

Results. Table 2 reports the results of prompting the models with each combination of the three building blocks described in the above paragraph. In the cases where *cpa* is not mentioned the *describe* task description is used. The results show that including the definition of the CPA task into the prompt does not help the GPT-3.5 model. This can be seen from the combinations of the *cpa* prompt which are all below the score of 61% for both datasets. In opposite, SOLAR seems to benefit from including the task name and for both datasets the highest score is achieved in this case. We can observe, mostly from the results of T2Dv2, that simply changing the wording in the classification message improves the Micro-F1 score by up to 13% when comparing the *classify* and the *relationships* keyword. In SOTAB V2, this gap ranges from 2–4% for GPT-3.5. Overall, the results show a prompt sensitivity of 3.95 and 7.49 in the case of GPT-3.5, while when looking at the results of SOLAR and GPT-4, we notice a lower sensitivity to the different formulations, especially for GPT-4 which is the most stable model amongst the three. We calculate prompt sensitivity as the standard deviation of the scores of the different prompts. Regarding SOTAB V2, the

Table 2. Micro-F1 performance of different zero-shot prompts for the CPA task.

Prompt	SOTAB V2 CPA			T2Dv2 CPA		
	GPT-3.5	GPT-4	SOLAR	GPT-3.5	GPT-4	SOLAR
instr-classify	64.99	80.31	49.56	56.64	80.36	75.23
cpa-instr-classify	60.14	80.38	53.59	52.55	79.76	69.72
instr-annotate	66.06	79.88	50.56	65.08	80.00	77.30
instr-determine	64.76	80.19	50.25	64.43	82.35	77.68
instr-relationships	66.42	79.30	50.58	73.12	81.48	72.56
less-instr-classify	62.86	80.19	52.57	60.50	78.55	76.83
less-instr-annotate	65.67	79.78	52.61	62.33	81.57	75.38
less-instr-determine	64.82	79.51	52.02	56.34	81.48	73.94
less-instr-relationships	66.49	80.07	52.13	73.58	79.76	71.60
cpa-less-instr-classify	56.73	81.36	53.60	50.56	80.86	78.29
Prompt sensitivity	3.95	0.64	1.30	7.49	1.06	2.60

average OOV answers for GPT-3.5 is 300, 23 for GPT-4 and for SOLAR this average is 350. For T2Dv2 the averages are 40, 1 and 5 for GPT-3.5, GPT-4 and SOLAR respectively. The token length of the "less-instr-relationships" prompt is 428,528, which results in an API usage fee of $ 0.00012 per annotation for GPT-3.5 and $0.0025 per annotation for GPT-4 with prices as of March 2024.

Table 3. Few-shot performance (Micro-F1) using two demonstration selection methods and their prompt token lengths (Tokens).

Method	shots	Tokens	SOTAB V2 CPA			T2Dv2 CPA		
			GPT-3.5	GPT-4	SOLAR	GPT-3.5	GPT-4	SOLAR
random	1	547,493	68.99	81.24	53.42	76.69	84.24	78.55
random	5	994,400	70.23	82.45	-	78.55	83.38	-
similar	1	617,256	70.68	82.62	58.21	76.13	84.77	82.67
similar	5	1,337,839	74.39	84.10	-	76.82	86.09	-

4   In-context Learning via Demonstrations

The related work explores different methods of selecting demonstrations for in-context learning [13,22]. To conduct few-shot experiments for CPA, we employ two methods for selecting demonstrations from the training sets listed in Table 1: randomly and based on similarity. The first method randomly selects examples from the training set as demonstrations. In the similarity method, we embed the test examples without labels as well as the available training examples using the embedding model *text-embedding-ada-002*[9] and select for each test example a number of most similar examples determined using cosine similarity. The prompt that we use for running the few-shot experiments is the *less-instr-relationships* prompt which overall gave a decent score for all models. To perform few-shot, we pass the demonstrations with the help of a message with the role of user that contains the demonstration table and an assistant role message that contains the classification output for the demonstration. These messages are passed to the model before passing the last user message which contains the test table. The results of the few-shot experiments are listed in Table 3. Due to memory issues, we could run SOLAR only in a one-shot setting. From the table, we can observe that in the case of GPT-3.5 and GPT-4 the similarity method outperforms the random method by at least 2% for SOTAB V2, while for T2Dv2 the results are close for both methods. Lastly, SOLAR benefits from the similar demonstrations by 5 and 4% for SOTAB V2 and T2Dv2 respectively.

5   Fine-Tuning the LLM

We fine-tune the *gpt-3.5-turbo-0613* model using the down-sampled training sets of SOTAB V2 CTA and CPA and the *instr-classify* prompt. We fine-tune the model with different combinations of training sets: First, we fine-tune the model using only the SOTAB V2 CTA training set. Second, we fine-tune the model only on the CPA dataset therefore only on the CPA task. As third approach, we fine-tune the model using the CTA and CPA datasets from the two previous steps merged together to fine-tune on both tasks simultaneously. As the last approach, we fine-tune again on both tasks but with both datasets halved to make the number of fine-tuning examples comparable with the first two setups. We refer to these models as *cta-ft*, *cpa-ft*, *cta-cpa-ft* and *cta-cpa-ft-small* respectively.

Table 4. Micro-F1 fine-tuning results on CTA and CPA compared to GPT-3.5 zero-shot results. F-Tokens reports the number of tokens of the fine-tuning dataset, while F-Cost reports the cost of fine-tuning the model with prices as of March 2024.

	F-Tokens	F-Cost	SOTAB V2		T2Dv2	
			CTA	CPA	CTA	CPA
zero-shot	-	-	64.35	66.49	69.85	73.58
cta-ft	1,787,364	$14.92	81.22	63.98	69.43	72.34
cpa-ft	2,341,017	$18.72	70.95	83.55	65.74	72.95
cta-cpa-ft	4,128,381	$33	82.01	84.08	72.92	76.36
cta-cpa-ft-small	2,081,448	$16.65	80.35	80.80	71.97	69.51

---

[9] https://platform.openai.com/docs/models/embeddings.

Results. The results of fine-tuning are shown in Table 4. From them we conclude that fine-tuning for a specific task significantly increases the Micro-F1 score for the task and dataset that was used for fine-tuning, while decreasing the performance on the unseen T2Dv2 datasets. When fine-tuning for both tasks with the larger set, we observe that the model generalizes better to all datasets. On the other hand, when using the small CTA and CPA dataset for fine-tuning, the resulting model performs good on only the datasets that have been used for fine-tuning and not on the unseen T2Dv2 datasets. By comparing the results in Table 3 and Table 4, we can conclude that when using GPT-3.5 it is more beneficial to use the training set for fine-tuning the model, which results in 83.55% Micro-F1, rather than using the training set as a pool for selecting demonstrations which reaches 74.39% for SOTAB V2. In addition, fine-tuning also helps reduce the number of OOV answers to around 20–30 for SOTAB V2.

6   Comparison to PLM Baselines

We compare the previous zero-shot prompts for GPT-3.5, GPT-4 and fine-tuned GPT-3.5 (FT-GPT-3.5) to three baselines. The first baseline is a fine-tuned RoBERTa model with the maximum token length set to 512 and a batch size of 32. The pairs of columns are concatenated together and passed to RoBERTa which we train for 30 epochs. The second baseline TURL [3] is pre-trained using table corpora and uses TinyBERT [6] in its architecture. For this baseline we use CrossEntropy as a loss function and train the model for 50 epochs. The last PLM baseline DODUO [19] uses a new serialization method where a single table is serialized into one sequence. For this model, we use a batch size of 32 and run training for 30 epochs. We train all the baselines using a learning rate of 5e-5 and report the average performance of three runs with different random seeds.

Table 5. F1 results of fine-tuned PLM baselines compared to zero-shot results of LLMs.

Method	shots	SOTAB V2 CPA	shots	T2Dv2 CPA
GPT-3.5	0	66.49	0	73.58
GPT-4	0	81.43	0	82.35
FT-GPT-3.5	2160	83.55	2160	72.95
TURL	2160	60.75	170	59.23
DODUO	10,496	70.34	170	4.08
RoBERTa	2160	71.45	170	81.52

Results. The results of the PLM baselines are summarized in Table 5. Comparing RoBERTa and FT-GPT-3.5 which were both fine-tuned on the SOTAB V2 CPA dataset, GPT-3.5 achieves 11% higher in Micro-F1 than RoBERTa. On the other hand, for the T2Dv2 dataset, FT-GPT-3.5 fine-tuned on SOTAB V2 does not generalize well and the score compared to RoBERTa fine-tuned with the full T2Dv2 training set is 8% lower. Comparing to TURL, FT-GPT-3.5 achieves 23% higher Micro-F1, while comparing it to DODUO which is fine-tuned with more data, FT-GPT-3.5 still achieves 11% more in F1.

7 Conclusion

Our experiments using different zero-shot prompts have shown that GPT-4 reaches a F1 score of around 80% for the CPA task, outperforming the other models while also being less sensitive to variations of the prompt. Fine-tuning GPT-3.5 for the CPA task enables the model to reach a similar performance as GPT-4 while costing less API usage fees per annotation. Our experiments further show that if training data is available, it is better to use the data for fine-tuning rather than as a pool for choosing demonstrations.

Acknowledgments. The authors acknowledge support by the state of Baden-Württemberg through bwHPC for running the open-source model SOLAR.

References

1. Auer, S., Bizer, C., Kobilarov, G., Lehmann, J., Cyganiak, R., Ives, Z.: DBpedia: a nucleus for a web of open data. In: Aberer, K., et al. (eds.) ASWC/ISWC -2007. LNCS, vol. 4825, pp. 722–735. Springer, Heidelberg (2007). https://doi.org/10.1007/978-3-540-76298-0_52

2. Cannaviccio, M., Barbosa, D., Merialdo, P.: Towards annotating relational data on the web with language models. In: Proceedings of the 2018 World Wide Web Conference, pp. 1307–1316 (2018)

3. Deng, X., Sun, H., Lees, A., Wu, Y., Yu, C.: TURL: table understanding through representation learning. In: Proc. VLDB Endow. **14**(3), 307–319 (2020)

4. Devlin, J., Chang, M.W., Lee, K., Toutanova, K.: BERT: pre-training of deep bidirectional transformers for language understanding. In: Proceedings of the 2019 Conference of the North American Chapter of the Association for Computational Linguistics: Human Language Technologies, vol. 1, pp. 4171–4186 (2019)

5. Feuer, B., Liu, Y., Hegde, C., Freire, J.: ArcheType: a novel framework for open-source column type annotation using large language models. arXiv preprint arXiv:2310.18208 (2023)

6. Jiao, X., et al.: TinyBERT: distilling BERT for natural language understanding. In: Findings of the Association for Computational Linguistics EMNLP 2020, pp. 4163–4174 (2020)

7. Jiménez-Ruiz, E., Hassanzadeh, O., Efthymiou, V., Chen, J., Srinivas, K.: SemTab 2019: resources to benchmark tabular data to knowledge graph matching systems. In: Proceedings of the International Semantic Web Conference, pp. 514–530 (2020)

8. Kayali, M., Lykov, A., Fountalis, I., Vasiloglou, N., Olteanu, D., Suciu, D.: CHORUS: foundation models for unified data discovery and exploration. arXiv preprint arXiv:2306.09610 (2023)

9. Korini, K., Bizer, C.: Column type annotation using ChatGPT. In: Joint proceedings of workshops at the 49th International Conference on Very Large Data Bases, CEUR-WS, vol. 3462, pp. 1–12 (2023)
10. Korini, K., Peeters, R., Bizer, C.: SOTAB: the WDC schema.org table annotation benchmark. In: Proceedings of the Semantic Web Challenge on Tabular Data to Knowledge Graph Matching (SemTab), CEUR-WS, vol. 3320, pp. 14–19 (2022)
11. Li, P., et al.: Table-GPT: table-tuned GPT for diverse table tasks. arXiv preprint arXiv:2310.09263 (2023)
12. Limaye, G., Sarawagi, S., Chakrabarti, S.: Annotating and searching web tables using entities, types and relationships. Proc. VLDB Endow. 3(1–2), 1338–1347 (2010)
13. Liu, J., Shen, D., Zhang, Y., Dolan, W.B., Carin, L., Chen, W.: What makes good in-context examples for GPT-3? In: Proceedings of Deep Learning Inside Out (DeeLIO 2022), pp. 100–114 (2022)
14. Liu, J., Chabot, Y., Troncy, R., Huynh, V.P., et al.: From tabular data to knowledge graphs: a survey of semantic table interpretation tasks and methods. J. Web Semant. 76, 100761 (2023)
15. Liu, J., Troncy, R.: DAGOBAH: an end-to-end context-free tabular data semantic annotation system. In: Proceedings of the Semantic Web Challenge on Tabular Data to Knowledge Graph Matching (SemTab), CEUR-WS, vol. 2553, pp. 41–48 (2019)
16. Nguyen, P., Kertkeidkachorn, N., Ichise, R., Takeda, H.: Mtab: matching tabular data to knowledge graph using probability models. In: Proceedings of the Semantic Web Challenge on Tabular Data to Knowledge Graph Matching (SemTab), CEUR-WS, vol. 2553, pp. 7–14 (2019)
17. Ouyang, L., et al.: Training language models to follow instructions with human feedback. In: Advances in Neural Information Processing Systems, vol. 35, pp. 27730–27744 (2022)
18. Ritze, D., Lehmberg, O., Bizer, C.: Matching HTML tables to DBpedia. In: Proceedings of the 5th International Conference on Web Intelligence, Mining and Semantics, pp. 1–6 (2015)
19. Suhara, Y., et al.: Annotating columns with pre-trained language models. In: Proceedings of the 2022 International Conference on Management of Data, pp. 1493–1503 (2022)
20. Touvron, H., et al.: Llama 2: open foundation and fine-tuned chat models. arXiv preprint arXiv:2307.09288 (2023)
21. Venetis, P., et al.: Recovering semantics of tables on the web. Proc. VLDB Endow. 4(9), 528–538 (2011)
22. Ye, X., Iyer, S., Celikyilmaz, A., Stoyanov, V., Durrett, G., Pasunuru, R.: Complementary explanations for effective in-context learning. In: Findings of the Association for Computational Linguistics: ACL 2023, pp. 4469–4484 (2023)
23. Zhang, T., Yue, X., Li, Y., Sun, H.: TableLlama: towards open large generalist models for tables. arXiv preprint arXiv:2311.09206 (2023)
24. Zhao, W.X., Zhou, K., Li, J., Tang, T., Wang, X., et al.: A survey of large language models. arXiv preprint arXiv:2303.18223 (2023)

Can LLMs Generate Competency Questions?

Youssra Rebboud[1] , Lionel Tailhardat[1,2] , Pasquale Lisena[1(✉)] ,
and Raphael Troncy[1]

[1] EURECOM, Sophia Antipolis, France
pasquale.lisena@eurecom.fr
[2] Orange, Paris, France

Abstract. Large Language Models have shown high performances in a
large number of tasks, being recently applied also to support Knowledge
Graphs construction. An important step for data modeling consists in
the definition of a set of competency questions, which are often used as
a guide for the development of an ontology and as a mean to evaluate
the resulting schema. In this work, we investigate the suitability of LLMs
for the automatic generation of competency questions given an existing
ontology. We compare different large language models under various settings in order to give a comprehensive overview of what LLMs can do to
support the knowledge engineer.

Keywords: LLMs · Knowledge Graphs · Ontology · Data Modeling

1 Introduction

Ontologies – as explicit representations of a discourse domain through concepts
and relationships – and their instantiation as knowledge graphs, enable data
analysis and inference techniques to handle heterogeneous data and reason about
the context of represented objects. Despite these advantages and proven knowledge engineering methods [15,17], designing an ontology represents a significant
upfront cost for application designers willing to build and leverage a knowledge
graph. Indeed, modeling an application domain requires knowledge engineers to
immerse themselves in the domain over a long period of time and engage with
numerous domain experts. Simultaneously, the recent explosive success of generative AI methods and the widespread use of large language models (LLMs) as
a crucial component in industrial and consumer applications – particularly in
the field of generating code from user-expressed intentions in natural language
(and vice versa) – suggests that abstracting a domain into a specific formalism
from a textual corpus is an achievable goal that could assist knowledge engineers in their work. Simple experiments, accessible to anyone via ChatGPT or
similar tools, demonstrate that it is indeed possible to generate a skeleton of
an OWL/RDF ontology implementation using a prompt that briefly describes

A. Meroño Peñuela et al. (Eds.): ESWC 2024, LNCS 15344, pp. 71–80, 2025.
https://doi.org/10.1007/978-3-031-78952-6_7

the targeted concepts. However, the reliability and scalability of this intuition still need to be explored, which leads us to ask the question of how much LLMs could co-contribute in the knowledge engineering process together with usual knowledge engineering methodologies (competency questions, ontology re-use, authoring tests, etc.).

In order to thoroughly explore the intricacies of this question, we have identified six sub-tasks, which are presented in Table 1. In this paper, we delve into the details of the sub-task #1, assuming that insights gained from this research will likely contribute to advancements in the other sub-tasks. Our approach consists in analyzing the quality of the Competency Questions (CQs) [17] generated by LLMs through prompt-engineering experiments. These experiments are conducted on a dataset of RDF-based ontologies, along with their corresponding set of CQs and evaluation queries provided by the authors of each ontology. Through this work, we contribute to boosting the adoption of Semantic Web technologies and research on LLMs by defining a methodology for exploring the coupling of LLMs and Knowledge Graphs (KGs) with a focus on ontologies. In practice, using CQs generated by an LLM, an ontology designer could accelerate development and expand validation with unforeseen CQs. We also highlight which ontology characteristics or LLM parameter settings are crucial in facilitating knowledge engineering tasks. The dataset and code related to this work is available at https://github.com/D2KLab/llm4ke.

Table 1. 6 sub-tasks essential in the knowledge engineering process

#	Research questions – Could a LLM ...
1	reverse engineer an ontology and find out what good competency questions (CQ) could be derived?
2	take as input the CQ and generate parts of the ontology?
3	take as input the CQ and extend an existing ontology?
4	take as input the CQ and generate ontology design patterns?
5	write an authoring test (a SPARQL query) given the ontology and the CQ?
6	generate an adequate set of RML rules for data ingestion given a dataset and an ontology?

The remainder of this paper is organized as follows. In Sect. 2, we review some related work. In Sect. 3, we provide details of our approach by focusing on the LLM-based data processing pipeline and describing how to perform prompting. In Sect. 4, we present the experiments conducted and their results on a subset of five RDF ontologies and six LLMs. We conclude and outline some future work in Sect. 5.

2   Related Work

Different works have so far investigated the performance of LLMs in classic tasks in the Knowledge Graph domain [2]. *SPIRES* [6] is a method that utilizes GPT-3 to produce structured data from an input text and schema. In [20], the authors use the Overall Execution Accuracy (OEA) to assess the performance of a LLM in converting questions to queries (SQL or SPARQL). The OEA is computed on an ad-hoc benchmark, where an execution is considered accurate if the query result matches the corresponding answer.

Several works address the usage and production of competency questions. The study of patterns in competency questions [25] has inspired the realization of AgOCQs [3] in which CQs are automatically generated. The evaluation has been performed with an expert group, which highlighted the validity of the method. The patterns can be filled by *Glossary of terms* – which can be automatically extracted such as in ReqTagger [26] – or used to automatically generate SPARQL queries from CQs [4,24].

3   Methodology

In this section, we provide details of our approach by focusing on the LLM-based data processing pipeline (Sect. 3.1) and on the prompt details (Sect. 3.2).

3.1   Implementation

To standardize and automate experiments, we developed a platform in Python, whose workflow is depicted in Fig. 1. The platform relies on the LangChain framework[1] [7] to interact with various LLMs. Specifically, we integrated models from LangChain providers for Ollama, HuggingFace, and OpenAI into our workflow, allowing for querying within the same pipeline.

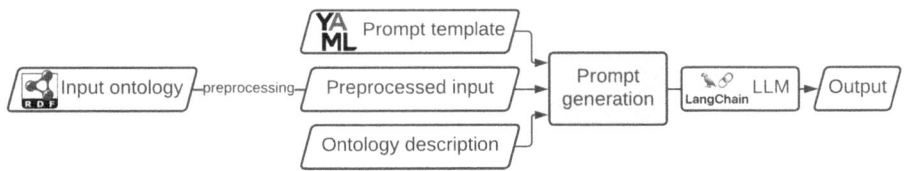

Fig. 1. Workflow of the platform

We make use of a prompt configuration in the form of a YAML file, including:

- the description of the task TD (for documentation purposes);
- the list of required input fields;
- the prompt template, in which placeholders are marked by curly brackets as in the documentation of LangChain, e.g. {name}, {classes}.

Additionally, each process can be further customized by specifying the LLM to use, the path of the input ontology, whether to include the ontology description in the prompt or not, and the number of required output results.

In order to avoid to ingest the full RDF representation in the prompt[2], we parse the ontology using RDFlib [11] and extract either:

---

[1] https://python.langchain.com/.

[2] During some preliminary experiments, we realised that including the full ontology in Turtle format was producing a long prompt, which has shown to confuse the LLMs and produce hallucination.

- the list of class labels C;
- the list of property labels P;
- a summary schema of the interconnection of classes and properties S.

This schema S is represented as triples in the format (C_x, p_y, C_z), where $C_x, C_z \in C$ are class labels, and $p_y \in P$ is the label of an object property which has C_x as domain and C_z as range. An example taken from the FOAF ontology is (foaf:Group, foaf:member, foaf:Agent). Please note that C_x and C_z are not necessarily two different classes, because the domain and range can coincide, e.g. in (foaf:Person, foaf:knows, foaf:Person). In the case of a data property $p_d \in P$, we include the triple $(C_x, p_d, \text{``}literal\text{''})$, e.g. in (foaf:Person, foaf:lastName, ``literal''').

When the dimension of the ontology is large, it is processed in batches of 20 classes. In such a case, in each iteration, C is composed of a maximum of 20 classes, P includes all properties which have C as domain or range, and S encompasses all interconnections involving C and P.

3.2 Prompting

We primarily utilized three templates for our work. The first template outlines the classes within the ontology, the second includes both classes and properties, and the final template integrates the ontology's schema. Each of these templates encompasses:

- Task Description (TD): 'Generate a set of competency questions (CQ) which are relevant for the ontology called {name of onto logy}'.
- Ontology Description (OD): provides a general overview of the ontology and specifies the domain it belongs to, e.g., 'Odeuropa ontology represents' odours and their experiences from Cultural Heritage perspective.
- Examples (EXP): examples of CQs of the desired ontology, e.g., 'Which scents were linked to the idea of heaven in X period?'.
- Notes(N): guidelines provided to the model for brevity and clarity, e.g., 'Do not include any text except the competency question'.

Based on the prompt configuration technique described in Sect. 3.1, we propose to generate prompts for a given ontology with various features (Table 2) depending on the overall experiment goals and following best practice in prompt structuring.

4   Experiments

In this section, we present the experiments conducted based on the method described in Sect. 3. We first provide details of the dataset used in Sect. 4.1, then on the LLMs used in Sect. 4.2, and finally report on the evaluation results in Sect. 4.3.

Table 2. Prompt features as a function of the evaluation goal.
For the classes feature, the *"The {name} ontology has the following set of classes:"* is used in the prompt. For the "Properties" feature, it is the *"and the following set of properties:"* sentence. For "Schema" it is the *"The {name} ontology has the following schema"* sentence. "opt." stands for optional (i.e. w. and w.o definition).

Evaluation goal	Definition	Classes	Properties	Schema	Examples	Constraints
All classes	opt.	✓			n	✓
All classes + properties	opt.	✓	✓		n	✓
Logic	opt.			✓	n	✓

4.1   Investigated Ontologies

For our experiments, we selected a subset of five ontologies (Table 3) with a publicly available implementation based on the following two criteria: *1)* these ontologies were modeled following explicitly the Competency Questions (CQs) methodology [17]; *2)* these ontologies have well-phrased CQs with associated Authoring Tests (ATs) in the form of SPARQL queries. Once the subset was established, we created a dataset by recording a versioned copy of the ontologies' implementation, as well as their companion set of CQs and ATs. To generalize the approach described in Sect. 3 to all the ontologies of the subset, we normalized the representation of the CQs by storing them in a YAML data structure including – if relevant – the reference to the corresponding ATs. The dataset is publicly available in our repository, with annotation on the origin for each component of it and explanations on the normalization process.

Table 3. Subset of ontologies for the LLM4KE experiments.
Ontologies in our dataset, along with additional details such as the number of classes (#Classes) and properties (#Props), associated competency questions (CQ count), associated authoring tests (AT count), and a coverage measure (AT/CQ coverage) indicating the extent to which ATs are effectively defined and implemented for each CQ. For Polifonia, we count CQs from their "default group" and indicate "?" for the AT count as no obvious set of ATs was found. For Demcare, the CQ2SPARQLOWL [14] dataset served as a reference for building our dataset. For the remaining ontologies, the dataset was directly constructed from each project's repository.

Data-model	Ref.	Full ontology name or topic	#Classes	#Props	CQ count	AT count	AT/CQ coverage
DemCare	[10]	Dementia Ambient Care Ontology.	290	115	107	60	56%
DOREMUS	[1]	Music catalogues on the web of data.	218	705	58	30	52%
NORIA-O	[21]	IT networks and operations for anomaly detection and IT service management.	55	135	26	25	88%
Odeuropa	[12]	Odours and their experiences from a Cultural Heritage perspective.	13	10	74	74	100%
Polifonia	[5]	Polifonia Ontology Network (PON) for queries in the music domain.	247	299	194	?	0%

4.2   Investigated LLMs

We explored various Large Language Model (LLM) options, including both open-source and proprietary models. For open-source models, we considered their performances according to the Hugging Face leaderboard,[3] in particular across three specific datasets, which we consider relevant for this research:

- ARC2018 [8] (AI2 Reasoning Challenge), a question-answering dataset;
- HellaSwag [27], created to challenge model common sense reasoning abilities;
- Winogrande [18], a dataset designed to evaluate commonsense reasoning capabilities in AI systems.

We selected these models based on their architectures, aiming to choose one from each architectural category. Each model was chosen for its superior performance within its respective architecture, as indicated by their positions on the leaderboard at the time of selection. Due to resource limitations, we have opted to confine our selection of open-source LLMs to those with a parameter count equal to or less than 13 billion. Table 4 summarises the used LLMs.

Table 4. Used LLMs for Experiments. B refers to billion parameters.

Model	Architecture	Size (B)	Access Paradigm
DPO (see footnote 6)	MixtralForCausalLM	12.9	Open-source
Solar (see footnote 8)	LlamaForCausalLM	10.7	Open-source
UNA (see footnote 10)	MistralForCausalLM	7	Open-source
Zephyrβ (see footnote 12)	MistralForCausalLM	7	Open-source
GPT 3.5	Transformer Decoder	175	proprietary
GPT-4-0125-preview	Transformer Decoder	1500	proprietary

We have used `Truthful_DPO_TomGrc_FusionNet_7Bx2_MoE_13B`[4] (we refer to it as *DPO*), which is an instance of `FusionNet_7Bx2_MoE_14B` fine-tuned on the Truthy-DPO dataset[5].

Additionally, we leveraged `SOLAR-10B-OrcaDPO-Jawade`, which we shortcut to *Solar*, a finetuned version of `SOLAR-10.7B-Instruct-v1.0`[6] [9], finetuned on the `dpo pairs` dataset.[7] Furthermore, we have used `UNA-TheBeagle-7b-v1`[8], that we call simply *UNA*, a 7B LLM trained on The Bagel dataset.[9] On the other hand, we opted for zephyrβ[10] [23], because of its performance that surpassed Llama2 70B [22] on different benchmarks.

---

[3] https://huggingface.co/spaces/HuggingFaceH4/open_llm_leaderboard.
[4] https://huggingface.co/yunconglong/Truthful_DPO_TomGrc_FusionNet_7Bx2_MoE_13B.
[5] https://huggingface.co/datasets/jondurbin/truthy-dpo-v0.1.
[6] https://huggingface.co/bhavinjawade/SOLAR/-10B/-OrcaDPO/-Jawade.
[7] https://huggingface.co/datasets/Intel/orca_dpo_pairs.
[8] https://huggingface.co/fblgit/UNA-TheBeagle/-7b/-v1.
[9] https://huggingface.co/datasets/jondurbin/bagel-v0.3.
[10] https://huggingface.co/HuggingFaceH4/zephyr/-7b/-beta.

Moreover, we included in our study API-only access models, and in particular the GPT series from OpenAI[11]. We used both GPT3.5[12] and GPT4 [13].

4.3   Evaluation

Comparative analysis of generated CQs with ground-truth. To perform the evaluation of our approach, we utilize the dataset presented in Sect. 4.1 and consider the CQs provided by the authors of each ontology as the ground truth. We compare the output CQs from the LLMs (CQ_o) to each CQ in the ground-truth (CQ_{gt}) and consider a CQ_o as valid if it is sufficiently similar to at least one CQ_{gt}. For the similarity score, we use cosine similarity between the embeddings of CQ_o and CQ_{gt} computed using SentenceBERT [16]. We define a threshold θ above which we consider a CQ_o valid (Eq. 1):

$$x \in CQ_o^{valid} \Leftrightarrow x \in CQ_o \land \exists\{y \in CQ_{gt} : \text{cosine similarity}(y, x) > \theta\} \quad (1)$$

with $CQ_o^{valid} \subset CQ_o$. We then compute the precision $P = \frac{\text{number of } CQ_o^{valid}}{\text{number of } CQ_o}$ of each experiment.

Results and Discussion. The results of the experiments are reported in Table 5, using a threshold of $\theta = 0.6$, chosen empirically for better showing the differences between the models. As a first outlook, we observe that the precision scores are generally low. From the perspective of the LLMs, Zephyr consistently shows the best scores across a majority of ontologies with at least two different modalities, with the exception of some experiments on Odeuropa (in particular with only classes) and NORIA-O (classes and properties) where UNA performs better. For Odeuropa, this can be due to the fact that the dimension of Odeuropa is lower that the used batch size, and it is consequently included entirely in the prompt; reducing the batch size to 5, improves the results of Zephyr for Odeuropa to 0.90 (C), 0.91 (P) and 0.70 (S). Future work will investigate the effect of the batch size on the different LLMs and ontologies.

From the perspective of prompt features, we observe that providing examples (few-shot) generally leads to better precision (compared to zero-shot), although not always. Future work will investigate the performances of other numbers of shots, e.g. 1-shot or 5-shot. Similarly, using properties in prompts results in a greater increase in precision. Conversely, prompting with the schema does not generally improve precision and may even decrease it, as in the case of GPT4, DPO and Zephyr.

Even though the absolute scores are generally quite low, it should not be concluded that the generated CQs are irrelevant. In fact, the generation process may have resulted in new competency questions that can be a valuable addition to the ground truth dataset. To properly evaluate the relevance of these competency questions, an expert panel should be involved, which will be the focus of

---

[11] https://openai.com/.

[12] https://platform.openai.com/docs/models/gpt-3-5-turbo.

Table 5. The precision scores for the experiments, reporting the LLM name, the number of included exemplary CQs and, for each ontology, the modality {C = all classes, P = classes and properties, S = summary schema}

Ontology→		DOREMUS			DemCare			Odeuropa			Polifonia			NORIA-O		
LLM	Ex	C	P	S	C	P	S	C	P	S	C	P	S	C	P	S
GPT3	0	0.02	0.01	0.01	0.15	0.14	0.00	0.00	0.00	0.10	0.08	0.08	0.20	0.00	0.00	0.03
	3	0.04	0.01	0.04	0.17	0.13	0.00	0.90	0.30	0.00	0.20	0.30	0.32	0.00	0.03	0.03
GPT4	0	0.00	0.00	0.02	0.14	0.23	0.01	0.20	0.50	0.30	0.21	0.24	0.30	0.00	0.03	0.00
	3	**0.10**	0.11	0.11	**0.21**	0.17	0.01	0.40	0.90	0.90	0.32	0.32	0.32	0.03	0.03	0.00
dpo	0	0.00	0.00	0.00	0.04	0.08	0.00	0.70	0.30	0.00	0.05	0.09	0.11	0.00	0.00	0.00
	3	0.03	0.04	0.01	0.15	0.13	0.04	0.75	0.82	**1.00**	0.22	0.22	0.22	0.04	0.06	0.00
solar	0	0.00	0.00	0.00	0.08	0.06	0.00	0.20	0.00	0.20	0.07	0.04	0.12	0.00	0.03	0.00
	3	0.00	0.12	0.07	0.11	0.17	0.00	0.30	0.30	0.30	0.20	0.22	0.24	0.04	0.00	0.03
una	0	0.00	0.03	0.05	0.10	0.10	0.00	0.50	0.00	0.64	0.08	0.05	0.10	0.03	0.00	0.00
	3	0.09	0.15	0.12	0.20	0.24	**0.27**	**1.00**	0.70	**1.00**	0.34	**0.38**	0.33	**0.31**	**0.07**	0.00
zephyr	0	0.01	0.01	0.00	0.05	0.09	0.00	0.90	**1.00**	0.00	0.16	0.08	0.15	0.00	0.00	0.00
	3	0.03	**0.58**	**0.56**	**0.21**	**0.33**	0.00	0.40	0.00	**1.00**	**0.36**	**0.38**	**0.34**	0.00	0.00	**0.20**

future work. Due to variations in the number of classes among the ontologies in our dataset (Table 3), it is important to note that the LLMs used in the experiments may have been queried more frequently for certain ontologies and less frequently for others, because of the subdivision in batches.

A first qualitative assessment let us notice that the configurations obtaining the lower scores have some common characteristics: the strict reuse of class and property labels instead of periphrasis, the inclusion of the ontology name in the output CQ, the presence of generic connections between concepts ("involve", "influence", "associate", "relate") instead of semantically meaningful ones. Future work will investigate possible patterns with the help of domain experts.

5   Conclusion and Future Work

This work aimed to understand how knowledge engineering can benefit from large language models (LLMs). We identified six sub-tasks and developed a methodology to explore the coupling of LLMs with knowledge graphs, specifically focusing on ontologies. Using a data processing pipeline with six LLMs, three prompting strategies, and five ontologies, we assessed the ability of LLMs to generate Competency Questions (CQs), which are crucial in ontology development. In conclusion, providing examples of competency questions and utilizing relationship information from ontologies in prompts is important for improving LLM performance. It is interesting to note that providing more details for certain ontologies can decrease LLM performance, which requires further investigation.

Future work will focus on understanding the characteristics of ontologies that impact the accuracy of LLM responses. This includes investigating the relevance of LLMs trained on general language for ontologies with specialized vocabulary. Additionally, research will explore the role of Competency Question formulation and the influence of properties, including their names, descriptions, and associated logic. Evaluating the capability of LLMs to handle ontologies that reuse other data models will also be explored. To provide more generalizable results, the work will be extended to other ontologies with well-formulated Competency Questions and Authoring Tests, such as using the CQ2SPARQLOWL dataset [14] and the SILKNOW ontology [19]. Involving a panel of experts to generate CQs without prior knowledge on data models and comparing them with the CQs generated by LLMs, or refining the performance measurement of LLMs by removing any redundant or low-quality generated CQs, are other tasks to be carried out as well.

Acknowledgements. This work is supported by the French National Research Agency (ANR) within the kFLOW project (Grant n°ANR-21-CE23-0028).

References

1. Achichi, M., Lisena, P., Todorov, K., Troncy, R., Delahousse, J.: DOREMUS: a graph of linked musical works. In: 17th International Semantic Web Conference (ISWC). Monterey, CA, USA (2018)
2. Allen, B., Stork, L., Groth, P.: Knowledge engineering using large language models. Trans. Graph Data Knowl. (2023). https://doi.org/10.4230/TGDK.1.1.3, https://drops.dagstuhl.de/entities/document/10.4230/TGDK.1.1.3
3. Antia, M.J., Keet, C.M.: Automating the generation of competency questions for ontologies with AgOCQs. In: Ortiz-Rodriguez, F., Villazón-Terrazas, B., Tiwari, S., Bobed, C. (eds.) KGSWC 2023. LNCS, vol. 14382, pp. 213–227. Springer Nature Switzerland, Cham (2023). https://doi.org/10.1007/978-3-031-47745-4_16
4. Benhocine, K., Hansali, A., Zemmouchi-Ghomari, L., Ghomari, A.R.: Towards an automatic SPARQL query generation from ontology competency questions. Int. J. Comput. Appl. **44**(10), 971–980 (2022). https://doi.org/10.1080/1206212X.2022.2031722
5. de Berardinis, J., et al.: The Polifonia ontology network: building a semantic backbone for musical heritage. In: The Semantic Web – ISWC 2023 (2023)
6. Caufield, J.H., et al.: Structured prompt interrogation and recursive extraction of semantics (SPIRES): a method for populating knowledge bases using zero-shot learning. Bioinformatics **104** (2024). https://doi.org/10.1093/bioinformatics/btae104
7. Chase, H.: LangChain (2022). https://github.com/langchain-ai/langchain
8. Clark, P., et al.: Think you have solved question answering? Try ARC, the AI2 reasoning challenge. arXiv abs/1803.05457 (2018). https://api.semanticscholar.org/CorpusID:3922816
9. Kim, D., et al.: SOLAR 10.7B: scaling large language models with simple yet effective depth up-scaling (2023)
10. Kompatsiaris, I.: Dementia ambient care: multi-sensing monitoring for intelligent remote management and decision support (2012). https://demcare.eu/

11. Krech, D., et al.: RDFLib (2023). https://doi.org/10.5281/zenodo.6845245, https://github.com/RDFLib/rdflib
12. Lisena, P., et al.: Capturing the semantics of smell: the Odeuropa data model for olfactory heritage information. In: Ortiz-Rodriguez, F., Villazón-Terrazas, B., Tiwari, S., Bobed, C. (eds.) KGSWC 2023. LNCS, vol. 14382, pp. 387–405. Springer, Cham (2022). https://doi.org/10.1007/978-3-031-47745-4_16
13. OpenAI: GPT-4 Technical report (2023)
14. Potoniec, J., Wiśniewski, D., Ławrynowicz, A., Keet, C.M.: Dataset of ontology competency questions to SPARQL-OWL queries translations. Data Brief (2020). https://doi.org/10.1016/j.dib.2019.105098
15. Poveda-Villalón, M., Fernández-Izquierdo, A., Fernández-López, M., García-Castro, R.: LOT: an industrial oriented ontology engineering framework. Eng. Appl. Artif. Intell. Eng. Appl. Artif. Intell. **111**, 104755 (2022). https://doi.org/10.1016/j.engappai.2022.104755
16. Reimers, N., Gurevych, I.: Sentence-BERT: sentence embeddings using Siamese BERT-networks. In: Proceedings of the 2019 Conference on Empirical Methods in Natural Language Processing. Association for Computational Linguistics (2019)
17. Ren, Y., Parvizi, A., Mellish, C., Pan, J., van Deemter, K., Stevens, R.: Towards competency question-driven ontology authoring. In: 11th European Semantic Web Conference (ESWC) (2014). https://doi.org/10.1007/978-3-319-07443-6_50
18. Sakaguchi, K., Bras, R.L., Bhagavatula, C., Choi, Y.: WinoGrande: an adversarial winograd schema challenge at scale. Commun. ACM **64**(9), 99–106 (2021). https://doi.org/10.1145/3474381
19. Schleider, T., Troncy, R., Gaitan, M., Alba, E., et al.: The SILKNOW knowledge graph. Semant. Web J. Spec. Issue Cultural Herit. Semant. Web March 2021. IOS Press (2021)
20. Sequeda, J., Allemang, D., Jacob, B.: A Benchmark to Understand the Role of Knowledge Graphs on Large Language Model's Accuracy for Question Answering on Enterprise SQL Databases (2023)
21. Tailhardat, L., Chabot, Y., Troncy, R.: NORIA-O: an ontology for anomaly detection and incident management in ICT systems. In: Semantic Web – 21st International Conference, ESWC 2024, Hersonissos, Crete, Greece, 26–30 May 2024, Proceedings (2024)
22. Touvron, H., et al.: Llama 2: Open Foundation and Fine-Tuned Chat Models (2023)
23. Tunstall, L., et al.: Zephyr: Direct Distillation of LM Alignment (2023)
24. Wisniewski, D., Potoniec, J., Lawrynowicz, A.: SeeQuery: an automatic method for recommending translations of ontology competency questions into SPARQL-OWL. In: 30th ACM International Conference on Information and Knowledge Management (CIKM), pp. 2119–2128. Association for Computing Machinery (2021). https://doi.org/10.1145/3459637.3482387
25. Wisniewski, D., Potoniec, J., Lawrynowicz, A., Keet, C.M.: Competency questions and SPARQL-OWL queries dataset and analysis. J. Web Semant. **59**, 100534 (2019). https://doi.org/10.1016/j.websem.2019.100534, https://www.sciencedirect.com/science/article/pii/S1570826819300617
26. Wiśniewski, D., Potoniec, J., Ławrynowicz, A.: ReqTagger: a rule-based tagger for automatic glossary of terms extraction from ontology requirements. Found. Comput. Decis. Sci. **47**(1), 65–86 (2022). https://doi.org/10.2478/fcds-2022-0003
27. Zellers, R., Holtzman, A., Bisk, Y., Farhadi, A., Choi, Y.: HellaSwag: can a machine really finish your sentence? In: Proceedings of the 57th Annual Meeting of the Association for Computational Linguistics (2019)

12 Shades of RDF: Impact of Syntaxes on Data Extraction with Language Models

Célian Ringwald[1]([⊠]) [iD], Fabien Gandon[1,2]([⊠]) [iD], Catherine Faron[1] [iD],
Franck Michel[1] [iD], and Hanna Abi Akl[1,2] [iD]

[1] Université Côte d'Azur, Inria, CNRS, I3S, Sophia Antipolis, France
{celian.ringwald,fabien.gandon}@inria.fr
[2] Data ScienceTech Institute, Paris, France

Abstract. The fine-tuning of generative pre-trained language models (PLMs) on a new task can be impacted by the choice made for representing the inputs and outputs. This article focuses on the linearization process used to structure and represent, as output, facts extracted from text. On a restricted relation extraction (RE) task, we challenged T5 and BART by fine-tuning them on 12 linearizations, including RDF standard syntaxes and variations thereof. Our benchmark covers: the validity of the produced triples, the performance of the model, the training behaviours and the resources needed. We show these PLMs can learn some syntaxes more easily than others, and we identify a promising "Turtle Light" syntax supporting the quick and robust learning of the RE task.

Keywords: Data extraction · RDF · Linearization · Language Model

1 Introduction: Targeted Data Properties Extraction

Relation extraction (RE) – the task of retrieving relations from unstructured text – was drastically improved recently by two main changes: (1) the construction of massive corpora aligning texts and facts from Knowledge graphs (KG) e.g. Wikipedia articles with corresponding Wikidata or DBpedia subgraphs, and (2) the usage of pre-trained language models (PLM) to carry out this task. However, Wikidata and DBpedia still struggle with coverage and quality issues [6,24]. In this context, extracting from Wikipedia the missing information in KGs is an important task. A promising research direction is to design a system allowing adaptability and fine-grained quality control. Now that we have end-to-end off-the-shelf methods, we have the opportunity to directly produce RDF serialization from natural language, and specify and control the output with constraints (e.g. with SHACL, ShEx). However, to the best of our knowledge, no LLM-based system currently performs RE directly from Wikipedia articles with a specific RDF syntax. Formally, let $Db \subseteq W \times G$ be a dual base, where W is a set

© The Author(s), under exclusive license to Springer Nature Switzerland AG 2025
A. Meroño Peñuela et al. (Eds.): ESWC 2024, LNCS 15344, pp. 81–91, 2025.
https://doi.org/10.1007/978-3-031-78952-6_8

of Wikipedia articles and G a set of corresponding KGs. Our goal is to learn a pattern-based extractor leveraging generative PLM: $E_{Db} \colon W \times S \to G; (t, s) \mapsto g$, where $t \in W$ is an input text, $s \in S$ is a set of SHACL shapes, and g is an RDF graph implied by t and valid against s.

Generative PLMs are very flexible but variations in prompts and output formats can impact their performances. In this paper, we focus on RE for the most common datatype properties of DBpedia resources of type dbo:Person. In this simplified setup, we challenged two encoder-decoder models trained on twelve RDF syntax flavours. Hence our research question: *How does the choice of a syntax impact the generation of RDF triples using datatype properties?*

After reviewing the related works (Sect. 2) we present a method to extract RDF from Wikipedia (Sect. 3) and the experiments we conducted (Sect. 4) before discussing the results (Sect. 5).

2   Related Works: RDF Extraction with Language Models

Before investing in generative PLMs, the research community focused on systems built on top of encoder-only PLMs (derived from BERT [2]), where relations were decoded by design in a discriminative manner [19]. Since 2021, generative PLMs have gained interest after demonstrating their ability to solve complex tasks in an end-to-end design. The solutions based on pre-trained generative transformer models rely either on encoder-decoder or decoder-only models. (1) Encoder-decoder models traditionally proposed for translation or summarization tasks also demonstrate several successes in Question Answering (QA) and RE tasks which were achieved by finetuning BART [13] and T5 models [22]. For RE we can cite: REBEL [7], TALN [20], DEEPstruct [28] or UIE [16]. (2) Decoder-only models have interesting generalization properties but generally work at large scale and need dedicated resources to be adapted to a specific task. Few-shot and zero-shot approaches were studied for these reasons. But few-shot learning does not seem sufficient to solve the relation extraction task [4]. Parameter-efficient fine-tuning (PEFT) approaches [3] allow the adaptation of large models to a specific task but do not necessarily perform as well as fine-tuned models [14].

The use of generative pre-trained models allows us to learn the triple syntax implicitly from the examples submitted during training [29]. The question of the structure of the output was initially referred to as "Answer Engineering" [15], but in the domain of graph extraction, the community refers to it as the "linearization process" i.e. the transformation of a graph structure into a raw sequence of tokens. This allows the usage of a generative model pre-trained on natural language texts [9]. Until now, different methods have been investigated but they were not rigorously compared. The two main solutions proposed represent a relation as a list of triples [28]: $((s1, p1, o1), (s2, p1, o2), ...)$ or a sequence of tags [12] where each element of the triple is preceded by a special token e.g. H, R, T in $\langle H \rangle s1 \langle R \rangle p1 \langle T \rangle o1 \langle H \rangle s2 \langle R \rangle p1 \langle T \rangle o2$. [7] and [11] proposed a triple linearization method (subject-collapsed) where triples sharing the same subject are grouped to avoid repetition.

In this article, we will also consider the syntaxes recommended by the W3C to serialize RDF triples, namely, RDF/XML, N-Triples, Turtle, and JSON-LD.

3   Methodological Framework: Definitions and Notations

Our pipeline takes as input a DBpedia dump[1] which is filtered to check that the values of the triples we target are mentioned in the corresponding Wikipedia abstracts and comply with a SHACL shape (Sect. 3.1). The selected triples are ordered and the URIs they use are cleaned. The dataset is then linearized into 12 syntaxes (Sect. 3.2) and each version is used in a K-fold approach. (Sects. 3.3 and 4).

3.1   Dataset and Ground Truth

Our experiment focuses on a simplified relation extraction task to better analyse the impact of the syntax. To avoid any entity linking step related to object properties, we only focused on datatype properties that relate to numbers, string values and dates. This is a good starting point because LLM hallucination generally affects these literal values [8]. Moreover, until now, the proposed generative models mostly focused on object properties, allowing for constrained decoding [10] that cannot be envisaged in the case of datatypes properties.

We focused on the DBpedia subgraphs describing instances of one of the most represented DBpedia classes, `dbo:Person`, and their corresponding Wikipedia abstracts. The instances of this class include the highest number of datatype properties, among which: `rdfs:label`, `dbo:alias`, `dbo:birthName`, `dbo:birthDate`, `dbo:deathDate`, `dbo:birthYear`, `dbo:deathYear`. Our original set was composed of 1 833 493 entities and 3 249 446 related triples, but this is over-scaled compared to our task. Preliminary trials [23] shown that a smaller set could be sufficient to learn the graph pattern captured by a SHACL shape.

Several works mention the noise caused by the massive alignment of facts with text [25], which also impacts T-Rex or REBEL [14]. More specifically, two problems are pointed out: the triple values do not necessarily appear in the text and, conversely, the facts of the text may not have counterpart triples in the knowledge base. To solve the first one, we keep only the triples describing values that could be found in the Wikipedia abstract of a given entity. To answer the second problem, we designed a SHACL shape targeting `dbo:Person` and specifying which property is mandatory and which is optional, and we kept only the graphs valid against this shape. By applying these two pre-processing steps to a random sample of 1000 entities, we found that 80% of the triples contain values that can be found in the Wikipedia abstract, but that only 45% of the entities have a description graph valid against the shape.

Our pipeline includes two additional pre-processing steps: (1) Triple ordering: [17] demonstrated the importance of having in the first place the triples

---

[1] https://databus.dbpedia.org/dbpedia/collections/dbpedia-snapshot-2022-09.

typing the entity. As RDFlib[2] does not ensure this on every syntax, we added an ordering step. (2) URI encoding: the Turtle syntax uses tokens that can be found in URIs (dots and parenthesis) but their usage is forbidden in local names. We had to encode them systematically

3.2   RDF Syntaxes and Alternative Linearizations

Our benchmark covers three types of syntaxes. First we consider the four W3C RDF syntaxes: XML-RDF (noted $_x$), Turtle (noted $_T$), N-Triples (noted $_n$) and JSON-LD (noted $_j$). Second, we include the classical syntaxes of the literature: the List (noted $_l$) and the Tags (noted $_g$). Finally, we propose *Turtle light*, a simplified Turtle syntax where namespaces, prefixes, and datatypes are considered as already defined (noted $_t$). We also consider two variations. The first one is the triple subject factorisation (noted $_f$). It is naturally integrated into Turtle, JSON-LD and RDF-XML and we also apply to the Turtle Light, the List and the Tags. A second variation is the single-line writing (noted $_1$) to evaluate the impact of the carriage return[3]. Finally, we consider the use of vocabulary extension (noted $_v$) which first ensures that syntax-related tokens will not be considered as unknown by the tokenizer, but also allows us to detach these tokens from the pre-trained embedding space because they relate to another semantic space, e.g. a comma in Turtle vs. a comma in a text in natural language. For each W3C syntax, we added all the tokens specified in its recommendation.

3.3   Pre-trained Language Models: the Choice of Frugal Sizes

We focused our benchmark on the two encoder-decoder models traditionally used in the literature (see Sect. 2), BART (noted B) and $T5$, and we limited our experiment to the "base" size of these pre-trained models that can be seen as small or frugal LLMs compared to decoder-only models: today's LLMs count billions of parameters [18], where BART base uses 140M parameters and T5 base 220M. When comparing BART and T5, they were pre-trained on different datasets and in a different manner. Each model is given a specific Task Prompt, where $Abstract is a Wikipedia abstract and $Syntax the targeted RDF syntax: (1) BART: "$entity_URI : $Abstract"; and (2) T5: "Translate English to $Syntax: [$entity_URI] $Abstract". In the next sections, we use the notations introduced in this section to name each possible configuration. For instance, a BART model trained on *Turtle Light* syntax, with factorization and multi-lines will be written B_{tf}, and a $T5$ model trained on lists with a vocabulary will be written $T5_{vl}$.

---

[2] https://rdflib.readthedocs.io/en/stable/.

[3] The "\n" special token.

4   Experimental Set-Up

4.1   Fine-Tuning Details

Our code[4] is published under an open license and based on a fork of REBEL[5], which we extended and adapted to our task. For each standard RDF syntax, we developed a specific parser and integrated the metrics we present below.

Data Split: we follow a 5-fold cross-validation based on 5 000 rotated examples split into 4 000 training examples and 1 000 test examples. In addition, 250 disjoint examples are used for the evaluation. **Configuration:** The BART model was fine-tuned using the inverse square root scheduler with an initial learning rate of 0.00005. For T5 we used the Adafactor scheduler with an initial learning rate of 0.001. Both models were fine-tuned with 1000 steps of warmup and configured with an early stop mode with patience of 5 steps. Both models were trained on a single GPU, Tesla V100-SXM2-32GB for BART and NVIDIA A100 80 GB PCIe for T5 (able to manage bf16). **Management of Tokenization Inconsistencies:** As underlined in [1,26], both T5 and BART tokenizers may duplicate or delete spaces before or after special tokens. For this reason, we controlled the token consistency during the evaluation with a typographic checker and cleaner. This is applied to the learning examples and to the predicted output when both are compared.

4.2   Evaluation Metrics

The first stage of this experiment is to evaluate the ability of the model to produce a given syntax without generating any parsing error. This is measured by the rate of Parsed Triples R_{PT}. We also introduce the rate of Correct Subject R_{CS}: the choice of the URI for the subject of a generated triple depends on the ability of a model to copy from the input the targeted entity. In addition, we define the rate of SHACL-Validated Triples R_{SVT}.

$$R_{PT} = \frac{Nb_{output\ parsed}}{Nb_{output\ generated}} \qquad R_{CS} = \frac{Nb_{URI\ found}}{Nb_{output\ parsed}} \qquad R_{SVT} = \frac{Nb_{output\ Valid}}{Nb_{output\ parsed}}$$

Non-parsable triples are evaluated using the Levenstein edit distance $lev(r_g, r_t)$ where r_g is the generated RDF code, r_t is the one targeted. The result is the number of editions needed to transform r_g into r_t.

Traditionally, RE focuses on *precision* (P), *recall* (R), F_1 score, or *top@k* metrics. Following [5], only parsed outputs are evaluated with these metrics and we focus on macro-measures (P^+, R^+, F_1^+) that better account for the imbalanced distribution of properties.

These metrics follow the *Strict Mode* evaluation [27], comparing predicted and ground truth values and verifying their strict equality. The strict evaluation-based metrics are not the most appropriate to evaluate datatype properties with

---

[4] https://github.com/datalogism/12ShadesOfRDFSyntax.
[5] https://github.com/Babelscape/rebel.

values of type xsd:String, where we may accept semantically close values. For this reason, we also compute the BLEU score [21] (B): the closer B is to 1, the greater the similarity between string values.

To assess the training process itself based on cross-entropy loss objective, we define meta-metrics to monitor the behaviour of the R_{PT} and F_1 metrics. The three meta-metrics are defined as: (1) the learning velocity V is the number of epochs needed to reach the first saturation (> 0.9) of a given metric, e.g. $V_{F_1^-}$ is the number of epochs needed to reach the first saturation when $F_1^- > 0.9$; (2) the stability of a learning process is defined as the ratio of epochs during which a metric remains stable after the first saturation, e.g. for F_1^- we note the stability $S_{F_1^-}$; (3) the final divergence of the learning process is defined as the number of folds for which there is a final divergence, e.g. the divergence $D_{F_1^-}$ is the number of folds for which the final F_1^- is lower than the value of its first saturation. In some folds, the learning behaviours metrics may have no value. First, when saturation never happens on a fold, the average velocity ($\overline{V}$) and stability ($\overline{S}$) cannot be computed. For this reason, we focus on the micro-F1 (F_1^-), because the macro-F1 (F_1^+) metric never saturates[6]

Finally, we define a global grade G_g that will allow us to compare the overall performances of our configurations. It combines the performance of the model in terms of parsability, SHACL validity and subject validity on one side, and in terms of macro F_1 on the other side: $G_g = \overline{R_{PT}} \times \overline{R_{CS}} \times \overline{R_{SVT}} \times \overline{F_1^+} \times 100$ where, for instance, $\overline{F_1^+}$ is the average of F_1^+ over the splits.

Additionally, we monitored the training time T_t (in minutes) and the carbon cost[7] C_c (emissions of CO_2-equivalents in kg) for training a model.

5   Results and Discussions: The Best Syntaxes

Table 1 compiles the results for the best-performing configurations; additional details are online[8]. As the configurations using a vocabulary systematically perform better, we only report these in the table. Starting with the **triple validity** metric, almost every configuration produces triples that could be parsed ($\overline{R_{PT}}$); except $T5$ that struggles to produce the Turtle and N-Triples syntaxes.

Considering the $\overline{lev}$ computed on the triples with syntax errors, we observe the ability of some models to extract close to perfect triples. Moreover, a lot of models record negligible $\overline{lev}$ distances ($\overline{lev} \approx 0$) and in these cases the parsing mainly fails because of forgotten or misplaced tokens that break the syntax (see examples online (See footnote 8)). In contrast, high values of the $\overline{lev}$ also allow us to identify models producing triples that can be far from the well-formed triples ($T5_{vT}, T5_{vn}, T5_{vlf}, T5_{vt1}$). Once the results are parsable, they are always valid

---

[6] A formalisation of the computation of those three metrics is detailed on GitHub: https://github.com/datalogism/12ShadesOfRDFSyntax/tree/main/eval.

[7] https://codecarbon.io/.

[8] https://wandb.ai/celian-ringwald/12ShadesOfRDF.

against the shape ($\overline{R_{SVT}}$). The subject URI is also generally easily copied from the prompt by the model, even if we can find some exceptions ($T5_{vgf}$ and $T5_{vlf}$).

The **RE** metrics are computed on valid triples and, in that respect, the best models have a $\overline{F_1^+}$, $\overline{P^+}$ and $\overline{R^+}$ close to 0.95. This is a good result since the macro metrics are generally less optimistic and more informative than the micro ones, where every configuration seems to reach an almost perfect extraction. From that point of view, $T5_{vj}$ is our best result, closely followed by B_{vgf}, B_{vtf1}, B_{vT}, $T5_{vtf1}$ and $T5_{vgf}$. Considering the BLUE score B, we can see that $T5_{vj}$ is always perfectly predicting string values of datatype properties, and other models generally perform well, except $T5_{vtl}$.

The **training behaviour** metrics show that the models generally saturate at the first epoch. Velocity metrics ($\overline{V_{R_{PT}}}$ and $\overline{V_{F_1^-}}$) also demonstrate that models learn the relation extraction task slightly before they learn to produce syntactically correct triples. Considering the stability ($\overline{S_{R_{PT}}}$ and $\overline{S_{F_1^-}}$), we observed that

Table 1. Results for the best-performing configurations. This table is ordered based on the G_g score taking into account both triple validity and performances. In bold are the best results. In italics are the second-best results. The worse results are underlined. Averages are calculated over the 5 folds. The mean μ and standard deviation σ are provided for each metric. As a reminder the syntax notation is: XML-RDF ($_x$), Turtle ($_T$), Turtle Light ($_t$), N-Triples ($_n$), JSON-LD ($_j$), list ($_l$) and tags ($_g$).

Config	Triple Validity			RE performances ×100				Edition m.		Training behaviors							Resources		G_g
	R_{PT}	R_{CS}	R_{SVT}	F_1^-	F_1^+	P^+	R^+	B	lev	Nb_{epochs}	$V_{R_{PT}}$	$S_{R_{PT}}$	$\sum D_{R_{PT}}$	$V_{F_1^-}$	$S_{F_1^-}$	$\sum D_{F_1^-}$	C_c	T_t	
$T5_{vj}$	1	1	1	**99.75**	**95.63**	**100.00**	**94.37**	**1.00**	0	13	0.2	∅	0	0.2	∅	2	0.252	137	**96**
B_{vgf}	1	1	1	99.69	*95.47*	*99.29*	94.28	0.97	0	15	0	∅	0	0	∅	1	0.042	29	**95**
B_{vtf1}	1	1	1	99.72	94.54	97.09	93.20	0.93	0	12	0	∅	0	0.2	∅	2	*0.035*	27	**95**
B_{vT}	1	1	1	*99.73*	94.43	96.39	*93.42*	0.97	11	22	0	∅	0	0	∅	1	0.104	75	*94*
$T5_{vtf1}$	1	1	1	99.51	93.94	95.48	93.13	0.96	0	14	0.2	∅	0	0	∅	3	0.099	56	*94*
$T5_{vx}$	1	1	1	99.58	92.86	96.81	91.91	0.95	2	18	0.4	∅	1	0.4	∅	2	0.324	206	93
B_{vg}	1	1	1	99.62	92.57	96.34	91.08	0.94	0	17	0	∅	0	0	∅	0	0.053	46	93
$T5_{vl}$	1	1	1	99.55	92.34	95.19	91.40	0.97	0	11	0.8	∅	1	0.6	∅	1	0.118	75	92
B_{vlf}	1	1	1	99.63	91.99	96.68	90.49	**1.00**	2	12	0	∅	0	0	∅	1	0.04	29	92
B_{vl}	1	1	1	99.62	92.03	94.75	90.37	0.90	18	18	0	∅	0	0	∅	1	0.064	54	92
B_{vtf}	1	1	1	99.49	90.72	95.45	89.13	0.97	0	12	0	∅	0	0	∅	0	**0.029**	26	91
$T5_{vgf}$	1	0.96	1	99.57	94.18	96.76	92.51	0.98	1	13	0.2	∅	0	0.2	∅	1	0.087	45	91
$T5_{vtf}$	1	1	1	99.33	90.72	95.81	88.72	0.96	1	10	0.8	∅	1	0.4	∅	1	0.072	44	90
B_{vj}	1	1	1	99.52	90.27	95.14	88.85	0.96	47	11	0.2	∅	0	0	∅	0	0.093	74	90
B_{vx}	1	1	1	99.46	89.87	96.69	88.85	0.97	17	14	0	∅	0	0.2	∅	1	0.092	75	90
$T5_{vtl}$	0.97	1	1	99.34	91.73	95.32	89.68	0.97	99	10	0	∅	0	0	∅	2	0.109	56	89
$T5_{vlf}$	1	0.98	1	99.32	90.32	94.28	89.43	0.88	205	11	1	∅	1	0	∅	4	0.081	49	88
B_{vn}	1	1	1	99.36	87.73	97.01	85.48	0.99	81	24	0	∅	0	0.4	∅	1	0.134	119	88
$T5_{vg}$	0.98	1	1	99.29	88.72	96.15	86.28	0.94	18	15	0.4	∅	1	0	∅	1	0.107	76	87
$T5_{vt}$	0.97	1	1	99.24	88.41	92.60	86.61	0.94	29	14	0.2	∅	1	0.2	∅	3	0.115	79	90
B_{vtl}	0.97	1	1	99.32	86.15	94.13	83.89	0.99	20	16	0	∅	0	0	∅	1	0.047	41	83
B_{vt}	0.97	1	1	99.34	85.68	93.52	83.64	0.98	13	14	0	∅	0	0	∅	1	0.053	43	83
$T5_{wT}$	0.82	1	1	99.25	88.41	92.60	86.61	0.97	810	15	0.8	0.5	2	0.4	∅	3	0.221	139	72
$T5_{vn}$	0.75	1	1	99.39	90.61	97.98	88.17	0.97	137	13	1.6	0.4	3	0.2	0.5	3	0.25	160	67
μ	0.98	1.00	1	99.49	91.42	96.02	89.87	0.96	63	14	0.3	∅	0.5	0.1	∅	1.5	0.11	73	89
σ	0.1	0.0	0	0.2	2.7	1.7	3	0.0	163	3	0.4	∅	0.7	0.2	∅	1	0.1	46	6.8

two models $T5_{vT}$ and $T5_{vn}$ experience difficulties to converge. As for the divergence metrics ($\sum D_{R_{PT}}$ and $\sum D_{F_1^-}$), we see that the forgetting effect could be reached, but BART-based models are less impacted.

The **resources metrics** also show important discrepancies between models, that could be explained by the verbosity of some syntaxes, the resources needed for each model, and the ability of the latter to learn a given syntax without divergences. Indeed T5 models are greedier than BART models and simple syntaxes are thriftier than RDF ones. Model training costs vary from 29 g of CO_2, reached by B_{vtf} to 300 g of CO_2 emitted by T_{vx}.

Globally, BART generally writes syntactically better triples than T5, where T5 needs less training epochs but requires more resources. The factorisation variation has shown a positive impact on the performance of the models, except on $T5_{vl}$ configurations. On the Turtle Light variations, the one-line option also improves quality but the best configuration seems to be the combination of both factorisation and one-line writing. In the end, B_{vtf1} offers good performances, at a low cost with a standard and human-readable syntax.

Finally, the experiment conducted has some limitations. T5 and BART were pre-trained partially on Wikipedia, which means they may already have been exposed to some of the knowledge we want to extract. The second limitation is our dependency on the tokenization method which, if changed, could impact the effectiveness of a given syntax to capture relations.

6   Conclusion: a Light Turtle Goes a Long Way

In this article, we evaluated how the choice of a syntax impacts the generation of RDF triples focusing on datatype properties extraction from text. We showed that basic syntaxes (list and tags) are generally easily parsed but lead to average performances. While learning W3C RDF syntaxes is more resource-consuming, the best-performing configuration $T5_{vj}$ outperforms the others at the cost of 2 h of training on an A100 GPU and 250g of CO_2 produced. An interesting compromise is the use of simplified syntaxes, close to standards, robust and quick to learn, in particular **inline factorised Turtle Light** (B_{vtf1} and $T5_{vtf1}$).

Our experiments also showed the limits of full fine-tuning in some training configurations: $T5_{vn}$ or $T5_{vT}$, underlining that Turtle and N-Triples may require better-fitted adaptation. Several directions could be explored, including the use of a loss or an iterative learning process designed to take into account the syntax and the task, as well as models specialized on code.

Acknowledgments. This work is supported by 3IA Côte d'Azur (ANR-19-P3IA-0002) and UCAJEDI (ANR-15-IDEX-01) and the OPAL infrastructure and Université Côte d'Azur's Center for High-Performance Computing.

References

1. Banerjee, D., Nair, P.A., Kaur, J.N., Usbeck, R., Biemann, C.: Modern baselines for sparql semantic parsing. In: Proceedings of the 45th International ACM SIGIR Conference on Research and Development in Information Retrieval. SIGIR '22, pp. 2260–2265. Association for Computing Machinery, New York, NY, USA (2022). https://doi.org/10.1145/3477495.3531841
2. Devlin, J., Chang, M.W., Lee, K., Toutanova, K.: BERT: pre-training of deep bidirectional transformers for language understanding. In: Burstein, J., Doran, C., Solorio, T. (eds.) Proceedings of the 2019 Conference of the North American Chapter of the Association for Computational Linguistics: Human Language Technologies, Volume 1 (Long and Short Papers), pp. 4171–4186. Association for Computational Linguistics, Minneapolis, Minnesota (2019). https://doi.org/10.18653/v1/N19-1423, https://aclanthology.org/N19-1423
3. Ding, N., et al.: Parameter-efficient fine-tuning of large-scale pre-trained language models. Nat. Mach. Intell. **5**(3), 220–235 (2023). https://doi.org/10.1038/s42256-023-00626-4, https://www.nature.com/articles/s42256-023-00626-4, number: 3 Publisher: Nature Publishing Group
4. Han, R., Peng, T., Yang, C., Wang, B., Liu, L., Wan, X.: Is information extraction solved by ChatGPT? An analysis of performance, evaluation criteria, robustness and errors (2023). https://doi.org/10.48550/arXiv.2305.14450, http://arxiv.org/abs/2305.14450, arXiv:2305.14450 [cs]
5. Harbecke, D., Chen, Y., Hennig, L., Alt, C.: Why only micro-f1? Class weighting of measures for relation classification. In: Shavrina, T., Mikhailov, V., Malykh, V., Artemova, E., Serikov, O., Protasov, V. (eds.) Proceedings of NLP Power! The First Workshop on Efficient Benchmarking in NLP, pp. 32–41. Association for Computational Linguistics, Dublin, Ireland (2022). https://doi.org/10.18653/v1/2022.nlppower-1.4, https://aclanthology.org/2022.nlppower-1.4
6. Hofer, M., Obraczka, D., Saeedi, A., Köpcke, H., Rahm, E.: Construction of knowledge graphs: state and challenges (2023). https://doi.org/10.48550/arXiv.2302.11509, http://arxiv.org/abs/2302.11509, arXiv:2302.11509 [cs]
7. Huguet Cabot, P.L., Navigli, R.: REBEL: relation extraction by end-to-end language generation. In: Moens, M.F., Huang, X., Specia, L., Yih, S.W.T. (eds.) Findings of the Association for Computational Linguistics: EMNLP 2021, pp. 2370–2381. Association for Computational Linguistics, Punta Cana, Dominican Republic (2021). https://doi.org/10.18653/v1/2021.findings-emnlp.204, https://aclanthology.org/2021.findings-emnlp.204
8. Ji, Z., et al.: Survey of hallucination in natural language generation. ACM Comput. Surv. **55**(12) (2023). https://doi.org/10.1145/3571730
9. Jin, B., Liu, G., Han, C., Jiang, M., Ji, H., Han, J.: Large language models on graphs: a comprehensive survey (2023). http://arxiv.org/abs/2312.02783, arXiv:2312.02783 [cs]
10. Josifoski, M., De Cao, N., Peyrard, M., Petroni, F., West, R.: GenIE: generative information extraction. In: Carpuat, M., de Marneffe, M.C., Meza Ruiz, I.V. (eds.) Proceedings of the 2022 Conference of the North American Chapter of the Association for Computational Linguistics: Human Language Technologies, pp. 4626–4643. Association for Computational Linguistics, Seattle, United States (2022). https://doi.org/10.18653/v1/2022.naacl-main.342, https://aclanthology.org/2022.naacl-main.342

11. Josifoski, M., Sakota, M., Peyrard, M., West, R.: Exploiting asymmetry for synthetic training data generation: SynthIE and the case of information extraction. In: Bouamor, H., Pino, J., Bali, K. (eds.) Proceedings of the 2023 Conference on Empirical Methods in Natural Language Processing, pp. 1555–1574. Association for Computational Linguistics, Singapore (2023). https://doi.org/10.18653/v1/2023.emnlp-main.96, https://aclanthology.org/2023.emnlp-main.96

12. Ke, P., et al.: JointGT: graph-text joint representation learning for text generation from knowledge graphs. In: Zong, C., Xia, F., Li, W., Navigli, R. (eds.) Findings of the Association for Computational Linguistics: ACL-IJCNLP 2021, pp. 2526–2538. Association for Computational Linguistics, Online (2021). https://doi.org/10.18653/v1/2021.findings-acl.223, https://aclanthology.org/2021.findings-acl.223

13. Lewis, M., et al.: BART: denoising sequence-to-sequence pre-training for natural language generation, translation, and comprehension (2019). https://doi.org/10.48550/arXiv.1910.13461, http://arxiv.org/abs/1910.13461, arXiv:1910.13461 [cs, stat]

14. Li, X., Polat, F., Groth, P.: Do Instruction-tuned Large Language Models Help with Relation Extraction? (2023)

15. Liu, P., Yuan, W., Fu, J., Jiang, Z., Hayashi, H., Neubig, G.: Pre-train, prompt, and predict: a systematic survey of prompting methods in natural language processing. ACM Comput. Surv. **55**(9) (2023). https://doi.org/10.1145/3560815

16. Lu, Y., et al.: Unified structure generation for universal information extraction. In: Muresan, S., Nakov, P., Villavicencio, A. (eds.) Proceedings of the 60th Annual Meeting of the Association for Computational Linguistics (Volume 1: Long Papers), pp. 5755–5772. Association for Computational Linguistics, Dublin, Ireland (2022). https://doi.org/10.18653/v1/2022.acl-long.395, https://aclanthology.org/2022.acl-long.395

17. Mihindukulasooriya, N., et al.: Knowledge graph induction enabling recommending and trend analysis: a corporate research community use case. In: Sattler, U., et al. (eds.) ISWC 2022. LNCS, vol. 13489, pp. 827–844. Springer, Cham (2022). https://doi.org/10.1007/978-3-031-19433-7_47

18. Minaee, S., et al.: Large language models: a survey (2024)

19. Nayak, T., Majumder, N., Goyal, P., Poria, S.: Deep neural approaches to relation triplets extraction: a comprehensive survey. Cogn. Comput. **13**, 1215–1232 (2021). https://api.semanticscholar.org/CorpusID:232427782

20. Paolini, G., et al.: Structured prediction as translation between augmented natural languages. In: 9th International Conference on Learning Representations. ICLR 2021 (2021)

21. Papineni, K., Roukos, S., Ward, T., Zhu, W.J.: Bleu: a method for automatic evaluation of machine translation. In: Isabelle, P., Charniak, E., Lin, D. (eds.) Proceedings of the 40th Annual Meeting of the Association for Computational Linguistics, pp. 311–318. Association for Computational Linguistics, Philadelphia, Pennsylvania, USA (2002). https://doi.org/10.3115/1073083.1073135, https://aclanthology.org/P02-1040

22. Raffel, C., et al.: Exploring the limits of transfer learning with a unified text-to-text transformer (2023). http://arxiv.org/abs/1910.10683, arXiv:1910.10683 [cs, stat]

23. Ringwald, C., Gandon, F., Faron, C., Michel, F., Abi Akl, H.: Well-written knowledge graphs: most effective RDF syntaxes for triple linearization in end-to-end extraction of relations from texts (student abstract). In: Proceedings of the AAAI Conference on Artificial Intelligence, vol. 38, pp. 23631–23632 (2024)

24. Shenoy, K., Ilievski, F., Garijo, D., Schwabe, D., Szekely, P.: A study of the quality of Wikidata. J. Web Semanti. **72**, 100679 (2022). https://doi.org/10.1016/j.websem.2021.100679, https://www.sciencedirect.com/science/article/pii/S1570826821000536

25. Smirnova, A., Cudré-Mauroux, P.: Relation extraction using distant supervision: a survey. ACM Comput. Surv. **51**(5) (2018). https://doi.org/10.1145/3241741

26. Sun, K., Qi, P., Zhang, Y., Liu, L., Wang, W.Y., Huang, Z.: Tokenization consistency matters for generative models on extractive NLP Tasks (2023). https://doi.org/10.48550/arXiv.2212.09912, http://arxiv.org/abs/2212.09912, arXiv:2212.09912 [cs]

27. Taillé, B., Guigue, V., Scoutheeten, G., Gallinari, P.: Let's stop incorrect comparisons in end-to-end relation extraction! In: Webber, B., Cohn, T., He, Y., Liu, Y. (eds.) Proceedings of the 2020 Conference on Empirical Methods in Natural Language Processing (EMNLP), pp. 3689–3701. Association for Computational Linguistics, Online (2020). https://doi.org/10.18653/v1/2020.emnlp-main.301, https://aclanthology.org/2020.emnlp-main.301

28. Wang, C., Liu, X., Chen, Z., Hong, H., Tang, J., Song, D.: DeepStruct: pre-training of language models for structure prediction. In: Muresan, S., Nakov, P., Villavicencio, A. (eds.) Findings of the Association for Computational Linguistics: ACL 2022, pp. 803–823. Association for Computational Linguistics, Dublin, Ireland (2022). https://doi.org/10.18653/v1/2022.findings-acl.67, https://aclanthology.org/2022.findings-acl.67

29. Ye, H., Zhang, N., Chen, H., Chen, H.: Generative knowledge graph construction: a review. CoRR abs/2210.12714 (2022). https://doi.org/10.48550/arXiv.2210.12714

Validating Semantic Artifacts with Large Language Models

Nilay Tufek[1(✉)] , Aparna Saissre Thuluva[1] , Valentin Philipp Just[2] ,
Fajar J. Ekaputra[3,4] , Tathagata Bandyopadhyay[1] , Marta Sabou[3] ,
and Allan Hanbury[4]

[1] Technology Department, Siemens AG, Munich, Germany
ntufek@gmail.com
[2] Institute of Computer Engineering, TU Wien, Vienna, Austria
[3] Institute of Data, Process and Knowledge Management, WU Vienna, Vienna, Austria
[4] Institute for Information Systems Engineering, TU Wien, Vienna, Austria

Abstract. As part of knowledge engineering workflows, semantic artifacts, such as ontologies, knowledge graphs or semantic descriptions based on industrial standards, are often validated in terms of their compliance with requirements expressed in natural language (e.g., ontology competency questions, standard specifications). Key to this process is the translation of the requirements in machine-actionable queries (e.g., SPARQL) that can automate the validation process. This manual translation process is time-consuming, error-prone and challenging, especially in areas where domain experts might lack knowledge of semantic technologies. In this paper, we propose a Large Language Models (LLMs) based approach to translate requirements texts into SPARQL queries and test it in validation use cases related to SAREF and OPC UA Robotics. F1 scores of 88–100% indicate the feasibility of the approach and its potential impact on ensuring high quality semantic artifacts and further uptake of the semantic technologies (industrial) domains.

Keywords: Semantic Artifacts · Validation · LLM · OPC UA

1 Introduction

Knowledge Engineering (KE) aims to elicit, capture, conceptualise and formalise knowledge in the form of *semantic artifacts* that support information systems, in particular in the area of Artificial Intelligence. A semantic artifact is a "machine-actionable formalisation of a conceptualisation, enabling sharing and reuse by humans and machines" [7]. Examples of such artifacts range from taxonomies and thesauri, to ontologies and knowledge graphs.

Ensuring the quality of a semantic artifact is often achieved by validating that it complies with certain requirements. For example, in ontology engineering, ontologies are validated against competency questions or requirements elicited

A. Meroño Peñuela et al. (Eds.): ESWC 2024, LNCS 15344, pp. 92–101, 2025.
https://doi.org/10.1007/978-3-031-78952-6_9

when building (or reusing already existing) ontologies [18]. We represent this process graphically in Fig. 1a: given a set of competency questions or requirements expressed in natural language, a semantic artifact is built (or selected for reuse). The validation of the semantic resource happens by translating the requirements from natural language to a machine-actionable language such as SPARQL (or SHACL) and applying these to the artifacts. Validation fails when the queries return no answer, as the information expressed by the requirements could not be found in the semantic artifact.

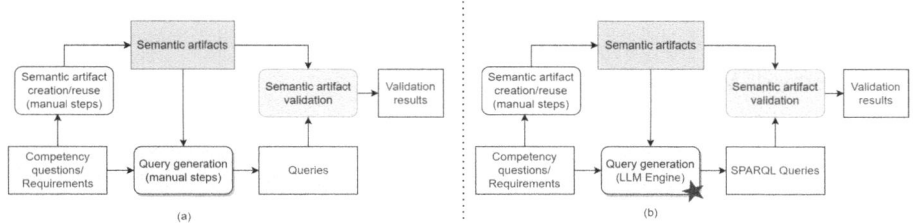

Fig. 1. Validation of semantic artifacts: (a) traditional approach; (b) with LLMs.

Interestingly, this pattern of validating semantic artifacts through the formalisation of requirements can also be found more broadly in communities that adopt semantic technologies [8]. This is the case with industrial standards such as ISA, IEC, OPC UA, etc., which provide standardized semantics for the industry automation field [6]. These standards provide the specification of their semantics in textual documents (e.g., in PDF format). Their adopters create information artifacts (e.g., descriptions of devices e.g., in XML format) in compliance with the standard's rules to ensure interoperability and integration in their domain. To benefit from formal and machine-actionable semantics in terms of automated query and reasoning capabilities, several of these standards are aligned to the Semantic Web (SW) technology stack [11,12,19,20]. As a result, standard adopters create *semantic artifacts* (expressed in RDF), which need to comply with the textual requirements expressed in the standard specification (aka compliance rules). Compliance is checked by validating these industrial semantic artifacts through formal queries derived from the standard specification.

The key *challenge* in all these validation settings is that translating textual requirements into formal queries manually is time consuming, tedious and error-prone [22]. In industrial settings, this is exacerbated by *scale* (e.g., OPC UA alone has about 140 specification documents each containing 30–100 textual compliance rules) and reduced expertise with semantic technologies [3]. LLMs such as GPT-3, have shown a versatile applicability for performing language processing tasks [5]. While their use to address KE tasks is being investigated [2, 15,16], there is, so far limited focus on semantic artifact validation.

To fill this gap, we investigate how to automatically generate SPARQL queries from textual requirements using LLMs (Fig. 1b) as a key enabler for semantic artifact validation. We describe our methodology for devising suitable prompts and experimentally investigate the feasibility of this approach in two uses cases: (i) the open source Smart Applications REFerence (SAREF) ontology [1] and (ii) an OPC UA Robotics ontology derived from OPC UA Robotics nodeset file[1] using the formal mapping to RDF defined in [19]. The experimental data and the source code are publicly available [21]. Results of F1 score ranging between 88–100% demonstrate the feasibility of the approach.

An overview of related work (Sect. 2), is followed by the description of our methodology (Sect. 3), its adaptation to the two use cases and the experiments conducted (Sect. 4). We close with lessons learned and conclusions (Sect. 5).

2   Related Work

The support of LLMs for KE has attracted much research interest in recent years. Allen et al. [2] highlights two possible uses of LLMs for KE: (i) LLM as a component in a hybrid neuro-symbolic system to support the KE process, and (ii) LLM as a stand-alone approach to KE. Further, they emphasize the capability of LLM as a general-purpose technology to transform natural language into formal language. Meyer et al. [13] elaborate their experiments on potential application areas where LLMs can assist with Knowledge Graph (KG) engineering.

However, much of these recent works are focused on KG construction and completion, marked with the availability of benchmarks (e.g., Text2KGBench [14]) and challenges (e.g., LLM-KBC[2]). In contrast, support for other KE tasks, including the validation of semantic artefacts, is limited or only reported as part of a larger process.

The identification of incorrect KG triples has been briefly discussed in [10] as part of a KG generation process. Meyer et al. conducted experiments with SPARQL query generation where their initial results show that the standard prompt engineering is not sufficient [13].

Therefore, there is a need for a methodology to support validation of semantic artefacts, including generating SPARQL queries from textual requirements.

3   Proposed Methodology

LLMs are pre-trained models on billions or trillions of parameters [9]. Therefore, in general, they can generate SPARQL queries from natural language sentences and questions, in other words, Natural Language Query (NLQ). The generated queries are sometimes syntactically correct. However, in most cases they may not be semantically correct as they still lack the context and instructions to generate the queries desired by the user [13]. In this work, we developed a methodology to improve the syntactic and semantic correctness of SPARQL queries generated

---

[1] https://github.com/OPCFoundation/UA-Nodeset/blob/latest/Robotics/Opc.Ua. Robotics.NodeSet2.xml.

[2] https://lm-kbc.github.io/challenge2023/.

from LLMs. We mainly use prompt engineering, which means giving knowledge required by an LLM (e.g., in the form of additional context such as text documents, excel sheets, knowledge graphs, etc.) and giving it instructions or guidelines in the form of natural language text to perform the task a user wants.

There are several ways to provide instructions to LLMs [17]. Our methodology relies on prompt engineering with zero-shot learning
and has three steps:

- *Step 1: Schema preparation*: provides context/schema to the LLM such as the semantic artifact, based on which the queries should be generated;
- *Step 2: Instruction template adaptation*: a list of instructions for the LLM is created by adaptation of an instruction template, and
- *Step 3: LLM configuration* towards optimal and consistent results.

The development of this methodology was an iterative process that involved performing multiple experiments on LLMs for SPARQL query generation. At every iteration, we extended the context and fine-tuned the instructions to the LLM to improve the correctness and accuracy of the generated SPARQL query. As part of our methodology, we developed a prompt template for the SPARQL query generation (cf. Listing 1.1). The prompt template contains three placeholders: SCHEMA of the semantic artefacts (for Step 1), Domain-Specific-Instructions (for Step 2), and NLQ to be translated into SPARQL.

Listing 1.1. Prompt template for SPARQL query generation using LLMs

```
By using this ontology:
{SCHEMA}
Instructions:
1. First, generate the paths and relations.
2. Then generate SPARQL query using those paths and relations.
3. Define all the necessary prefixes fully and use only those
     prefixes in the query.
4. Use precise prefixes while generating a SPARQL query; do not give
     multiple options for prefixes in the query.
5. Do not use '/' or '\textbackslash' inside the WHERE clause; define
     the full path in prefix.
6. Do not include any explanations or apologies in your responses.
7. Do not respond to any questions that ask for anything else than
     for you to construct a SPARQL query.
8. Do not include any text except the SPARQL query generated.
{Domain-Specific-Instructions}
{NLQ}
```

3.1   Step 1: Schema Preparation

The schema part of the prompt is the semantic artifact. Should the artifact contain ontologies with complex (OWL) axioms, this leads to challenges for the LLM. Therefore, a pre-processing step is required to simplify the OWL axioms and present them as simple triples prior to being used by the LLM. In this case, there is a token limit for the schema. In our case, we used OpenAI's GPT-4 [5] LLM engine where the token size limit is 8192 tokens. In contrast to this approach, the schema can be given to an LLM by uploading documents. In this way, the token limit can be further extended. However, when the size of the schema is larger, it should be divided into chunks and it should be kept in a vector database. Moreover, appropriate chunks should be given to the LLM for query generation, however, this is a part of our future work.

3.2   Step 2: Instruction Template Adaptation

Listing 1.1 shows a prompt template containing the list of instructions provided to an LLM for query generation. The instruction part is divided into two sections.

General Instructions (Instructions 1–8): are domain agnostic and can be used to generate SPARQL queries in any domain. They were enriched in an iterative way through experiments. Therefore, this list is not complete, but rather a baseline to be further extended. The instructions have these roles:

– *Instructions 1–2* define the main goal of the prompt, i.e., query generation. In the case of semantic artifacts with complex query paths between entities with multiple levels, it is challenging for an LLM to generate the paths and relations between entities correctly. Therefore, these first two instructions ensure that the LLM first summarizes the paths and relations between entities before using them in SPARQL queries. This leads to better results.
– *Instruction 3–5* instruct on how the prefixes should be defined and used in the generated query to provide accurate results.
– *Instructions 6–8* request that only a SPARQL query is returned so that it can be executed on a triple store without further processing. .

Listing 1.2. An example of domain-specific instructions for OPC UA domain

```
9. Use 'hasProperty' relation while generating the SPARQL query to
     get to a variable node.
10. Use 'hasComponent' relation while generating the SPARQL query to
     get to an object node.
11. Subjects and objects are entities in a generated SPARQL query, so
     they should always start with a capital letter.
```

Domain Specific Instructions: the LLM requires domain specific instructions to generate accurate queries for domain specific use cases. In our experiments, we mainly focused on generating the SPARQL queries OPC UA where the structure of information models is complex. Therefore, we also might need to provide domain specific instructions such as in Listing 1.2. In OPC UA there are mainly two types of relations between entities: "hasComponent" (refers from an Object node to another Object node) and "hasProperty" (refers from an Object node to a variable node). We observed that the LLM could not use these relationships correctly to generate SPARQL queries before being explicitly instructed on how to make use of these domain specific information (*instructions 9–11*). A general lesson learned from our experiments is that, when complex domain knowledge is present in the use cases, additional instructions need to be provided that ensure a correct interpretation of this knowledge.

3.3   Step 3: LLM Configuration

Besides making use of a prompt template, it is crucial to configure the LLM appropriately for each use case. For query generation purposes, the LLM needs to be accurate rather than creative, i.e., deterministic in its answers. Therefore, the temperature of the LLM for this use case should be set to zero in order to enable producing consistent results across several executions. In this project, we used Azure OpenAI Service with GPT 4.0 Engine.

4   Experimental Evaluation

The aim of these experiments is to evaluate the quality of SPARQL queries produced using LLM. To this end, we evaluated our method in the following two use cases
according to the evaluation strategy described in Sect. 4.1. The result of the evaluation is reported in Sect. 4.2.

Use Case 1 (UC1): Validation with Compliance Rules. In our prior work, we described the process of extracting compliance rules from OPC UA companion specifications [22]. These compliance rules fulfill a similar role to competency questions as they describe the requirements to comply with an OPC UA companion specification. The information model of an OPC UA companion specification can be converted from XML into an OWL ontology and subsequently can be queried with SPARQL queries [19]. To convert these textual compliance rules to SPARQL queries the LLM-based semantic artifact validation method can be used.

In UC1, we chose the OPC UA Robotics companion specification and its information model for our evaluation. Robotics information model describes the components of a robot and how they should interact and communicate with each other. The compliance rules, to comply with the information model are explicitly and implicitly stated in the text and tables in the specification document. We extracted 25 compliance rules in textual form. The related template file and compliance rules can be found in [21].

Use Case 2 (UC2): Validation with Competency Questions. Competency Questions represent the requirements of ontologies [4] and can be used to ensure the capability of an ontology in answering them. The competency questions are normally formulated in natural language and have to be converted into SPARQL queries to validate the ontology. Therefore this use case can also be addressed with the methodology presented in this paper.

For our evaluation purpose, we chose the SAREF ontology for UC2 since it covers similar domains as OPC UA with its companion specifications but is less complex than OPC UA. To this end, we instantiated data and developed a set of 15 competency questions related to the TemperatureSensor concept in SAREF Core. The related template file, competency questions list, and end-to-end implementation are located in [21].

4.1 Evaluation Strategy

First, for both use cases, the NLQs and their expected, corresponding SPARQL query outputs were established as ground truth. Then the NLQ and the semantic artifacts were provided to the LLM-based semantic artifact validation system. The received <SPARQL;result> pairs, were then compared with the ground truth. Differing results were marked as *False* and matching results were evaluated with SPARQL and ontology experts. Following this, results matching the expectation were labelled as *True*, and finally, all results were evaluated in terms of precision, recall, and F1 score.

Furthermore, there are two different ways of using GPT 4.0 in our evaluation context: GPT Web UI and APIs. The first method involved running each sentence through the Azure-based GPT 4.0 Web UI, with prepared prompts using a consistent template populated with the ontology and the question. The second method was to execute the same NLQs through GPT 4.0 API Calls. We tested each use case with both methods and evaluated the results.

4.2 Experimental Results

We evaluated the LLM-based semantic artifact validation methodology on both SAREF and OPC UA robotics following the evaluation design explained above.

The OPC UA Robotics KG was evaluated with 25 compliance rules pertaining to validation. Out of the compliance rules, 13 correspond to a valid implementation on the knowledge graph, while there is no implementation for 12 of them on the relevant knowledge graph.

Table 1. Semantic Artifact Validation Results (Compliance Rules, OPC UA Robotics)

Source & Sending Method	Number of NLQ	Type of NLQ	Precision	Recall	F1 score
Robotics (over Azure Web UI)	25 (13/12)	Compl. Rules	.88	.88	.88
Robotics (over Azure API)	25 (13/12)	Compl. Rules	.88	.88	.88
Robotics* (whole experiment)	50 (26/24)	Compl. Rules	.88	.88	.88

Similarly, 15 competency questions for validating the SAREF KG were used. Among these, 10 were identified as valid questions, while 5 were not as shown in Table 2. Although everything remained consistent in terms of sentences, template, ontology, the LLM engine, and configurations, minor discrepancies are noticed between the Web UI results and API Call results.

4.3   Discussion

The main lessons we learned during our work include:

- *Verified prompt templates play a crucial role.* The main challenge of our work was optimizing the prompt template, as even small changes to the template showed deviation in the results. Templates that worked for some sentences in the dataset, may not work for other sentences. Therefore, we optimized the template iteratively to derive the template in Listing 1.1, which was successfully applied for all the sentences in our datasets. Consistently using this template lead to improved quality and accuracy of the generated queries, and is one of the key reusable results of our work.
- *In-depth domain and modeling semantics are challenging for LLMs.* The modeling semantics of OWL axioms and the domain knowledge decided in the OPC UA relations could only be processed in our workflow when these semantic structures were rewritten and presented in a simplified manner.
- *Execution modality impacts on results.* The query generation experiments were conducted using API and web-page based execution modalities (Sect. 4.1). In general, the results were better on the Web UI. Identifying the reason for this still requires deeper investigation.
- *The complexity of the semantic artifact negatively impacts the results' quality.* The macro average F1 score results for UC1 are 88% across all experiments (Table 1). Moreover, 100% F1 score result was achieved through Web UI, but this fell to 93% when using the API call (Table 2). The overall average result for UC2 is 96%. OPC UA Robotics had a more complex NLQ and semantic artifacts and achieved a lower score.

Table 2. Semantic Artifact Validation Results over Competency Questions for SAREF

Source & Sending Method	Number of NLQ	Type of NLQ	Precision	Recall	F1 score
SAREF (over ChatGPT UI)	15 (10/5)	Competency Q.	1.00	1.00	1.00
SAREF (over ChatGPT API)	15 (10/5)	Competency Q.	0.92	0.95	0.93
SAREF* (whole experiment)	30 (20/10)	Competency Q.	0.95	0.97	0.96

5   Conclusion and Future Work

We proposed a methodology to support semantic artifact validation task with LLMs. We evaluated our approach with two different semantic artifacts from the industry domain and open source artifacts. We investigated how to use textual requirements, such as competency questions and compliance rules, for the task. Consequently, we generated SPARQL queries through LLM (ChatGPT Web UI and API Calls). F1 score ranged between 88% and 100%, which can be considered promising for the future. In our work, we found how important prompt engineering is in the new era of LLM usage for KE, especially on semantic artifact validation, and its challenges.

In the future, we plan to develop and evaluate our approach for scalability and robustness within the industry domain and beyond. Furthermore, we plan to continue our research on LLMs for other KE tasks in the industry domain.

Acknowledgments. The FWF HOnEst project (V754-N) supported this work.

References

1. ETSI 2021: Official ETSI portal for SAREF (2021). https://saref.etsi.org/index.html
2. Allen, B.P., Stork, L., Groth, P.: Knowledge engineering using large language models. Trans. Graph Data Knowl. **1**(1), 3:1–3:19 (2023). https://doi.org/10.4230/TGDK.1.1.3. https://drops.dagstuhl.de/entities/document/10.4230/TGDK.1.1.3
3. Bareedu, Y.S., et al.: Deriving semantic validation rules from industrial standards: an OPC UA study. Semantic Web (Preprint), 1–38 (2022)
4. Bezerra, C., Freitas, F., Santana, F.: Evaluating ontologies with competency questions. In: 2013 IEEE/WIC/ACM International Joint Conferences on Web Intelligence (WI) and Intelligent Agent Technologies (IAT), vol. 3, pp. 284–285 (2013). https://doi.org/10.1109/WI-IAT.2013.199
5. Brown, T., et al.: Language models are few-shot learners. Adv. Neural. Inf. Process. Syst. **33**, 1877–1901 (2020)
6. Burns, T., Cosgrove, J., Doyle, F.: A review of interoperability standards for industry 4.0. Procedia Manuf. **38**, 646–653 (2019)
7. Corcho, O., et al.: A maturity model for catalogues of semantic artefacts. Working paper, June 2023. https://doi.org/10.48550/arXiv.2305.06746
8. Huaman, E., Kärle, E., Fensel, D.: Knowledge graph validation. arXiv preprint arXiv:2005.01389 (2020)
9. Jozefowicz, R., Vinyals, O., Schuster, M., Shazeer, N., Wu, Y.: Exploring the limits of language modeling. arXiv preprint arXiv:1602.02410 (2016)
10. Khorashadizadeh, H., Mihindukulasooriya, N., Tiwari, S., Groppe, J., Groppe, S.: Exploring in-context learning capabilities of foundation models for generating knowledge graphs from text. arXiv preprint arXiv:2305.08804 (2023)
11. Leclerc, J.C., Tetard, G., Keraron, Y., Fauconnet, C.: Use of ontologies to structure and manage digital technical data of industrial assets: first steps towards an ecology of knowledge in multi-energies industry. Proceedings (2022). http://ceur-ws.org. ISSN 1613, 0073
12. Listl, F.G., Fischer, J., Sohr, A., Dittler, D., Jazdi, N., Weyrich, M.: Utilizing ISA-95 in an industrial knowledge graph for material flow simulation-semantic model extensions and efficient data integration. Procedia CIRP **120**, 1558–1563 (2023)
13. Meyer, L.P., et al.: LLM-assisted knowledge graph engineering: experiments with chatgpt. arXiv preprint arXiv:2307.06917 (2023)
14. Mihindukulasooriya, N., Tiwari, S., Enguix, C.F., Lata, K.: Text2KGBench: a benchmark for ontology-driven knowledge graph generation from text. In: Payne, T.R., et al. (eds.) ISWC 2023. LNCS, vol. 14266, pp. 247–265. Springer, Cham (2023). https://doi.org/10.1007/978-3-031-47243-5_14

15. Pan, J.Z., et al.: Large language models and knowledge graphs: opportunities and challenges. Trans. Graph Data Knowl. **1**(1), 2:1–2:38 (2023). https://doi.org/10.4230/TGDK.1.1.2. https://drops.dagstuhl.de/entities/document/10.4230/TGDK.1.1.2

16. Pan, S., Luo, L., Wang, Y., Chen, C., Wang, J., Wu, X.: Unifying large language models and knowledge graphs: a roadmap. IEEE Trans. Knowl. Data Eng., 1–20 (2024). https://doi.org/10.1109/TKDE.2024.3352100

17. Polat, F., Tiddi, I., Groth, P.: Testing prompt engineering methods for knowledge extraction from text

18. Poveda-Villalón, M., Fernández-Izquierdo, A., Fernández-López, M., García-Castro, R.: LOT: an industrial oriented ontology engineering framework. Eng. Appl. Artif. Intell. **111**, 104755 (2022)

19. Schiekofer, R., Grimm, S., Brandt, M.M., Weyrich, M.: A formal mapping between OPC UA and the semantic web. In: 2019 IEEE 17th International Conference on Industrial Informatics (INDIN), vol. 1, pp. 33–40. IEEE (2019)

20. Seyedamir, A., Ferrer, B.R., Lastra, J.L.M.: An ISA-95 based ontology for manufacturing systems knowledge description extended with semantic rules. In: 2018 IEEE 16th International Conference on Industrial Informatics (INDIN), pp. 374–380. IEEE (2018)

21. Tufek, N.: Siemens-OKE/LLM-query-pipeline (2024). https://github.com/Siemens-OKE/llm-query-pipeline

22. Tufek, N., Thuluva, A.S.S., Just, V.P., Sabou, M.: Towards extraction of validation rules from OPC UA companion specifications. In: 2023 IEEE 28th International Conference on Emerging Technologies and Factory Automation (ETFA), pp. 1–8. IEEE (2023)

OntoChat: A Framework
for Conversational Ontology Engineering
Using Language Models

Bohui Zhang[1(✉)] [iD], Valentina Anita Carriero[2] [iD], Katrin Schreiberhuber[3] [iD],
Stefani Tsaneva[3] [iD], Lucía Sánchez González[4] [iD], Jongmo Kim[1] [iD],
and Jacopo de Berardinis[1] [iD]

[1] Department of Informatics, King's College London, London, UK
`bohui.zhang@kcl.ac.uk`
[2] Cefriel – Politecnico di Milano, Milan, Italy
[3] Vienna University of Economics and Business, Vienna, Austria
[4] Ontology Engineering Group, Universidad Politécnica de Madrid, Madrid, Spain

Abstract. Ontology engineering (OE) in large projects poses a number
of challenges arising from the heterogeneous backgrounds of the various stakeholders, domain experts, and their complex interactions with
ontology designers. This multi-party interaction often creates systematic ambiguities and biases from the elicitation of ontology requirements,
which directly affect the design, evaluation and may jeopardise the target reuse. Meanwhile, current OE methodologies strongly rely on manual
activities (e.g., interviews, discussion pages). After collecting evidence on
the most crucial OE activities, we introduce **OntoChat**, a framework
for conversational ontology engineering that supports requirement elicitation, analysis, and testing. By interacting with a conversational agent,
users can steer the creation of user stories and the extraction of competency questions, while receiving computational support to analyse the
overall requirements and test early versions of the resulting ontologies.
We evaluate OntoChat by replicating the engineering of the Music Meta
Ontology, and collecting preliminary metrics on the effectiveness of each
component from users. We release all code at https://github.com/King-
s-Knowledge-Graph-Lab/OntoChat.

Keywords: Ontology Engineering · Large Language Models ·
Competency Questions · Computational Creativity

1 Introduction

Ontology Engineering (OE) encompasses a number of activities defining a collaborative effort to design, evaluate, and reuse ontologies of general or domain-
specific purposes [20, 26]. Depending on the intended reuse by one or more stakeholders, the process starts with ontology designers eliciting requirements from
the former, while interacting with experts to validate their formal understanding

© The Author(s), under exclusive license to Springer Nature Switzerland AG 2025
A. Meroño Peñuela et al. (Eds.): ESWC 2024, LNCS 15344, pp. 102–121, 2025.
https://doi.org/10.1007/978-3-031-78952-6_10

of the domain. Although the way OE activities are organised may vary depending on the methodology adopted [10, 27], these interactions are frequent and iterative throughout the development cycle. In large projects, ontology designers engage in a number of manual activities and interact with multiple parties to make sure requirements are collected consistently and comprehensively, seeking clarification from domain experts to formalise and test them [12]. This multi-party interaction may require substantial resources and create systematic ambiguities and biases arising from potentially conflicting or ill-formulated requirements [6]. Not only does this affect the ontology design and evaluation, but it may also jeopardise their reuse by the same stakeholders. In other cases, a blurry line exists among stakeholders, domain experts, and ontology designers, which is common to multidisciplinary and highly collaborative projects, such as Wikidata [30].

OE has long faced arguments about its technical challenges and costs. Despite the development of collaborative methodologies (c.f. Sect. 2), the field still faces concerns about positively impacting the liveliness, evolution, and reusability of ontologies [21]. Meanwhile, Large Language Models (LLMs) have received increasing attention in the Semantic Web due to their language understanding capabilities. These provide generalisation across various tasks (e.g., question answering, text summarisation), making it possible to effectively generate, process, and annotate text to address knowledge engineering tasks [4, 31].

Here, we hypothesise that LLMs can assist and facilitate OE activities to implement conversational workflows and prompt-driven functionalities that can reduce the complex interactions between domain experts and ontology designers, while accelerating the analysis and formalisation of requirements. To confirm our motivations and collect insights for the design of such a framework, we put forth the following research questions.

- **RQ1**: Which ontology engineering activities are the most in need of computational support?
- **RQ2**: How can LLMs enable a conversational ontology engineering framework to support these activities?

To address RQ1, we conducted a survey asking ontology engineers to rate OE activities in relation to their difficulty and the manual effort required. We reuse the insights collected from the survey to implement a conversational workflow where different categories of users interact independently with the system and produce intermediate artefacts and documentation throughout the various stages of the OE process (RQ2). In sum, this work contributed:

- An investigation of which OE activities are most in need of computational support, gathered from a survey involving participants with OE expertise.
- **OntoChat**, a conversational framework for ontology engineering providing support for (i) *requirement elicitation* (user story creation, competency question extraction), (ii) *analysis* (competency question verification, reduction, and clustering), and for (iii) *testing* preliminary versions of an ontology.
- A preliminary evaluation of an online prototype of OntoChat where participants were asked to replicate the OE of the Music Meta ontology [7] and measure the effectiveness of their outcomes and interactions.

2   Related Work

Various OE methodologies have been proposed over the years, with their focus shifting towards collaborative approaches [26]. Early works include METHON-TOLOGY [15], based on requirements elicitation from [28] and providing support for conceptualisation, implementation, and maintenance steps; and DILIGENT [24] which also account for the involvement of different stakeholders. More recent work incorporated Agile principles to support iterative ontology development, such as NEON [27], SAMOD [23], and *eXtreme Design* (XD) [9,10]. The latter also provides guidelines for requirement elicitation and is strongly test-based.

In [6], ontology requirements are collected from *customers* in the form of *user stories*. A story[1] contains three main components: the *persona* portrays a typical user, including their name, occupation, skills, and interests; the *goal* captures the persona's aims in the story; the *scenario* describes how the persona's goals are currently addressed, to contextualise the gap with the resource being developed. Through the collection of stories, ontology requirements can then be defined by extracting competency questions (CQs) – the natural language counterpart of structured queries that the resulting knowledge graph (KG) should answer [17].

CQs are central to OE. They facilitate the collection of requirements, drive the implementation of the ontologies (e.g., in XD, they are mapped to ontology design patterns) and are used for testing [11]. Nonetheless, despite the level of experience in a particular OE methodology, bottlenecks, ambiguities, and domain jargon can still hamper progress from the requirement collection stage [12]. This especially happens when several stakeholders and domain experts are involved. To mitigate this issue, [6] introduced IDEA – a tool supporting the iterative elicitation and improvement of CQs via NLP methods.

Recently, LLMs have been applied to support and augment knowledge engineering tasks. Applications range from representing domain knowledge and generating examples of classes and relations to providing explanations and recommendations on ontologies after verbalising them into plain text [22]. For ontology engineering, LLM-based approaches have shown promising results for ontology matching and alignment [18,19,25]. Other studies have focused on ontology construction and learning from text, using LLMs to suggest relevant subconcepts [16] and to automatically extract and structuring knowledge [5]. In the context of requirement elicitation, new methods were contributed for retrofitting CQs from ontologies to promote reuse [3] and extracting CQs directly from KGs [14]. Overall, these works demonstrated great potential for LLM-driven knowledge engineering, but also acknowledged significant issues such as hallucination, poor non-linguistic reasoning, and the high cost of fine-tuning.

3   OntoChat: Towards Conversational Ontology Engineering

To address RQ1 and inform the design of our framework, we conducted an online survey asking participants to rank OE activities for complexity and need of

---

[1] Examples of user stories at https://github.com/polifonia-project/stories.

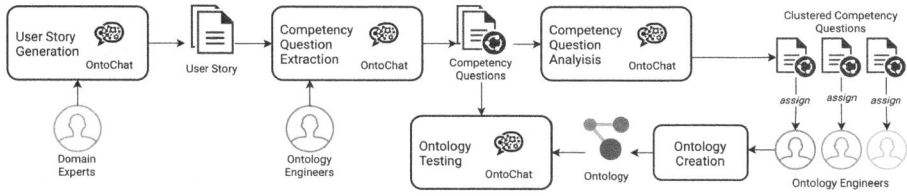

Fig. 1. Illustration of the workflow alongside the main features in OntoChat.

computational support. The survey was conducted via Google Forms (without recording any personal data from participants) and was distributed to Semantic Web practitioners. Participants were asked to quantify the agreement of statements on a 5-point Likert scale, with each statement expressing an OE activity.

We gathered responses from $N = 23$ participants with various level of experience and familiarity with OE methodologies (primarily Neon, Ontology 101, Linked Open Terms). Results are detailed in Appendix A. Given the size of our sample, we decided to rely on strong evidence ($\geq 75\%$ positive responses using 4–5 scores), finding that the most demanding OE tasks in need of computational support are: the collection of ontology requirements (86.4%), the extraction of CQs from textual ontology requirements (81.8%), the analysis of ontology requirements (77.3%), and ontology testing (81.8%).

Based on these findings, and building upon the IDEA approach [6], we designed OntoChat to support such OE activities. The workflow, illustrated in Fig. 1, leverages LLMs as knowledge elicitators to reduce the demand and complexity of the multi-party interactions with ontology designers, and aims at accelerating OE tasks. To collect requirements, the process starts with stakeholders and domain experts co-creating user stories by interacting with our conversational agent. Ontology engineers can then extract CQs by iteratively refining the model's recommendations; reduce redundant requirements, and analyse the resulting CQs via clustering. Finally, OntoChat also allows testing preliminary versions of ontologies via verbalisation and unit prompting.

3.1   Assisted Persona and Story Creation

To enable the collaborative user story generation OntoChat follows steps below.

Step 1: LLM role definition (back-end). The LLM behaviour is primed to emulate a knowledge elicitator aiming to gather information from the user about each user story component – the persona definition, specification of concrete goals & addressed scenario, and the provision of data examples (back-end).

Step 2: Knowledge elicitation (user involvement). The user is guided through a series of questions focusing on a particular story aspect. For instance, to gather insights about the persona's background, OntoChat asks *"What are the name, occupations, skills, interests of the user?"* Whenever the user does not provide enough details or gives partial answers, the LLM continues to elicit additional insights until all necessary information is gathered (c.f. Fig. 7b, Appendix C.1).

Step 3: User story generation (back-end) The initial user story draft is created following a one-shot learning approach [13]. The LLM is supplied with a user story example, and is prompted to follow the same structure for generating a *user story draft* summarising the information extracted in the elicitation step.

Step 4: Refinement (user involvement). The user is presented with the user story draft and is encouraged to provide feedback. The refinement stage is iterative and continues until the user no longer requests further changes. Possible refinements include the correction of factual inconsistencies, additions to the user stories, removal of irrelevant details, etc. We provide some exemplary refinement requests in Fig. 8 (Appendix C.1).

3.2   Competency Question Extraction

The main objective of this module is to assist ontology engineers in extracting CQs from user stories. The procedure is organised as follows.

Step 1: Instructing the LLM for CQ extraction (back-end). The model is provided with examples of pairs of user story fragments and expected CQs, to align its outputs to the expectations of ontology engineers.

Step 2: First extraction of CQs (user involvement). The ontology engineer is asked to provide a user story for CQ extraction. The user story may be manually crafted, or obtained from the previous step (see Fig. 9, Appendix C.1). As output, OntoChat provides an initial list of CQs (see Fig. 10, Appendix C.2)

Step 3: Competency question refinement (back-end). The LLM is provided with a series of prompts (hidden from the user) to perform two *refinement steps*.

– *Step 3.1: Split not atomic CQs.* If the example data is complex, users may get non-atomic questions from a single example. As these usually entail nested requirements, complex CQs need to be split. Following a few-shot learning approach, the LLM is asked whether each CQ has a complex form, hence triggering the simplification. For example, from the data *"The musical work Penny Lane has genre/style baroque pop and psychedelic pop."*, the LLM generated *"What genres/styles are associated with Penny Lane?"*. After this step, the LLM replaces it with two distinct CQs: *"What genres are associated with Penny Lane?"* and *"What styles are associated with Penny Lane?"*.
– *Step 3.2: Named entities abstraction.* As an example, the previous CQs replaced the specific genres with the interrogative pronoun "what" (genres/styles). However, it did not remove the real-world entity "Penny Lane". Within this step, the LLMs is prompted to check again the CQs, and, guided by examples, remove possible named entities. This yields abstract CQs like *"What genres are associated with the musical work?"* and *"What styles are associated with the musical work?"*.

Step 4: User confirmation (user involvement). Finally, OntoChat asks the user whether the number of CQs and their formulation are sound. If not, by leveraging knowledge acquired from previous prompts (see Step 3), the model repeats the refinement steps until the user is satisfied (see Fig. 11, Appendix C.2).

3.3 Competency Question Filtration and Analysis

As some CQs may be redundant or show negligible semantic variations that are of little interest to ontology engineers, OntoChat provides support for their filtration and analysis. This is achieved through: *paraphrase identification*, to remove equivalent CQs; and *CQ clustering*, to identify groups of similar requirements. In [14], the former was found to have two benefits: (i) it mitigates the noise and the artefacts introduced in the previous steps; (ii) it reduces the number of CQs that will be presented to ontology engineers.

In contrast to [6,14], which both rely on sentence embeddings and specialised models, this functionality is entirely supported by LLMs, which is motivated by recent findings demonstrating that LLMs possess clustering capabilities [2,29, 32]. Given a list of CQs, the LLM is asked to remove redundant questions and find meaningful groups of CQs sharing the same thematic focus and intent. The latter is expected to support ontology designers in understanding requirements and possibly organising their Agile teams (e.g., a team receiving a CQ cluster based on their familiarity with the sub-domain). In the current version, this step does not require user supervision.

3.4 Ontology Testing Support

While the previous functionalities focus on requirement elicitation and analysis, this component provides support for testing preliminary or iterative versions of an ontology. Ontology testing efforts are often categorised into three methodologies: CQ verification, inference verification, and error provocation. The first two are concerned with verifying the correct implementation of a requirement, whereas the latter is needed to find cases where the ontology should fail [11]. These are typically done by formalising CQs into SPARQL queries.

To test preliminary versions of an ontology, we aim for a SPARQL-free approach to achieve fast CQ verification and inference, while supporting error provocation. This is achieved in two steps: *ontology verbalisation*, and prompt-driven *CQ unit testing*. Our verbalisation converts a OWL ontology into plain text by documenting classes, properties, named entities, and their relationships in a descriptional manner. The method follows a simple algorithmic procedure and assumes that the ontology is well commented to produce an expressive verbalisation. Then, using the verbalisation, the LLM is prompted to asses the coverage of each CQ by replying *Yes/No*. To prevent prompt leakage and ensure independence in the model's predictions, this is done separately for each CQ.

3.5 Implementation Details

OntoChat is implemented in `Python 3.11` and is released on GitHub[2] (code, prompts, experiments) under the MIT license. To facilitate its use and collect user feedback, we implemented an interface prototype using Gradio [1]. This can

---

[2] https://github.com/King-s-Knowledge-Graph-Lab/OntoChat.

be launched on a local server, also hosted on Hugging Face Spaces[3]. The interface has four tabs that wrap all the functionalities within the same environment. The current version uses OpenAI's API and has been evaluated on the GPT-3 family of models (`gpt-3.5-turbo`, and `gpt-3.5-turbo-16k` for larger contexts).

4   Evaluation

We performed a component-based evaluation of OntoChat to measure the effectiveness of each functionality and collect user feedback based on their experiences. The evaluation was organised to replicate the OE activities of the Music Meta ontology [7]. It was chosen as a benchmark/testbed for three reasons: it required considerable OE efforts and was already the source of ambiguities in the Polifonia project [8]; it was complemented by high-quality material (user stories, CQs, documentation, queries, etc.) from [6] to use as ground truth; the authors had access to a pool of domain experts for evaluation.

4.1   Experimental Methodology

To ensure each component is evaluated individually by the intended target users, we evaluate the more generative components by collecting feedback on their use from domain experts and ontology engineers through questionnaires. All questions ask participants to quantify the agreement with the statement made from 1 (strongly disagree) to 5 (strongly agree), with 3 being a neutral response (NR). No personal information is collected throughout the evaluation. The ontology testing feature, instead, is evaluated experimentally for accuracy.

User Story Questionnaire (Domain Experts). We recruited $N = 6$ music experts in the Polifonia project to create user stories summarising their requirements on music metadata using OntoChat. Our goal is to evaluate the model's success in producing satisfactory user stories. Additionally, we gather insights on OntoChat's usability and its effectiveness in minimising manual effort.

CQ Extraction and Clustering Questionnaires (Ontology Engineers). We recruited $N = 8$ ontology engineers to evaluate the model's performance in generating CQs that are consistent with the given story, well-formulated, and consistent with the intended scope of the ontology. Users are first introduced to the concept of the user story, then asked to familiarise with the *Linka – Music Knowledge* story[4]. Their task is to extract and analyse CQs from the story using OntoChat.

---

[3] https://huggingface.co/spaces/b289zhan/OntoChat.
[4] https://github.com/polifonia-project/stories/tree/main/Linka_Computer_Scientist.

Ontology Testing Evaluation. Given the OWL definition of Music Meta, and the 28 (manually produced) CQs driving its implementation, we evaluate this component as a classification task. This is done by extending the CQ set with the same number of negative CQs (requirements that are not yet supported by Music Meta). We expect OntoChat to correctly discriminate between these groups.

4.2   Preliminary Results

Feedback collected from domain experts confirmed that the user stories generated with OntoChat captured the intended goal and requirements and always provided relevant information (Fig. 3). More than 80% of participants enjoyed using the tool and found the final stories well-structured and easily understandable. While users acknowledged the model's ability to improve intermediate drafts through their feedback, only 50% were satisfied with the example data generated. Overall, 4/6 experts recognised the tool's potential to accelerate this task (2 NR), and 5 of them would prefer it over manual curation.

From the evaluation with ontology engineers, OntoChat was found to generate CQs that are comprehensive, reflective of the intended ontology scope, and easy to understand (Fig. 4). However, 2/8 participants noted the extraction of entities outside the story's scope; and only 50% observed the potential to reduce possible author bias. While 6/8 participants expressed satisfaction with OntoChat and recognised its time-saving benefits, all agreed it holds promise for streamlining CQ generation, indicating a preference over fully manual creation.

The clustering feature proved advantageous for understanding and organising ontology requirements when compared to full manual inspection (Fig. 5). Participants found the interaction intuitive (62.5%) and the resulting clusters expressed meaningful groupings of CQs (87.5%). While the feature offers time-saving benefits by providing an aggregated view of ontology requirements, there were indications that it may not fully support comprehensive analysis on its own.

Finally, for ontology testing, we found that OntoChat can correctly classify supported requirements with an accuracy of 87.5% (P=88%, R=85.7%), and often provides explanations and examples to support its prediction (Appendix B.4).

5   Conclusions

This work addresses the challenges of ontology engineering in large collaborative projects by implementing a conversational workflow to streamline the process. The proposed framework, OntoChat, leverages LLMs to facilitate requirement elicitation, analysis, and ontology testing. Our preliminary evaluation efforts demonstrate a positive response from domain experts and ontology engineers, indicating potential for accelerating conventional ontology engineering tasks.

Nonetheless, several limitations still exist, notably those inherent to the use of LLMs in specialised domains due to their limited or potentially obsolete knowledge. Additional challenges include addressing biases in persona creation and enhancing the framework to provide insights into implementation costs and timelines. This will allow us to measure the amount of user supervision and involvement (e.g., number of interactions with the LLM, specificity of user feedback) during the refinement steps, needed to achieve a reasonable output from OntoChat (e.g., a user story, a list of competency questions), in contrast to full manual curation. Future work will focus on addressing these challenges, while enhancing the generation of examples in user stories, refining named entity scope in competency question creation, and broadening analysis support.

Acknowledgements. This project has received funding from the European Union's Horizon 2020 research and innovation programme under grant agreement No 101004746. This work was partly funded by the HE project MuseIT, which has been co-founded by the European Union under the Grant Agreement No 101061441.

A   Survey Results

As outline in Sect. 3, the design of OntoChat relies on our first research question presented in the introduction and recapitulated as follows: **RQ1** Which ontology engineering activities are the most in need of computational support?

To address RQ1, we run an online survey to collect feedback from ontology engineers. Based on their experience with OE tasks, they were asked to express their agreement with our statements. The latter were designed in order to understand the perceived complexity and the need of computational support for OE activities. Our survey received $N = 23$ responses.

The majority of participants (60.8%) declared to have strong knowledge and expertise in Ontology Engineering (OE). Participants have formerly used the following OE methodologies: NEON (47.4%), Ontology 101 (47.4%), eXtreme Design (42.1%), Linked Open Terms (42.1%), METHODOLOGY (31.6%), and SAMOD (5.3%). They have experience working an OE projects with ontology design teams of various size: **1** (23.8%), **2–3** (47.6%), **4–6** (33.3%), and **7+** (14.3%). Analogously, they have worked on OE projects involving teams of stakeholders and domain experts of the various size: **1** (15%), **2–3** (45%), **4–6** (40%), and **7+** (25%). The results of this survey are detailed in Fig. 2 for consultation.

B   Evaluation Results

B.1   Collaborative User Story Generation

This section provides more details on the evaluation of the *collaborative user story generation* feature in OntoChat. As outlined in Sect. 4, this evaluation was carried out by $N = 6$ domain experts who are familiar with the creation of user stories, and were actively involved in the OE activities behind of the Polifonia Ontology Network [6]. In line with our expectations, all participants confirmed their expert knowledge in the music (metadata) domain, and familiarity with the Music Meta Ontology. In addition, 50% of them acknowledge *some knowledge* of OE and have experience with the eXtreme Design methodology. The results of the evaluation are outlined in Fig. 3 for all the 10 questions.

B.2   Competency Question Extraction

Here, we provide more details on the evaluation of the *competency question extraction* feature in OntoChat. As outlined in Sect. 4, this evaluation was carried out by $N = 8$ participants with expertise in ontology engineering. The results of the evaluation are outlined in Fig. 4 for all the 8 questions.

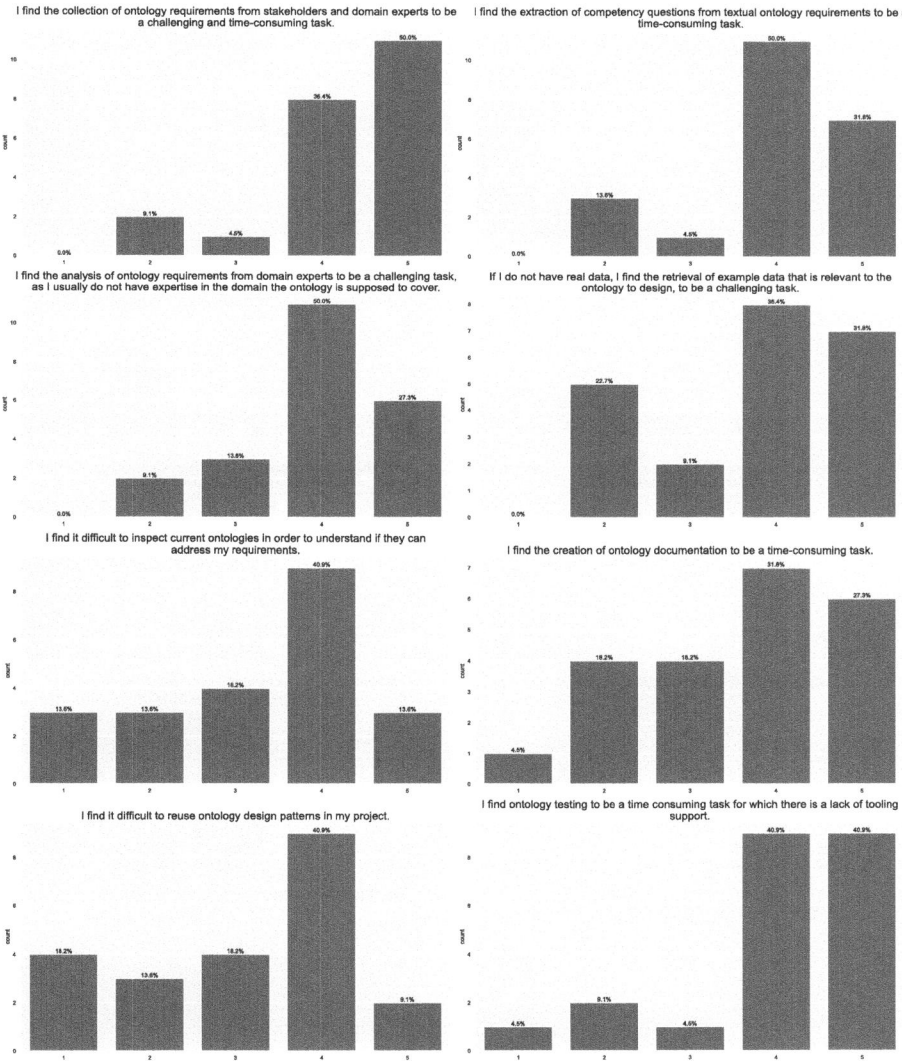

Fig. 2. Responses from the Ontology Engineering survey to address RQ1. Replies quantify the agreement of participants with respect to each statement on a 5-point Likert scale, where 1 (absolutely disagree) to 5 (absolutely agree), with 3 being a neutral response (neither agree nor disagree).

B.3 Competency Question Clustering

As this evaluation step was performed after Competency Question Extraction by the same participants, their background information is the same as reported Appendix B.2. The results of the evaluation are outlined in Fig. 5.

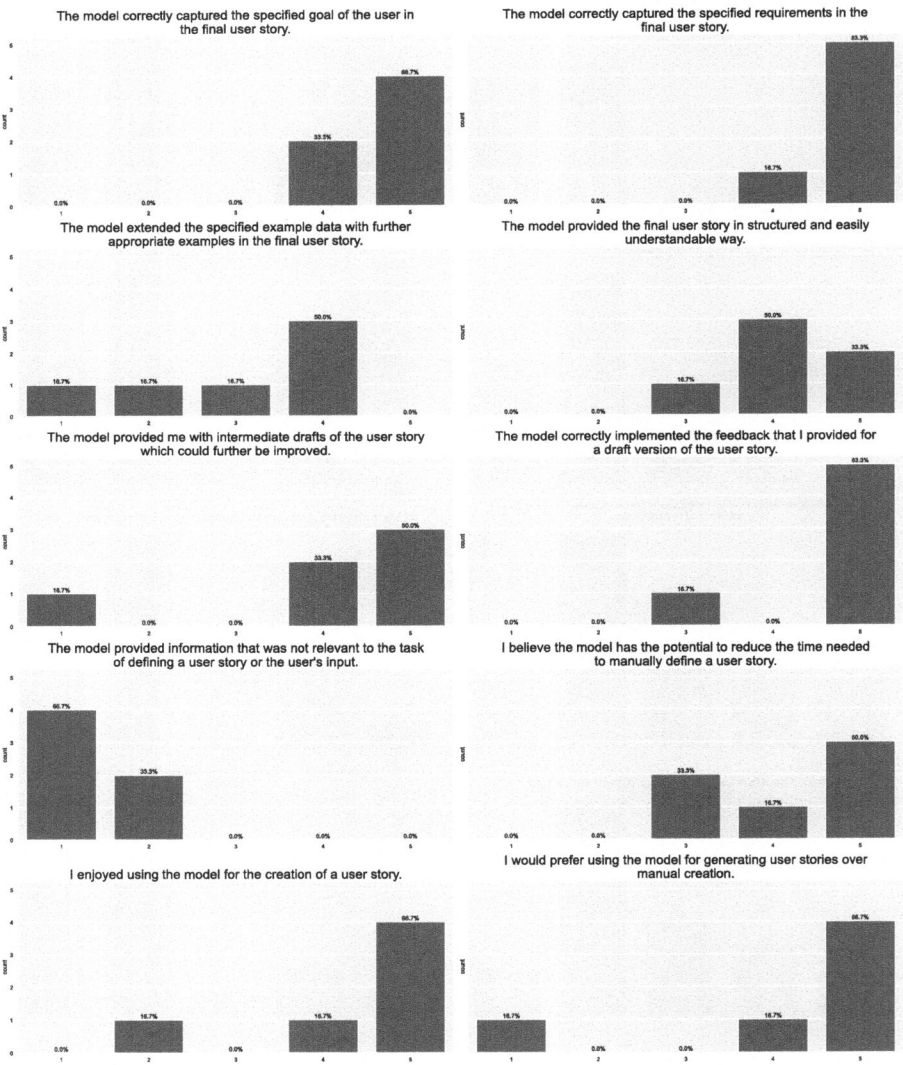

Fig. 3. User ratings on the *Collaborative User Story Creation* functionality of OntoChat. The evaluation was performed by $N = 6$ domain experts.

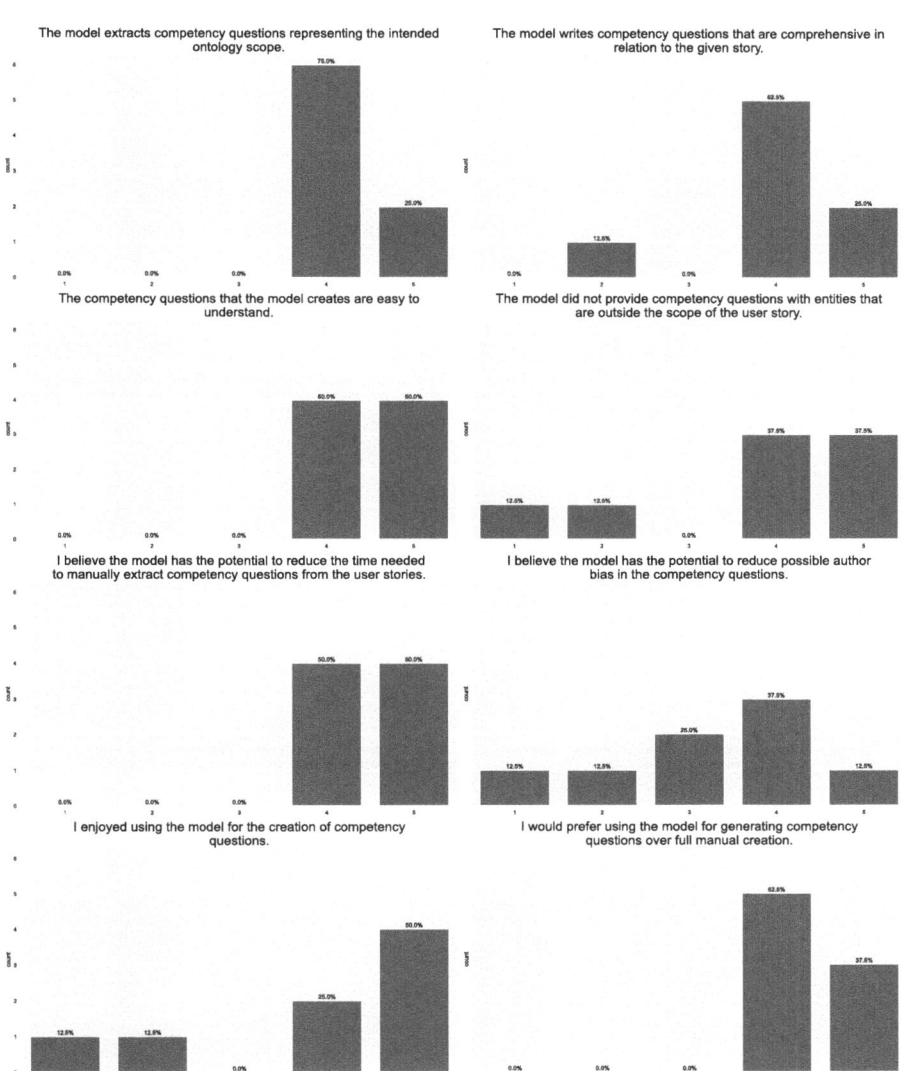

Fig. 4. User ratings on the *Competency Question Extraction* functionality of OntoChat. This evaluation was performed by $N = 8$ ontology engineers.

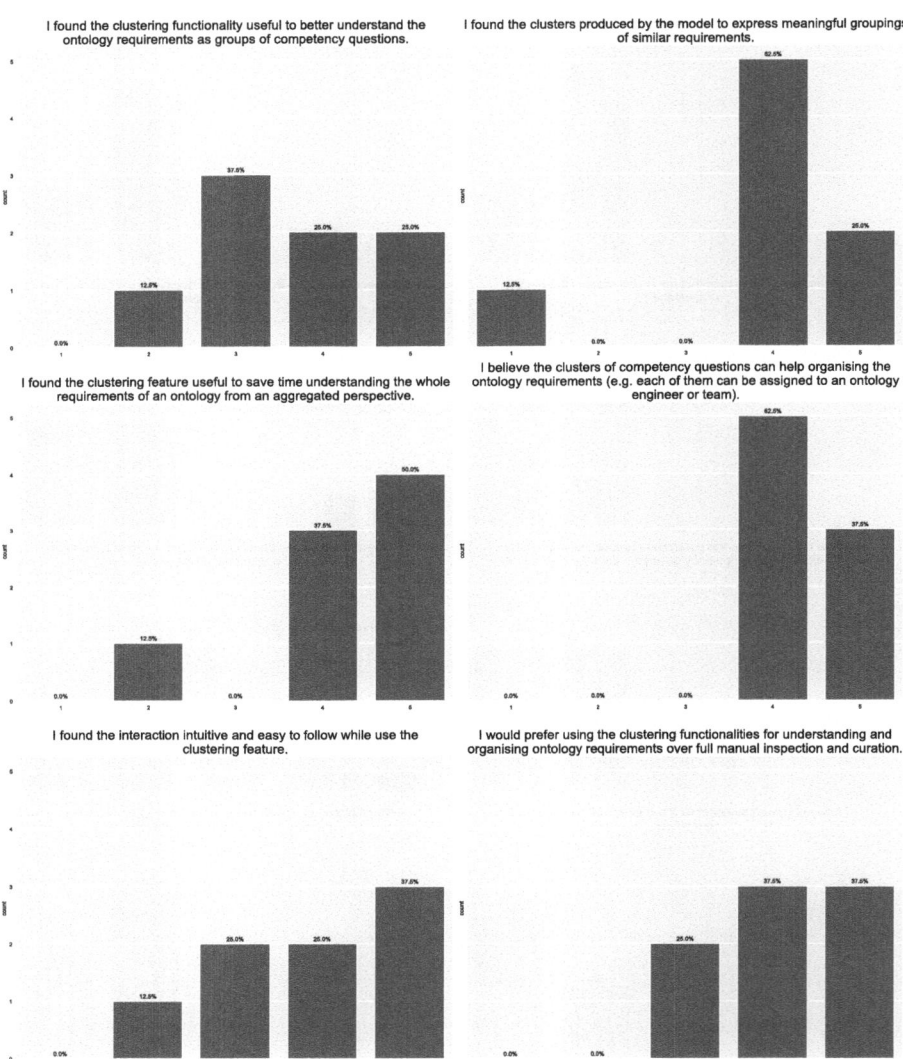

Fig. 5. User ratings on the *Competency Question Clustering* functionality performed by $N = 8$ ontology engineers.

B.4   Preliminary Ontology Testing

To complement our results for ontology testing, we report the confusion matrix in Fig. 6, expressing the number of correct predictions (25 true positives, 24 true negatives) and wrongly classified competency questions (3 false positives, 4 false negatives). Please, note that this can be seen as instance of competency question verification and error provocation for positive and negative CQs, respectively.

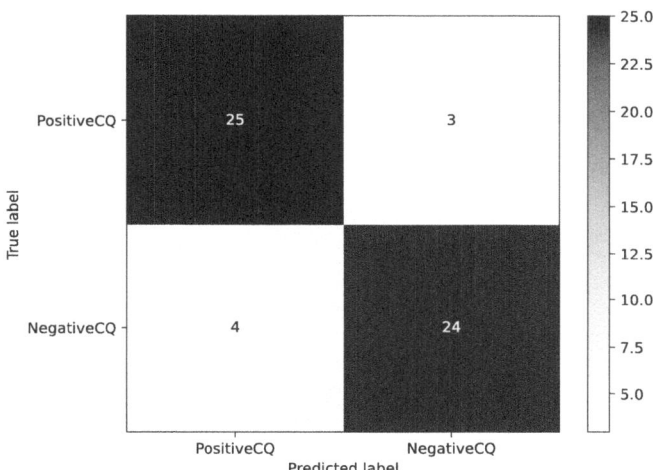

Fig. 6. Confusion matrix summarising our results for *prompt-driven CQ unit testing* (c.f. Sect. 3.4). Positive CQs (target label 1) denote competency questions that are expected to be addressed or covered by the ontology, whereas negative CQs (target label 0) are artificially created to express requirements that are not yet addressed by the ontology and should thus be predicted as such.

C   Examples

C.1   Collaborative User Story Generation

In this section, we provide several concrete example excerpts from the user story generation supported by OntoChat. Figure 7 provides outputs of the knowledge elicitation stage while story refinement examples are visualised in Fig. 8. A full user story created with the assistance of OntoChat is shown in Fig. 9.

C.2   Competency Question Extraction

In this section, we provide examples from the *Competency Questions Extraction* functionality supported by OntoChat. Figure 10 shows the first iteration of CQ extraction from a user story by OntoChat, while Fig. 11 illustrates the outputs after refinement (c.f. Sect. 3.2).

Hello! I am OntoChat, your conversational ontology engineering assistant. I will guide you step by step in the creation of a user story. Let's start with the persona. What are the name, occupations, skills, interests of the user?

Maria is an event producer. She has a degree in Computer Science but she is interested in compiling festival music programmes

Great! Now, what is the goal of Maria? Is she facing any specific issues in her work that could be addressed through a structured knowledge base?

Hello! I am OntoChat, your conversational ontology engineering assistant. I will guide you step by step in the creation of a user story. Let's start with the persona. What are the name, occupations, skills, interests of the user?

The user's name is Martin.

Great! Could you please provide Martin's occupation, skills, and interests?

(a) OntoChat collecting information of different story aspects.

(b) OntoChat dealing with partial answers and missing details,

Fig. 7. Example excerpts from the knowledge elicitation stage of the user story collaborative generation.

Feel free to provide any feedback or additional details to further refine the user story for Martin's needs.

I just remembered Martin also has a degree in Computer Science

Thank you for the additional information about Martin's background in Computer Science. Here is the updated user story:

Title: Music Program Compilation for Music Festivals
Persona: Martin, Event and Music Producer with a Degree in Computer Science

Please let me know if you would like to add more details or if you have any other feedback to improve the user story.

What I meant is that Maria is pursuing a Computer Science degree, she has not graduated yet

Title: Music Festival Program Compilation Assistance
Persona: Maria, Event Producer pursuing a degree in Computer Science and interested in compiling festival music programs

(a) Refinement by additional information.

(b) Refinement through clarification.

Fig. 8. Example excerpts from the story refinement stage of the user story collaborative generation.

User story

Title: Music Festival Program Compilation Assistance
Persona: Maria, Event Producer pursuing a degree in Computer Science and interested in compiling festival music programs
Goal: Maria aims to create cohesive and engaging festival music programs, leveraging her skill of selecting music pieces based on the current situation, but faces challenges in identifying relationships between different artists and songs.
Scenario: Maria, a student of Computer Science, is tasked with curating a music program for an upcoming festival. She needs to ensure a smooth flow between different artists and songs to create an enjoyable experience for the audience. Maria's ability to choose music based on the current situation is crucial. By using a structured knowledge base, Maria can access information on artists, songs, producers, and songwriters, helping her to make informed decisions on the sequencing and selection of music for the program, aligning with the event's atmosphere and audience preferences.
Example Data:
- Artist: Beyoncé
  - Songs: "Crazy in Love", "Single Ladies"
  - Producer: Timbaland
  - Songwriter: Beyoncé, Rich Harrison
- Artist: Ed Sheeran
  - Songs: "Shape of You", "Thinking Out Loud"
  - Producer: Benny Blanco
  - Songwriter: Ed Sheeran, Johnny McDaid

Let me know if you would like any further adjustments or additional details to be included in the user story.

Fig. 9. A user story generated with the assistance of OntoChat.

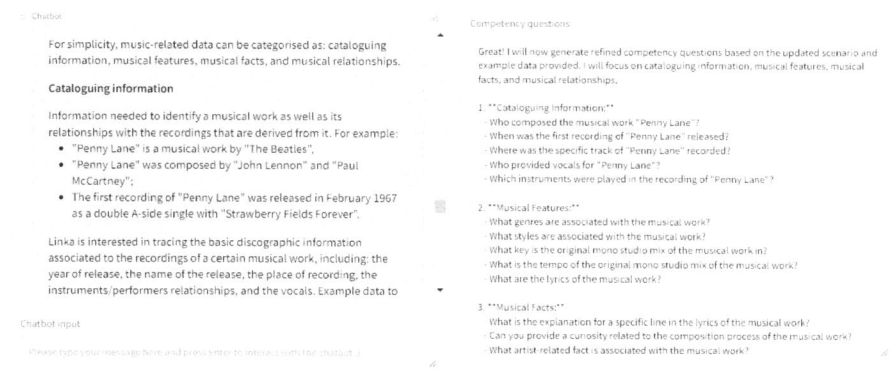

Fig. 10. Illustration of OntoChat's *competency question extraction* feature, first extraction of CQs.

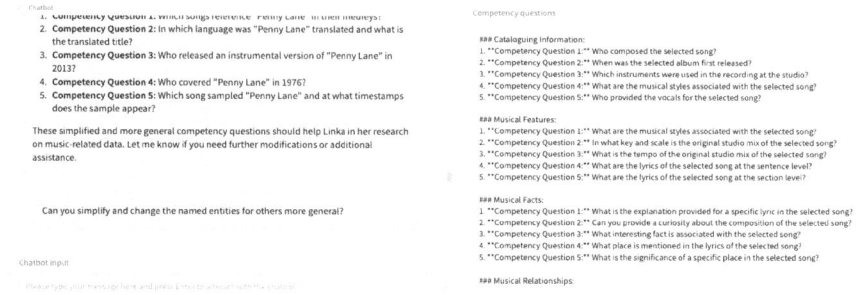

Fig. 11. Illustration of OntoChat's *competency question extraction* feature, refinement of the CQs.

C.3 Competency Question Clustering

We report an example of competency question clustering obtained after using this features on a selection of the original CQs driving the design of the Music Meta Ontology [7], which can be fully found online[5]. The clusters produced by OntoChat via the LLM Clustering option (no number of clusters is provided apriori), together with their label, are reported in Listing 1.1.

---

[5] https://github.com/polifonia-project/music-meta-ontology.

```
"Music Artists": [
    "Which is the name of a music artist?",
    "Which is the alias of a music artist?",
    "Which is the language of the name/alias of a music artist?",
    "Which award was a music artist nominated for?",
    "Which award was received by a music artist?",
    "Which music artists has a music artist been influenced by?",
    "Which music artist has a music artist collaborated with?",
    "Which is the start date of the activity of a music artist?",
    "Which is the end date of the activity of a music artist?"
],
"Musical Pieces and Composers": [
    "Which is the composer of a musical piece?",
    "Is the composer of a musical piece known?",
    "In which time interval did the creation process took place?",
    "Where did the creation process took place?",
    "Which task was executed by a creative action?",
    "Which are the parts of a musical piece?",
    "Which collection is a musical piece member of?"
],
"Music Ensembles": [
    "Which are the members of a music ensemble?",
    "Which role a music artist played within a music ensemble?",
    "Where was a music ensemble formed?"
],
"Musical Performances and Recordings": [
    "Where was a musical piece performed?",
    "When was a musical piece performed?",
    "Which music artists took part to a musical performance?",
    "Which is the recording process that recorded a musical performance?",
    "Which is the recording produced by a recording process?"
], ...
```

Listing 1.1. Example of CQ clusters generated from Music Meta's (human-annotated) competency questions using the LLM clustering option in OntoChat.

C.4   Ontology Testing

We provide a selection of tested competency questions, with expected and predicted outcome (Yes = 1 for supported CQs, and No = 0 for CQs that are not supported by the current definition of the Music Meta ontology). These are reported in Table 1, and are complemented by a supporting explanation informing the user on how the requirement can/cannot be addressed by the ontology (e.g. classes and relations that can be used.

Table 1. Examples of tested competency questions with predicted and expected outcome. These are complemented by a supporting explanation.

CQ	Which award was received by a music artist?
Test prediction	Yes
Expected test outcome	Yes (supported)
Explanation	The ontology includes the class "Award" and the relation "Received award" which connects a MusicArtist to the Award they have received. This allows for querying the ontology to find the award(s) received by a specific music artist.
CQ	In which time interval did the creation process took place?
Test outcome	
Expected test outcome	Yes (supported)
Explanation	The ontology described can address the competency question "In which time interval did the creation process take place?" The ontology includes classes and properties related to the creative process, such as CreativeProcess, CreativeAction, and AnnotationMethod. It also includes properties like "isDerivedFrom" and "Creates" that can be used to track the creation process and infer the time interval in which it took place.
CQ	Which is the recording process that recorded a musical performance?
Test prediction	Yes
Expected test outcome	Yes (supported)
Explanation	The ontology can address the competency question "Which is the recording process that recorded a musical performance?" The ontology includes the class "RecordingProcess" and the property "isRecordedBy" which connects a RecordingProcess to a MusicEntity or MusicalPerformance.
CQ	Does a music algorithm favor a specific genre?
Test prediction	Yes
Expected test outcome	No (not supported, but potentially plausible)
Explanation	The ontology includes the necessary classes and relations to represent music algorithms, music genres, and the relationship between them. By using the "isTrainedOn" and "isTrainedBy" relations, it is possible to infer whether a music algorithm has been trained on a specific music genre or if a music genre has influenced the training of a music algorithm.
CQ	Is a music work associated to any case of plagiarism?
Test prediction	No
Expected test outcome	No (not supported)
Explanation	The ontology focuses on describing music metadata related to artists, compositions, performances, and recordings, but it does not include specific concepts or relations related to plagiarism detection or identifying cases of plagiarism in music works. To address the competency question, additional concepts and relations related to plagiarism detection and analysis would need to be added to the ontology.
CQ	Which language is most used in a music artist's lyrics?
Test prediction	No
Expected test outcome	No (not supported)
Explanation	The ontology described does not include any classes or properties related to language or lyrics analysis. It focuses more on the structural and organisational aspects of music metadata, such as compositions, performances, recordings, and their relationships. To address the question of which language is most used in a music artist's lyrics, additional classes and properties related to language analysis and text processing would need to be included in the ontology.
CQ	When was the album first sold?
Test prediction	Yes
Expected test outcome	No (not supported)
Explanation	The ontology includes classes and properties related to albums, such as Release, Publication Situation, and Publisher. By using these classes and properties, it is possible to model the publication and release of albums, including the specific situation or context in which they are made available to the public. The ontology can capture information about the timing, location, and associated entities involved in the publication process, allowing for the inference of when the album was first sold.

References

1. Abid, A., Abdalla, A., Abid, A., Khan, D., Alfozan, A., Zou, J.: Gradio: hassle-free sharing and testing of ML models in the wild. arXiv preprint arXiv:1906.02569 (2019)
2. Aharoni, R., Goldberg, Y.: Unsupervised domain clusters in pretrained language models. In: Jurafsky, D., Chai, J., Schluter, N., Tetreault, J. (eds.) Proceedings of the 58th Annual Meeting of the Association for Computational Linguistics, pp. 7747–7763. Association for Computational Linguistics, Online (2020). https://doi.org/10.18653/v1/2020.acl-main.692
3. Alharbi, R., Tamma, V., Grasso, F., Payne, T.: An experiment in retrofitting competency questions for existing ontologies. arXiv preprint arXiv:2311.05662 (2023)
4. Allen, B.P., Stork, L., Groth, P.: Knowledge engineering using large language models. arXiv preprint arXiv:2310.00637 (2023)
5. Babaei Giglou, H., D'Souza, J., Auer, S.: LLMs4OL: large language models for ontology learning. In: Payne, T.R., et al. (eds.) ISWC 2023. LNCS, vol. 14265, pp. 408–427. Springer, Cham (2023). https://doi.org/10.1007/978-3-031-47240-4_22
6. de Berardinis, J., et al.: The Polifonia ontology network: building a semantic backbone for musical heritage. In: Proceedings of the 22nd International Semantic Web Conference (ISWC) (2023)
7. de Berardinis, J., Carriero, V.A., Meroño-Peñuela, A., Poltronieri, A., Presutti, V.: The music meta ontology: a flexible semantic model for the interoperability of music metadata. In: Proceedings of the the 24th International Society for Music Information Retrieval Conference (2023)
8. de Berardinis, J., et al.: Ontologies and knowledge graphs of music objects, patterns, and software package - 2nd version. Technical report, European Commission, The Polifonia consortium (2023)
9. Blomqvist, E., Hammar, K., Presutti, V.: Engineering ontologies with patterns - the eXtreme design methodology. In: Ontology Engineering with Ontology Design Patterns - Foundations and Applications, Studies on the Semantic Web, vol. 25. IOS Press, Amsterdam (2016). https://doi.org/10.3233/978-1-61499-676-7-23
10. Blomqvist, E., Presutti, V., Daga, E., Gangemi, A.: Experimenting with eXtreme design. In: Cimiano, P., Pinto, H.S. (eds.) EKAW 2010. LNCS (LNAI), vol. 6317, pp. 120–134. Springer, Heidelberg (2010). https://doi.org/10.1007/978-3-642-16438-5_9
11. Blomqvist, E., Seil Sepour, A., Presutti, V.: Ontology testing - methodology and tool. In: ten Teije, A., et al. (eds.) EKAW 2012. LNCS (LNAI), vol. 7603, pp. 216–226. Springer, Heidelberg (2012). https://doi.org/10.1007/978-3-642-33876-2_20
12. Bottini, T., et al.: D1.1 Roadmap and pilot requirements 1st version. Technical report, EU Commission, The Polifonia Consortium (2021)
13. Brown, T., et al.: Language models are few-shot learners. In: Advances in Neural Information Processing Systems, vol. 33, pp. 1877–1901 (2020)
14. Ciroku, F., de Berardinis, J., Kim, J., Meroño-Peñuela, A., Presutti, V., Simperl, E.: RevOnt: reverse engineering of competency questions from knowledge graphs via language models. Manuscript under review (2024)
15. Fernández-López, M., Gómez-Pérez, A., Juristo, N.: METHONTOLOGY: from ontological art towards ontological engineering. In: AAAI Conference on Artificial Intelligence (1997)

16. Funk, M., Hosemann, S., Jung, J.C., Lutz, C.: Towards ontology construction with language models. arXiv preprint arXiv:2309.09898 (2023)
17. Grüninger, M., Fox, M.S.: The role of competency questions in enterprise engineering. In: Rolstadås, A. (ed.) Benchmarking—Theory and Practice. IAICT, pp. 22–31. Springer, Boston, MA (1995). https://doi.org/10.1007/978-0-387-34847-6_3
18. He, Y., Chen, J., Dong, H., Horrocks, I.: Exploring large language models for ontology alignment. arXiv preprint arXiv:2309.07172 (2023)
19. Hertling, S., Paulheim, H.: Olala: Ontology matching with large language models. In: Proceedings of the 12th Knowledge Capture Conference 2023, pp. 131–139 (2023)
20. Kendall, E.F., McGuinness, D.L.: Ontology Engineering. Morgan & Claypool Publishers, San Rafael (2019)
21. Mateiu, P., Groza, A.: Ontology engineering with large language models. arXiv preprint arXiv:2307.16699 (2023)
22. Meyer, L.P., et al.: LLM-assisted knowledge graph engineering: experiments with chatgpt. arXiv preprint arXiv:2307.06917 (2023)
23. Peroni, S.: A simplified agile methodology for ontology development. In: Dragoni, M., Poveda-Villalón, M., Jimenez-Ruiz, E. (eds.) OWLED/ORE -2016. LNCS, vol. 10161, pp. 55–69. Springer, Cham (2017). https://doi.org/10.1007/978-3-319-54627-8_5
24. Pinto, H.S., Staab, S., Tempich, C.: DILIGENT: towards a fine-grained methodology for DIstributed, Loosely-controlled and evolvInG engineering of oNTologies. In: ECAI, vol. 16, p. 393. Citeseer (2004)
25. Qiang, Z., Wang, W., Taylor, K.: Agent-OM: leveraging large language models for ontology matching. arXiv preprint arXiv:2312.00326 (2023)
26. Simperl, E., Luczak-Rösch, M.: Collaborative ontology engineering: a survey. Knowl. Eng. Rev. **29**(1), 101–131 (2014)
27. Suárez-Figueroa, M.C., Gómez-Pérez, A., Fernández-López, M.: The NeOn methodology for ontology engineering. In: Suárez-Figueroa, M.C., Gómez-Pérez, A., Motta, E., Gangemi, A. (eds.) Ontology Engineering in a Networked World, pp. 9–34. Springer, Heidelberg (2012). https://doi.org/10.1007/978-3-642-24794-1_2
28. Uschold, M., King, M.: Towards a methodology for building ontologies. Citeseer (1995)
29. Viswanathan, V., Gashteovski, K., Lawrence, C., Wu, T., Neubig, G.: Large language models enable few-shot clustering. arXiv preprint arXiv:2307.00524 (2023)
30. Vrandečić, D., Krötzsch, M.: Wikidata: a free collaborative knowledgebase. Commun. ACM **57**(10), 78–85 (2014). https://doi.org/10.1145/2629489
31. Zhang, B., Reklos, I., Jain, N., Peñuela, A.M., Simperl, E.: Using large language models for knowledge engineering (LLMKE): a case study on Wikidata. arXiv preprint arXiv:2309.08491 (2023)
32. Zhang, Y., Wang, Z., Shang, J.: ClusterLLM: large language models as a guide for text clustering. In: Bouamor, H., Pino, J., Bali, K. (eds.) Proceedings of the 2023 Conference on Empirical Methods in Natural Language Processing, pp. 13903–13920. Association for Computational Linguistics, Singapore (2023). https://doi.org/10.18653/v1/2023.emnlp-main.858

Industry

Dataset Management Powered by Semantic Web Technologies

Björn Andersson[1]([envelope]), Patrik Kompuš[2], Sachiko Lim[1], and Michaela Skans[1]

[1] Dun & Bradstreet Sweden AB, Solna, Sweden
mailtobjorn@gmail.com
[2] Prague University of Economics and Business, Prague, Czech Republic

1 Introduction

When developing data supply chains, more and more companies strive for *compliance by design*. This process aims to ensure that computer software meets business compliance rules and policies. Some examples of compliance questions that require an answer are *On what legal grounds can we store and process the data?*, *Does the data need to be encrypted at rest?*, *How long can we keep the data?* and *Who shall be able to access the data?*.

To automate these decisions in the data supply chain, the software needs to retrieve required policies and rules to be able to take appropriate actions. Also, to be able to request for policies, the software needs to be aware of the data asset that it is currently processing; i.e., the data needs an asset identifier.

Dun & Bradstreet is a leading global provider of business decisioning data and analytics for almost 200 years. In our Nordic data supply chain, we use Semantic Web technologies and knowledge graphs to govern which datasets are allowed to be processed. By assigning each dataset a unique identifier at the earliest stage in the data supply chain, any subsequent software decision point can retrieve the associated policies and take appropriate decisions. The information in the knowledge graph is governed and maintained by data owners and can be updated (when required) without changing any of the software in the data supply chain.

2 Related Work

Among previous work that utilized an approach based on Semantic Web technologies to ensure data compliance, Debruyne et al. proposed an ontology, an extension of the provenance ontology called PROVO, to represent collected informed consent and its changes over time [2]. Castro et al. introduced an autonomous data governance system building on semantic techniques and ontology-driven reasoning based on defined rules [1]. Palmirani et al. proposed a Privacy Ontology (PrOnto) representing the main legal norms of data protection under GDPR [3]. These proposed frameworks have not yet been fully implemented in production, however. Real-world validation with live datasets would enhance the practical applicability of Semantic Web technologies. Our paper introduces an approach that has been actively employed in large-scale production since 2017.

A. Meroño Peñuela et al. (Eds.): ESWC 2024, LNCS 15344, pp. 125–128, 2025.
https://doi.org/10.1007/978-3-031-78952-6_11

3   Dataset Management Framework

In our data supply chain, a dataset is defined as a collection of information elements that abide under the same judicial policies and share the same data controller/processor and data owner.

3.1   Dataset Ontology Model

The center of our dataset ontology model is the `Dataset` concept, which serves as the `rdfs:domain` for our properties. Several SPSVERBc3es are defined to represent finite lists of possible values where each value is defined as an `owl:NamedIndividual`. We use qualified cardinality restrictions (QCRs) to define the shape of a `Dataset` instance. Figure 1 shows an example of our model.

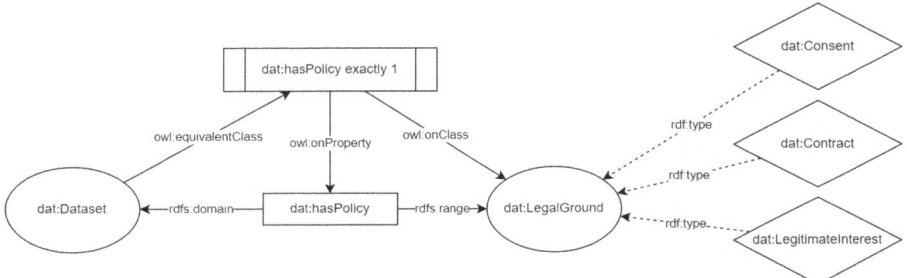

Fig. 1. An example of how some legal grounds are modelled in relation to a dataset

The properties in our dataset ontology model cover various metadata and data compliance policies divided into four categories; *General Information, Legal Framework, Information Security* and *Data Usage*. Figure 2 shows some of the properties in each category.

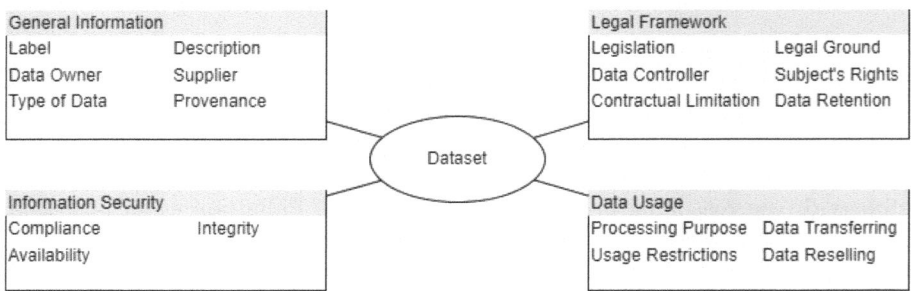

Fig. 2. Examples of properties within the dataset ontology model

3.2   System Design and Implemented Use Cases

The dataset management framework is implemented using Semantic Web technologies. The most important services, storage systems, clients and actors are depicted in Fig. 3 where the numbered use cases are further explained below.

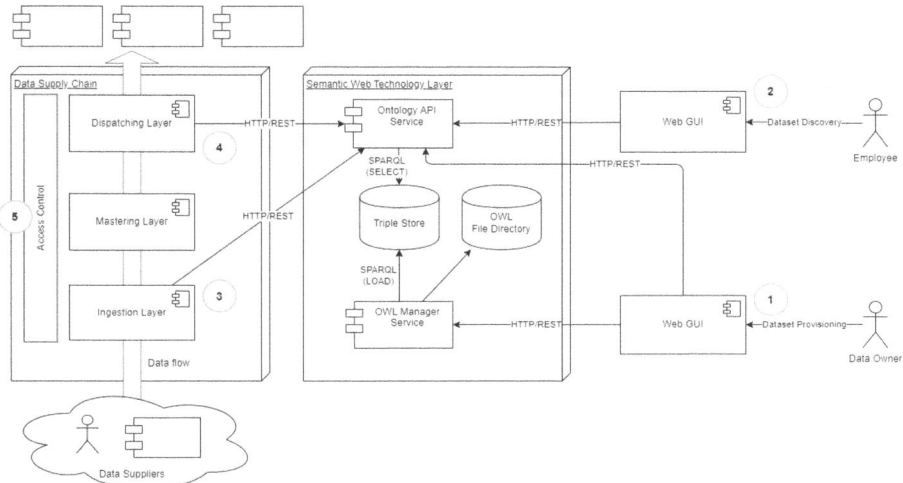

Fig. 3. High level system design of the dataset management framework

1. *Dataset Provisioning* Data owners use a `Web GUI` to create and update their datasets. The GUI renders a form based on the implemented QCRs. The form output is transferred to an `OWL Manager` service, which updates the appropriate OWL-file and finally loads the new version of the file into the `Triple Store`. Each instantiated dataset is assigned a globally unique IRI further used as the identifier across the data supply chain.
2. *Dataset Discovery* Employees may access a `Web GUI` where they can search for datasets and apply filters based on certain criteria selections, e.g., *"List all datasets in Finland that contain contact data"*. An `Ontology API` service executes a set of pre-defined SPARQL-queries towards the `Triple Store` and returns the content to the `Web GUI`. Also, the dataset IRI itself redirects any employee directly to the description of the dataset in the `Web GUI`.
3. *Dataset Ingestion* During the data ingestion process, every data content that shall be ingested is tagged with a dataset IRI. The `Ingestion Layer` verifies that the IRI exists, is active and that there is a provided legal ground for the dataset. If these checks are true, the data is ingested and further processed by the data supply chain; otherwise the data is rejected. The dataset IRI is now tagged to the ingested file and to all data messages originating from this file.

4. *Dataset Dispatching* Every data message is intercepted and inspected by the `Dispatching Layer`. The dataset IRI is retrieved from the message header and the `Ontology API` service is used to query the `Triple Store` for dispatching-related policies. Based on the returned policies, the `Dispatching Layer` distributes the data message to the appropriate and compliant destinations.
5. *Dataset Authorization* Access to operational tools and physical data within our data supply chain is authorized using attribute-based access control (ABAC) where the dataset IRI is one of the possible policy attributes.

4   Conclusion and Future Work

This dataset management framework has been in use since 2017, governing approximately 80 datasets. On a weekly basis over 25 million messages are processed in our Nordic data supply chain, all explicitly tagged as belonging to one of these datasets. Data owners, who previously had to manage their datasets using Excel or Word documents, have a modern user interface where they themselves can easily create new datasets or update existing ones if necessary, without needing any help from other resources such as developers. The user interface has over 100 active users.

By implementing this framework, we:

1. have a dataset registry that is centralized, unified, digitalized and accessible for humans and machines
2. ensure legal basis for data storage and processing
3. ensure information security by granting access to data per user/dataset to provide privacy by default
4. provide data compliance by design through automated data delivery decisions

To further standardize our solution, as future work we would like to explore using Shapes Constraint Language (SHACL) to steer the web forms in the user interface. Another future point of investigation could potentially be a dynamic data lineage solution.

References

1. Castro, A., Villagra, V.A., García, P., Rivera, D., Toledo, D.: An ontological-based model to data governance for big data. IEEE Access **9**, 109943–109959 (2021)
2. Debruyne, C., Pandit, H.J., Lewis, D., O'Sullivan, D.: "just-in-time" generation of datasets by considering structured representations of given consent for gdpr compliance. Knowl. Inform. Syst. **62**(9), 3615–3640 (2020)
3. Palmirani, M., Martoni, M., Rossi, A., Bartolini, C., Robaldo, L.: Pronto: privacy ontology for legal compliance. In: Proc. 18th Eur. Conf. Digital Government (ECDG), pp. 142–151 (2018)

Optimizing Aerospace Product Maintenance
A Novel Multi-Modal Knowledge Graph and LLM Approach for Enhanced Decision Support

Raed Awill[1,2]([✉]), Wajahat Ali Khan[1], Maqbool Hussain[1], and Ben Anderson[2]

[1] University of Derby, Derby, UK
100470771@unimail.derby.ac.uk
[2] Addqual Ltd., Derby, UK

Abstract. Siloed and inaccessible repair knowledge hinders the efficient maintenance of critical Turbine Engine components in the aerospace industry. This research introduces a novel multi-modal knowledge graph, leveraging Natural Language Processing (NLP) and Large Language Models (LLMs) to extract and structure repair rules from unstructured documents into a 131-node, 148-relationship graph. This advancement enables immediate access to essential information and facilitates data-driven decision-making, enhancing repair accuracy and efficiency. Implemented at AddQual Ltd., the knowledge graph reduced information retrieval times by 70%, increased repair speed by 20%, and is projected to yield 20% annual cost savings. These results highlight the transformative potential of integrating AI with knowledge graphs in aerospace maintenance. Future work will focus on advancing robust data validation frameworks and developing adaptive AI algorithms, extending the benefits across the aerospace sector and beyond.

Keywords: Knowledge Graph · Multi-Modal · Turbine Repair · Decision Support · Aerospace · Text2Cypher

1 Introduction

In the fast-paced aerospace industry, maintaining turbine engine components such as blades is essential for safety and optimal performance [1]. Building on our previous work [2] that highlighted the challenges in knowledge extraction from structured sources, our current research extends these capabilities to unstructured PDF documents [7], enhancing knowledge management in aerospace maintenance. Unstructured documents, traditionally difficult to navigate and integrate into decision-making processes, have impeded the effectiveness of repair strategies, impacting component reliability. Recognizing this issue, our research introduces an effective approach by developing a multi-modal knowledge graph. This graph is designed to systematically capture, structure, and make accessible the vast and previously hidden repair knowledge contained within unstructured

© The Author(s), under exclusive license to Springer Nature Switzerland AG 2025
A. Meroño Peñuela et al. (Eds.): ESWC 2024, LNCS 15344, pp. 129–132, 2025.
https://doi.org/10.1007/978-3-031-78952-6_12

documents. By leveraging NLP with LLMs capabilities, we have extracted, cate-gorized, and linked engine components, their images, repair rules, measurements, and actions related to engine component maintenance into a coherent, naviga-ble structure. Our proposed knowledge graph addresses three core challenges in aerospace maintenance: (1) enhancing the accessibility of repair knowledge, thus overcoming the limitations posed by traditional document formats; (2) enabling the utilization of existing data for improved decision-making, by structuring and linking measurement data within the graph; and (3) ensuring consistent and informed repair decisions through a standardized representation of knowledge that supports data-driven analysis. The adoption of our knowledge graph at AddQual Ltd. demonstrates its practical value, reducing information retrieval times and enhancing the consistency and efficiency of the repair processes.

2 Approach

Our system employs Neo4j, a graph database ideal for handling complex, multi-modal data (text, visuals, and numerical data) in aerospace maintenance. Its adaptability is essential for seamless data integration, continuous system devel-opment, and sustained effectiveness in dynamic operational environments [4]. Furthermore, Cypher, Neo4j's query language, enables precise and efficient data retrieval, preserving semantic integrity as the data landscape evolves [3].

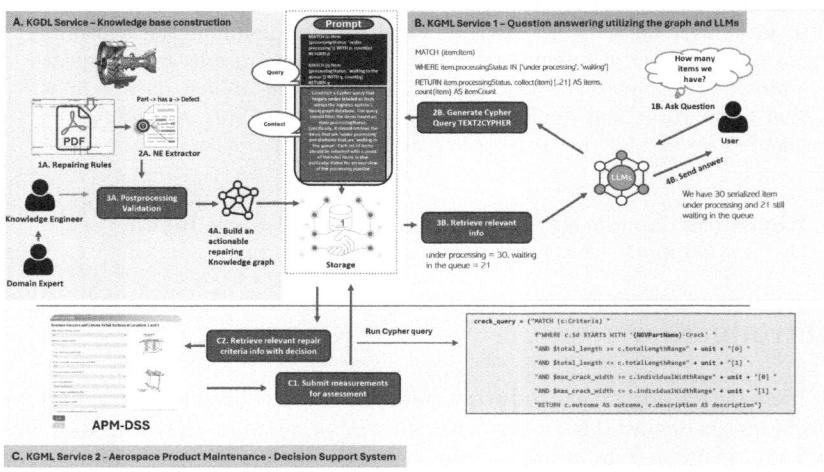

Fig. 1. Workflow Diagram of the Integrated Multi-Modal KG System

2.1   A: Knowledge Graph Definition Language Service (KGDL)

The system integrates multi-modal data from unstructured documents into a structured graph, extracting key repair rules, measurements, and images of engine components for maintenance. The LLM parses and organizes these data types per the input schema, enhancing the semantic depth of the graph for better usability. It starts with a domain expert converting a PDF with KG schema into a Neo4j graph using an LLM. The PDF is segmented, and processed by the LLM to extract data, and Cypher queries are generated and executed in Neo4j. This forms the basis of a DSS system [6], detailed in Fig. 1, which shows the steps to build a validated knowledge base. Additionally, our semantic technologies not only store data but also enable advanced reasoning. By extracting entities like 'compressor' from PDFs and using iterative prompting with GPT-4, which improved based on the aerospace domain experts' feedback, precise Cypher queries are generated. For instance, it identifies necessary inspections and retrieves relevant maintenance actions for components like 'Gas Turbine blades', ensuring the data meets domain-specific needs for aerospace maintenance decision-making.

2.2   B: Knowledge Graph Manipulation Language Services (KGML)

KGML, illustrated in Fig. 1, comprises two interconnected subsystems designed to maximize the knowledge graph's utility. KGML Service 1 facilitates user interaction through an NLP feature. This service allows users to submit queries about engine components using natural language, and KGML automatically translates these queries into Cypher queries suitable for the underlying graph database. This seamless integration enables users to receive clear and accurate information promptly. The KGML Service 2 serves as a dedicated Decision Support System (DSS) for aerospace product maintenance, streamlining the maintenance decision-making process. It automates the retrieval of relevant repair rules and efficiently stores and analyzes user-entered measurements. The system then executes complex Cypher queries to align the outcomes with established maintenance standards. By providing a deep analysis of technical data, this subsystem empowers users to make decisions. To address trust and reliability concerns, the KGML serves as a decision-support tool, complementing rather than replacing human judgment. Technicians use the outputs from the LLM to efficiently repair engine defects, benefiting from the knowledge graph's explainable insights for transparent decision-making. Our approach includes documented procedures for technician verification and managerial oversight, ensuring responsible integration of LLM outputs into the critical maintenance workflows.

3   Results, Insights, and Future Work

Implementing our multi-modal knowledge graph at AddQual Ltd. has substantially improved the efficiency and accuracy of aerospace engine maintenance. The knowledge graph displayed high entity recognition accuracy at 96.5% and relationship extraction accuracy at 95.2%, evaluated using a validation set of 500 entities, encompassing engine components, components images, and repair procedures. This thorough validation approach included automated data extraction by LLM algorithms, supplemented by critical evaluations from domain experts, ensuring the results are practically applicable. Drawing on the Holistic Evaluation of Language Models (HELM) [5], GPT-4 exhibits a Robustness score of 88% in Cypher Query Construction from the extracted entities, demonstrating reliable performance in handling the complex linguistic challenges found in aerospace maintenance texts. The validation set was specifically designed to challenge the system with complex scenarios typical in aerospace maintenance, thereby proving the knowledge graph's capability to manage, categorize, and retrieve complex information accurately. This led to a marked improvement in operational efficiency: repair technicians experienced a 70% faster retrieval of necessary maintenance data, and the system handled over 2,000 user queries with an impressive average response time of just 4 s. Furthermore, leveraging historical user-entered measurement data has optimized repair decision-making, boosting the consistency of repair actions across different tasks by 35% and enhancing overall operational efficiency by 20%. These improvements have significantly reduced maintenance time, saving 240 h over six months. Additionally, end-user feedback has been overwhelmingly positive, with a 90% satisfaction rate among repair personnel, underscoring the system's usability and effectiveness in improving decision-making processes. This research has illuminated the critical role of structured knowledge integration in improving decision-making within aerospace maintenance, offering a profound lesson on the interplay between domain-specific knowledge and AI technologies. We learned that the efficacy of AI-driven systems heavily relies on the depth and accuracy of the underlying data models, as evidenced by our knowledge graph's significant impact on operational efficiency and decision-making precision. Moving forward, it is essential to prioritize robust data validation frameworks and adaptive AI algorithms to further enhance the reliability and applicability of such systems across varied industrial landscapes.

References

1. Addqual | non-destructive testing inspection (2024). https://www.addqual.com/
2. Awill, R., Khan, W.A., Hussain, M., Zada, S., Anderson, B.: Aerospace qualification services knowledge graph: a leap towards enhanced data management. In: Proceedings of the International Semantic Web Conference 2023 (Nov 2023)
3. Holzschuher, F., Peinl, R.: Performance of graph query languages: comparison of cypher, gremlin and native access in neo4j. In: International Conference on Extending Database Technology (2013)
4. Kaur, K., Rani, R.: Modeling and querying data in nosql databases. In: 2013 IEEE International Conference on Big Data, pp. 1–7 (2013). https://doi.org/10.1109/BigData.2013.6691765
5. Liang, P., Bommasani, R., et al., T.L.: Holistic evaluation of language models (2023)
6. Peng, C., Xia, F., Naseriparsa, M., Osborne, F.: Knowledge graphs: opportunities and challenges. Artif. Intell. Rev. **56**(11), 13071–13102 (2023)
7. Zhao, H., Pan, Y., Yang, F.: Research on information extraction of technical documents and construction of domain knowledge graph. IEEE Access **8**, 168087–168098 (2020)

LLM-Based Guided Generation of Ontology Term Definitions

Stefan Bischof[ID], Erwin Filtz[ID], Josiane Xavier Parreira[ID],
and Simon Steyskal[(✉)][ID]

Siemens AG Österreich, Vienna, Austria
simon.steyskal@siemens.com

Abstract. This paper describes our approach for leveraging LLMs to generate definitions and descriptions for ontology terms. Our approach is grounded in the need for detailed and accurate representation of (domain-specific) Knowledge Graphs, and it aims at speeding up the process of generating such text. We outline our approach, including the problems that we encountered, and the solution we propose to overcome them. Our approach is currently in use in an industrial setting.

Keywords: Ontology Engineering · Large Language Models · Text Generation

1 Introduction

Knowledge graphs currently experience an increased uptake by industries. Different companies are turning to ontologies and Knowledge Graphs to enable interoperability within their businesses. In this modelling process, providing accurate term definitions and thorough descriptions of terms in an ontology is crucial, as they support users in having a common understanding of the underlying schema.

Writing such terms' definitions is, however, a labour-intensive task, requiring extensive manual labour to check domain literature and standards for accuracy. This process is also not only time-consuming but also prone to errors and inconsistencies, due to the subjective interpretation of the literature. Therefore, ontology terms will often lack a proper description.

The rise of Large Language Models (LLMs) in the past years has heavily influenced research in multiple domains. LLMs offer powerful features, such as the means to automate certain tasks, therefore saving time and effort of users and developers. In particular, a number of code libraries or library extensions have been proposed to support ontology engineering with the use of LLMs. OntoGPT [1] is a Python library capable of extracting entities and their relationships from natural text and transforming them into another structured format, for instance OWL. Similarly, a Protege plugin [2] converts natural language into OWL. Furthermore, there are tools available (e.g., [3,4]), which take advantage of LLMs for automatically populating a Knowledge Graph, by extracting the entities from text documents, given an existing ontology.

© The Author(s), under exclusive license to Springer Nature Switzerland AG 2025
A. Meroño Peñuela et al. (Eds.): ESWC 2024, LNCS 15344, pp. 133–137, 2025.
https://doi.org/10.1007/978-3-031-78952-6_13

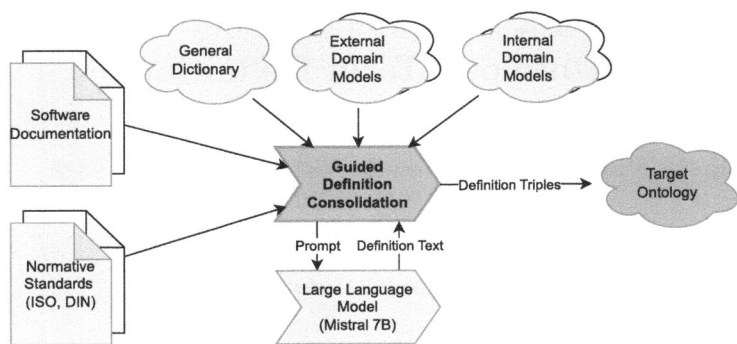

Fig. 1. Architecture of our proposed solution with different types of authoritative input, the main component, the LLM and the target ontology.

While LLMs provide a promising solution to the tedious manual labour involved in ontology engineering, they are not without their own set of challenges. The quality of the output they generate is often inconsistent and unpredictable. Instances of "hallucinations", or the generation of inaccurate or irrelevant information are common. These issues not only undermine the accuracy and reliability of the generated term definitions, but also complicate the process of ontology development, as significant time and resources must be then spent on reviewing and correcting these errors. Consequently, these challenges, if not addressed properly, might negate the benefits of using LLMs in the first place. Therefore, a more efficient and reliable approach is needed.

In this paper we propose leveraging LLMs to generate text for definitions for ontological terms, to significantly expedite the process and decrease the time domain experts need to complete such tasks. The approach was developed and tested and it is currently being used in an industrial setting.

In the following section we will outline our approach, which involves a combination of authoritative input and guided text generation.

2   Proposed Solution

In order to take advantage of LLMs and avoid their pitfalls, we propose a solution which guides LLMs by feeding them authoritative input on the terms, similar to existing retrieval-augmented generation (RAG) approaches. This approach aims to steer the generation process, reducing hallucinations and improving the overall quality of the output. An overview of our approach is shown in Fig. 1.

Authoritative Input. Authoritative input refers to credible and reliable information sources on the terms. This input serves as a reference guide for the LLMs, helping them generate accurate and relevant content. By providing the LLMs with a concrete foundation, we can reduce the likelihood of hallucinations and improve the consistency of the generated content. The authoritative

Listing 1. Sample Prompt Template

```
You are a domain expert for %domain% tasked with providing an
insightful definition of specific concepts in the context of %context%.

Rules to be followed while generating the definition:
- Desired Length: Short: 1 sentence
- Format: Single sentence
-----------------------------------------------
Generate Definition for:
- Concept Name: %label%
- Definition to be generated:
  As a domain expert, Provide a definition for the concept '%label%'.
  Use the following existing definitions as a basis for yours.
- Existing Definitions:
    * %existing definition 1%
    * %existing definition 2%
    * ...
```

input sources can be classified into the following groups: (*i*) External dictionaries, providing descriptions for terms; (*ii*) External domain models, containing descriptions of terms, such as ASHRAE Standard 223P[1], Brick[2], or Project Haystack[3]; (*iii*) Internal domain models, developed within Siemens; (*iv*) Software documentation; and (*v*) Normative standards, containing a section defining the used terms in the respective standards.

Guided Generation. Guided generation involves using the authoritative input as a guide or reference for the LLMs. Instead of generating content from scratch, the LLMs use the input to inform their generation process. This approach ensures that the generated content aligns with the authoritative input, thereby improving the accuracy and reliability of the definitions. Furthermore, by limiting the scope of the generation process to the parameters defined by the authoritative input, we can significantly reduce the likelihood of hallucinations and improve the overall efficiency of the process. A sample prompt for the generation of a description for a term, setting the scene for the LLM, and including definitions taken from the authoritative input is shown in Listing 1. Algorithm 1 describes the ontology annotation process using our proposed approach. After loading the data, for each ontology concept, definitions are searched in the data sources. In case no definition is found, the LLM is also asked for a definition. After that, the returned definitions are used as an input for the prompt generation by the LLM. Finally, a consolidated definition of the returned results is generated by the LLM.

---

[1] https://explore.open223.info/.

[2] https://brickschema.org/.

[3] https://project-haystack.org/.

Algorithm 1. Ontology Annotation Process

1: **Input:**
  – `data_sources`: List of data sources
  – `llm_models`: List of Language Learning Models (LLMs)
  – `external_definitions_url`: URL for external definition source
  – `output_file`: Name of the output file
2: **Output:** annotated concepts
3: **Abstract Steps:**
  1. Load data sources, and build indices.
  2. Query indices for information, fetch external definitions.
  3. **for** each concept in ontology **do**
  4.   Query external definitions (fallback to LLM if needed).
  5.   Create prompts and use LLM to generate definitions.
  6.   Condense generated definitions using LLM (fallback if needed).
  7. **end for**

Application and Benefits. We have implemented our approach and tested it within a project in our company, which involves creating an ontology for a domain in the smart building area. We have observed that our solution produces very good suggestions for concept definitions in the ontology. As a last step an expert reviews the generated definitions to ensure their soundness and correctness. First tests show considerably less time is required for this reviewing process compared to creating the descriptions manually in the first place. A thorough evaluation will be conducted in future work.

3   Conclusions

This paper addressed the task of generating descriptions for terms in an ontology. We have presented our approach which leverages LLMs to support domain experts in executing this task more efficiently. Our approach makes use of authoritative input to guide the text generation process, and it is currently being used in a industrial setting with clear benefits.

References

1. Caufield, J.H., et al.: Structured prompt interrogation and recursive extraction of semantics (SPIRES): a method for populating knowledge bases using zero-shot learning. Bioinformatics **40**(3) (2024). https://doi.org/10.1093/bioinformatics/btae104
2. Mateiu, P., Groza, A.: Ontology engineering with large language models. CoRR abs/2307.16699 (2023). https://doi.org/10.48550/ARXIV.2307.16699

3. Mihindukulasooriya, N., Tiwari, S., Enguix, C.F., Lata, K.: Text2KGBench: a benchmark for ontology-driven knowledge graph generation from text. In: ISWC'23. LNCS, vol. 14266, pp. 247–265 (2023). https://doi.org/10.1007/978-3-031-47243-5_14

4. Yu, S., Huang, T., Liu, M., Wang, Z.: BEAR: revolutionizing service domain knowledge graph construction with LLM. In: ICSOC'23. LNCS, vol. 14419, pp. 339–346 (2023). https://doi.org/10.1007/978-3-031-48421-6_23

Towards Solid-Based B2B Data Value Chains

Andreas Both[1,2]([✉]), Dustin Yeboah[1], Thorsten Kastner[1], Daniel Schraudner[3], Sebastian Schmid[3], Christoph Braun[4], Andreas Harth[3], and Tobias Käfer[4]

[1] DATEV eG, Nuremberg, Germany
[2] Leipzig University of Applied Sciences, Leipzig, Germany
andreas.both@htwk-leipzig.de
[3] Friedrich-Alexander University (FAU), Nuremberg, Germany
[4] Karlsruhe Institute of Technology (KIT), Karlsruhe, Germany

Abstract. In the paper, we describe the data sharing within a data-driven B2B ecosystem using Solid technologies. Using a real-world use case, we describe our approach and implementation, as well as the (previously non-existent) referencing of a purpose ontology to fully express the intended use of shared data in a machine-readable and analyzable form. We follow the intention of establishing a safe, robust, and traceable linked-data-driven B2B ecosystem based on Solid, where high standards of data privacy and thriftiness have to be met.

Keywords: Solid · Data Value Chains · Zero Trust · Data Sovereignty

1 Introduction

In this section, we will describe the use case of data-based ecosystems (data value chain, cf. [2]), Solid technologies [4], and the challenges in such ecosystems (in particular, regarding GDPR [7] and zero-trust architectures [5,6]) that are unique regarding the strong need for a technological solution that enables data-driven value chains and could fulfill the requirements for safety, robustness, and traceability. In particular, Solid provides a standardized machine-processable process for data exchanged based on Linked Data. In addition, the separation of data, applications, and identities facilitates the simple reuse of software components. The standardization of process steps in the form of semantic data representations and linked-data-driven implementations is therefore not limited to one use case but has a leverage effect for the entire industrial landscape.

Here, we focus on B2B data collaborations as a central use case of all businesses. Figure 1 shows an example of typical data exchange operations in B2B collaborations, where a small or medium enterprise (SME) requires data from its tax advisory office (TAO) to hand it over to the bank for creating a credit offer (that would finally be handed as data to the SME). There, only the directly communicating actors know about each other and are not aware of any other hidden participants in the data value chain. In general, in such an ecosystem,

A. Meroño Peñuela et al. (Eds.): ESWC 2024, LNCS 15344, pp. 138–142, 2025.
https://doi.org/10.1007/978-3-031-78952-6_14

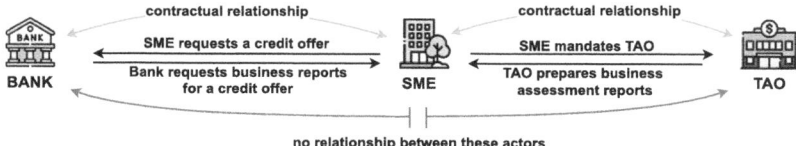

Fig. 1. Use case: Personas and contractual relationships.

the collaboration of organizational actors is expressed while providing data to a service provider to perform computations (i.e., contract data processing) and provide data to the original data provider (process and return) or hand the data safely to another partner (data transmission). The automation of such processes is crucial for businesses. Therefore, several technical challenges have to be fulfilled to be able to fully exploit the potential of data-driven services: (C_1) All data exchange process data has to be represented machine-readable, s.t., the process can be automated (e.g., while asking automatically for a data instance of a particular data format); (C_2) For the exchanged data additional metadata needs to be provided, s.t., the legal requirements are fulfilled (e.g., to provide the purpose of the data exchange). Solid technologies already provide some standards to address both challenges. In this paper, we describe our solution to extend the process by a standardized process driven by Linked Data and enable a universal and integrated solution supporting end-to-end data value chains. Hence, we provide here a (possible) cornerstone for a data-driven B2B ecosystem in the form of requirements, modeling, and a Solid app implementation.

2   Solid-Based Data Value Chains

Linked Data is a profound solution to represent semantic data on the web and in enterprises. However, while publishing and interlinking data works well in the context of public data (e.g., public company register [3]), the same approaches cannot be applied to B2B environments where business partners cannot share all data nor are allowed to reveal information about their business partners that are part of their data providers (actually, this strong data protection requirements often apply to units inside companies too, e.g., in case of a data trustee scenario). Therefore, a technology is needed that enables the exchange of data on demand, s.t., the B2B potential of Linked Data can be exploited. The W3C Solid Community Group's Application Interoperability [1] (INTEROP) provides a method to describe data representations and data access within so-called Solid Pods (Web storage) with information about the access grants and the affected data items. Following [7] all data processing needs a valid data processing purpose P (cf. C_2) that represents the minimum possible and necessary rights; typically that is also true within business environments extended with additional constraints (e.g., data re-sharing only within a particular business domain or administrative regions); the INTEROP vocabulary is not providing such a resolvable property.

Fig. 2. Chain of sharing business assessment reports.

Given our exemplary scenario (cf. Fig. 2), the TAO has provided data to the SME for a particular purpose of data processing P_0. The SME has provided the data to the Bank also defining a purpose P_1. Additionally, re-sharing data of the TAO to the Bank is not allowed to reveal information about the TAO as this might uncover business secrets of the SME. INTEROP is standardizing only the direct data exchange processes.

We can derive two technical requirements for future data value chains. (RQ1) The data purpose needs to be represented in an unambiguous, machine-readable form. Accordingly, the following must always apply to all data shared with P_i and passed on with P_j: P_j is equal to or more restrictive than P_i. (RQ2) Providing the received data to another business partner has to hide the original source (i.e., each identifier needs to be concealed), s.t., such data is treated in the same way as data produced by the data provider internally. However, the data receivers need to document if and how data was re-distributed to third parties (traceability, e.g., as evidence for external auditors of the data value chain).

To fulfill the aforementioned requirements, we model (see the complete modeling in our online appendix[1]) the following data representations and extend the process with the intention of establishing end-to-end data value chains within a B2B environment. For RQ1 we have extended the INTEROP classes for data sharing and data access with the predicate gdprp:purposeForSharing linking to a purpose class, in order to facilitate documentation and passing on purposes throughout the data chain. RQ2 is addressed by the classes delegatedAccess-Authorization and delegatedDataAuthorization to indicate that the given access and data grants are based on grants given by a third party. Further, the additional class FacadeDataRegistration enables hiding the Data Registration of the original data provider when passing on data and access authorizations. As shown in Fig. 3 (cf. online appendix), the modeled data enables businesses to fulfill the requirements and enables automatic processing as all metadata of the data value chain is represented in a machine-readable, semantic form. The implementation of the extended Solid-based data sharing is available online[2] and can be used to establish conform B2B data value chains.

3   Discussion and Conclusions

In this paper, we addressed the challenges of establishing B2B data-driven ecosystems. Our modeling and implementations aim to enable end-to-end

---

[1] https://doi.org/10.6084/m9.figshare.25424635.

[2] https://purl.archive.org/mandatb2b/ESWC2024.

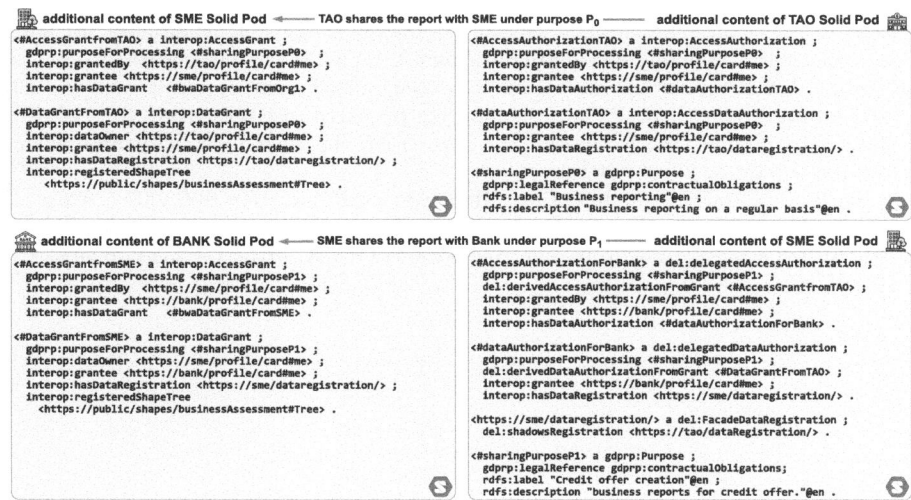

Fig. 3. Solid compatible chain of sharing business assessment reports.

processing of B2B data sharing/re-distributing while leaving the data granting control to the users (cf. Data Sovereignty). Following our approach, data value chains would be represented completely by Linked Data, enabling businesses to automatically process data while still providing crucial features like traceability and protection of business secrets. While doing so, we address a core blocker for applying Linked Data in distributed data-driven ecosystems with a strong interest in data protection and business secrets (e.g., supply chains, data value-added service). Our goal is to grow this solution into a global B2B ecosystem of data stores (i.e., Solid Pods) with linked data that can be connected on demand to help companies thrive through collaboration based on their semantic data.

Although our approach is applicable and represents a cornerstone for such ecosystems, further research is needed to achieve this goal, e.g., the reasoning on instances of purposes ontology needs to be safe and sound to establish completely automatable processes. Another issue is the redirect chain that is enforced by hiding (cf. `FacadeDataRegistration`) the original source of data items, which might lead to implementing a data trustee for better scalability and availability.

Acknowledgments. This work has been supported in part by the German ministry BMBF under grant 16DTM107B (*MANDAT*).

References

1. Bingham, J., Prud'hommeaux, E., Pavlik, E.: Solid Application Interoperability. W3C Editor's Draft (Nov. 2023)
2. Kano, L., Tsang, E.W.K., Yeung, H.W.C.: Global value chains: a review of the multi-disciplinary literature. J. of Inter. Bus. Stud. **51**(4) (2020)

3. Roman, D., et al.: The euBusinessGraph ontology: a lightweight ontology for harmonizing basic company information. Semantic Web **13**(41–68), 1 (2022)
4. Sambra, A.V., et al.: Solid: a platform for decentralized social applications based on linked data. MIT CSAIL & Qatar Computing Research Institute, Tech. Rep. (2016)
5. Shore, M., Zeadally, S., Keshariya, A.: Zero trust: the what, how, why, and when. Computer **54**(11), 26–35 (2021)
6. Stafford, V.: Zero trust architecture. NIST Special Publication **800**, 207 (2020)
7. The European Parliament and the Council of the European Union: Regulation (EU) 2016/679 (General Data Protection Regulation) GDPR. https://gdpr-info.eu/

Rapid Graph Generation from Job Descriptions: Combining Taxonomies and LLMs

Kaan Karakeben, Henri Egle Sorotos$^{(\boxtimes)}$, Alisa Milchevskaya, and Ahmad Assaf

Beamery, London, UK
{kaan.karakeben,henri.egle-sorotos,alisa.milchevskaya,ahmad}@beamery.com
https://beamery.com/

Abstract. Job Descriptions are a common currency for hiring talent. Whilst they are ubiquitous, they are also unstructured, difficult to analyse, and have no common format. In this paper, we present a novel approach to generate knowledge graphs from job descriptions by utilising a bespoke Large Language Model to extract and reconcile concepts to our ground truth taxonomy of HR entities.

Keywords: knowledge graph · unstructured data · taxonomies · LLM

1 Introduction

Human Resources (HR) is a core business function of almost all organisations. They manage the most important asset of many companies, its people. HR is a data-rich, but consistently data-poor function. This is not a trivial problem to solve because the causes are multi-faceted. HR data is unstructured, and often qualitative. Artefacts include performance reviews, resumes, and job descriptions (JDs). This data needs to be structured before being used as input for AI, analytics, and reporting.

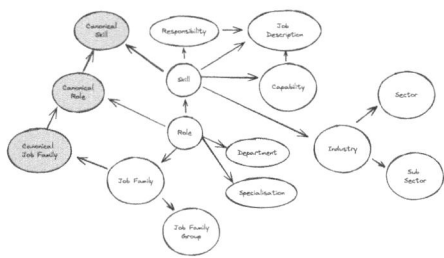

Fig. 1. Beamery's HR Domain Model

Another problem is that HR data is often siloed. Systems are often not integrated, and data is not shared across the organisation. To confront the intricate challenge of how data is interconnected, we have developed a graph domain model [4] to represent concepts found in the HR domain. This is represented in Resource Description Framework (RDF) format, and is conceptually shown in Fig. 1.

Crucially, it provides a common language of canonical taxonomies for HR data, and can be used to reconcile data across different systems. This domain model can be used to structure and reconcile data from HR artefacts, such as JDs. Notice that skills are the central concept in the domain model, and are related to other concepts such as qualifications, required capabilities, and responsibilities. JDs are a key source of this data and are found in companies globally. The paper will discuss our approach using an in-house fine-tuned Large Language Model (LLM) to extract these domain concepts from JDs, and reconcile them to our domain model.

2   Approach

Our approach to generating a knowledge graph from job descriptions is a two-step process:

1. **Concept Extraction and Reconciliation:** We use a bespoke LLM to extract concepts from job descriptions and reconcile to our canonical domain model.
2. **Graph Generation:** We generate a graph from the extracted raw concepts with relationships to canonical skills in our domain model.

2.1   Concept Extraction and Reconciliation

Job vacancy datasets are now abundantly available across various platforms. They provide insights into the dynamic demands of the labour market and enhance job matching processes [1]. A JD is a document containing unstructured and semi-structured natural language. This is a mix of free text and lists. There is no common format for JDs, and they can vary widely in length and content. They contain wealth of information about the skills, qualifications, competencies and prior experience required for a role.

The advancement of generative LLMs, particularly those that are instruction-tuned, has led to their widespread application across a broad spectrum of fields [2]. These applications frequently achieve highly competitive outcomes, factually demonstrated by OpenAI's GPT-4 upon release in 2023 [3]. Our fine-tuned LLM was trained on Beamery's talent graph [4] which contains proprietary data from a variety of HR artefacts. These concepts are found in our domain model, and the LLM is built to extract only these specific concepts from JDs. Prompt Engineering [5] is used to prime the bespoke system to act as a highly experienced HR professional with experience extracting key terms from JDs. The task is shown to the model as a system prompt via few-shot learning [6], which prepares the LLM to extract concepts from the JD. This enables in-context learning of the system to successfully extract the following concepts 1) skills, 2) capabilities, and 3) responsibilities. Our work builds upon that by Zhang et al. [7]. From the perspective of the system, the JD is a prompt, and the concepts are the completion.

We assume skills are the most granular and important concept in model. Capabilities and responsibilities are the sum of the skills required for a role, as per the domain model in Fig. 1. Because of this, we send the extracted capability and responsibility concepts to the system again, and ask it to extract skills from these concepts. This creates a complete graph of skills, capabilities and responsibilities.

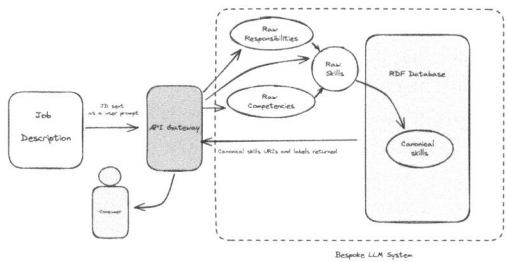

Fig. 2. Bespoke LLM System Diagram

2.2   Graph Generation

Underlying the bespoke LLM is a taxonomy of "canonical skills" that are designed to be mutually exclusive and collectively exhaustive (MECE). These are stored using the Simple Knowledge Organisation System (SKOS) [9] in graph. The canonical taxonomies are the common language understood by our AI and downstream applications.

What makes this approach unique is that the LLM returns extracted concepts as concepts in our canonical domain model of specific skills. These terms returned have associated graph URIs. Whilst extracting concepts using a generic LLM is a useful tool, it would not reconcile to our canonical skills in the domain model. Generic LLMs result in a high degree of cardinality of concepts extracted. For instance, any vanilla LLM could extract "Python" and "Python programming" as separate skill concepts. Previously seen and reconciled concepts are used to train and improve the LLM system and are persisted in the graph.

Edges between the raw skills concepts and the canonical skills are created and persisted with edges to common URIs. This allows us to generate a graph of the original JD, extracted concepts, and their relationships to the canonical skills. Each group of concepts extracted from a JD is stored as a named graph using both graph per source and graph per resource [8]. Provenance is a key value add. All JDs are stored in a common format, and linked to canonical skills.

3   Conclusion

JDs are a common currency for hiring talent. As initially stated, they are unstructured, difficult to analyse, and have no common format. The method in this paper allows us to generate a graph from JDs, and have a common currency for applications. It has been shown that by linking these concepts to a canonical taxonomy, we can reconcile data across different systems and feed data into AI, analytics and reporting. The benefits of linked data can be realised, such as SPARQL queries. At Beamery, this approach is in production and used to power AI applications such as matching and ranking candidates to jobs [12].

The method proposed is not without its limitations. Some potential problems include the fact the LLM may not always extract the correct concepts from the JD. We may see hallucinations or incorrect concepts extracted. Additionally, the reconciliation model may not always reconcile the concepts to the correct canonical skills. There may be concepts in the JD that are not in the canonical skill taxonomy. Despite this, the method proposed is significantly more efficient than manual methods. It allows results to power AI, analytics and reporting with JD data. In future, a similar mechanism could be used to link JD data to existing skills data such as ESCO [10] or ONET [11]. Additionally, there is the potential to see new insights from the data, and to power new applications that were not possible before.

References

1. Balog, K., Fang, Y., De Rijke, M., Serdyukov, P., Si, L.: Expertise retrieval. Found. Trends Inf. Retr. **6**(2–3), 127–256 (2012)
2. Ouyang, L., et al.: Training language models to follow instructions with human feedback, arXiv preprint, arXiv:2203.02155 (2022)
3. OpenAI, "GPT-4 technical report," arXiv preprint, arXiv:2303.08774 (2023)
4. Beamery (2022). https://beamery.com/resources/blogs/knowledge-graphs-the-future-of-talent-management
5. Saravia, E.: Prompt Engineering Guide (2022). https://github.com/dair-ai/Prompt-EngineeringGuide.
6. Brown, T., et al.: Language Models are Few-Shot Learners, arXiv preprint. arXiv:2005.14165v4 (2020)
7. Zhang, M., Jensen, K.N., Sonniks, S.D., Plank, B.: SkillSpan: Hard and Soft Skill Extraction from English Job Postings, arXiv preprint arXiv:2204.12811 (2022)
8. Dodds, L., Davis, I.: Linked Data Patterns: A pattern catalogue for modelling, publishing, and consuming Linked Data (2022). https://patterns.dataincubator.org/book/
9. W3C, SKOS Simple Knowledge Organization System Reference (2009). https://www.w3.org/TR/skos-reference/
10. ESCO (2024). https://ec.europa.eu/esco/portal/home
11. O*NET (2024). https://www.onetonline.org/
12. Beamery AI Talent Match (2024). https://support.beamery.com/hc/en-us/articles/9671611196305-Beamery-AI-Explained

FAIR Internet of Things Data: Enabling Process Optimization at Munich Airport

Michael Freund[1]([✉])[iD], Julian Rott[2][iD], Rene Dorsch[1][iD],
and Andreas Harth[1,3][iD]

[1] Fraunhofer Institute for Integrated Circuits IIS, Nürnberg, Germany
{michael.freund,rene.dorsch,andreas.harth}@iis.fraunhofer.de
[2] Munich Airport, Munich, Germany
[3] Friedrich-Alexander-Universität Erlangen-Nürnberg, Nürnberg, Germany

Abstract. We present how data collected from Internet of Things (IoT) devices adhering to the FAIR data principles forms the foundation for data analytics applications at Munich Airport. We describe how the collected IoT data is annotated, how our APIs are structured, present two data analytics applications currently in use to analyze FAIR IoT data for process optimization, and share lessons learned.

Keywords: FAIR data principles · Internet of Things · Solid

1 Introduction

The Internet of Things (IoT) has become an integral part of enterprise process monitoring systems, enabling improved transparency of operational processes through the collection of additional data. In general, IoT devices operate continuously and generate large amounts of heterogeneous data [1]. For instance, our IoT system at Munich Airport has been in operation for about 9 months and is installed at a baggage check-in counter. The IoT system consists of three RGB stereo depth IoT cameras and processes approximately 2,700 pieces of baggage on a typical day, resulting in approximately 8,100 timestamps, 8,100 RGB images and 8,100 depth images.

Managing, integrating, and using the raw data produced by our IoT system presents challenges, especially data fusion complexities [5], as the images and timestamps require additional provenance data and need to be integrated with existing datasets. Furthermore, there are difficulties in efficiently finding images and provenance data associated with a particular piece of baggage and in securely accessing the found data segments with access control. Challenges related to Findability, Accessibility, Interoperability, and Reusability (FAIR) are prevalent not only in enterprise IoT environments but also across various domains. As a potential solution, the use of FAIR data principles [6] has proven to be effective.

A. Meroño Peñuela et al. (Eds.): ESWC 2024, LNCS 15344, pp. 147–151, 2025.
https://doi.org/10.1007/978-3-031-78952-6_16

Listing 1. RDF data describing an image and provenance data.

```
1    @prefix sosa: <http://www.w3.org/ns/sosa/>.
2    @prefix prov: <http://www.w3.org/ns/prov#>.
3    @prefix dc: <http://purl.org/dc/elements/1.1/>.
4    @prefix rdfs: <http://www.w3.org/2000/01/rdf-schema#>.
5    @prefix xsd: <http://www.w3.org/2001/XMLSchema#>.
6    @prefix : <http://www.munich-airport.de/ontology/fmo#>.
7    @base <http://www.munich-airport.de/iotdata> .
8
9    <#image1> a prov:Entity;
10      dc:format "image/png"; dc:creator <#cam37>;
11      prov:generatedAtTime "2023-12-14T11:54:01"^^xsd:dateTime;
12      dc:source
            <http://munich-airport.de/cam37/20240114/150340.png>.
13
14   <#cam37> a sosa:Sensor;
15      sosa:observers <#baggageTop>;
16      rdfs:label "Camera 37";
17      sosa:isHostedBy <platform1>.
18
19   <#baggageTop> a sosa:ObservableProperty;
20      rdfs:label "Top view of transported baggage.".
21
22   <#imageProcessingAgent> a prov:Agent;
23      rdfs:label "Image Processing Agent".
24
25   <#imageProcessingActivity> a prov:Activity;
26      prov:wasAssociatedWith <#imageProcessingAgent>;
27      prov:used <#image1>.
28
29   <#processedData20231214115401876282> a prov:Entity;
30      prov:wasGeneratedBy <#imageProcessingActivity>;
31      :baggageHeight "0.1"^^xsd:decimal; :color "FF0000".
```

2   Approach

In our setup at Munich Airport, we use an IoT architecture introduced in previous work [2]. A key component of the architecture is the use of Solid [4]. Solid is a specification enabling secure and decentralized data storage built on the Linked Data Platform (LDP). The use of Solid forms the basis for ensuring that our IoT data adheres to FAIR principles. A snippet of the stored RDF data can be seen in Listing 1 and is used as a reference in the following.

Findability. To ensure findability, we assigned each collected image a unique identifier in the form of a URI. We added RDF descriptions to the image data, such as the data format and creator of the image (line 10), the timestamp when the image was generated (line 11), and the URI of the image resource (line 12). Both the RDF metadata file and the images are stored in Solid and linked to the camera that created the image, which in turn is linked to the entire IoT platform. This allows us to use link following to discover and find images.

Accessibility. Using Solid allows us to use HTTP as a means to securely access our IoT data, and allows us to use access control lists to restrict access to unauthorized users. By separating the RDF metadata files from the images, we ensure that the metadata remains available even if the image data is no longer accessible. Using HTTP not only provides easy access to the data, but also ensures that the required ports are not blocked by typical firewall configurations.

Interoperability. Metadata is stored using RDF in combination with standard and open vocabularies such as Dublin Core, SOSA/SSN, and PROV-O (lines 10, 15, 26) to describe the data and ensure interoperability. In addition, we use a custom ontology developed for Munich Airport specific entities using the LOT methodology [3] (line 31).

Reusability. We organized the IoT data according to the airport's established internal data structures to promote data reuse. In addition, we annotated the image data with provenance information to track the data processing steps and algorithms involved (line 22), thereby clarifying and documenting how the data was generated.

Solid API. The HTTP API of the Solid storage is based on the hierarchical structure of IoT devices. For example, the data collected by `cam37` is stored in an LDP container for the camera, which contains LDP containers for each day the system has been running, each containing image data named by its creation timestamp (line 12). In addition, each date-specific LDP container has its own metadata file containing RDF data, similar to Listing 1.

3   Applications

The FAIR-compliant images and metadata stored in the Solid storage form the basis for applications. The applications are designed to consume the FAIR data, extract additional information useful for process improvement, and generate new FAIR data. Currently, we have implemented and deployed two such applications:

Size and Color Feature Extraction. The first application queries the metadata of the images stored in Solid to identify groups of images that correspond to a single piece of baggage, and retrieves all identified images via HTTP. The application then uses the group of images to create a 3D point cloud of the baggage. The 3D point cloud is then used to estimate the dimensions of the baggage and to extract the four most dominant colors. The extracted information, along with metadata such as provenance data, is added back to the Solid storage as RDF triples using HTTP PATCH requests.

Baggage Type Classification. The second application also queries the metadata of the images stored in Solid and retrieves the color image taken from the top perspective via HTTP. The application uses a pre-trained image classification algorithm to perform inference on the retrieved image to identify different types of baggage, such as suitcases or backpacks. The classified category, along with the associated probability score and provenance data, is added as RDF triples to the Solid storage using HTTP PATCH requests.

The information stored in Solid is then linked and integrated with existing RDF process data. The integrated process information enables optimization of operations, such as evaluating lead times for handling specific types of baggage or creating loading plans based on estimated baggage dimensions.

4   Lessons Learned

During the implementation of FAIR principles for IoT data at Munich Airport, we, the responsible project team, gained several insights:

- The initial process of making IoT data FAIR-compliant is more complex than traditional methods. But the FAIR approach offers long-term benefits, especially in application development and data integration.
- Provenance data can be central to troubleshooting and understanding nested processing steps because data aggregation steps and analysis algorithms used are documented along with the actual data.
- Using Solid for data storage supports FAIR compliance through the restrictions of the Solid protocol, such as the use of HTTP and RDF, and provides an actively maintained, mature server software implementation.
- Combining HTTP with access control lists simplifies data access for everyday users by enabling data retrieval using standard web browsers.

5   Conclusion and Future Work

In this paper, we detailed our approach to making IoT data FAIR at Munich Airport. We presented two deployed applications that consume and produce FAIR data, and shared lessons learned during the implementation of the project. Looking ahead, we plan to deploy more IoT devices and develop additional analytics applications.

Acknowledgements. This work was funded by the Bayerisches Verbund-forschungsprogramm (BayVFP) des Freistaates Bayern through the KIWI project (grant no. DIK0318/03).

References

1. Cai, H., et al.: IoT-based big data storage systems in cloud computing: perspectives and challenges. IEEE Internet Things J. **4**(1), 75–87 (2016)
2. Freund, M., et al.: WoT2Pod: an architecture enabling an edge-to-cloud continuum. International Conference on Internet of Things (2023)
3. Poveda-Villalón, M., et al.: LOT: an industrial oriented ontology engineering framework. Engineering Applications of Artificial Intelligence (2022)

4. Sambra, A.V., et al.: Solid: a platform for decentralized social applications based on linked data. MIT CSAIL & Qatar Computing Research Institute, Tech. Rep. (2016)
5. Wang, L.: Heterogeneous data and big data analytics. Automatic Control Inform. Sci. **3**(1), 8–15 (2017)
6. Wilkinson, M.D., et al.: The FAIR guiding principles for scientific data management and stewardship. Sci. Data **3**(1), 1–9 (2016)

Product Information Management Systems Powered by Knowledge Graphs

Amir Laadhar[1]([✉]), Nikhil Acharya[1], Johann Wagner[1], and Martin Ley[1,2]

[1] PANTOPIX GmbH & Co. KG, Josephine-Hirner-Str. 2, 88131 Lindau, Germany
{amir.laadhar,nikhil.acharya,johann.wagner,martin.ley}@pantopix.com
[2] Munich University of Applied Sciences, LothstraSSe 34, 80335 München, Germany
martin.ley@hm.edu

1   Introduction

Companies rely on Product Information Management (PIM) [1] systems to create, manage, and distribute product information across various channels. Traditional PIM platforms encounter numerous issues due to the complexity of product portfolios and an increasing heterogeneity of data sources. Moreover, there is the need to compare competitors' product offerings with the current product offering to achieve market and portfolio intelligence. Other issues include inconsistent data quality and cumbersome manual workflows faced by sales managers when there is no centralized source of truth. This leads to inefficiency in accessing necessary product data by company departments, detrimental to decision-making and competitiveness. Exploring potential solutions to these challenges led us to develop PIM systems based on Knowledge Graphs [5] for our industrial clients.

2   Product Navigator Application for Sales Managers

Sales managers are often faced with the hard task of collecting product offering information from multiple sources, which is a time-consuming and error-prone process. In addition to navigating several internal data sources, they have the added responsibility of manually tracking competitor product offerings across different external websites, further complicating their task. This makes it difficult to find accurate information quickly, deteriorating the ability to build strong customer relationships and stay competitive.

To cope with the mentioned issues, we employ a knowledge graph as the heart of the PIM system. The knowledge graph contains or integrates product information originating from different data silos, represented in a unified structure in a central location. The product navigator web application serves as a tailor-made point of access to the knowledge graph for the specific needs of the sales managers. A sales manager using a PIM system backed by a knowledge graph can effortlessly navigate complex product hierarchies and get rich information about products. This leads to the identification of hidden connections between

A. Meroño Peñuela et al. (Eds.): ESWC 2024, LNCS 15344, pp. 152–156, 2025.
https://doi.org/10.1007/978-3-031-78952-6_17

products and tracking the origin of information. Additionally, by accessing centralized and reliable information from multiple sources, sales managers can make informed decisions about product offerings and informed recommendations for customers.

3 PIM Network of Ontologies

We rely on a set of five ontologies as the backbone of the PIM knowledge graph. Figure 1 shows the main classes and properties of the PIM network of ontologies. This network integrates five ontologies to improve maintainability.

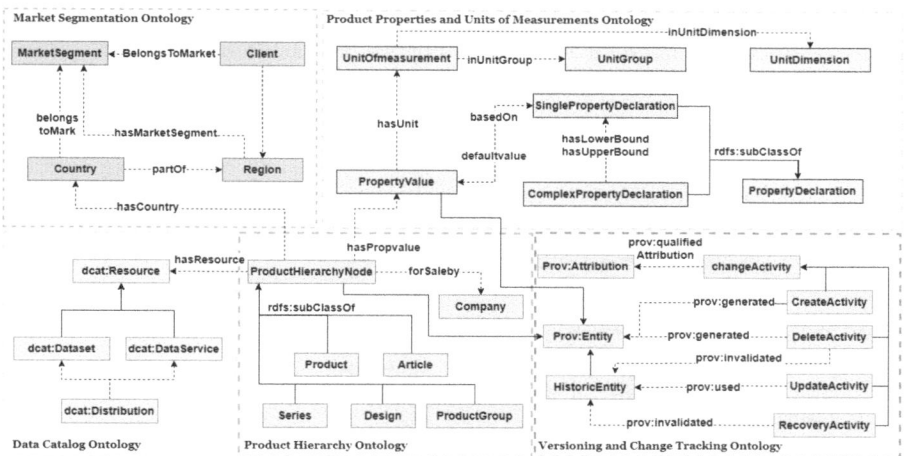

Fig. 1. PIM ontologies network

The main class of the product hierarchy ontology is `ProductHierarchyNode`. This class has sub-classes referring to different levels of the product hierarchy. This class serves as a superclass for the product hierarchy and cannot be directly instantiated. Its subclasses inherit object and data properties. The relationship between product hierarchy nodes is hasChild and hasParent. The `ProductHierarchyNode` superclass is integrated with the other ontologies. It can be associated with `PropertyValue`, which is the value related to a specific product technical feature (e,g., pressure level of 6 bar). This ontology can reuse existing ontologies such as Building Product Ontology [6] or PRONTO [7].

The product properties and units of measurement ontology aim to model property values (`PropertyValue`) related to a given property declaration. A property declaration defines a technical feature to describe products, such as a nominal engine power. A product can be represented with a number of property values associated to property declarations. Property values can require a reference to a unit of measurement. For example, an article can be associated with a property value with a value of 24.58 via the object property `hasPropvalue`. This Property value is `basedOn` a single property declaration "engine power".

We define a versioning and change tracking ontology based on the W3C PROV Ontology [2]. It records change activities made to the set of articles as well as their associated property values and property declarations. For instance, we can track historical changes made to an Article by the users.

We integrate the W3C Data Catalog Vocabulary (DCAT) [3] in the PIM ontologies network. A `ProductHierarchyNode` can also be associated with a `dcat:Resource` via the object property `hasResource`. For instance, we can associate an article with data sheets, images, and datasets.

The market segmentation ontology models the different markets (i.e., construction market), countries, and regions. For example, a product can be sold for a specific country by a specific company. This allows the comparison of articles sold by competitors made for different countries or market segments.

4   PIM System Architecture

In Fig. 2, we define the PIM system architecture overview, which has mainly four main layers: data sources, data onboarding, middleware, and serving layer. An initial alpha version of the PIM system is deployed for several users.

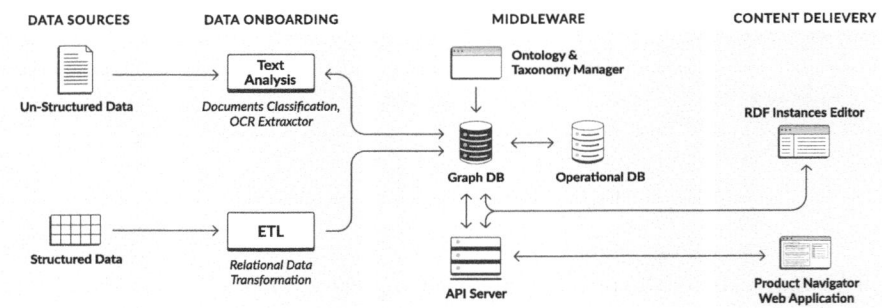

Fig. 2. PIM system architecture overview

4.1   Data Sources

We distinguish between two types of data sources: structured data and unstructured data. Unstructured data comprises mainly competitors' technical documents and websites. They contain paragraphs mixed with tables related to the technical features of different products and articles. We mainly use these documents to extract competitors' specific products and property descriptions for products that can be stored as RDF in the Knowledge Graph. The structured data comprises product datasheets and relational data sources containing pre-defined attributes having continuous or categorical values for each property of specific products like refrigerators and dryers. These structured data sources may contain product property information like engine power.

4.2   Data Onboarding

The goal of the unstructured data onboarding pipeline is to continuously extract competitors' products data and store it in the PIM knowledge graph. The stages to achieve unstructured data onboarding comprise documents crawling, documents classification, data extraction, and RDF generation. We begin by scraping competitors' websites searching and storing relevant public technical product documents. These documents provide a rich description of competitors' products. Then, we use a trained machine learning classifier to separate relevant product documents from irrelevant documents. Next, we rely on a trained OCR model to fetch relevant information from technical product documents. This data includes the article name, its technical properties, market, region, and manufacturer. The data quality of the extracted information from unstructured sources depends on the trained OCR model, which has an accuracy of 99%. However, mappings of all the extracted information to the knowledge graph remain a challenge due to updated information. We finally generate RDF triples from the extracted data and store them as competitors' articles in the knowledge graph. Structured data primarily from ERP systems, with technical properties originating in the R&D department, are synced into the PIM knowledge graph for further enrichment with additional properties, texts, and media assets.

4.3   Middleware

The middleware layer includes an ontology and a taxonomy manager, a triple-store, a relational database, and an API server. The ontology and taxonomy manager maintains the PIM vocabularies. The relational database stores operational data such as access and control lists. The API server defines a set of API calls used by different applications.

5   Evaluation and Lessons Learned

To assess the knowledge graph's quality, we employed automated testing with predefined SPARQL templates. We have also used SHACL [4] for periodic valida-tions of the knowledge graph. Building a knowledge graph within an agile devel-opment methodology represents both benefits and challenges. Agile methodol-ogy allows adaptability to changing requirements, which takes advantage of the knowledge graph flexibility to onboard changes. This flexibility also brings the challenge of maintaining the integrity of the knowledge graph data. Therefore, we define three working environments (i.e., development, quality assessment, and deployment), and each of them is divided into three graph repositories (i.e., ingestion, maintenance, and consumption). Knowledge graphs are advantageous for PIM systems since they allow the handling of complex product portfolios and competitor data. This positions the PIM as a company's central hub for product information over a growing amount of use cases.

References

1. Forza, C., et al.: Product Information Management for Mass Customization: Connecting Customer, Front-Office and Back-Office for Fast and Efficient Customization (2006)
2. W3C PROV-O Working Group. PROV-O: The PROV Ontology. W3C Recommendation, W3C, April 2013
3. W3C Data Catalog Vocabulary (DCAT) Working Group. Data Catalog Vocabulary (DCAT) – Version 2. W3C Recommendation, W3C, December 2020
4. W3C Data Shapes Working Group. Shapes Constraint Language (SHACL). W3C Recommendation, W3C, July 2017
5. Hogan, A., et al.: Knowledge graphs. ACM Comput. Surv. **54**, 4 (2022)
6. Wagner, A., et al.: BPO: the building product ontology for assembled products. In: Proceedings of the 7th Linked Data in Architecture and Construction Workshop (LDAC 2019), Lisbon, Portugal (2019)
7. Vegetti, M., et al.: PRONTO: an ontology for comprehensive and consistent representation of product information. Eng. Appl. Artif. Intell. **24**(8) (2011)

Posters and Demos

ArtSampo – Finnish Art on the Semantic Web

Annastiina Ahola[1]([✉])[iD], Heikki Rantala[1]([✉])[iD], and Eero Hyvönen[1,2]([✉])[iD]

[1] Semantic Computing Research Group (SeCo), Aalto University, Espoo, Finland
{annastiina.ahola,heikki.rantala,eero.hyvonen}@aalto.fi
[2] Helsinki Centre for Digital Humanities (HELDIG), University of Helsinki, Helsinki, Finland
https://seco.cs.aalto.fi

Abstract. This paper presents first results of ARTSAMPO, a collaborative Finnish Linked Open Data (LOD) infrastructure for publishing fine art collections on the Semantic Web and for facilitating Digital Humanities (DH) research. The infrastructure consists of a Knowledge Graph (KG) whose initial version was compiled from the metadata of the three art museums of the Finnish National Gallery. A semantic ARTSAMPO portal was built on top of the KG for searching, browsing, and analyzing the underlying data. The Finnish ontology infrastructure and international datasets are used for harmonizing and enriching the data.

Keywords: digital humanities · fine art · cultural heritage · portals

1 Introduction

Art is an important part of cultural identity. Contrary to the fears that web services showcasing information on museum collections would cause a decrease in museum visitors, these kind of services have instead become an important tool for marketing and distributing information for museums, and the number of visitors has been growing, e.g., in Finland. These collections, however, have been divided between both public museums of various types as well as private collections. This makes it hard for the visitor to get a general picture of national collections and access a particular art object at a suitable time and place.

Though not an comprehensive replacement to physically going to view an art object, a web service containing information on the collections could alleviate these problems and enrich the physical visit experience by providing additional insightful information that can be accessed without the limitations based on time and place. Another use case for web services would be for the curators of these art collections to be able to get a good overview on what their collections consist of. Various ontologies and vocabularies already exist for describing art, such as the Getty Research Institute's[1] Art & Architecture Thesaurus (AAT), Universal List of Artist Names (ULAN) and Getty Iconography Authority, as well as

---

[1] www.getty.edu/research/tools/vocabularies/.

A. Meroño Peñuela et al. (Eds.): ESWC 2024, LNCS 15344, pp. 159–163, 2025.
https://doi.org/10.1007/978-3-031-78952-6_18

the ICONCLASS [1] iconography classification system and Chinese Iconography Thesaurus CIT[2] for describing the contents of art works. Linked Data (LD) on art has also been published as part of projects like Europeana[3] as well as the Linked Art [2] project involving various high-profile international museums.

ARTSAMPO is a LOD service and semantic portal for Finnish art collections. It facilitates an easy way of searching, browsing, and analyzing fine art data for both the general public as well as researchers. The idea is to combine collection data from different museums into one KG and utilize Semantic Web technologies to enhance the users' experience and to provide means for studying art. In this work, collection data is transformed into RDF and made available as a LOD service for DH research. A user interface (UI) utilizing faceted search [6] and offering integrated data-analytic tools is also built on top of the data to make it accessible and explorable without SPARQL knowledge. ARTSAMPO is one of the Sampo systems[4] [3] for publishing cultural heritage data on the Semantic Web.

2   ArtSampo Knowledge Graph and User Interface

The current version of the ARTSAMPO KG is based on the metadata on the collections of Finnish National Gallery provided as open data[5]. These collections include over 58,000 art objects and 6,400 artists and span multiple different museums (Ateneum Art Museum, Museum of Contemporary Art Kiasma and Sinebrychoff Art Museum). This data was transformed from the original JSON files to Turtle-serialized RDF data. The transformation was done using simple, custom Python scripts with the rdflib[6] library that read the original data and created the necessary triples based on the JSON data. As the data for the different museums came all from the same source, the same script could be used for all the data without need for alignment between the data of different collections. Basic data type casting for relevant values (e.g., dimensions as decimals) and language tagging labeling was done during the process, but the values itself were not touched.

The initial version of the KG consists of approximately 1,100,000 triples. The triples in the KG are stored on a Apache Jena Fuseki[7] SPARQL server on the Linked Data Finland platform[8] and is accessible from a restricted, read-only SPARQL endpoint. The KG uses three classes for modeling the data: *Art Object*, *Person* and *Multimedia*. All types of art objects are instances of the *Art Object* class. People are modeled with the *Person* class and linked to art objects via the art object instance. Images of art objects are modeled through the *Multimedia* class and linked to the art objects similarly to the artists. All other metadata

---

[2] https://chineseiconography.org/.
[3] https://www.europeana.eu/.
[4] https://seco.cs.aalto.fi/applications/sampo/.
[5] https://www.kansallisgalleria.fi/en/api-sovelluskehittajille.
[6] https://rdflib.readthedocs.io/en/stable/.
[7] https://jena.apache.org/documentation/fuseki2/.
[8] https://ldf.fi/.

related to the aforementioned classes is modeled through properties getting literal values. This data model structure is not intended to be the final structure, but rather just an initial version to get a better idea of what can be done with the data, and the final data model design and usage of existing vocabularies will be iterated upon as further data sources and their interoperability with the original data set is explored in more detail.

The user interface (UI) for the ARTSAMPO KG is built with the Sampo-UI framework [5] to facilitate an easy way of browsing, exploring, and searching the data as well as to provide integrated data-analytic tools for analyzing the data without the need for technical expertise. The UI queries the data from the restricted SPARQL endpoint. The landing page of the portal lists the *application perspectives* available in the portal. The portal is split into two different perspectives: *art objects* and *persons*: By choosing the *art objects* perspective the user is presented the data as rows of art objects, while the *persons* perspective lists all the people related to various art objects in the data.

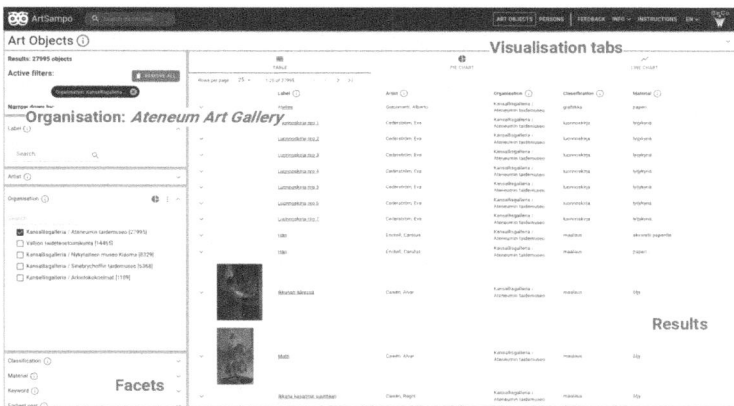

Fig. 1. The faceted search view of the portal with *Ateneum Art Museum* selected in the *Organisation* facet

The user can filter the search results in the faceted search view by using the provided facets to select the wanted values for various properties. For example, in Fig. 1 the use has selected *Ateneum Art Museum* as the wanted organisation in the *Organization* facet on the left, and all results are thus from the collections of the Ateneum Art Museum. The search results are listed as a table on the right and any of them can be selected for close reading and browsing for further information. With the provided data-analytic tools available as tabs the user can also easily visualize the result set as a whole. For example, Fig. 2 visualizes the most common art object materials for the selected subset of data (i.e., Ateneum Art Museum's collections) as a pie chart, while Fig. 3 visualizes a temporal aspect of the data, the years the creation processes of works have been started, on a timeline.

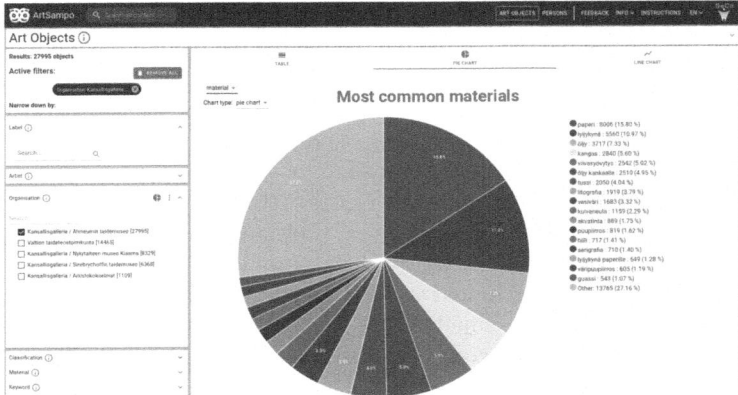

Fig. 2. A pie chart visualization showcasing the most common materials for works belonging to the Ateneum Art Museum's collections

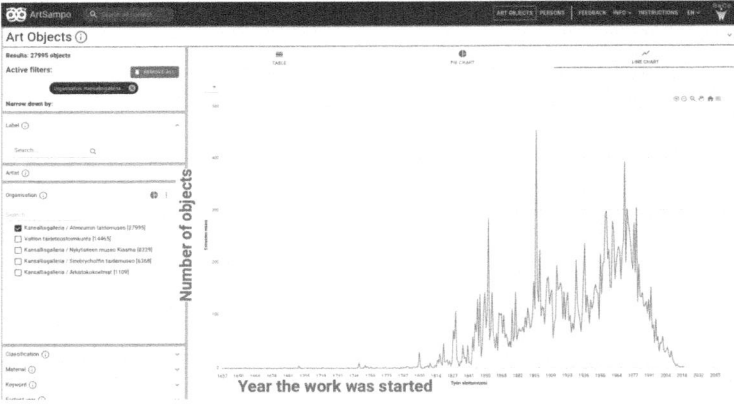

Fig. 3. A line chart visualization showcasing the distribution of years when the works belonging to Ateneum Art Museum's collections have been started by the artists

3   Discussion and Future Work

The ArtSampo adds Finnish art and art history to the growing number of Finnish Cultural Heritage (CH) "Sampo" KGs and portals. Our plan is to expand the current data included in the KG by integrating openly available data from other Finnish museums and galleries as well as from international collections featuring Finnish art. With the new UI for faceted searching, browsing, and analyzing the data, the collection contents are more accessible to the common art museum visitor, DH researcher, and museum curator in comparison to publishing the data dump and using the current legacy search system online[9].

---

[9] https://www.kansallisgalleria.fi/en/search.

An integral part of the ARTSAMPO project is to connect it to other data sources, such as other Sampos, Wikidata and ULAN, to contextually enrich the existing data. For example, biographies about 1,900 of the 6,400 artists can be found in other Sampo KGs, such as BiographySampo [4]. In CoCoSampo[10] [7], there is a letter correspondence KG of more than 10,000 letters of Finnish artists from the archives of the Finnish Art Society and the Finnish National Gallery. Outside links to, e.g., Wikidata can be extracted using person instances from Sampo KGs where these links are already available.

Another aspect of the project is to look into automatic content description by analyzing the available images and generating iconographic descriptions of those to supplement the possibly already-existing keywords that have been used for those particular art objects. The goal is to release the finalized KG from the project as LOD for use in research on the Linked Data Finland[11] platform.

Acknowledgements. This work has received partial funding from the European Union – NextGenerationEU instrument and is funded by the Research Council of Finland under grant number P3C3I6. Computing resources provided by the CSC – IT Center for Science were used in our work.

References

1. Couprie, L.D.: Iconclass: an iconographic classification system. Art Libr. J. **8**(2), 32–49 (1983)
2. Delmas-Glass, E., Sanderson, R.: Fostering a community of pharos scholars through the adoption of open standards. Art Libr. J. **45**(1), 19–23 (2020)
3. Hyvönen, E.: Digital humanities on the semantic web: Sampo model and portal series. Semant. Web **14**(4), 729–744 (2023)
4. Hyvönen, E., et al.: BiographySampo – publishing and enriching biographies on the semantic web for digital humanities research. In: Hitzler, P., et al. (eds.) ESWC 2019. LNCS, vol. 11503, pp. 574–589. Springer, Cham (2019). https://doi.org/10.1007/978-3-030-21348-0_37
5. Ikkala, E., Hyvönen, E., Rantala, H., Koho, M.: Sampo-UI: a full stack JavaScript framework for developing semantic portal user interfaces. Semant. Web J. **13**(1), 69–84 (2022). https://doi.org/10.3233/SW-210428
6. Tunkelang, D.: Faceted Search. Morgan & Claypool Publishers, San Rafael (2009)
7. Tuominen, J., et al.: Constellations of correspondence: a linked data service and portal for studying large and small networks of epistolary exchange in the grand duchy of Finland. In: CEUR Workshop Proceedings, vol. 3232, pp. 415–423. RWTH Aachen University (2022)

---

[10] https://seco.cs.aalto.fi/projects/coco/.
[11] https://www.ldf.fi/.

Towards Semantic Annotation
for Scientific Datasets

Alsayed Algergawy[1,2(✉)] (iD), Hamdi Hamed[1] (iD), Sven Thiel[1] (iD),
and Birgitta König-Ries[1,3] (iD)

[1] Heinz-Nixdorf Chair for Distributed Information Systems, Institute for Computer
Science, University of Jena, Jena, Germany
{alsayed.algergawy,hamdi.hamed,sven.thiel,
birgitta.koenig-ries}@uni-jena.de
[2] Chair of Data and Knowledge Engineering, University of Passau, Passau, Germany
[3] German Centre for Integrative Biodiversity Research (iDiv), Leipzig, Germany

Abstract. Semantic Web resources provide essential means to support dataset search, findability and interoperability. This becomes especially important in long-running and large scale collaborative projects, as semantic annotations promote a common understanding of central terms within the project. To this end, in this paper, we introduce a new tool developed to (semi-)automatically annotate scientific datasets collected within the framework of CRC AquaDiva (http://www.aquadiva.uni-jena.de/). To validate the powerful data annotation, we demonstrate the deployment of data annotation to enhance dataset search and analysis.

1 Introduction

As the complexity and amount of data collected within the context of long-running and large scale projects, e.g. the Collaborative Research Center (CRC) AquaDiva, increases there is a growing need to make use of semantic web methods to standardize data. The annotation of scientific datasets with ontology entities provides unique opportunities to improve data findability and interoperability [4]. To demonstrate the importance of semantic annotation for scientific data, we introduce a simple example in Fig. 1a. It represents a set of samples (*samp_ID*) collected at different locations (*loc*) and at different dates (*date*) and times (*time*). From each sample, a number of observations have been measured, such as *pH* and *Fe2+*. After the dataset has been stored into the associated data portal, a new user requests datasets about "observations referring to the alkaline milieu", but as expected she will not get any answer. However, if the dataset were correctly annotated by a semantic resource, e.g. an ontology as shown in Fig. 1b, the system would be able to answer the user query using a simple reasoner. However, providing such annotations is not trivial; thus tool support is needed.

In this work, we introduce a such (semi-)automated tool that allows dataset owners to annotate their datasets during the upload process. Furthermore, the

A. Meroño Peñuela et al. (Eds.): ESWC 2024, LNCS 15344, pp. 164–167, 2025.
https://doi.org/10.1007/978-3-031-78952-6_19

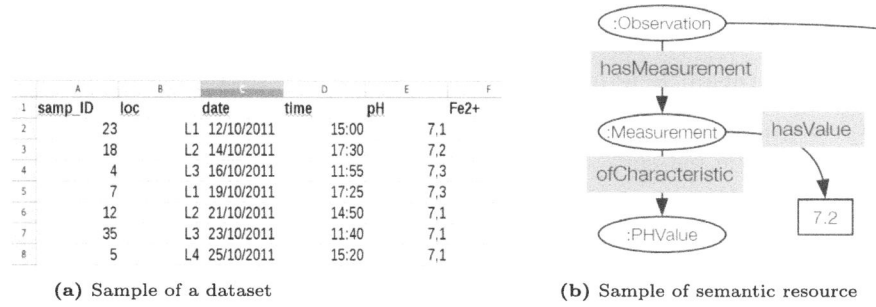

(a) Sample of a dataset   (b) Sample of semantic resource

Fig. 1. Sample example

tool supports editing and modifying existing annotations to correct and enhance the dataset interpretation. We develop our own domain-specific ontology, called AquaDiva Ontology, *ADOn*, as the semantic resource used for annotation. To demonstrate the deployment of the annotation tool, we describe its use to enhance dataset search and semantic analysis.

2   Methodology

A dataset is defined as a tuple of primary data and metadata organized for a specific purpose. The primary data represents the actual data organized according to a specific structure, called *data structure*. Each data structure consists of a set of data attributes, each data attribute has a name, datatype, (optional) unit, and description. Each tuple in the primary data is a collection of data cells containing the actual data values (called *data points*) [2]. The metadata contains information about the data owner, data curators, the methodology used to produce primary data, etc. In the implementation, we are going to annotate data attributes of available datasets with corresponding concepts from the domain-specific ontology (*ADOn*). In the following, we are going to elaborate more on two main components: *ontology development* and *annotation scheme*.

2.1   Ontology Development

To develop the domain specific ontology for the CRC AquaDiva, we make use of the fusion/merge strategy, where the new ontology is developed by assembling and reusing one or more (parts of) existing ontologies. To this end, we make use of the available resources in the project, such as project proposals, as well as we collected numerous research (competency) questions from the project scientists. We analyzed these resources and extracted main terms that cover the project domains, such as ecology, biology and aquatic. These terms have been used as input to the JOYCE tool [3] implemented within the project. The current

AquaDiva ontology (*ADOn*) has 78.840 axioms, 8.892 concepts, and 245 object properties.

2.2 Annotation Scheme

Data annotation is the process of associating a dataset component with a concept from the *ADOn* ontology. It is possible by using this annotation to search and explore data repositories as it links collection of datasets in a data repository to well-defined concepts. However, annotating scientific datasets is a hard process, as it is mandatory to not only link the data attribute with a concept, but also it is required to identify the data attribute context. Consider, two datasets $\mathcal{DS}_1$ and $\mathcal{DS}_2$ stored in a data repository, e.g., the AquaDiva data repository. The first dataset $\mathcal{DS}_1$ contains `weather and soil monitoring` data. It has a data structure with 50 data attributes including *"soil temperature"* annotated with the concepts soil (http://purl.obolibrary.org/obo/ENVO_00001998) and characteristic temperature (http://purl.obolibrary.org/obo/PATO_0000146). The second dataset $\mathcal{DS}_2$ provides information about `soil moisture` in the Hainich forest. $\mathcal{DS}_2$ has a data structure with 13 data attributes. The *"mean_theta_forestbottom"* data attribute is also annotated with the concept soil and the characteristic soil moisture (http://www.aquadiva.uni-jena.de/ad-ontology/ad-ontology.0.0/ad-ontology-characteristics.owl#SoilMoisture). Analyzing the dataset annotation, a possible relationship of the two datasets $\mathcal{DS}_1$ and $\mathcal{DS}_2$ can be determined.

Once we have the AquaDiva ontology, we can use it to annotate datasets on the data portal. We provide two ways for the annotation:

- During dataset upload: The first option is to support the annotation of a dataset during the uploading process. To this end, we collect needed information, such as data attribute' name, data types, and description (if available) to create a recommended list of concepts from the AquaDiva ontology. The list is created by computing the relatedness of a data attribute with ontology concepts by measuring the similarity between collected information and context information of ontology concepts, such as concept' label and definition. To compute this similarity, we make use of three different similarity measures, Levenstein, Jaro, and Jaccard, as each can compute the similarity from one aspect. As shown in Fig. 2, the recommended list of concepts are shown to the user (assuming that the person who uploads the dataset has enough knowledge to achieve the annotation task). The figure shows that the sample dataset shown in Fig. 1 is being uploaded through the data portal. During the uploading process we annotate the dataset as shown in Fig. 2. For example, the data attribute "samp_ID" has a list of recommended annotations, each associated with a score. After that, the user can either select a concept from the list or select another concept from the ontology.
- After uploading dataset: In some cases, the user who uploads the dataset does not have enough knowledge to annotate the dataset, so we need to manually annotate the dataset and then we update the annotation tables.

Furthermore, the annotation tool supports editing the existing annotations.

2.3   Semantic Annotation Deployment

To demonstrate the effectiveness and usability of semantic annotations to datasets collected in the AquaDiva project, we briefly outline two main applications:

- Semantic search: using the annotation we can move from keyword search to semantic search looking for not only the requested term but also for its context and the intended meaning for the user request. Furthermore, it supports the possibility to search through the term hierarchy.
- Dataset linking and exploration [1]: In this application, we classify a given dataset into a domain topic. With this topic, we then extract hidden links between different datasets in the repository making use of machine learning and semantic annotation.

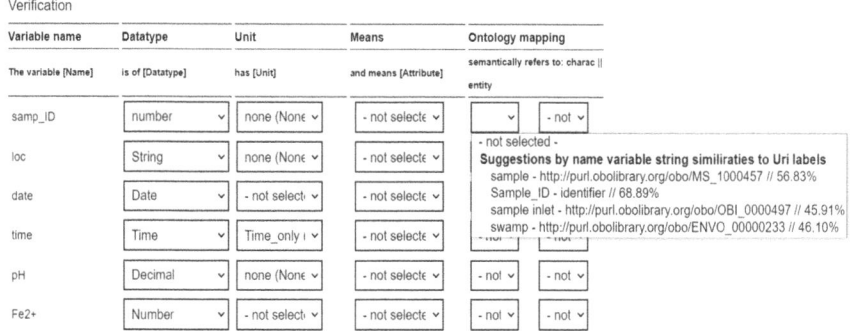

Fig. 2. Annotation process

Acknowledgments. This work has been funded by the *Deutsche Forschungsgemeinschaft (DFG)* as part of CRC 1076 AQUADIVA (Projectnumber 218627073).

References

1. Algergawy, A., Hamed, H., König-Ries, B.: Towards scientific data synthesis using deep learning and semantic web. In: Verborgh, R., et al. (eds.) ESWC 2021. LNCS, vol. 12739, pp. 54–59. Springer, Cham (2021). https://doi.org/10.1007/978-3-030-80418-3_10
2. Chamanara, J., Owonibi, M., Algergawy, A., Gerlach, R.: An extensible conceptual model for tabular scientific datasets. In: The Fifth International Conference on Advances in Information Mining and Management (2015)
3. Faessler, E., Klan, F., Algergawy, A., König-Ries, B., Hahn, U.: Selecting and tailoring ontologies with JOYCE. In: Ciancarini, P., et al. (eds.) EKAW 2016. LNCS (LNAI), vol. 10180, pp. 114–118. Springer, Cham (2017). https://doi.org/10.1007/978-3-319-58694-6_12
4. Paton, N.W., Chen, J., Wu, Z.: Dataset discovery and exploration: a survey. ACM Comput. Surv. **56**(4), 1–37 (2023)

A Framework for Question Answering on Knowledge Graphs Using Large Language Models

Caio Viktor S. Avila[1]([✉]), Marco A. Casanova[2], and Vânia M.P. Vidal[1]

[1] Federal University of Ceará, Fortaleza 60440-900, Brazil
caioviktor@alu.ufc.br, vvidal@lia.ufc.br
[2] Department of Informatics, Pontifical Catholic University of Rio de Janeiro,
Rio de Janeiro 22451-900, Brazil
casanova@inf.puc-rio.br

Abstract. Currently, large language models (LLMs) are the state of the art for pre-trained language models. LLMs have been applied to many tasks, including question and answering over Knowledge Graphs (KGs) and text-to-SPARQL, that is, the translation of Natural Language (NL) questions to SPARQL queries. This paper introduces Auto-KGQA, an autonomous domain-independent framework based on LLMs for text-to-SPARQL. The framework uses as context, fragments of the KG, which the LLM uses to translate the user's NL question to a SPARQL query on the KG. Finally, it generates a natural language response for the user, based upon the result of the execution of SPARQL query over the KG.

Keywords: Question Answering · Knowledge Graph · Large Language Model

1 Introduction

Question Answering. (QA) systems are computational systems that can answer questions typically asked in Linguagem Natural (LN) [5]. Among the types of QA systems, *Knowledge Graph Question Answering* (KGQA) systems stand out for their ability to generate curated and deep responses. KGQA systems are QA systems that are based on a *Knowledge Graph* (KG) [9].

Currently, Large Language Models (LLMs) are the state of the art for pre-trained language models. LLMs achieve good results in tasks like question and answering over KGs and text-to-SPARQL [2], which opens an opportunity to develop KGQA systems based on LLMs [8]. However, for the LLM to be able to generate SPARQL queries on a specific KG it is necessary that it has knowledge about the vocabulary and structure of the KG being queried. A possible strategy for passing on such knowledge could be passing the KG via prompt, exploiting the LLM's ability to learn with the context present in the prompt (in-context learning) [3]. However, given the size limitation of the LLM prompt, passing the

A. Meroño Peñuela et al. (Eds.): ESWC 2024, LNCS 15344, pp. 168–172, 2025.
https://doi.org/10.1007/978-3-031-78952-6_20

entire KG proves to be unfeasible in real-world scenarios. Thus, fragments must be selected, forming a sub-graph, relevant to the user's original question to be passed to the LLM, via prompt.

This paper introduces Auto-KGQA, an autonomous domain-independent framework based on LLMs for text-to-SPARQL. Given a KG K and a user's NL question Q, the framework selects fragments of the T-Box and A-Box of K, providing these as contextual input for the Large Language Model (LLM). Auto-KGQA proceeds to generate n potential SPARQL queries that interpret Q, subsequently selecting the most suitable query S based on the outcomes derived from executing these queries on K. Finally, it generates a natural language response for the user, based upon the result of the execution of S over K. The key feature of Auto-KGQA is its ability to select smaller KG fragments without prior knowledge of the expected outcome, thus reducing the number of input tokens to the LLM.

The remainder of this article is structured as follows. Section 2 covers related work. Section 3 introduces Auto-KGQA. Finally, Sect. 4 contains the conclusions.

2   Related Work

An approach to translate NL queries to SPARQL, called SGPT, is proposed in [7]. SGPT encodes a vector of linguistic embedding features, such as parts-of-speech (POS) and the dependency tree, in addition to the corresponding sub-graph of the question. Then, the embeddings are passed as training to a Transformers model based on GPT-2 to generate the SPARQL query.

The *Knowledge Solver* (KSL) paradigm was proposed in [4] to teach LLMs to fetch essential knowledge from external knowledge bases. In this approach, the LLM receives as input question-and-answer pairs (of the multiple choice type), where the LLM task is to learn to select the KG subgraph required to answer the original NL question.

SPARQLGEN is a one-shot approach that generates SPARQL queries by enhancing LLMs with context in a single prompt [6]. The prompt includes the question, an RDF subgraph needed for the query, and an example SPARQL query for a different question. Subgraph selection for each question is done through reverse engineering of expected correct SPARQL queries.

To the best of our knowledge, LLM-based approaches already receive a sub-graph of the KG relevant to the question as input or use information from the expected response to derive it. Therefore, this current work has the advantage of being able to autonomously select the relevant sub-graph, given only the user's question.

3   Auto-KGQA

The framework[1] is composed of six components: (1) Chat Web Interface, an instant messenger web interface for sending and receiving messages to the system

---

[1] https://github.com/CaioViktor/Auto-KGQA.

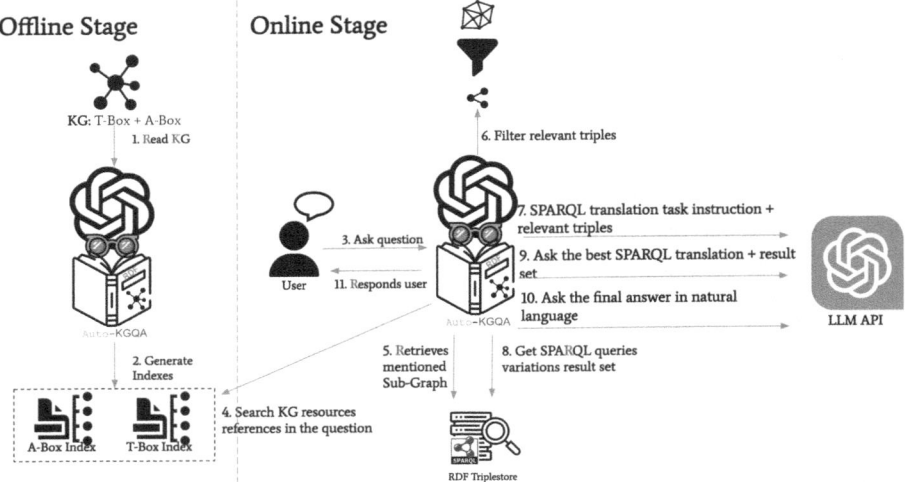

Fig. 1. Auto-KGQA framework

implemented in React; (2) Conversation API, question processing system accessible via API in Flask Python; (3) Knowledge Graph Endpoint; (4) Resources indexes, indices used to find references to KG resources in natural language questions; (5) Example dataset of queries collected during users interactions; and (6) LLM API (ChatGPT by default).

Below is a brief description of the processes carried out in the framework depicted in the Fig. 1. A more detailed explanation and initial experiments of the approach, can be found in [1].

Off-line Stage. The offline stage receives the KG (T-Box and A-Box) as input via a SPARQL endpoint and creates two indexes, used in the online stage to find references to KG resources in the input question. The first index generates mappings from labels of classes and properties to their URIs. The second index generates mappings from A-Box (instances) resource labels to their URIs.

The indexes generated in this step can be of three types: (1) full-text search engine, using the Whoosh ; (2) Sentences vector embedding based, using FAISS library ; (3) DBpedia Spotlight, using the DBpedia API. The first two indices can be used in any KG, both to index the T-box and the A-box. In turn, the third party can only be used when performing queries on DBpedia, indexing only its A-box.

On-line Stage. Figure 1 shows the workflow followed during the online stage. At this stage, the system uses the indexes created in the offline stage to find references to KG resources present in the user's question Qi (step 3). Then, for each referenced resource, all its triples are recovered, along with those of their neighbors up to depth 2 in the KG (step 4), building a set of Ti triples. Next, the framework builds the **Query Sub-graph** (presented in more detail in the next section), Gq, a subgraph of Ti that will be passed to LLM to build the SPARQL query . In the next step, a request is made to LLM to generate five translation variations of Qi to SPARQL over Gq (step 5). For each valid query generated by LLM, the system retrieves the result set from its execution on the KG endpoint (step 6). Next, the LLM is asked to choose the SPARQL translation that best represents the original query, also considering the previously obtained result sets (step 7). Finally, the system asks LLM to generate the final response in NL based on the SPARQL query and its result set selected in the previous step (step 8).

Query Sub-graph Construction. The selected triples, Ti, are filtered to remove triples irrelevant to the question Qi. For this, all triples of Ti are grouped by subject and property , then, for each group, a single phrase will be generated that represents a pseudo verbalization of these triples. The generated sentences follows the structure "**Subject verb complement**". The subject and verb will be formed by the labels of the resources in the original triples, while the complement will be a list of values representing the different RDF objects of each triple of the group, separated by "commas". When the RDF object is an RDF resource, it will be represented in the sentence by its label, when it is a literal, it will be used directly in the sentence. Next, the embedding vectors of all sentences are computed, which will be used to construct a langchain's faiss index, which will be used to get the sentences closest to Qi, Sc. The triples associated with Sc generate a set of triples relevant to the question, called Tr. The resources referenced in Tr are then passed as input to run a steiner-tree algorithm on Ti, to construct a connected graph Gc. Finally, the Ti triples are joined to the Gc triples, generating the Query Sub-graph, a connected graph with the most relevant triples for queries, called Gq. The Gq triples are then serialized to Turtle RDF notation so that they can be passed as a string to the LLM.

Demonstration. The Fig. 2 shows a demonstration of interaction via the Auto-KGQA web interface (the image was originally one vertically). In this demo, a KG described in [1] and available in the project's github repository is used, about which questions are asked in sequence about a specific resource (someone called "John"). At the link[2] you will find a video with a demonstration in greater detail.

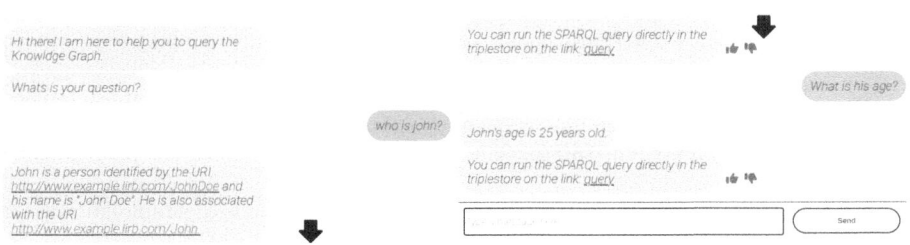

Fig. 2. Auto-KGQA interface demonstration.

---

[2] https://youtu.be/GFSHySDitzU.

4   Conclusions

This paper introduced Auto-KGQA, an autonomous domain-independent framework based on LLMs for text-to-SPARQL. The main goal of Auto-KGQA is the selection of smaller KG fragments thereby reducing the number of tokens passed as input to the LLM. Experiments with Auto-KGQA suggest that the framework achieved this goal, without sacrificing performance.

Future work includes experiments using opensource LLMs in place of OpenAI's ChatGPT, as well as using a RAG engine to utilize examples acquired via user feedback to improve system performance.

Acknowledgment. This work was partly funded by FAPERJ under grants E-26/200.834/2021, by CAPES under grant 88881.134081/2016-01 and 88882. 164913/2010-01, and by CNPq under grant 305.587/2021-8.

References

1. Avila, C.V.S., Vidal, V.M., Franco, W., Casanova, M.A.: Experiments with text-to-sparql based on chatgpt. In: 2024 IEEE 18th International Conference on Semantic Computing (ICSC). pp. 277–284. IEEE (2024)
2. Brown, T., Mann, B., Ryder, N., Subbiah, M., Kaplan, J.D., Dhariwal, P., Neelakantan, A., Shyam, P., Sastry, G., Askell, A., et al.: Language models are few-shot learners. Adv. Neural. Inf. Process. Syst. **33**, 1877–1901 (2020)
3. Dong, Q., Li, L., Dai, D., Zheng, C., Wu, Z., Chang, B., Sun, X., Xu, J., Sui, Z.: A survey for in-context learning. arXiv preprint arXiv:2301.00234 (2022)
4. Feng, C., Zhang, X., Fei, Z.: Knowledge solver: Teaching llms to search for domain knowledge from knowledge graphs. arXiv preprint arXiv:2309.03118 (2023)
5. Hirschman, L., Gaizauskas, R.: Natural language question answering: the view from here. natural language engineering **7**(4), 275–300 (2001)
6. Kovriguina, L., et al.: SPARQLGEN: one-shot prompt-based approach for SPARQL query generation. In: Proc. of the Posters and Demo Track of the 19th International Conference on Semantic Systems, Leipzing, Germany, September 20 to 22, 2023. CEUR Workshop Proceedings, vol. 3526. CEUR-WS.org (2023), https://ceur-ws.org/Vol-3526/paper-08.pdf
7. Rony, M.R.A.H., Kumar, U., Teucher, R., Kovriguina, L., Lehmann, J.: Sgpt: a generative approach for sparql query generation from natural language questions. IEEE Access **10**, 70712–70723 (2022)
8. Tan, Y., Min, D., Li, Y., Li, W., Hu, N., Chen, Y., Qi, G.: Can chatgpt replace traditional kbqa models? an in-depth analysis of the question answering performance of the gpt llm family. In: International Semantic Web Conference. pp. 348–367. Springer (2023)
9. Yani, M., Krisnadhi, A.A.: Challenges, techniques, and trends of simple knowledge graph question answering: a survey. Information **12**(7), 271 (2021)

KinGVisher – Knowledge Graph Visualizer

Andreas Both[1,2], Aleksandr Perevalov[1(✉)], and Aleksandr Gashkov[1]

[1] Leipzig University of Applied Sciences, Leipzig, Germany
aleksandr.perevalov@htwk-leipzig.de
[2] DATEV eG, Nuremberg, Germany

Abstract. Knowledge Graphs rely on conceptional knowledge (TBox) and concrete data instances (ABox). Both types of statements are represented by RDF triples, hence, they are located in the same data storage. As this is an advantage from the aspect of generalization, it might become difficult to distinguish between the purpose of the triples when exploring a knowledge graph. Additionally, the success of knowledge graphs leads to larger data sets that might make it also harder to identify and recognize the information of interest, its connections, and patterns. KinGVisher was designed and developed as a visual explorer for knowledge graphs, providing automatic graph layouts and supporting users in creating a clear view of the knowledge graph. We publish this as a full-fledged, open-sourced web application online, which is freely available to all users.

Keywords: Knowledge Graphs · Data Visualization · Graph Visualization · Data Exploration

1 Introduction

Visualizations are useful and necessary to improve the accessibility and under-standability of any data. This is particularly the case when dealing with large amounts of data, for instance, RDF knowledge graphs (KGs), in which distribution, differentiation, and stored content are constantly growing. This is not only the case for the general-domain KGs (e.g., DBpedia [1] and Wikidata [7]), but also for the domain-specific ones, as their structures are often difficult to understand. However, the advantage of linked data, which lies in reusing existing vocabularies and creating many instances of the same classes, might become problematic when many triples contain the same resource, and therefore a visualization might become heavily centralized (e.g., in DBpedia, `dbo:Place` is currently part of 804796 triples) or tightly packed. In turn, this may affect resource consumption and efficiency, especially if the visualizations are created in a web browser. Based on this observation, there is a need for a convenient KG visualization tool easily accessible to its users. We set the following requirements for such a tool: (1) The data in a KG must be *filterable* so that the number and both expected resources and unexpected resources can be defined; (2) A visualization

A. Meroño Peñuela et al. (Eds.): ESWC 2024, LNCS 15344, pp. 173–177, 2025.
https://doi.org/10.1007/978-3-031-78952-6_21

of a KG needs to provide access to *layout configurations*, s.t., users can adapt to many different scenarios; (3) A visualization needs to be enabled to work with *large knowledge graphs* (e.g., DBpedia or Wikidata). Additionally, for the sake of applicability and standardization, the tool should use only SPARQL to interact with a KG.

In this work, we introduce KinGVisher – a web application for efficient KG visualizations that supports the aforementioned requirements and enables users to dive into the data like a Kingfisher[1]. We release our tool as a full-fledged web application, which is freely available to all users online[2].

Several implementations exist dedicated to the visualizations of KGs and linked data. For example, work by Kerdjoudj et al. [5], Lohmann et al. [6], Ghosh [3] et al., the non-dynamic UML-styled visualization OWLGrEd [2], the domain-specific SNIK Graph [4], or a KG explorer by the Zazuko company [8]. In contrast to these approaches, we favor a dynamic view of the KG's data that can be filtered and searched interactively (and would not focus on the TBox visualization). Therefore, we define the following features to let the users stay in control of their visualizations: *Whitelist properties* – a list of properties of the knowledge graph can be defined that only should be shown in the visualization, *Blacklist properties* – a list of properties of the knowledge graph can be defined that should not be shown in the visualization, and *Important resources* – a list of resources of the knowledge graph that has to be part of the visualization, i.e., they are used as a starting point of the exploration.

As our approach is using SPARQL only, *the exploration of a KG is to be done iteratively* (in particular, if users have defined important resources), which is done by creating SPARQL queries based on previously discovered resources.

2   Demonstration of KinGVisher

Our demonstrator (cf. Fig. 1) provides the option of connecting to any public SPARQL endpoint and optionally defining a specific graph (not required for Wikidata or DBpedia, but common while using triplestores like Stardog[3]) ① of which the data should be evaluated. A core attribute is the user-defined number of maximal edges ② to keep the number of visualized triples within reasonable limits. Several visualization parameters are provided for directly controlling the layout for the current data ③. Moreover, several non-standard visualization configuration parameters are provided ④:

– Show resource labels: in case of being activated, no labels are shown in the visualization to reduce the number of rendered elements.
– Hierarchical layout: might improve the rendering of currently selected subgraphs with chains of connected edges (i.e., high depth).

---

[1] cf. https://en.wikipedia.org/wiki/Kingfisher.

[2] https://wse-research.org/kingvisher/.

[3] https://www.stardog.com/.

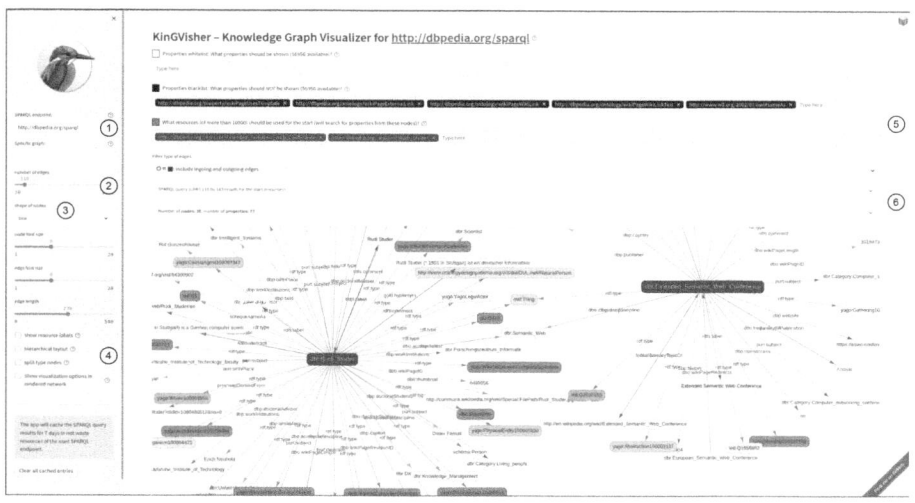

Fig. 1. Screenshot of the KinGVisher UI using the DBpedia SPARQL endpoint.

– Split type nodes: while being activated, for all triples of the form _:a rdf:type ?type, the type nodes (?type) are intentionally rendered separately as it might lead otherwise to a centralization around types nodes.
– Show visualization options: This will provide an additional control panel (below the visualization) for defining parameters of the used rendering to create customized visualizations. All parameters of the renderer are provided here for individual adjustments by users (e.g., for solving rendering problems).

Additionally, the definition of blacklist (s.t., users can remove unwanted properties that might pollute the graph visualization) and whitelist properties (s.t., users can focus on just a limited set of properties) is possible ⑤. It is worth mentioning here that it is also possible to define specific, "important" resources that should always be included in the visualization. In this case, the knowledge graph is searched iteratively (using SPARQL) so that connections between these resources can be determined and displayed. These nodes of the visualization are colorized using solid blue. All other nodes are colorized by a shade of green depending on the maximum calculated from the input degree and output degree of the node, i.e., the more important nodes are displayed in a darker color (s.t., users can identify the well-connected nodes easily).

The internal process is made transparent by providing the used SPARQL queries ⑥, a short statistics of the found properties is shown (that can be fold-out to see the ranking of the properties by appearance in the currently shown sub-graph), as well as the ingoing and outgoing edges of a (clicked) node.

Note, that the performance is highly dependent on the responsiveness of the SPARQL endpoint as – for the sake of general applicability – only SPARQL queries are used to retrieve data. A rudimentary cache has also been integrated to minimize the triggered workload on the SPARQL endpoint which is particularly speeding up the runtime regarding very large knowledge graphs.

Other useful functionalities include the ability to export the image of the rendered Knowledge Graph as a PNG file and to share the current configuration via a URI.

The implementation was done using the Python library Streamlit[4] that provides an integrated technology stack for frontend and backend while serving as a bridge between Python and the React[5] library (JavaScript/TypeScript) to generate a

The application is available as an online demo[6] and pre-bundled as Docker images published on Dockerhub[7] for free usage. The source code is available[8] on GitHub and is published under the MIT open-source license.

3   Conclusions

In this paper, we presented KinGVisher – a web-based Knowledge Graph Visualizer – that can interact with any available SPARQL endpoint. Our demonstrator serves to help users interactively visualize and explore knowledge graphs. In contrast to other visualization tools, our implementation is by design capable of working with data (iteratively) retrieved from very large knowledge graphs. Due to the challenges of creating visualizations for (large) knowledge graphs, our tool offers many configuration options to put users in control (e.g., while allowing them to manipulate the complete configuration parameters). Many of these options were never introduced in other tools. Hence, we assume several benefits for the research community, e.g., while working with large knowledge graphs where filtering resources and properties is helpful, or for better understanding the patterns and data available in the context of particular data artifacts of a given knowledge graph.

Acknowledgments. This work has been supported in part by the German ministry BMWi under grant 16DTM107B (*ASAGuR*) and a research project of ITZBund (Germany): "Entwicklung und Erforschung von IT-basierten Lösungen im Rahmen des ChatBot-Frameworks des Bundes (Question-Answering-Komponenten zur Erweiterung des ChatBot-Frameworks)".

References

1. Auer, S., Bizer, C., Kobilarov, G., Lehmann, J., Cyganiak, R., Ives, Z.: DBpedia: a nucleus for a web of open data. In: Aberer, K., et al. (eds.) ASWC/ISWC -2007. LNCS, vol. 4825, pp. 722–735. Springer, Heidelberg (2007). https://doi.org/10.1007/978-3-540-76298-0_52

---

[4] https://streamlit.io/.
[5] https://react.dev/.
[6] https://wse-research.org/kingvisher-knowledge-graph-visualizer/.
[7] https://hub.docker.com/r/wseresearch/knowledge-graph-visualizer.
[8] https://github.com/WSE-research/KinGVisher-Knowledge-Graph-Visualizer.

2. Čerāns, K., Ovčiņņikova, J., Liepiņš, R., Grasmanis, M.: Extensible visualizations of ontologies in OWLGrEd. In: Hitzler, P., et al. (eds.) ESWC 2019. LNCS, vol. 11762, pp. 191–196. Springer, Cham (2019). https://doi.org/10.1007/978-3-030-32327-1_38
3. Ghosh, D., Rajabi, E.: KG-Visual: a tool for visualizing RDF knowledge graphs. In: Garoufallou, E., Ovalle-Perandones, M.-A., Vlachidis, A. (eds.) MTSR 2021. CCIS, vol. 1537, pp. 126–136. Springer, Cham (2022). https://doi.org/10.1007/978-3-030-98876-0_11
4. Jahn, F., Höffner, K., Schneider, B., Lörke, A., Pause, T., Ammenwerth, E., Winter, A.: The SnIK graph: visualization of a medical informatics ontology. In: MEDINFO 2019: Health and Wellbeing e-Networks for All, pp. 1941–1942. IOS Press (2019). https://doi.org/10.3233/SHTI190724
5. Kerdjoudj, F., Curé, O.: RDF knowledge graph visualization from a knowledge extraction system. In: Joint Proceedings of the 1st International Workshop on Summarizing and Presenting Entities and Ontologies and the 3rd International Workshop on Human Semantic Web Interfaces (SumPre 2015, HSWI 2015) co-located with the 12th ESWC, 2015. CEUR Workshop Proceedings, vol. 1556. CEUR-WS.org (2015)
6. Lohmann, S., Link, V., Marbach, E., Negru, S.: WebVOWL: web-based visualization of ontologies. In: Lambrix, P., et al. (eds.) EKAW 2014. LNCS (LNAI), vol. 8982, pp. 154–158. Springer, Cham (2015). https://doi.org/10.1007/978-3-319-17966-7_21
7. Vrandečić, D., Krötzsch, M.: Wikidata: a free collaborative knowledgebase. Commun. ACM **57**(10), 78–85 (2014). https://doi.org/10.1145/2629489
8. Zazuko: Graph Explorer (2024). https://github.com/zazuko/graph-explorer, Accessed 01 Mar 2024

Gotta Catch'em All: From Data Silos to a Knowledge Graph

Oleksandra Bruns[1,2], Linnaea Söhn[3], Tabea Tietz[1,2(✉)], Jonatan Jalle Steller[3], Etienne Posthumus[1], Torsten Schrade[3], and Harald Sack[1,2]

[1] FIZ Karlsruhe – Leibniz Institute for Information Infrastructure, Hermann-von-Helmholtz-Platz 1, 76344 Eggenstein-Leopoldshafen, Germany
{oleksandra.bruns,tabea.tietz,harald.sack}@fiz-karlsruhe.de
[2] Karlsruhe Institute of Technology (AIFB), Kaiserstr. 89, 76133 Karlsruhe, Germany
[3] Academy of Sciences and Literature Mainz, Geschwister-Scholl-Straße 2, 55131 Mainz, Germany
{linnaea.sohn,jonatan.steller,torsten.schrade}@adwmainz.de

Abstract. Diverse research questions, perspectives, standards and formats across culture subject areas have led to the emergence of numerous data silos. NFDI4Culture seeks to overcome this by building a unified KG, facilitating enhanced discoverability and interoperability of distributed and heterogeneous research data. This paper outlines a pipeline for accessing and harvesting cultural heritage meta data from legacy repositories, it discusses the development of a lightweight ontology to facilitate interoperability.

Keywords: research data · knowledge graphs · infrastructure

1 Introduction

Behind every artifact lies a story that can only be uncovered when placed within the context of its cultural and historical surroundings. NFDI4Culture[1] is a consortium within the framework of the German national research data infrastructure programme (NFDI[2]) with the goal to establish an information infrastructure for cultural heritage (CH) research data. Its primary objective is to ensure the findability and interoperability of distributed and heterogeneous research data across five subject areas: architecture, art history, performing arts, musicology, and media sciences [1]. Currently, the consortium manages 68 data portals, which provide access to hundreds of diverse culture datasets[3]. This encompasses a diverse array of tangible and intangible data, ranging from architectural plans and art descriptions to music compositions, historical manuscripts and theatrical events. However the data is contextually related, each discipline approaches

---

[1] https://nfdi4culture.de/.
[2] https://www.nfdi.de.
[3] https://nfdi4culture.de/resources/dataportals.

A. Meroño Peñuela et al. (Eds.): ESWC 2024, LNCS 15344, pp. 178–182, 2025.
https://doi.org/10.1007/978-3-031-78952-6_22

data management from its own unique perspective, answering different research questions. This results in the use of a range of standards and formats tailored to specific community needs. Such diversity enhances CH understanding, offering detailed data descriptions and facilitating research. Yet, it poses challenges for data discovery, harvesting, and integration across subjects.

One of the objectives of the NFDI4Culture is to build a Knowledge Graph (KG) to aggregate diverse and isolated meta data from the research landscape and thereby enable discoverability, interoperability and reusability of CH data. One way to achieve this is, following the established initiatives in the cultural domain, e.g. DDB[4], Europeana[5], to build a centralised infrastructure that consolidates data in one location. However, maintaining and updating such a centralized system is very resource-intensive, requiring data providers to regularly compile and contribute their data using a shared standard to access current content. Alternatively, federated infrastructures prioritize a shared API instead of shared formats. Thus, the data providers are required to create their own reliable endpoint that can be accessed and queried from the outside (e.g. CLARIN[6]). However, querying via federation can pose challenges for users, as, for the successful search, they need to be familiar with the various standards used across different data sources. Additionally, much of the data within NFDI4Culture still remains unindexed and inaccessible for querying and federation. It resides in isolated silos within legacy repositories, often challenging to even locate and harvest.

This paper reports on current efforts towards extending the NFDI4Culture-KG, in particular, it presents a KG-based workflow of harvesting research data from legacy repositories, indexing the data, and developing a lightweight ontology for data representation that facilitates easy access and search.

2   From Silos to the NFDI4Culture-KG

The NFDI4Culture-KG interconnects research data within NFDI4Culture. It comprises the Research Information Graph (RIG) and the Research Data Graph (RDG). While the RIG describes metadata about resources, e.g. publishers, contact points, standards, licences, data portals, the RDG aims to harvest and interconnect the content meta data of the resources, e.g. making individual items within data portals accessible for search. Taking into account the challenges and objectives of NFDI4Culture to aggregate and unify CH research data for improved accessibility and interoperability, an ETL (Extract, Transform, Load) environment has been designed. It consists of six modular workflow components, adaptable for independent use or within a comprehensive automated ingest routine. Once harvested and integrated, resources are accessible through a SPARQL endpoint[7] and SHMARQL[8] - a SPARQL endpoint explorer devel-

---

[4] https://www.deutsche-digitale-bibliothek.de/.
[5] https://www.europeana.eu/.
[6] https://www.clarin.eu/.
[7] https://nfdi4culture.de/sparql.
[8] https://nfdi.fiz-karlsruhe.de/shmarql.

oped in NFDI4Culture, as well as a dashboard[9] for analysis and visualizations. This section will shortly describe the components of the environment (for more details see[10]).

Step 1: Action. The goal of this step is to define a structured process for harvesting and transforming data feeds[11] into a standardized format compatible with the NFDI4Culture-KG. This involves creating an action RDF/Turtle file with schema.org-based step definitions, connecting the data feed to its metadata (in the RIG), and generating persistent identifiers for imported resources. Ensuring harmonisation and interoperability across harvested data requires mapping to a shared scheme, particularly due to a large amount of formats of sourced data such as CGIF [3], LIDO[12], MEI[13], and other unique annotation schemes. To address this, mapping to the Culture Ontology (see Sect. 3) is provided for each data format outside the pipeline's scope.

Step 2: Cleaning. To ensure harmonisation between the harvested data feed and associated data files while preventing conflicts with information in the consumed resources that may contradict action file definitions, triples are added or deleted based on the information in the action file.

Step 3: Update. After several procedures, e.g. status checks, branch switching, managing bulk operations, and supporting various modes, the changes are pushed to the repository.

Step 4: Stash. If changes in a data feed are pushed, data directories (often called "stashes") are automatically updated or created in response to changes in the data feed. The new version is then made available via a SPARQL endpoint.

Step 5: Endpoint. To prevent downtimes, the construction of a new endpoint is realized through a Docker-based delivery workflow. If a new endpoint must be built, environment variables are adjusted to reference the new container and port for initiating the deployment. Once the new SPARQL endpoint becomes operational, the old container is stopped and removed.

Step 6: Analysis. The last component provides statistics about the integrated data feeds through the Culture Knowledge Graph Dashboard. It supports data analysis and visualizations based on the execution of provided SPARQL queries.

3   Ontologies of NFDI4Culture

The primary objective of the NFDI4Culture-KG is to link research data across NFDI4Culture subject domains through the utilization of ontologies. Every NFDI consortium shares a commitment to creating an interoperable research data infrastructure for a consortium's specific domain. The NFDIcore ontology[14]

---

[9] https://nfdi4culture.de/go/kg-kitchen-dashboard.

[10] https://gitlab.rlp.net/adwmainz/nfdi4culture/knowledge-graph/culture-kg-kitchen.

[11] In the context of the ETL process, discussions often revolve around data feeds rather than datasets due to the emphasis on continuous streams.

[12] https://www.lido-schema.org/schema/latest/lido.html.

[13] https://music-encoding.org/.

[14] https://github.com/ISE-FIZKarlsruhe/nfdicore.

was developed to be used across consortia [2] to represent metadata about NFDI resources, e.g. persons, projects, data portals, etc., answering shared questions, e.g. "Who is a contact point of a resource?". To answer domain-specific research questions, the NFDIcore ontology is extended following a modular approach, as e.g. with the culture ontology module (CTO)[15]. This allows for providing additional metadata to describe culture resources, as e.g. property `cto:ddbAPI` enables linking a resource, e.g. a dataset, in the NFDI4Culture Portal to its corresponding entry in the German Digital Library (DDB).

While the RIG facilitates exploration and retrieval of index and metadata for NFDI4Culture resources, the primary objective of the RDG is to represent and interconnect the content of distributed data collections to address domain related research questions, e.g. "Which historical books are written by librettists and include prints showing the iconographic subject "Hercules at the Crossroads?" " [4]. The CTO provides semantics to achieve this level of research granularity in the RDG: the ontology establishes a connection between a data resource (stored and described in the RIG) and its individual component - `cto:DatafeedElement`. The ontology provides light-weight vocabulary for describing element types, subject concepts, and related concepts, including creative works, persons, locations, and temporal information by linking an element to the corresponding concepts in the external vocabularies such as GND[16], Wikidata[17], and ICONCLASS[18]. Additionally, for more detailed research, each data feed element is linked to its source file, where all the information contributed by a data provider is stored and represented using the domain-appropriate standard.

Compared to a generalist model like SCHEMA.org[19], the Culture Ontology (CTO) offers tailored advantages perfectly suited to the intricate landscape of cultural heritage research data. Specifically tailored to meet the unique requirements of the NFDI4Culture community, CTO allows for capturing the nuanced data requirements of each discipline while enabling interoperability across a wide array of cultural datasets. In contrast, utilizing domain-specific ontologies such as CIDOC-CRM[20] requires a comprehensive representation of cultural heritage information. While CIDOC-CRM provides a detailed framework, CTO distinguishes itself by its lightweight design, prioritizing flexibility and adaptability to the dynamic needs of the NFDI4Culture consortium. The primary objective of CTO is not to represent every fine-grained aspect of cultural objects, but rather to integrate the most relevant information essential for ensuring interoperability across cultural domains. This approach allows for efficient data management and harmonization while accommodating the diverse and evolving nature of cultural heritage research within the NFDI4Culture framework.

---

[15] https://gitlab.rlp.net/adwmainz/nfdi4culture/knowledge-graph/culture-ontology.
[16] https://www.dnb.de/EN/Professionell/Standardisierung/GND/gnd/_node.html.
[17] https://www.wikidata.org/.
[18] https://iconclass.org/.
[19] https://schema.org/.
[20] https://www.cidoc-crm.org/.

4   Conclusion

Cultural research data is critical for the understanding of our shared human history and preserving artifacts and sites. However, it is usually dispersed across multiple legacy systems that lack interoperability. In this paper, a KG-based workflow is presented for integrating cultural content into the NFDI4Culture and thus, improving its findability and accessibility.

Both the Culture Kitchen and the Culture Ontology (CTO) are significant steps towards addressing the challenge of integrating and harmonizing diverse data sources within NFDI4Culture. By providing a common vocabulary and framework for representing cultural data, the CTO ontology facilitates standardization and interoperability. Similarly, the Culture Kitchen environment offers a practical approach for data management and integration, providing tools and workflows for aggregating, harmonizing, and exploring cultural research data. Together, these efforts contribute to the ongoing process of improving accessibility and usability within the NFDI4Culture.

In future work, the focus is on the integration of further cultural research data into the NFDI4Culture-KG, further enhancing its findability and interoperability. Additionally, efforts will continue to improve the components of the NFDI4Culture infrastructure, including the SPARQL endpoint, dashboard, SHMARQL, and other tools, to enhance their usability and functionality to accomodate users' requirements.

Acknowledgements. This work is funded by Deutsche Forschungsgemeinschaft (DFG), project number 441958017.

References

1. Bruns, O., et al.: What's cooking in the NFDI4Culture kitchen? A KG-based research data integration workflow. In: 4th Workshop on Metadata and Research (objects) Management for Linked Open Science (DaMaLOS), co-located with ESWC (2024)
2. Sack, H., et al.: Knowledge graph based RDM solutions: NFDI4Culture - NFDI-MatWerk - NFDI4DataScience. In: 1st Conference on Research Data Infrastructure (2023)
3. Steller, J.J., et al.: Communities, harvesting, and CGIF: building the research data graph at NFDI4Culture. In: DHd2024: Quo Vadis (2024)
4. Tietz, T., et al.: From floppy disks to 5-Star LOD: FAIR research infrastructure for NFDI4Culture. In: 3rd Workshop on Metadata and Research (objects) Management for Linked Open Science (DaMaLOS), co-located with ESWC 2023. Publisso (2023)

The Helmholtz Knowledge Graph: Driving the Transition Towards a FAIR Data Ecosystem in the Helmholtz Association

Jens Bröder[1], Gabriel Preuß[2], Fiona D'Mello[1], Said Fathalla[1],
Volker Hofmann[1][✉], and Stefan Sandfeld[1]

[1] Forschungszentrum Jülich GmbH, Institute of Advanced Simulation - Materials
Data Science and Informatics (IAS-9), Aachen, Germany
{j.broeder,f.dmello,s.fathalla,v.hofmann,s.sandfeld}@fz-juelich.de
[2] Helmholtz-Zentrum Berlin für Materialien und Energie, Berlin, Germany
gabriel.preuss@helmholtz-berlin.de
https://ror.org/02nv7yv05

Abstract. The Helmholtz Knowledge Graph aggregates metadata
about digital assets and research output from the various institutional
and siloed digital infrastructures within the Helmholtz association. It is
part of the technical backbone of the Helmholtz FAIR data space, that
is established by the "Helmholtz Metadata Collaboration" (HMC). It is
used to drive change towards better metadata practices, increase visibility of data and provide useful data-based services. In this paper, we
present how metadata describing Helmholtz's digital assets and research
outputs are harvested and uplifted. The data is made publicly accessible
to both humans and machines through a user interface based text search
and a SPARQL endpoint, respectively.

Keywords: Knowledge Graph · Linked Data · FAIR · Helmholtz
Metadata Collaboration · Schema.org · JSON-LD · Data Mining ·
Metadata

1 Introduction

Research in the Helmholtz Association is carried out in inter- and multidisciplinary collaborations that span between its 18 independently operating non-
university research centers across Germany. Helmholtz digital infrastructure is
institutional, and thus Helmholtz's research data and other digital assets are
stored and maintained in independent silos, lack visibility and accessibility with
their full value remaining unavailable to scientists, managers, strategists, and
policy makers. Metadata on the web is typically used to track citations not
data. It often lacks completeness and semantic quality and therefore, published
research data often fails to satisfy FAIR principles [7] resulting in a lack of interoperability and re-usability. The "Helmholtz Metadata Collaboration" (HMC)[1]

---

[1] https://helmholtz-metadaten.de/en.

A. Meroño Peñuela et al. (Eds.): ESWC 2024, LNCS 15344, pp. 183–187, 2025.
https://doi.org/10.1007/978-3-031-78952-6_23

is taking on this challenge by developing innovative technologies and tools for a sustainable handling of research data through high-quality metadata. HMC launched the "unified Helmholtz Information and Data Exchange (unHIDE)"[2] - an initiative to network and harmonize Helmholtz digital infrastructure, and connect Helmholtz data through a lightweight interoperability layer in form of the Helmholtz Knowledge Graph. With this, we envision to (1) provide a better cross-organizational access to Helmholtz's (meta)data and information assets on an upper semantic level, (2) harmonize and optimize the related metadata across the association, and (3) form a basis from where semantic quality and depths of metadata descriptions can be improved and extended into domain and application levels. The institutional focus and defined domain boundaries within the Helmholtz's research fields[3] differentiate the Helmholtz KG from other graphs with wider scopes, such as e.g. the OpenAIRE graph [6]. These graph partners we approach for graph-graph exchange of data and developed technologies.

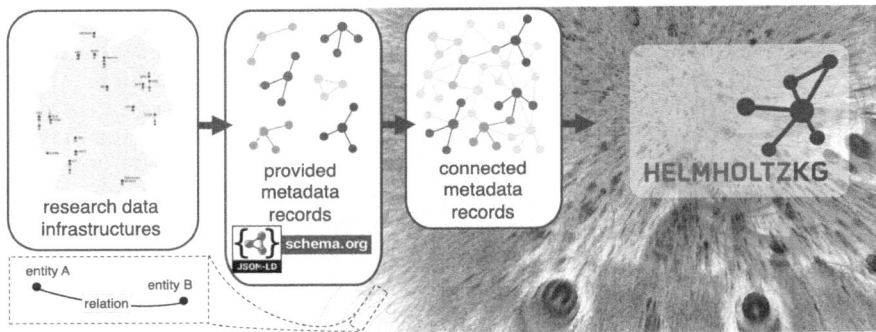

Fig. 1. Aggregation of the Helmholtz Knowledge Graph: Data records (schema.org / JSON-LD) are continuously harvested from Helmholtz data providers and run through our data pipelines for initial uplifting, de-duplication and integration into the Helmholtz KG. The graph on the right displays the sub graph of the 2.26 mil. main entities and their connections as a semi relaxed force atlas layout using Gephi[1].

2   Data Aggregation and Statistics

To aggregate the Helmholtz KG, metadata records are harvested from Helmholtz data providers and integrated (Fig. 1): we developed a library of harvesters [2] that harvests records recurrently through common web standards, such as OAI-PMH, sitemaps, feeds, or from the APIs of established data providers (DataCite, GitHub, GitLab). The data in the Helmholtz KG is aligned along https://schema.org semantics, for which exposed metadata records are preferably provided as Linked Data (e.g. serialized in JSON-LD documents). All harvested

---

[2] https://helmholtz-metadaten.de/en/unhide_helmholtz-kg.
[3] https://www.helmholtz.de/en/research/research-fields/.

records are processed through a data pipeline utilizing the workflow manager Prefect (v2.15.0)[4], during which records are initially uplifted with inferable semantic annotations and then de-duplicated. Then, records are uploaded into an OpenLink Virtuoso triple store, and indexed into an Apache Solr database to support full federated text search. The graph is exposed as a set of triples through a SPARQL endpoint[5]. In addition, users can search the graph data through a user-friendly web front end[6] as well as an API[7]. The aggregation and deployment design was inspired by the Ocean InfoHub (OIH) project [4] whose open code base kick-started our development. The graph is deployed first on the HDF Cloud [5] and now on the JSC Cloud at the Jülich Supercomputing Centre. The first release of the Helmholtz KG contains 2.15 million metadata

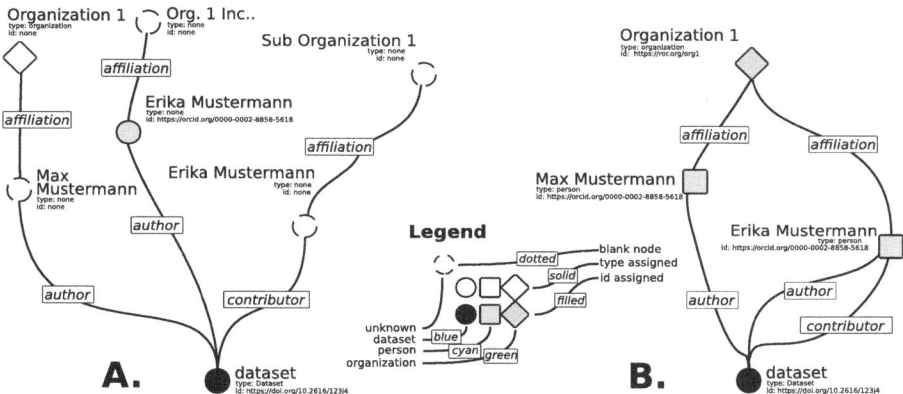

Fig. 2. Uplifting data records: A. Often, metadata is not systematically typed or assigned with persistent identifiers (PIDs). The resultant connections show that the same entities appear as duplicated blank nodes in several instances. **B.** The same data with assigned types and PIDs allows resolution of entities leading to a higher connectivity of the data in the graph.

records, which were harvested from 32 Helmholtz data providers. At the graph level, this results in 72 million RDF triples. Of these, 16.35 million entities are associated with a semantic type (approximately seven typed entities per record). Currently, the most frequent types of entities are persons, organizations, documents, datasets, software and events. Of these, 793k entities are associated with a persistent identifier (PID) or URL. PIDs as well as correct semantic annotation (e.g. of entity types) are important to increase the connectivity in the graph by resolving entities as shown in Fig. 2. Data with poor semantic quality often lacks

---

[4] https://www.prefect.io/.

[5] SPARQL endpoint: https://sparql.unhide.helmholtz-metadaten.de.

[6] Web front end: https://search.unhide.helmholtz-metadaten.de.

[7] Web API: https://api.unhide.helmholtz-metadaten.de.

PIDs (Fig. 2A) resulting in duplicated instances of the same nodes within the same record. This impairs search queries up to a level where duplicated instances might not be recognized and returned as separate results for a given query. By assigning PIDs (Fig. 2B) entities can be resolved leading to an increased number of connections to a single node. PID usage with data varies with entity types: ORCID and ROR PIDs are used to refer to persons respectively organizations exclusively, in contrast DOI PIDs are used heterogeneously to refer to research outputs including data and scholarly communications.

3   Outlook

In the future, we plan to continuously grow the graph by connecting more infrastructures as data providers from within Helmholtz. We further look to integrate data from Helmholtz FAIR digital objects. Through consulting and assisting data providers to expose high-quality metadata on the web, we will (1) increase their search engine optimization and (2) harmonize how top-level metadata is used in our association. Further, we will use the graph data to uplift and semantically enrich the provided data records. This will be achieved by type inference and entity resolution through logic and the application of machine learning methods. This uplifted data will be contrasted with the original data and provided back to the authoritative source of the metadata. We aim to keep the graph semantics and technology interoperable with other scientific knowledge graphs - such as the semantic pedigree ODIS [4] - to allow graph-to-graph interaction of data and federated querying.

Data and Software Availability. All software related to the Helmholtz Knowledge Graph is open source and freely available [2] under MIT license. The metadata and graph data can be fully extracted via API and the SPARQL endpoints and is available under the Creative Commons Attribution 4.0 International license. Versioned dumps of the graph data are pushed to Zenodo [3].

Acknowledgments. This project was funded by the Helmholtz Metadata Collaboration (HMC), an incubator-platform of the Helmholtz Association within the framework of the Information and Data Science strategic initiative. The authors acknowledge the Helmholtz Data Federation (HDF) for providing services and compute on the HDF Cloud at the Jülich Supercomputing Centre (JSC). We thank our colleagues Pier Luigi Buttigieg, Thomas Jejkal, Oonagh Mannix, Anton Pirogov, Silke Gerlich and Mustafa Soylu for contributions to the unHIDE initiative, as well as the ODIS/ OceanInfoHub team for advice and sharing their architecture code.

Disclosure of Interests. The authors have no competing interests to declare that are relevant to the content of this article.

References

1. Bastian, M., Heymann, S., Jacomy, M.: Gephi: an open source software for exploring and manipulating networks. In: Proceedings of the International AAAI Conference on Web and Social Media, vol. 3, pp. 361–362 (2009)
2. Bröder, J., et al.: Software repositories of unhide and the knowledge graph. https://codebase.helmholtz.cloud/hmc/hmc-public/unhide
3. Bröder, J., Preuß, G., D'Mello, F., Fathalla, S., Hofmann, V., Sandfeld, S.: The helmholtz knowledge graph dataset (2024). https://doi.org/10.5281/zenodo.10948205
4. Fils, D., et al.: Ocean InfoHub: a global knowledge network for the ocean data and information system (ODIS). In: AGU Fall Meeting Abstracts, vol. 2021, pp. IN45H–0523 (2021)
5. Hagemeier, B.: HDF cloud–helmholtz data federation cloud resources at the jülich supercomputing centre. J. Large-scale Res. Facil. JLSRF **5**, A137–A137 (2019). https://doi.org/10.17815/jlsrf-5-173
6. Manghi, P., et al.: Openaire graph dataset (2024). https://doi.org/10.5281/zenodo.10488385
7. Wilkinson, M.D., et al.: The fair guiding principles for scientific data management and stewardship. Sci. Data **3**(1), 1–9 (2016). https://doi.org/10.1038/sdata.2016.18

Data Search and Discovery in RDF Sources

Zoé Chevallier[1,2(✉)], Zoubida Kedad[1], Béatrice Finance[1],
and Frédéric Chaillan[2]

[1] David Lab. University of Versailles Paris-Sclay, Versailles, France
[2] Grand Paris Sud, Evry-Courcouronnes, France
`f.chaillan@grandparissud.fr`
`{zoe.chevallier,zoubida.kedad,beatrice.finance}@uvsq.fr,`
`z.chevallier@grandparissud.fr`

Abstract. The RDF data sources published on the Web represent an unprecedented amount of knowledge. However, querying these sources to extract the relevant information for some specific needs represented by a target schema is a complex task, as the alignment between the target and the source schemas might not be provided or may be incomplete. This paper presents a system that aims to automatically populate the classes of a target schema from RDF data sources by identifying candidate instance patterns. This identification process relies on a semi-supervised learning algorithm and the system automatically generates the SPARQL queries that populate the target schema.

Keywords: RDF data sources · Target Schema Instantiation · SPARQL Query Generation · Semi-supervised learning

1 Introduction

The Web represents a huge space of available data from which various applications can extract meaningful knowledge. However, finding relevant data for some specific need is not obvious, especially for irregular data sources. This problem has been addressed by dataset discovery approaches [1,3], which aim at discovering the relevant datasets that could complement a given target dataset. These approaches are designed for structured datasets.

Considering that the specific needs of an application are described by a target schema, our problem is the identification and the extraction of relevant data to populate this target schema. A similar problem is the one of mapping generation which has been the subject of several works [2,4], targeting relational or XML data. Sacramento et al. [5] have addressed the problem of expressing an RDF data source in the terms defined by an ontology, which consists in generating a mapping between a source and this ontology. This requires the alignment between the source schema and the target schema, which is not always provided.

A. Meroño Peñuela et al. (Eds.): ESWC 2024, LNCS 15344, pp. 188–192, 2025.
https://doi.org/10.1007/978-3-031-78952-6_24

In this paper, we present a system that identifies candidate instances from RDF data sources to populate a given target schema. It relies on a semi-supervised learning algorithm to extract candidate instance patterns from an RDF data source and automatically generates the queries that extract these instances. This paper is organized as follows. Section 2 presents the architecture of our system. Section 3 details a use-case scenario, and Sect. 4 presents some future works.

2   System Architecture

Figure 1 depicts the architecture of our system. We consider that the target schema is described in RDFS[1] /OWL[2] . The alignment between the source schemas and the target schema can be exploited if they are available, but they are not required.

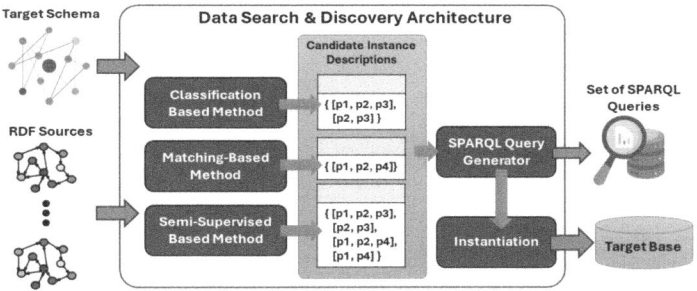

Fig. 1. The Data Search and Discovery System Architecture

Our system identifies in RDF sources candidate instance patterns in order to populate the target schema. Each pattern is a property set which describes some candidate instances in the data source. Given a candidate pattern, a SPARQL Query is generated to retrieve all the candidate instances and automatically populate the target schema.

We assume that each class C of the target schema is described by a set of properties, $Prop(C)$, such that $Prop(C) = \{p \mid < p, rdfs\!:\!domain, C > \in T\}$. An entity e in an RDF data source S is a resource that is neither a class, a property, a literal, or a blank node; it is characterized by a set of properties, $Prop(e)$, such that: $Prop(e) = \{p \mid < e, p, * > \in S\}$.

A straightforward way to identify candidate instance patterns is to compute the similarity between source entities and a target class C. If the similarity is higher than a threshold, then $Prop(e)$ is a candidate pattern for C. We refer to this process as ***classification-based***. If the output of some schema matching

---

[1] https://www.w3.org/TR/rdf-schema/.

[2] https://www.w3.org/TR/owl-features/.

tool is provided, and if a target class C_T is equivalent to a source class C_S, then all the instances of C_S are candidate instances for C_T. We refer to this process as **matching-based** instantiation.

However, these correspondences are not always provided. Besides, the schema in RDF sources is only descriptive, and an instance can be characterized by a property set that is different from the one defined in the schema for its class. Therefore, new candidate instance patterns should be identified based on the class description in the target schema, but also based on the candidate instance patterns already identified for a class. To do so, we propose an approach based on a semi-supervised learning algorithm [6] to identify candidate patterns.

An entity which is similar to a candidate pattern already identified for a class C could also be a candidate instance for C. We propose an approach that iteratively computes the similarity between each entity and the candidate patterns already identified. If the similarity between e and the candidate instance patterns of C is above a predefined threshold, then $Prop(e)$ is considered as a candidate instance pattern for C. We introduce the notion of candidate instance description that represent the patterns of candidate instances for a target class C. It is such that:

$$\mathcal{D}(C) = \{\mathcal{D}_i \mid \mathcal{D}_i = Prop(e), \text{e candidate instance of C}\} \tag{1}$$

If $\mathcal{D}(C) = \{ \mathcal{D}_1, ..., \mathcal{D}_n \}$ is a set of candidate instance descriptions, the similarity based on the instances is denoted $Sim_I(e, \mathcal{D}(C))$, and is defined as follows:

$$Sim_I(e, \mathcal{D}(C)) = MAX_{1 \leq i \leq n} \left(\frac{|Prop(e) \cap \mathcal{D}_i|}{|Prop(e) \cup \mathcal{D}_i|} \right) \tag{2}$$

The semi-supervised algorithm first computes candidate instance descriptions using both the matching-based and classification-based approaches. For a target class C, the similarity between each entity e and C, Sim_I is computed. If the similarity is higher than a given threshold, then $Prop(e)$ is a candidate instance description of C. If new candidate instance descriptions are identified, a new iteration is started. This identification process iterates until no more new candidate instance descriptions are found.

Consider $\mathcal{D}_i$ a candidate instance description of C such that $\mathcal{D}_i = \{ p_1, ..., p_n \}$. A SPARQL query is generated for $\mathcal{D}_i$ in order to extract from the considered dataset S all the entities characterized by a property set identical to $\mathcal{D}_i$, i.e., the set in which each entity e is such that $Prop(e) = \mathcal{D}_i$.

The entities and their associated triples are extracted, and a type declaration is defined for each of them stating that their corresponding type is C. This is represented by adding the triple pattern <?e, rdf:type, C> in the basic graph pattern.

In addition, if p is a property in $\mathcal{D}_i$, then the triple pattern <?e, p ?o_p > is added to the basic graph pattern.

We implement an exclusion mechanism to filter out the entities which are characterised by a superset of $\mathcal{D}_i$. We used a *minus* operator in the query that exclude the entities that are described by properties which are not contained in the description, i.e. $<?e, ?prop, ?o>$, where $?prop \notin \mathcal{D}_i$.

Figure 2 depicts the SPARQL query generated for the description: $\mathcal{D}(t{:}Person) = \{$ firstname, lastname $\}$.

```
CONSTRUCT {                                    𝒟(t:Person) = { firstname, lastname }
    ?e rdf:type t:Person .
    ?e firstname ?o_name .
    ?e lastname ?o_lastname . }

WHERE {
    ?e firstname ?o_name .
    ?e lastname ?o_lastname .

    MINUS { ?e ?prop ?o .
        FILTER (?prop NOT IN (firstname, lastname))
    }
}
```

Fig. 2. A Candidate Instance Description and the Corresponding SPARQL Query

3   Demonstration Scenario

Our system is implemented in Java, using Apache Jena. An online presentation of the demonstration is available[3]. The demonstration will proceed in four phases:

1. **Configuration.** The process starts by selecting a project composed of a RDFS/OWL target schema, RDF sources, and optionally a set of correspondences between the target schema and the RDF sources. A graphical representation of both the target schema and the data sources is presented.
2. **Identification of Candidate Instance Descriptions.** In this phase, we will show the generation of candidate instance descriptions using the different approaches. The candidate instance descriptions identified for each target class will be presented as well as their provenance, i.e. the data source from which they have been extracted. Moreover, a visualization tool allow the user to highlight the candidate instances identified in the source.
3. **Generation of SPARQL Queries.** We will then demonstrate the query generation process, and show the queries generated for each candidate instance description and the execution result, such as the one depicted in Fig. 3.
4. **Comparison of the Candidate Instance Sets.** In order to highlight the quality of the semi-supervised approach, we will compare its resulting candidate instance sets with the ones extracted using a baseline method which consists in extracting the candidate instance descriptions obtained using both the matching-based approach and the classification-based approach.

---

[3] https://mega.nz/folder/QK0lRSha#dSW_77ur0QBPNp7ff4_qXg.

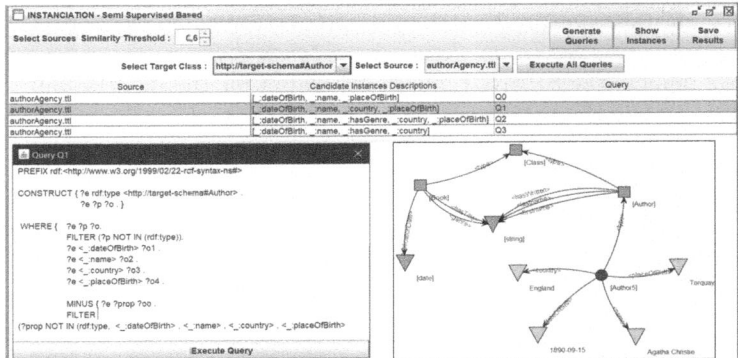

Fig. 3. A Screenshot of the Query Generated from a Candidate Description

4   Future Works

In future works, we will improve the query generation process in our data discovery system by taking into account some constraints defined on the target schema so as to extract only the source instances for which the constraints are verified. These constraints will be expressed in SHACL[4], and exploited during query generation. We will also explore the possible ways of minimizing the number of generated queries by grouping the candidate instance descriptions that share some properties before generating the queries.

References

1. Castro Fernandez, R., Abedjan, Z., Koko, F., Yuan, G., Madden, S., Stonebraker, M.: Aurum: a Data Discovery System. In: 2018 IEEE 34th International Conference on Data Engineering (ICDE), pp. 1001–1012. IEEE, Paris (2018)
2. Fagin, R., Haas, L.M., Hernandez, M., Miller, R.J., Popa, L., Velegrakis, Y.: Clio: schema mapping creation and data exchange | SpringerLink. In: Conceptual Modeling: Foundations and Applications, Lecture Notes in Computer Science, vol. 5600, pp. 198–236 (2009)
3. Koutras, C., et al.: Valentine: evaluating matching techniques for dataset discovery. In: 2021 IEEE 37th International Conference on Data Engineering (ICDE), pp. 468–479 (2021)
4. Mazilu, L., Paton, N.W., Fernandes, A.A., Koehler, M.: Schema mapping generation in the wild. Inf. Syst. 104, 101904 (2022)
5. Sacramento, E.R., Vidal, V.M.P., de Macêdo, J.A.F., Lóscio, B.F., Lopes, F.L.R., Casanova, M.A.: Towards automatic generation of application ontologies. J. Inf. Data Manag. 1(3), 535–550 (2010)
6. Yarowsky, D.: Unsupervised word sense disambiguation rivaling supervised methods. In: Proceedings of the 33rd annual meeting. Association for Computational Linguistics, Cambridge, Massachusetts (1995)

---

[4] https://www.w3.org/TR/shacl/.

MLSeascape: Search over Machine Learning Metadata Empowered by Knowledge Graphs

Ioannis Dasoulas(✉) , Duo Yang , and Anastasia Dimou

KU Leuven – Leuven.AI – Flanders Make@KULeuven, Leuven, Belgium
{ioannis.dasoulas,duo.yang,anastasia.dimou}@kuleuven.be

Abstract. As Machine Learning (ML) continuously grows in numbers, complexity and components, online ML platforms that gather and serve ML-related knowledge become increasingly important. However, available knowledge is fragmented with each platform representing distinct parts of the ML lifecycle using their own unique representation. In this demo paper, we present MLSeascape, an online application that leverages the MLSea-KG knowledge graph. The MLSea-KG knowledge graph incorporates ML metadata from multiple platforms, such as Kaggle, OpenML and Papers with Code. MLSeascape enables seamless search for ML metadata without needing to be an expert in semantic web technologies.
License: Apache-2.0
MLSeascape: https://w3id.org/mlseascape
Source Code: https://github.com/dtai-kg/MLSeascape
Video: https://youtu.be/jn-GGwm52EM

Keywords: Machine Learning · Knowledge Graphs · Search Systems

1 Introduction

Due to the continuous advancements of Machine Learning (ML), the number and complexity of ML pipelines keep on increasing. ML pipelines incorporate numerous sophisticated components, including datasets, hyper-parameters, algorithms and software, which can hinder their discoverability. Online platforms (e.g., OpenML[1], Kaggle[2] or Papers with Code[3]) play a pivotal role in cataloging ML experiments and metadata. Yet, these platforms vary in their data representations, captured metadata, interfaces and search functionalities, making it challenging for users to efficiently discover and retrieve relevant information.

Recent works demonstrated how ML knowledge discovery can be facilitated by semantically annotating and serving ML metadata from various sources [1,2].

---

[1] https://www.openml.org.
[2] https://www.kaggle.com.
[3] https://paperswithcode.com.

© The Author(s), under exclusive license to Springer Nature Switzerland AG 2025
A. Meroño Peñuela et al. (Eds.): ESWC 2024, LNCS 15344, pp. 193–196, 2025.
https://doi.org/10.1007/978-3-031-78952-6_25

However, existing works require knowledge of semantic web technologies and the underlying data model to effectively use them for ML discovery. A user-friendly abstraction layer is needed to make ML search more accessible to a wider audience while leveraging the underlying ML knowledge graph.

In this paper, we introduce **MLSeascape**[4], a knowledge graph-enhanced web application that provides an abstraction layer for discovering ML metadata from online platforms. **MLSeascape** serves diverse ML components and is able to demonstrate their properties and relationships between them, as well as to provide the original sources they are found. By leveraging semantic web technologies, **MLSeascape** aims to streamline the process of accessing and exploring ML resources, facilitating ML artifact discovery.

In the rest, we detail the architecture of **MLSeascape** (Sect. 2), describe the system's functionalities (Sect. 3) and conclude with future work (Sect. 4).

2   MLSeascape as Part of the MLSea Ecosystem

MLSeascape is a web application that aims to facilitate the discovery of ML metadata from various online platforms. It is a search-based platform where users can explore different ML components and view their properties, the relationships between components and their original sources. The data is retrieved from a public SPARQL endpoint[5] hosted by a GraphDB[6] triple store, which is enhanced with a built-in Lucene Connector[7] that accelerates text searches over the triple store while ensuring synchronization with it.

MLSeascape leverages the Machine Learning Knowledge Graph (MLSea-KG)[8] [1] to retrieve ML metadata which are hosted in a GraphDB triple store. MLSea-KG is a comprehensive and regularly updated knowledge graph containing over 1.44 billion RDF triples of ML experiments. It encompasses ML metadata from OpenML, Kaggle and Papers with Code, including datasets used in ML experiments, tasks, implementations, hyper-parameters, experiment executions, configuration settings, evaluation results, code notebooks, algorithms, publications, models, and information about scientists and practitioners.

MLSea-KG is based on the Machine Learning Sailor Ontology (MLSO[9]) and Taxonomies (MLST[10]) [1]. MLSO is an ontology that reuses and extends state-of-the-art ontologies (e.g., MLSchema [6], SDO [3], DCAT [4], FaBiO [5] to describe ML workflows, configurations, experimental results, models, datasets, software implementations and citations. MLST are SKOS taxonomies of ML-related concepts (e.g., task types, evaluation measures).

---

[4] https://w3id.org/mlseascape.

[5] https://193.190.127.194:7200.

[6] https://graphdb.ontotext.com.

[7] https://graphdb.ontotext.com/documentation/10.6/lucene-graphdb-connector.html.

[8] Paper accepted by ESWC 2024 Resource Track.

[9] http://w3id.org/mlso.

[10] https://github.com/dtai-kg/MLSO/tree/main/ontology/Taxonomies.

3   Demonstration of MLSeascape

MLSeascape allows users to search for different types of ML artifacts including datasets, models, software, tasks, algorithms, implementations and publications by traversing MLSea-KG. Users first select the type of ML artifact (e.g., datasets) they are interested to search for and input a related keyword (Fig. 1a). **MLSeascape** then presents potential matches for their search input in the MLSea-KG. For instance, in (Fig. 1b) some results for the search "NAS CVPR" are displayed. When the users select one of the matches, they are led to a new page that presents all generic metadata about their choice (e.g., date published, creators, description, original source) as well as related ML entities (e.g., similar datasets, related software, related ML tasks, publications) for the corresponding artifact. For instance, in (Fig. 2), the user selected the "NAS" dataset and MLSeascape retrieved and presented the dataset's metadata as well as relationships with other ML artifacts found online, such as similar datasets, related code repositories, and the publication that introduced the dataset.

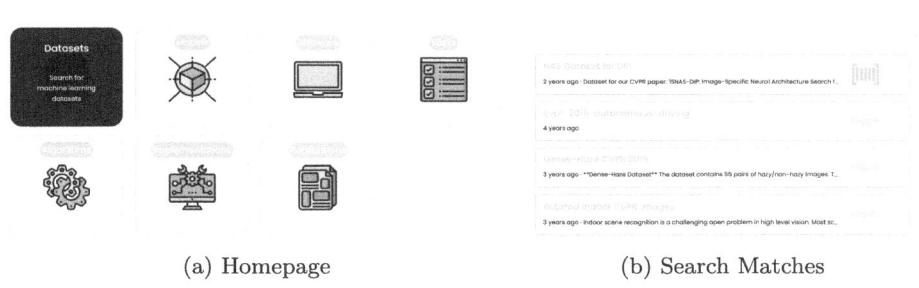

(a) Homepage   (b) Search Matches

Fig. 1. Artifacts Search

MLSeascape harnesses MLSea-KG's coverage of different ML platforms and its sophisticated relationships between ML artifacts. It emphasizes on revealing interconnections between artifacts that will help users get a more holistic view of the existing works that utilize them. It also focuses on simplicity, allowing non-experts to traverse through MLSea-KG with a single user input.

In the demo, we will demonstrate the full process of searching and browsing ML artifacts. All available types of artifacts and metadata will be demonstrated using prominent ML artifacts, as well as user inputs given during the presentation by the attendees.

4   Conclusion

In this paper, we introduce **MLSeascape**, a user-friendly web application designed to facilitate the exploration of ML artifacts and resources from diverse

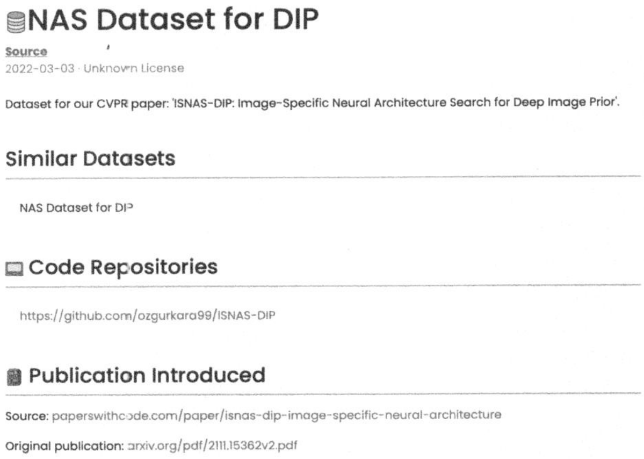

🗄 NAS Dataset for DIP

Source

2022-03-03 · Unknown License

Dataset for our CVPR paper: 'ISNAS-DIP: Image-Specific Neural Architecture Search for Deep Image Prior'.

Similar Datasets

NAS Dataset for DIP

🖵 Code Repositories

https://github.com/ozgurkara99/ISNAS-DIP

🗄 Publication Introduced

Source: paperswithcode.com/paper/isnas-dip-image-specific-neural-architecture

Original publication: arxiv.org/pdf/2111.15362v2.pdf

Fig. 2. Dataset Metadata Presentation Snippet

platforms. **MLSeascape's** coverage over ML metadata empowers practitioners and researchers to explore ML more effectively, aiming to promote innovation and advancements in the field. In the future, we aim to expand the coverage of **MLSeascape** by incorporating additional information or platforms that will be available through MLSea-KG. Additionally, we will enhance the search functionalities and improve **MLSeascape** by implementing artifact recommendations.

Acknowledgements. This research was partially supported by Flanders Make (REX-PEK project), the strategic research centre for the manufacturing industry and the Flanders innovation and entrepreneurship (VLAIO – KG3D project).

References

1. Dasoulas, I., Yang, D., Dimou, A.: MLSea: a semantic layer for discoverable machine learning. In: The Semantic Web, vol. 14665, pp. 178–198 (2024)
2. Färber, M., Lamprecht, D.: Linked papers with code: the latest in machine learning as an RDF knowledge graph. In: ISWC 2023 Posters and Demos (2023)
3. Garijo, D., Osorio, M., Khider, D., Ratnakar, V., Gil, Y.: OKG-Soft: an open knowledge graph with machine readable scientific software metadata. In: 15th International Conference on eScience (eScience), pp. 349–358 (2019)
4. Maali, F., Erickson, J.: Data Catalog Vocabulary (DCAT). Recommendation, World Wide Web Consortium (W3C) (2014). https://www.w3.org/TR/vocab-dcat/
5. Peroni, S., Shotton, D.: FaBiO and CiTO: ontologies for describing bibliographic resources and citations. J. Web Semant. **17**, 33–43 (2012)
6. Publio, G.C., et al.: ML-Schema: Exposing the Semantics of Machine Learning with Schemas and Ontologies. arXiv preprint arXiv:1807.05351 (2018)

SCOOP-UI: SHACL Shape Extraction in Just a Click!

Xuemin Duan[1(✉)], David Chaves-Fraga[1,2], and Anastasia Dimou[1]

[1] KU Leuven – Flanders Make@KULeuven – Leuven.AI, Leuven, Belgium
{xuemin.duan,anastasia.dimou}@kuleuven.be
[2] Departamento de Electrónica e Computación, Universidade de Santiago de
Compostela, Santiago de Compostela, Spain
david.chaves@usc.es

Abstract. The proliferation of knowledge graph validation using the
Shapes Constraint Language (SHACL) has catalyzed significant efforts
toward automating the extraction of SHACL shapes. These shapes may be
derived from RDF graphs, or the various components which are involved
in their creation, e.g., ontologies, raw data schemas, and mapping rules. In
SCOOP, we integrate shapes extracted from these components, however,
no system exists that enables the users to streamline the extraction and
integration processes. In this work, we present SCOOP-UI, a web application built on top of SCOOP to provide an editor for the users to handle
the different component's resources to extract and integrate their SHACL
shapes. This work enables users to get directly involved in the translation
of various resources into SHACL shapes, as well as in the integration of
these shapes to produce a unified representation.

Keywords: SHACL · Shape integration · Web application

1 Introduction

Automatic extraction of shapes e.g., in the Shapes Constraint Language[1]
(SHACL), to validate RDF graphs is crucial to guarantee consistency in data
transformation. Extracting SHACL shapes leverage either the RDF graph directly
[5] or associated sources such as ontologies [1], raw data schemas [4], and mapping
rules [2] utilized in constructing the RDF graph. The former approach entails constraint extraction via direct analysis of the RDF graph, whereas the latter involves
the translation of pre-existing constraints into SHACL constraints.

While the majority of current research concentrates on extracting shapes
from an individual source [3], e.g., from RDF graphs, ontologies, raw data
schemas, and mapping rules, no attention has been given to the potential coexis-
tence of diverse sources related to RDF graph creation. SCOOP[2] [3], a shape integration framework, addressed this research gap. By leveraging SCOOP, SHACL

---

[1] https://www.w3.org/TR/shacl/.
[2] Paper accepted by ESWC 2024 Resource Track.

A. Meroño Peñuela et al. (Eds.): ESWC 2024, LNCS 15344, pp. 197–201, 2025.
https://doi.org/10.1007/978-3-031-78952-6_26

Fig. 1. SHACL shape extraction and integration via SCOOP-UI

shapes extracted from the raw data schema and ontology used to create an RDF graph according to a set of mapping rules, can be integrated into a unified SHACL shapes graph, facilitating comprehensive validation of RDF graphs.

This work presents the SCOOP-UI[3], an open-source web-based application built on top of SCOOP[4], aiming to facilitate the automatic extraction and integration of SHACL shapes. SCOOP-UI supports (i) the extraction of a shapes graph from a single file, such as XML Schema (XSD) via its XSD2SHACL component, RDF Mapping Language (RML) via its RML2SHACL component, and Web Ontology Language (OWL) via its OWL2SHACL component; (ii) the extraction and integration of a unified shapes graph from multiple files (integrate either shapes extracted or existing). Last, it offers various predefined integration strategies; and also allows user-defined integration source priority.

2 SCOOP-UI Features

This section presents the functions and configurations supported by SCOOP-UI.

Core functions SCOOP-UI may have a single file or multiple files as the input which can be raw data schemas, ontologies, mapping rules, or SHACL shapes.

Single file input. When a single file is given as input, e.g., a raw data schema, an ontology, or a set of mapping rules, the application automatically triggers the corresponding shapes extraction component to directly generate the corresponding SHACL shapes. As the layout illustrated in Fig. 1, if only the Mapping

---

[3] https://demos.citius.usc.es/scoop/.

[4] https://github.com/dtai-kg/SCOOP.

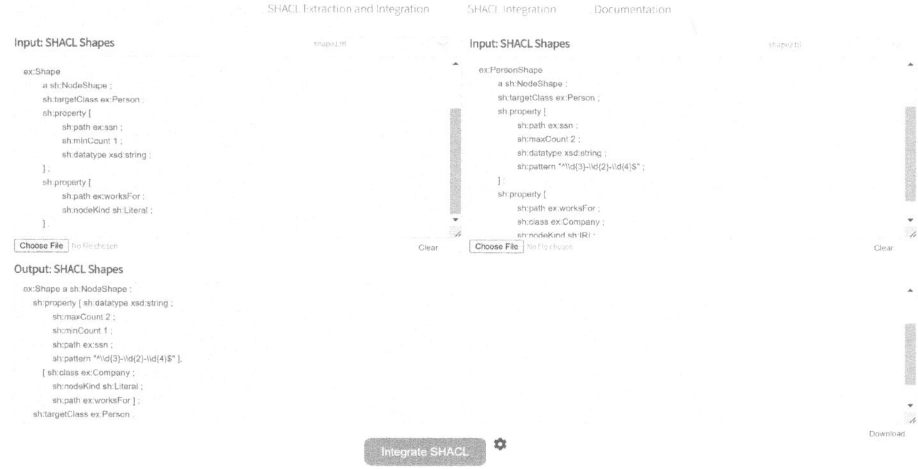

Fig. 2. SHACL shape integration via SCOOP-UI

Rules text area is filled while leaving other text areas empty, the SHACL shapes will be extracted via the RML2SHACL component.

Multiple files inputs. When multiple files from a single source or multiple sources are given as inputs, the application invokes the corresponding shape extraction components to extract the shapes (e.g., the XSD2SHACL component when files from the XSD source are given or the RML2SHACL component if some mapping rules from the XSD source are given). Subsequently, the shape integration module in SCOOP integrates the extracted shapes from various files into a unified shapes graph. As depicted in Fig. 1, upon giving multiple files by populating the text area or uploading files via the upload button, within Raw Data Schemas, Mapping Rules, and Ontologies, the application automatically performs the extraction and integration, then presents a unified shapes graph in the SHACL shapes text area.

Multiple SHACL shapes inputs. While SCOOP is designed to accommodate various input sources to extract and then integrate shapes, this application isolates the integration module of SCOOP to enable the support for integrating multiple files from SHACL shapes. As illustrated in Fig. 2, the application also caters to users who seek to integrate multiple existing SHACL shapes graphs without the need for extraction.

Configurations SCOOP-UI empowers users to select from three integration strategies: SCOOP-**All**, SCOOP-**Prior**, and SCOOP-**Prior-R**. The adoption of different strategies influences the resolution of inconsistent constraints. The **All** aims to integrate all constraints from extracted or existing shapes, utilizing logical constraint components (e.g., sh:or) to resolve potential inconsistencies. The **Prior** integrates constraints from lower-priority sources that are not inconsistent with constraints from higher-priority sources, based on user-defined priorities. The **Prior-R** is designed to filter out redundant shapes from the ontology source relative to higher-priority sources. If the SCOOP-Prior or SCOOP-Prior-R strategy is chosen, users have the flexibility to customize the priority of sources.

3 Architecture and Demonstration

SCOOP-UI[3] is comprised of a front-end user interface, back-end service, and API, facilitating an end-to-end workflow. The front-end interface is developed using HTML, CSS, and JavaScript. It encompasses text areas and upload buttons for inputs, clear buttons to clear given inputs, configuration options for shape integration, an output text area for displaying results, and a download button to download the generated shapes graph. The back-end service is constructed using the FastAPI framework[5], which receives requests from the front-end interface and invokes the corresponding SCOOP modules. SCOOP currently incorporates XSD2SHACL [4] for handling XSD files, RML2SHACL [2] for RML files, and Astrea [1] for OWL files.

The SCOOP-UI offers test examples about students and real-world use cases from railway infrastructure register[6] (RINF) for each input source, conveniently accessible through direct clicks, as depicted in Figs. 1 and 2. In the demo, we demonstrate the extraction of SHACL shapes from the single file of RML, XSD, or OWL, and illustrate the impact of different configurations on the extracted constraints when multiple files are given. We showcase the direct integration process when multiple SHACL shapes are provided as inputs.

4 Conclusion

Through SCOOP-UI, users can seamlessly extract and integrate a unified shapes graph directly from various sources without the need to familiarize themselves with multiple shape extraction tools. Presently, our application supports input from OWL, RML, XSD, and existing SHACL shapes. Its versatility allows for potential expansion to accommodate additional sources in the future, contingent upon the emergence of new shape extraction tools targeting other sources.

Acknowledgments. Xuemin Duan and Anastasia Dimou are partially supported by Flanders Make, the research centre for the manufacturing industry, and the Flanders innovation and entrepreneurship (VLAIO) through the KG3D project. David Chaves-Fraga is funded by the Galician Ministry of Education, University and Professional Training and the European Regional Development Fund (ERDF/FEDER program) through grants ED431C2018/29 and ED431G2019/04.

---

[5] https://fastapi.tiangolo.com/.

[6] https://www.rinf-ch.ch/documentation?lang=EN.

References

1. Cimmino, A., Fernández-Izquierdo, A., García-Castro, R.: Astrea: automatic generation of SHACL shapes from ontologies. In: European Semantic Web Conference, pp. 497–513. Springer (2020). https://doi.org/10.1007/978-3-030-49461-2_29
2. Delva, T., Smedt, B.D., Oo, S.M., Assche, D.V., Lieber, S., Dimou, A.: RML2SHACL: RDF generation taking shape. In: Proceedings of the 11th on Knowledge Capture Conference. ACM (2021). https://doi.org/10.1145/3460210.3493562
3. Duan, X., Chaves-Fraga, D., Derom, O., Dimou, A.: SCOOP all the constraints' flavours for your knowledge graph. In: Proceedings of the 21st Extended Semantic Web Conference (ESWC) (2024)
4. Duan, X., Chaves-Fraga, D., Dimou, A.: XSD2SHACL: capturing RDF constraints from XML schema. In: Proceedings of the 12th Knowledge Capture Conference 2023. K-CAP 2023, ACM (2023). https://doi.org/10.1145/3587259.3627565
5. Rabbani, K., Lissandrini, M., Hose, K.: SHACTOR: improving the quality of large-scale knowledge graphs with validating shapes. In: SIGMOD-Companion 2023. ACM (2023). https://doi.org/10.1145/3555041.3589723

Converter: Enhancing Interoperability in Research Data Management

Sefika Efeoglu[1,3]($\boxtimes$) (ID), Zongxiong Chen[2] (ID), Sonja Schimmler[1,2] (ID), and Bianca Wentzel[2] (ID)

[1] Technische Universität Berlin, Berlin, Germany
sonja.schimmler@tu-berlin.de
[2] Fraunhofer FOKUS, Berlin, Germany
{zongxiong.chen,bianca.wentzel}@fokus.fraunhofer.de
[3] Freie Universität Berlin, Berlin, Germany
sefika.efeoglu@tu-berlin.de

Abstract. Research Data Management (RDM) is essential in handling and organizing data in the research field. The Berlin Open Science Platform (BOP) serves as a case study that exemplifies the significance of standardization within the Berlin University Alliance (BUA), employing different vocabularies when publishing their data, resulting in data heterogeneity. The meta portals of the NFDI4Cat and the NFDI4DataScience project serve as additional case studies in the context of the NFDI initiative. To establish consistency among the harvested repositories in the respective systems, this study focuses on developing a novel component, namely the *converter*, that breaks barriers between data collection and various schemas. With the minor modification of the existing Piveau framework, the development of the converter, contributes to enhanced data accessibility, streamlined collaboration, and improved interoperability within the research community.

Keywords: Research Data Management · Interoperability · DCAT

1 Introduction

Research Data Management (RDM) plays a crucial role in the research field by facilitating the handling and organization of data. As the volume of data in research areas continues to expand, it becomes increasingly important to address the challenge of managing diverse metadata formats across different applications. One potential solution to this challenge is to standardize the general descriptive metadata into a common format, e.g., the Data Catalog Vocabulary Application Profile[1] (DCAT-AP) [1].

The Berlin University Alliance (BUA), a German excellency cluster, aims to foster collaboration and knowledge sharing among esteemed institutions: Freie Universität Berlin (FU Berlin), Humboldt-Universität zu Berlin (HU Berlin),

---

[1] DCAT: https://www.w3.org/TR/vocab-dcat-3/.

A. Meroño Peñuela et al. (Eds.): ESWC 2024, LNCS 15344, pp. 202–206, 2025.
https://doi.org/10.1007/978-3-031-78952-6_27

Fig. 1. An overview of three repositories from the institutions of the Berlin University Alliance on the Berlin Open Science Platform.

Technische Universität Berlin (TU Berlin), and Charité - Universitätsmedizin Berlin[2]. The BUA's main goal is to establish a digital research space that follows the FAIR (Findable, Accessible, Interoperable, and Reusable) principles, catering to a diverse community of researchers, including professors, scholars, and students. To achieve this, we developed a user-friendly meetup portal called Berlin Open Science Platform (BOP)[3] (see Fig. 1). This platform offers convenient access to data resources from the repositories of three universities, all on a single platform. It is based on Piveau[4], a well-established open source data ecosystem, which uses DCAT-AP. The portal brings together and organizes research data from the affiliated universities within the BUA. The research data stored in the BUA repositories encompasses diverse data types including doctoral theses, scientific papers, videos, images, and audio files.

Despite utilizing the oai_dc format[5], the universities within the BUA leverage distinct vocabularies when publishing their data. Using different vocabularies in its schemas causes interoperability problems [2,3]. The current version of the Piveau harvester requires the adaption of its metadata importer when harvesting data from the different repositories within the BUA. It also lacks the capability to establish the corresponding mapping between DCAT and the data retrieved from the different endpoints. These problems raise the need to convert the schemas of the repositories into DCAT before sending the metadata to the Piveau harvester.

In this work, we developed a novel pipeline that integrates data from different sources and in different schemas. Specifically, we federated data within the BOP in the context of the BUA[6]. The approach can be utilized in other projects,

---

[2] This institution's research data is stored in the HU Berlin and FU Berlin repositories.

[3] The metadata portal: https://meta4bua.fokus.fraunhofer.de/.

[4] Piveau is available at https://gitlab.com/piveau and https://github.com/piveau-data.

[5] OAI-DC Schema: http://www.openarchives.org/OAI/2.0/oai_dc.xsd.

[6] BUA: https://www.berlin-university-alliance.de/.

including NFDI4Cat[7] and NFDI4DataScience[8] within the NFDI initiative[9] to build a German National Research Data Infrastructure as well. By employing this pipeline, we can overcome the barriers posed by disparate data resources and harmonize the data into a cohesive and standardized framework.

In the following, we provide a detailed description of how the proposed converter is implemented and integrated into the Piveau framework. This integration is further extended to its application in the BOP project. The step-by-step process of implementing the converter and integrating it into Piveau is described, while its specific application within the BOP is highlighted. Finally, we summarize the contributions our implementation of the converter makes to the Piveau framework.

2 Methodology

We developed a *converter*[10], which finds the corresponding metadata between the schema of the harvested data and the DCAT vocabulary. The corresponding metadata between schemas is found by a schema matcher (see the GitHub repository). This *converter* facilitates the interoperability between DCAT and data resources using different schemas. After finding the corresponding metadata, it saves the harvesting data in the DCAT format replacing its original schema[11]. The *converter* acts as a bridge between repositories and the Piveau harvester [4,5] (see Fig. 2), offering a set of different importers, transformers and exporters. Despite having its own transformers, the Piveau harvester needs maintenance for various schemas due to receiving metadata in a different format from the DCAT vocabulary. The Piveau harvester in Fig. 2 exclusively receives data in the DCAT format after integrating the *converter*. As a result, there is no need for additional maintenance in the Piveau harvester, even when the incoming data from endpoints is in different schema formats. With regards to BOP, an example of the significance of standardization can be observed in the BUA. This variation poses a challenge in achieving consistency across the harvested repositories within the BOP. The converter transforms the different data formats and schemas into a standardized format, ensuring that data from the DSpace repositories[12] of HU Berlin, FU Berlin, and TU Berlin can be easily accessed and utilized, regardless of the specific vocabulary or schema employed by each university. For example, the repositories in the BUA utilize the term "subject" in their schemas to define keywords about the data, in contrast to the corresponding term "keywords" in DCAT. Another example is that FU Berlin's repository uses

---

[7] NFDI4Cat: https://nfdi4cat.org.

[8] NFDI4DataScience: https://www.nfdi4datascience.de.

[9] NFDI: https://www.nfdi.de.

[10] The converter is available at https://github.com/sefeoglu/dcat-converter.

[11] The sample output of the converter is available at https://github.com/sefeoglu/dcat-converter/blob/master/data/sample.rdf.

[12] The most commonly used repository solutions include DSpace, Zenodo and Dataverse (see https://www.re3data.org/.

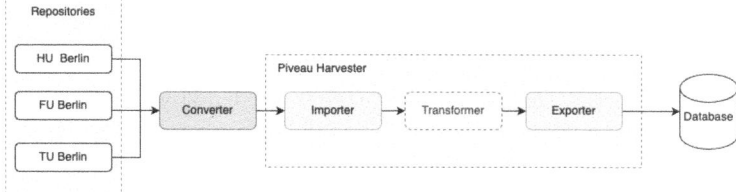

Fig. 2. Pipeline: The converter communicates with different repositories and transforms different schemas and vocabularies into a standardized format, i.e., DCAT, and harvester employs importer to fetch metadata from converter and exports to persistent datastore.

"abstract" to refer to the publication's abstract, while the other repositories in the BUA use "description" in their schemas. We investigated schema alignment among metadata of dcat, oai_dc, dc_terms, and dc_elements, considering their metadata's labels, comments, and definitions, along with prompting ChatGPT by OpenAI and computing cosine similarity with those models' embeddings. We conducted experiments[13] about prompt templates in [6]. Leveraging this tool, BOP can efficiently harmonize and integrate data from all three universities. By addressing the challenge of data heterogeneity, the converter promotes a unified and cohesive research environment.

In the context of the NFDI initiative, we plan to harvest a variety of data repositories in the future. One of the domain-independent repositories we already harvest is the NFDI4Cat Zenodo[14] community, which is based on the repository software Invenio. Another repository we harvest in the context of NFDI4Cat is a domain-specific Dataverse instance employed at the BasCat laboratory at TU Berlin. Both do not natively support the DCAT schema. In order to maintain a cohesive and standardized database, we can integrate new converter services that facilitate the transformation of arbitrary schemas into our targeted DCAT schema under the proposed framework. By utilizing this service into our data management workflow, we ensure that data from repositories like the Invenio and the Dataverse instance mentioned above can be harmoniously integrated into the NFDI4Cat Meta Portal using the DCAT format. This conversion process enables consistent data representation and enhances interoperability among the different NFDI projects. The flexibility of the converting script allows for the transformation of varying schemas, accommodating the unique characteristics and structures of different data sources within the research communities.

3   Conclusion

We developed a novel service, *converter*, which resolves the interoperability problem between the DCAT vocabulary and the harvested data before sending the

---

[13] The experiments and their results: https://github.com/sefeoglu/dcat-converter/tree/master/schema_matching_experiments.
[14] Zenodo is available at https://zenodo.org/.

retrieved data to the Piveau framework. Our main contributions are listed in the following.

- Without a converter, the Piveau importer is burdened with the task of managing multiple schemas, necessitating codebase adaption for each distinct schema. Moreover, the transformers currently available in the Piveau framework have limited capabilities in handling complex schema mappings. This limitation poses a challenge in effectively transforming and integrating data from different schemas.
- Our work offers a comprehensive solution for effectively managing different vocabularies within the same schema, e.g., oai_dc. Our proposal stands out due to its seamless deployment and easy integration as a pluggable service into the Piveau framework.
- Thanks to the converter introduced, we can eliminate the need for any extensive adaption of the Piveau harvester, streamlining the integration process and ensuring a smooth transition.

The proposed pluggable service, called *converter*, is initially used to demonstrate how the metadata of the institutes in the Berlin University Alliance (BUA) can be converted into the DCAT format. However, it can be extended to convert the metadata of other universities into the same format within the metadata portal.

Acknowledgement. This work has been funded by the German Federal Ministry of Education and Research (BMBF) and the state of Berlin and by the German Research Foundation (DFG) under project numbers 441926934 (NFDI4Cat) and 460234259 (NFDI4DataScience).

References

1. Dragan, A., Sofou, N.: DCAT application profile for data portals in Europe (2019), https://joinup.ec.europa.eu/sites/default/files/distribution/access_url/2019-05/e3f7bcdf-eaad-4741-9bf6-dc61327f4eea/DCAT_AP_1.2.1.pdf
2. Efeoglu, S.: Graphmatcher: a graph representation learning approach for ontology matching. In: The Semantic Web – ISWC 2022 (Workshop Proceedings), CEUR-WS (2022)
3. Jiménez-Ruiz, E., Cuenca Grau, B.: Logmap: logic-based and scalable ontology matching. In: Aroyo, L. (ed.) The Semantic Web - ISWC 2011, pp. 273–288. SBH, Berlin, Heidelberg (2011)
4. Kirstein, F., Dutkowski, S., Dittwald, B., Hauswirth, M.: The European data portal: scalable harvesting and management of linked open data. In: The Semantic Web – ISWC 2019 (Workshop Proceedings), CEUR-WS (2019)
5. Kirstein, F., Stefanidis, K., Dittwald, B., Dutkowski, S., Urbanek, S., Hauswirth, M.: Piveau: a large-scale open data management platform based on semantic web technologies. In: Harth, A. (ed.) The Semantic Web - ESWC 2020, pp. 648–664. Springer International Publishing, Cham (2020)
6. Norouzi, S.S., Mahdavinejad, M.S., Hitzler, P.: Conversational ontology alignment with chatgpt. arXiv preprint arXiv:2308.09217 (2023)

RDFminer: An Interactive Tool for the Evolutionary Discovery of SHACL Shapes

Rémi Felin$^{(\boxtimes)}$ ⓘ, Pierre Monnin ⓘ, Catherine Faron ⓘ, and Andrea G. B. Tettamanzi ⓘ

Université Côte d'Azur, Inria, CNRS, I3S, Sophia-Antipolis, France
{remi.felin,pierre.monnin,catherine.faron,andrea.tettamanzi}@inria.fr

Abstract. RDFminer is an open source Web application to automatically discover SHACL shapes through an evolutionary process. It takes an RDF data graph as input, from which shapes are mined and assessed using a probabilistic validation framework. The user can interact with RDFminer through a dashboard where they can launch and monitor the mining of shapes, and analyse the results in real time.

Keywords: RDF · SHACL · Shape Mining · Evolutionary Algorithm

1 Introduction

The continuous intensive production of RDF facts on the Web contributes to the availability of large knowledge graphs. Subsequently, the problem of inconsistencies in RDF data resulting from these efforts has emerged, which directly impacts the RDF data graph quality, validity and actionability. To identify inconsistencies in RDF data, the SHACL W3C recommendation allows to express constraints as *shapes* that RDF data must conform to. This shifts the problem to determining the domain constraints to be checked: it is well-known that acquiring SHACL shapes from large RDF data graphs is a tedious task [5]. In this paper, we present RDFminer, a Web application that makes it possible to discover SHACL shapes from an RDF graph. It implements an evolutionary approach and provides an interactive interface enabling the user to launch, monitor and analyse their shape discovery projects. Figure 1 presents the whole architecture of RDFminer.

2 Evolutionary Discovery of SHACL Shapes

RDFminer is a framework implementing the evolutionary approach based on Grammatical Evolution described in [3] to discover relevant SHACL shapes from an RDF data graph. The principle of this approach is to generate and manage a population of candidate shapes that evolve through mutation and crossover,

A. Meroño Peñuela et al. (Eds.): ESWC 2024, LNCS 15344, pp. 207–211, 2025.
https://doi.org/10.1007/978-3-031-78952-6_28

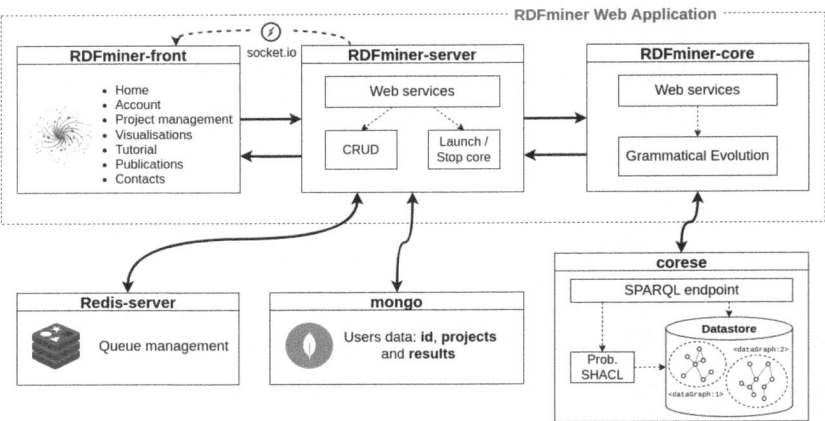

Fig. 1. Global architecture of *RDFminer*

with the aim of improving their fitness, *i.e.*, their adequacy to the data graph, over time. The main steps of the algorithm are presented in Fig. 2

The fitness of the shapes is calculated using a probabilistic framework for SHACL validation presented in [2]. That framework extends standard SHACL validation by declaring RDF graphs as valid w.r.t. a shape if they contain less than a given threshold of triples that do not conform to this shape. SHACL validation reports are extended accordingly with probabilistic metrics, using an extended vocabulary.[1]

RDFminer relies on the GEVA 2.0 [4] implementation of Grammatical Evolution for the generation of candidate SHACL shapes and on the Corese [1] semantic Web factory to query RDF data and validate RDF data against candidate shapes. We implemented a multi-threading system to assess candidate shapes as this is the most time-consuming task in the overall evolutionary discovery process.

3   A Web Application to Discover SHACL Shapes

Exploiting the RDFminer core engine to discover SHACL shapes is essentially a trial-and-error process. That is why we developed a Web application to provide users with an interface that allows them to control the mining process interactively: it enables to parameterize and launch the discovery process, monitor its execution, inspect and analyze its results.

3.1   Monitoring Dashboard

The connected user can discover shapes from a given RDF data graph by creating a project and defining the parameters of the mining process: the data

---

[1] Probabilistic SHACL vocabulary: http://ns.inria.fr/probabilistic-shacl/.

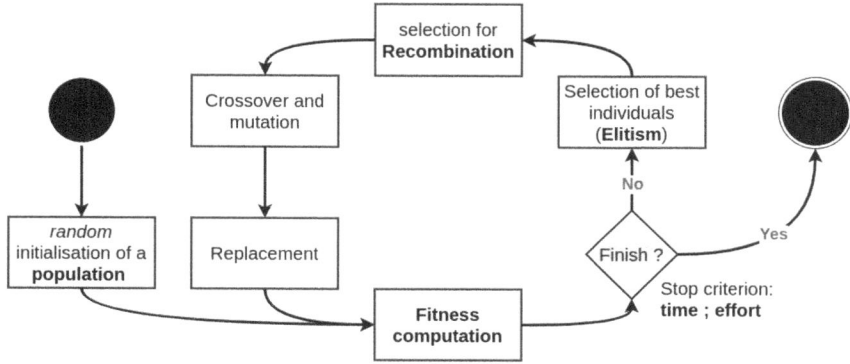

Fig. 2. Main steps of the Grammatical Evolution algorithm

graph, the SHACL constructs to be considered, and the hyper-parameters of the Grammatical Evolution algorithm. The status of the running project is updated in real time and can be interrupted if needed. This dashboard is presented in Fig. 3a.

3.2   Result Analysis Dashboard

Due to the nature of the evolutionary mining process, the population of candidate shapes evolves continuously. This dashboard thus allows the user to consult and analyze results both in real-time when evolution is underway or at the end of the process.

In more detail, every running project generates in real-time results which can be analysed through this dashboard. Completed projects are accessible as well. The user accesses the Results view and can analyse the current execution status (Fig. 3b), the discovered SHACL shapes and their characteristics (Fig. 3c) and the execution statistics as charts (Fig. 3d). The *population evolution* chart describes the rate of individuals (candidate shapes) that differ from one generation to the next one: this should be interpreted together with the *individuals with non-null fitness* and *fitness evolution* charts to determine if the chosen hyperparameters of the evolutionary algorithm lead to the discovery of relevant shapes. The *characteristics of the entities* chart provides information on the quality of the shapes: a colour gradient from red to green indicates the degree to which RDF data conform to the shapes. This real-time analysis of the mining process is an effective way of supervising its execution. For instance, the user can decide to stop it (Fig. 3a) if it appears to be stuck in a local optimum. At the end of an execution, the user can download the shapes graph in Turtle format and/or the complete results file (including individuals, their statistics and the algorithm's statistics) in JSON format for post-processing.

Fig. 3. Visualization dashboard of a shape mining project in progress

It should also be noted that `RDFminer` core can be used independently of the other components through its API.[2] The source code is available in a public repository[3] and an `RDFminer` service is available online.[4]

4 Proposed Demonstration

The demonstration will be as follows: We will connect to the `eswc_demo` account and show the results of a completed project aiming to discover shapes from the covid-on-the-web RDF data graph [3]. Then we will create and launch a new similar mining project but with less demanding hyper-parameters so that it can complete within a few minutes and we will show how the user can visualize in real-time the current state of the project: the current list of shapes discovered, the development rate, the proportion of individuals with a non-zero fitness score

---

[2] User guide: https://github.com/Wimmics/RDFminer/tree/main/RDFminer-core.
[3] Source code: https://github.com/Wimmics/RDFminer.
[4] Web application: https://ns.inria.fr/rdfminer/.

and the evolution of the fitness score. On completion of the project, we will download the results file and the shapes graph. A tutorial video corresponding to this demonstration is available on the `RDFminer` website.[5]

As future work, we aim to conduct a user evaluation of both the quality of the generated shapes considered as valid, with a special focus on shapes with a little support (*i.e.*, few triples that confirm them), and the usability of the RDFminer dashboard to monitor and tune the shape mining process.

Acknowledgements. This work has been partially funded by the 3IA Côte d'Azur "Investments in the Future" project managed by the National Research Agency (ANR) with the reference number ANR-19-P3IA-0002.

References

1. Cérès, R., et al.: Corese (2023). https://project.inria.fr/corese/
2. Felin, R., et al.: A framework to include and exploit probabilistic information in SHACL validation reports. ESWC (2023)
3. Felin, R., et al.: An algorithm based on grammatical evolution for discovering SHACL constraints. EuroGP (2024)
4. O'Neill, M., et al.: GEVA - Grammatical Evolution in Java (2011)
5. Rabbani, K., Lissandrini, M., Hose, K.: SHACL and SHEx in the wild: a community survey on validating shapes generation and adoption. In: WWW (Companion Volume) (2022)

---

[5] Tutorial video: https://ns.inria.fr/rdfminer/tutorial.

MusicBO, an Application of Text2AMR2FRED to the Musical Heritage Domain

Aldo Gangemi[1], Arianna Graciotti[1(✉)], Antonello Meloni[2], Eleonora Marzi[1], Andrea Nuzzolese[3], Valentina Presutti[1], Diego Reforgiato Recupero[2,3], Alessandro Russo[3], and Rocco Tripodi[4]

[1] University of Bologna, 40126 Bologna, Italy
Arianna.Graciotti@unibo.it
[2] University of Cagliari, Via Ospedale 72, 09124 Cagliari, Italy
[3] CNR, via San Martino della Battaglia 44, 00185 Rome, Italy
[4] Ca' Foscari University of Venice, Sestiere Dorsoduro, 3246, 30123 Venezia, VE, Italy

Abstract. Converting textual data into Knowledge Graphs (KGs) poses a significant challenge, particularly when dealing with multilingual and historical documents. In this paper, we describe the application of Text2-AMR2FRED to MusicBO corpus, the former being a tool for transforming text into RDF/OWL KGs via Abstract Meaning Representation (AMR), the latter being a diachronic collection of Musical Heritage (MH) texts.

Keywords: Abstract Meaning Representation · Natural Language Processing · Knowledge Graphs · Semantic Frames

1 Introduction

This paper describes the methods and tools applied for automatically transforming MusicBO, a multilingual and diachronic textual corpus about the role of Musical Heritage (MH) in the city of Bologna, into an OWL-compliant RDF Knowledge Graph (KG). The KG obtained is publicly accessible through a SPARQL endpoint[1], enabling the creation of visual data stories[2] using MELODY[3]. The resulting KG aims to enable scholars with different backgrounds to conduct large-scale qualitative analysis.

---

[1] https://polifonia.disi.unibo.it/musicbo/sparql.

[2] https://projects.dharc.unibo.it/melody/musicbo/music_in_bologna_knowledge_graph_overvi

[3] MELODY (Make mE a Linked Open Data storY) is a web portal that allows users to query Linked Open Data and create web-ready interactive data stories.

A. Meroño Peñuela et al. (Eds.): ESWC 2024, LNCS 15344, pp. 212–216, 2025.
https://doi.org/10.1007/978-3-031-78952-6_29

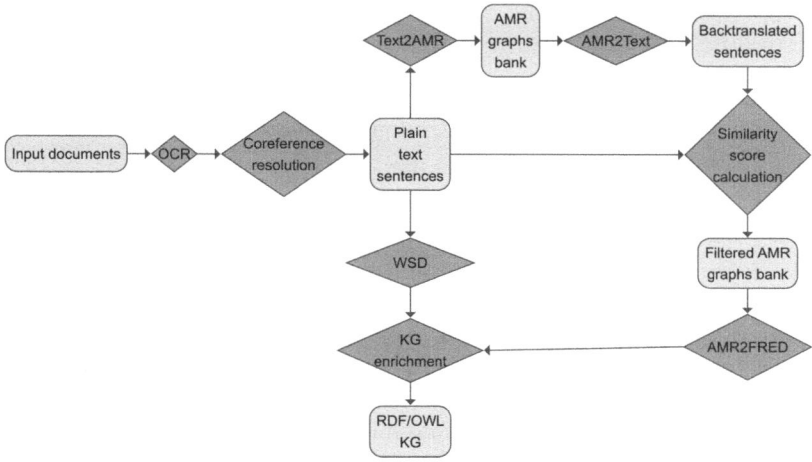

Fig. 1. The MusicBO KG creation pipeline schema.

2   The MusicBO Knowledge Graph

MusicBO corpus[4] contains 137 texts in 4 languages (Italian, English, French, and Spanish) published between 1700 to the current era[6].

Table 1. Statistics describing the MusicBO corpus' documents included in the scope of this study.

Language	#docs	total length (#tokens)	average length (#tokens)	median length (#tokens)
EN	47	1.873.030	40.718	9.964.5
ITA	51	2.329.054	44.789, 5	14.334

Our approach to transform plain text into a KG, depicted in Fig. 1, is based on Text2AMR2FRED[7][3], an enhanced version of FRED [4,5]. We include in the scope of this study only the MusicBO corpus' documents in English and in Italian (respectively 47 and 51). Statistics[8] of the documents processed in this study

---

[4] MusicBO corpus is part of the wider Polifonia Textual Corpus[5], a large-scale, multilingual and multigenre diachronic textual corpus.

[6] Due to copyright reasons, the documents of MusicBO corpus cannot be entirely disclosed. Still, we released metadata that allows the reproduction of the corpus https://doi.org/10.5281/zenodo.6672165.

[7] https://arco.istc.cnr.it/txt-amr-fred/.

[8] Statistics have been calculated using SpaCy (https://spacy.io) NLP library, employing the models `en_core_web_trf` for documents in English language and `it_core_news_lg` for documents in Italian language.

Table 2. Statistics describing the KG resulting from the application of Text2AMR2FRED to MusicBO corpus.

Language	#(sent, AMR graph) pairs (Text2AMR)	#(filtered sent, AMR graph) pairs (Automatic metrics evaluation)	#triples
EN	51.814	5.798	412.911
ITA	10.563	1.759	118.162
Overall	62.377	7.557	531.073

are reported in Table 1. The initial formats of these documents encompassed *.pdf*, *images*, or *.docx*. We extract plain text from them through customized Optical Character Recognition (OCR) technologies[9]. Subsequently, we carry out co-reference resolution[10], rule-based minimal post-OCR corrections[11], and sentence splitting on the extracted plain texts. Following this pre-processing stage, we submit the processed sentences to neural models (SPRING for English [1] and USeA for Italian [7]) for text2AMR parsing. AMR graphs, anchored to Prop-Bank *Frames*[12], function as an event-centric representation of the MusicBO corpus' sentences, suited for extracting 'who-did-what-to-whom' information from a text. Through the application of the AMR2FRED tool[13] [6], accessible via the Machine Reading suite[14], we transform AMR graphs into full-fledged RDF/OWL KGs aligned with FRED's theoretical framework. The outcome is a series of *named graphs*, enabling the tracking of each triple to its originating sentence in the corpus. We enrich the resulting KGs through Framester [2], which allows the alignment with external Knowledge Bases (KBs) such as DBPedia[15], Wikidata[2] and Verbatlas[2]. For instance, consider the following triples[16]:

---

[9] https://github.com/polifonia-project/textual-corpus-population.

[10] For English language documents, we implemented a co-reference resolution pipeline based on Spacy's *neuralcoref* (https://spacy.io/universe/project/neuralcoref). We are currently evaluating tools for Italian.

[11] https://github.com/polifonia-project/rulebased-postocr-corrector.

[12] PropBank Frames are the core lexicon of the PropBank paradigm and consist of predicate-argument structures named "rolesets".

[13] https://github.com/polifonia-project/amr2Fred.

[14] https://github.com/polifonia-project/machine-reading.

[15] https://www.dbpedia.org/, https://www.wikidata.org/, https://verbatlas.org/.

[16] Extrapolated from the KG originating from the sentence *"In the year 1814, Barbaja went to Bologna and offered Rossini a better engagement than before."*, taken from the MusicBO corpus document *The Life of Rossini (Edwards, 1869)*, available at: https://freeditorial.com/en/books/filter-author/henry-sutherland-edwards.

```
fred : Barbaja  a  amr : Person  ;
    owl : sameAs  dbpedia : Domenico_Barbaia ,
        wd : Q908235  .

fred : offer_1  a  pbdata : offer −01  ;
    pblr : benefactive_or_entity_offered_to  fred : Rossini  ;
    pblr : commodity  fred : engagement_1  ;
    pblr : entity_offering  fred : Barbaja  ;
    fschema : subsumedUnder  va : 0229f ,
        fnframe : Offering  .

fred : Rossini  a  amr : Person  ;
    owl : sameAs  dbpedia : Gioachino_Rossini ,
        wd : Q9726  .
```

The reported triples encode the event of an engagement offer delivered from Domenico Barbaja, an opera manager, to the composer Gioachino Rossini[17]. Such knowledge is what scholars who supported the corpus collection aimed to disclose, at scale, from MusicBO documents automatically. Independent scholars can leverage such knowledge encoded in the KG and create data stories through MELODY, such as the one created by University of Bologna students[18], focusing on the representation of Russian composers and classical music in the MusicBo corpus.

Processing non-standard texts may lead to potential inaccuracies of text2AMR parsers, as such data is scarce in their training sets. Manual validation is time-consuming, and no standard benchmarks exist for semantic parsing of historic and OCRed text. We followed a back-translation [8] methodology to address these challenges. We converted the AMR graphs back to sentences using SPRING for English and m-AMR2Text for Italian[19] , followed by similarity score computations using BLEURT [20] for English and cosine similarity for Italian. We posit that high-quality graphs are associated with generated sentences exhibiting high BLEURT or cosine similarity scores. All AMR graphs paired with AMR2Text-generated sentences with a negative BLEURT score or a cosine similarity below 0.90 were discarded. We provide in Table 2 the statistics regarding the KG resulting from the application of Text2AMR2FRED to the MusicBO corpus, including insights regarding the automatic filtering. Raw data to recreate the KG are stored in a dedicated repository[21].

---

[17] The named entities are automatically linked to their entry in Wikipedia by BLINK [9], the entity linker used by SPRING, and aligned to Wikidata and DBPedia in the AMR2RDF step of our pipeline.

[18] https://melody-data.github.io/stories/published_stories/story_1687714706.423208. html.

[19] https://github.com/UKPLab/m-AMR2Text.

[20] https://github.com/google-research/bleurt.

[21] https://github.com/polifonia-project/musicbo-knowledge-graph/tree/main.

Acknowledgements. The authors acknowledge the support of the European Union's Horizon 2020 research and innovation programme under grant agreement No. 101004746.

References

1. Bevilacqua, M., Blloshmi, R., Navigli, R.: One SPRING to Rule Them Both: Symmetric AMR Semantic Parsing and Generation without a Complex Pipeline. In: Proceedings of the AAAI Conference on Artificial Intelligence. vol. 35, no. 14, pp. 12564–12573 (2021). https://ojs.aaai.org/index.php/AAAI/article/view/17489
2. Gangemi, A., Alam, M., Asprino, L., Presutti, V., Recupero, D.R.: Framester: a wide coverage linguistic linked data hub. In: EKAW 2016, pp. 239–254. Springer International Publishing, Bologna, Italy (2016)
3. Gangemi, A., et al.: Text2AMR2FRED, a tool for transforming text into RDF/OWL Knowledge Graphs via Abstract Meaning Representation. In: 22nd ISWC, CEUR Workshop Proc., Athens, Greece (2023)
4. Gangemi, A., Hassan, E., Presutti, V., Recupero, D.R.: FRED as an event extraction tool. In: van Erp, M., Hollink, L., Troncy, R., van Hage, W.R., van de Laar, P., Shamma, D.A., Gao, L. (eds.) Proceedings of DeRiVE 2013, co-located with the 12th ISWC 2013, Sydney, Australia, October 21, 2013. CEUR Workshop Proceedings, vol. 1123, pp. 14–17. CEUR-WS.org (2013)
5. Gangemi, A., Presutti, V., Recupero, D.R., Nuzzolese, A.G., Draicchio, F., Mongiovì, M.: Semantic web machine reading with FRED. Semant. Web **8**(6), 873–893 (2017). https://doi.org/10.3233/SW-160240, https://doi.org/10.3233/SW-160240
6. Meloni, A., Reforgiato Recupero, D., Gangemi, A.: AMR2FRED, a tool for translating abstract meaning representation to motif-based linguistic knowledge graphs. In: The Semantic Web: ESWC 2017 Satellite Events, pp. 43–47. Springer International Publishing, Portorož, Slovenia (2017)
7. Orlando, R., Conia, S., Faralli, S., Navigli, R.: Universal semantic annotator: the first unified API for WSD, SRL and semantic parsing. In: Proceedings of the 13th LREC 2022, pp. 2634–2641. European Language Resources Association, Marseille, France (2022). https://aclanthology.org/2022.lrec-1.282
8. Sennrich, R., Haddow, B., Birch, A.: Improving neural machine translation models with monolingual data. In: Proceedings of the 54th Annual Meeting of the ACL (Volume 1: Long Papers), pp. 86–96. ACL, Berlin, Germany (2016). https://doi.org/10.18653/v1/P16-1009, https://aclanthology.org/P16-1009
9. Wu, L., Petroni, F., Josifoski, M., Riedel, S., Zettlemoyer, L.: Scalable zero-shot entity linking with dense entity retrieval. In: Webber, B., Cohn, T., He, Y., Liu, Y. (eds.) Proceedings of the 2020 Conference on Empirical Methods in Natural Language Processing (EMNLP), pp. 6397–6407. ACL, Online (2020). https://doi.org/10.18653/v1/2020.emnlp-main.519, https://aclanthology.org/2020.emnlp-main.519

RDF2vec Embeddings for Updateable Knowledge Graphs – Reuse, Don't Retrain!

Sang Hyu Hahn and Heiko Paulheim[✉][iD]

University of Mannheim, Data and Web Science Group, Mannheim, Germany
heiko.paulheim@uni-mannheim.de

Abstract. Most Knowledge Graph Embeddings, like RDF2vec, are designed to be trained on a fixed knowledge graph (KG). When that KG is updated, they usually need to be retrained from scratch, which takes quite a bit of time. In this paper, we introduce a method of incrementally updating an RDF2vec embedding instead of retraining it. We conduct an experiment using different snapshots of DBpedia, demonstrating that this is a competitive, yet faster method to obtain embedding vectors of an updated knowledge graph, which sometimes even yields better results than retraining from scratch.

Keywords: Updateable Knowledge Graphs · Embeddings · RDF2vec

1 Introduction

Knowledge Graph Embeddings (KGEs) are widely used, e.g., for link prediction in knowledge graphs, or to provide dense representations for other downstream tasks, such as node classification or recommender systems [7]. The vast majority of KGE approaches assume a *static* knowledge graph, i.e., upon an update of that graph, the embeddings have to be re-trained from scratch [1]. At the same time, training KGEs is usually a time and resource consuming process.

In this paper, we consider a widely used KGE technique, i.e., RDF2vec [5], and show how it can be adapted so that existing KGEs can be updated rather than re-trained. We look at four different snapshots of DBpedia [4], and compare embedding models which are trained on an earlier version and updated to a newer one to those freshly trained on the new version. We show that the results with updated KGEs on downstream tasks are en par or even superior, at much lower training efforts. Other than approaches like OUKE [2] and DKGE [9], it can also update embeddings of entities without changes in their direct context, and also supports the addition of new relations, not only new entities.

2 Approach

Our approach builds upon the capability of word2vec to resume training based on new sentences, updating both vectors for existing words, as well as learning

A. Meroño Peñuela et al. (Eds.): ESWC 2024, LNCS 15344, pp. 217–222, 2025.
https://doi.org/10.1007/978-3-031-78952-6_30

Data: W_{init} *an initial set of walks, d: walk depth*
Result: W_{final}: Set of walks
for *walk* $w \in W_{init}$ **do**
    while *w.length() < d* **do**
        if *(random()<0.5)* **then**
            edge = pickRandomFrom(getIngoingEdges(w.first()))
            add *edge* at beginning of *w*
        end
        else
            edge = pickRandomFrom(getOutgoingEdges(w.last()))
            add *edge* at end of *w*
        end
    end
end
add *w* to W_{final}

Algorithm 1: Overall walk generation algorithm for generating new walks

vectors for new words.[1] To that end, new walks reflecting the updates in a KG have to be extracted. We pursue three strategies to extract new walks for an updated KG.

All of them are inspired by the algorithm of RDF2vec Light, which extracts walks for specific entities [8]. With $G = (V, E)$ being the KG for which an embedding has already been trained, and $G' = (V', E')$ being the new version of the KG, the three strategies all call algorithm 1 with different sets of walks W_{init}:

Entity-based computes a set of n walks for each new entity. Calls algorithm 1 with W_{init} being the set of (0-hop) walks constituted by $V' \setminus V$.
Edge-based computes a set of n walks for each new edge. Calls algorithm 1 with W_{init} being the set of 1-hop walks constituted by $E' \setminus E$.
Combined computes a set of n walks for each new entity, and for each new edge connecting two existing entities. Calls W_{init} for the union of 0-hop walks constituted by $V' \setminus V$, and 1-hop walks constituted by $\{(e_1, r, e_2) \in E' \setminus E \mid e_1 \notin V' \setminus V \wedge e_2 \notin V' \setminus V\}$.

The last approach is faster than the edge-based approach for new entities, since it generates n walks per new entity in G', while the edge-based approach would generate $n \cdot d$ walks, where d is the degree of the new entity.

3   Experiments

In our experiments, we use four snapshots of DBpedia[2]. All three update scenarios start from the 2019-09 version (4.3M entities, 11.8M triples) and update the

---

[1] https://radimrehurek.com/gensim/auto_examples/tutorials/run_word2vec.html# online-training-resuming-training.
[2] https://databus.dbpedia.org/dbpedia/mappings/mappingbased-objects.

Table 1. DBpedia versions used in the experiments

Version	#Entities	#Triples	#relations
2019-09	4,256,911	11,799,129	621
2020-12	7,266,101	21,384,769	635
2021-12	7,347,010	22,072,275	634
2022-12	7,958,883	22,791,171	633

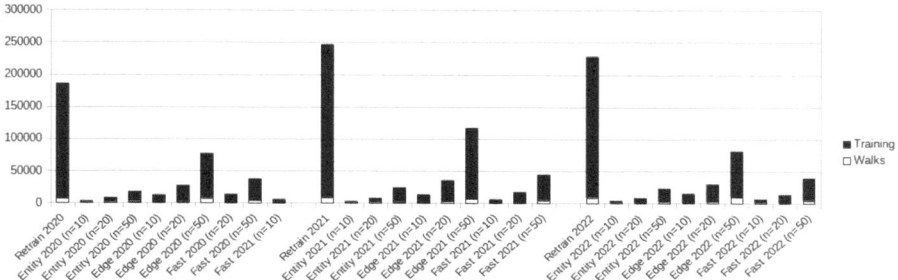

Fig. 1. Depiction of runtimes, split by walk generation (white) and model training/update (black).

embeddings to the 2020-12 (7.3M entities, 21.3M triples, 2021-12 (7.3M entities, 22.0M triples), and 2022-12 (8.0M entities, 22.8M triples) version, respectively. We run experiments with 10, 20, and 50 walks per new entity and/or edge. Statistics about the datasets are depicted in Table 1.

We use the gEval benchmark suite [6], which defines different tasks for evaluating and comparing KGEs, and the RDF2vec parameters reported to work best in past works[3].[4] The results are shown in Tables 2 and 3. The runtimes[5] for creating the KGEs are depicted in Fig. 1.

4   Summary and Limitations

The results show that the update mechanism can update RDF2vec representations for new versions of a KG, in most of the cases performing at least as good or even better than fully retrained ones, but with less consumption of computational resources. While the fact that updated embeddings may even outperform those retrained from scratch might come as a surprise, it can be explained by the fact that an updated KGE can reflect knowledge encoded in *both* versions of the KG, not just one, and, hence, may even encode more information.

---

[3] Skip-gram, 5 epochs, 200 dimensions, window size = 5, depth = 8.

[4] Code to reproduce experiments: https://github.com/sanghyu/RDF2vec-Update.

[5] Intel Xeon Gold 6230 (2.1 Ghz), using 8 cores with 300 GB RAM.

Table 2. Classification (C, accuracy) and regression (R, RMSE) results. The best performing results per DBpedia version are marked in bold; all results outperforming retraining from scratch are marked in grey.

Strategy	AAUP C	AAUP R	Cities C	Cities R	Forbes C	Forbes R	Albums C	Albums L	Movies C	Movies R
Baseline 2019	.670	71.965	.771	18.112	.568	40.738	.632	15.167	.733	22.525
Retrain 2020	.708	64.510	.776	14.340	.597	36.414	.659	15.698	.747	19.752
Entity 2020 (n=10)	.687	66.347	.789	14.668	.602	36.483	.682	15.163	.705	21.882
Entity 2020 (n=20)	**.713**	64.154	.772	14.112	.610	37.372	.726	14.154	.726	21.056
Entity 2020 (n=50)	.704	63.464	.757	13.869	.610	37.803	.742	14.369	.731	20.355
Edge 2020 (n=10)	.708	**62.061**	.770	12.595	**.625**	37.345	.760	13.338	**.756**	19.587
Edge 2020 (n=20)	.709	63.925	.791	12.238	.611	36.680	**.776**	13.526	.750	19.403
Edge 2020 (n=50)	.701	64.484	.778	**12.035**	.609	**35.941**	.757	13.368	.750	**19.148**
Comb. 2020 (n=10)	.704	62.572	**.783**	13.863	.621	37.083	.748	13.799	.733	21.143
Comb. 2020 (n=20)	.699	62.586	.778	12.832	.616	36.245	.764	13.158	.738	20.514
Comb. 2020 (n=50)	.693	63.594	.763	12.732	.617	36.414	.773	**12.691**	**.756**	19.748
Retrain 2021	**.715**	65.680	.776	14.255	.617	37.513	.649	14.927	.738	20.219
Entity 2021 (n=10)	.689	67.052	.794	14.137	.602	37.034	.680	15.413	.703	21.993
Entity 2021 (n=20)	.691	65.430	.782	13.931	.604	37.244	.717	14.359	.717	21.220
Entity 2021 (n=50)	.707	63.956	.780	14.140	.609	37.323	.727	14.536	.723	20.553
Edge 2021 (n=10)	.708	**63.069**	.785	13.937	.618	37.220	.752	13.664	**.753**	19.606
Edge 2021 (n=20)	.710	63.659	.786	13.719	.606	37.292	.772	13.198	.746	19.539
Edge 2021 (n=50)	.693	64.388	.787	13.594	.615	**36.057**	**.783**	**12.734**	.747	**19.481**
Comb. 2021 (n=10)	.699	65.351	**.807**	13.943	**.625**	37.597	.752	13.899	.732	21.237
Comb. 2021 (n=20)	.709	64.583	.785	**13.469**	.619	36.580	.770	13.198	.730	20.737
Comb. 2021 (n=50)	**.715**	64.684	.790	13.957	.621	36.263	.771	12.825	.743	19.964
Retrain 2022	.674	66.313	.773	16.639	.617	37.165	.691	14.830	.731	19.808
Entity 2022 (n=10)	.687	66.347	.789	14.668	.602	**36.483**	.682	15.163	.705	21.882
Entity 2022 (n=20)	.704	64.619	.786	14.221	.606	37.160	.727	14.402	.725	21.186
Entity 2022 (n=50)	.703	64.652	.781	13.611	.605	37.347	.722	14.202	.729	20.655
Edge 2022 (n=10)	**.707**	**62.957**	.785	13.043	**.619**	37.235	.742	13.664	**.755**	19.596
Edge 2022 (n=20)	.698	63.931	.783	13.113	.618	37.820	.748	13.284	.754	19.349
Edge 2022 (n=50)	.696	65.469	**.806**	**12.517**	.610	36.866	**.768**	13.256	.749	**19.289**
Comb. 2022 (n=10)	.696	64.327	.777	13.426	.618	37.215	.741	13.850	.729	21.033
Comb. 2022 (n=20)	.701	64.249	.779	13.437	.618	37.272	.765	13.151	.734	20.248
Comb. 2022 (n=50)	.702	64.351	.783	13.133	.616	36.888	.760	**12.954**	.744	20.248

Currently, the approach only supports *addition* of entities and edges. The case where entites and edges are *removed* is not directly addressed by our approach. For those cases, a combination with techniques that forget and reconstruct embeddings, as suggested in [3], might be useful.

The fact that, in many cases, using updated KGEs even outperforms using KGEs fully retrained from scratch yields the interesting question whether this should be considered a general training paradigm for RDF2vec on versioned knowledge graphs, as it indicates that incrementally training those embeddings might yield better embeddings than only training on the version for which the embedding is needed.

Table 3. Clustering (accuracy), Semantic Analogies (accuracy), Document Similarity (Kendall's Tau), and Entity Similarity (Harmonic Mean) results. The best performing results per DBpedia version are marked in bold; all results outperforming retraining from scratch are marked in grey.

Strategy	Clustering				Semantic Analogies				Ent. Rel.	Doc. Sim.
	cit/cou (2k)	cit/cou	5 cls.	teams	cap-cou	cap-cou (all)	curr	cit-stat		
Baseline 2019	.628	.593	.522	.862	.352	.263	.387	.356	.457	.293
Retrain 2020	.809	.590	.787	.502	.755	.677	.418	.336	**.513**	.346
Entity 2020 (n=10)	.730	.821	.781	**.864**	**.879**	.816	.299	**.485**	.430	.424
Entity 2020 (n=20)	.729	**.843**	.784	.781	.761	**.822**	.399	.446	.451	.405
Entity 2020 (n=50)	.733	.671	.756	.779	.715	.803	.491	.383	.486	.396
Edge 2020 (n=10)	.732	.741	.779	.783	.662	.783	.478	.334	.489	.414
Edge 2020 (n=20)	.756	.708	.782	.782	.642	.749	.510	.267	.508	.423
Edge 2020 (n=50)	**.828**	.636	**.790**	.778	.626	.725	**.528**	.198	.512	.414
Comb. 2020 (n=10)	.757	.739	.681	.862	.773	.789	.382	.469	.474	**.427**
Comb. 2020 (n=20)	.776	.708	.751	.783	.820	.788	.469	.319	.696	.419
Comb. 2020 (n=50)	.819	.663	.765	.780	.810	.793	.519	.350	.509	.420
Retrain 2021	.825	.633	**.772**	.490	.739	.683	.461	.347	**.547**	.425
Entity 2021 (n=10)	.748	**.823**	.719	.858	**.836**	.799	.363	**.466**	.426	.438
Entity 2021 (n=20)	.747	.726	.754	.782	.781	**.805**	.423	.409	.457	.430
Entity 2021 (n=50)	.785	.675	.746	.780	.670	.756	.464	.317	.473	.410
Edge 2021 (n=10)	.774	.736	.756	.787	.674	.740	.462	.218	.504	.444
Edge 2021 (n=20)	.803	.702	.763	.783	.652	.722	.479	.178	.506	.454
Edge 2021 (n=50)	**.864**	.655	.759	.777	.634	.668	**.488**	.140	.506	**.464**
Comb. 2021 (n=10)	.788	.735	.660	**.860**	.767	.764	.452	.363	.489	.451
Comb. 2021 (n=20)	.834	.706	.756	.820	.773	.761	.483	.309	.495	.463
Comb. 2021 (n=50)	.848	.655	.762	.780	.804	.683	.461	.347	.510	**.464**
Retrain 2022	.828	.653	.774	.476	.725	.635	.384	.343	**.532**	.392
Entity 2022 (n=10)	.730	.821	.781	**.864**	**.879**	**.816**	.299	**.485**	.430	.424
Entity 2022 (n=20)	.769	**.833**	.775	.804	.800	.811	.359	.438	.460	.422
Entity 2022 (n=50)	.741	.672	.776	.785	.739	.749	.428	.352	.494	.419
Edge 2022 (n=10)	.778	.736	.780	.794	.709	.743	.428	.295	.515	.433
Edge 2022 (n=20)	.797	.695	.768	.793	.682	.701	.431	.219	.510	.444
Edge 2022 (n=50)	**.849**	.641	**.783**	.780	.702	.692	**.448**	.165	.507	**.461**
Comb. 2022 (n=10)	.731	.738	.756	.860	.848	.801	.383	.435	.502	.429
Comb. 2022 (n=20)	.790	.712	.763	.792	.828	.769	.425	.377	.503	.422
Comb. 2022 (n=50)	.837	.645	.782	.775	.812	.746	.443	.316	.572	.442

Acknowledgement. Supported by the state of Baden-Württemberg through bwHPC.

References

1. Biswas, R., et al.: Knowledge graph embeddings: open challenges and opportunities. Trans. Graph Data Knowl. **1**(1), 1–4 (2023)
2. Fei, L., Wu, T., Khan, A.: Online updates of knowledge graph embedding. In: Complex Networks & Their Applications. pp. 523–535. Springer (2022). https://doi.org/10.1007/978-3-030-93413-2_44
3. Krause, F.: Dynamic knowledge graph embeddings via local embedding reconstructions. In: European Semantic Web Conference, pp. 215–223. Springer (2022). https://doi.org/10.1007/978-3-031-11609-4_36

4. Lehmann, J., et al.: Dbpedia-a large-scale, multilingual knowledge base extracted from wikipedia. Semantic web **6**(2), 167–195 (2015)

5. Paulheim, H., Ristoski, P., Portisch, J.: Embedding Knowledge Graphs with RDF2vec. Springer Nature (2023)

6. Pellegrino, M.A., Altabba, A., Garofalo, M., Ristoski, P., Cochez, M.: GEval: a modular and extensible evaluation framework for graph embedding techniques. In: Harth, A., et al. (eds.) ESWC 2020. LNCS, vol. 12123, pp. 565–582. Springer, Cham (2020). https://doi.org/10.1007/978-3-030-49461-2_33

7. Portisch, J., Heist, N., Paulheim, H.: Knowledge graph embedding for data mining vs. knowledge graph embedding for link prediction–two sides of the same coin? Semantic Web (2022)

8. Portisch, J., Hladik, M., Paulheim, H.: Rdf2vec light–a lightweight approach for knowledge graph embeddings. arXiv preprint arXiv:2009.07659 (2020)

9. Wu, T., Khan, A., Yong, M., Qi, G., Wang, M.: Efficiently embedding dynamic knowledge graphs. Knowl.-Based Syst. **250**, 109124 (2022)

Critical Path Identification in Supply Chain Knowledge Graphs with Large Language Models

Yaomengxi Han[1,2], Zifeng Ding[1,3(✉)], Yushan Liu[1,3], Bailan He[1,3], and Volker Tresp[3,4(✉)]

[1] Siemens AG, Munich, Germany
[2] Technical University of Munich, Munich, Germany
[3] Ludwig Maximilian University of Munich, Munich, Germany
zifeng.ding@campus.lmu.de
[4] Munich Center for Machine Learning, Munich, Germany
Volker.Tresp@lmu.de

Abstract. In the ever-evolving landscape of global commerce, supply chain management (SCM) has gained increasing significance. An important task in SCM is to find critical supply chain paths for a target company because these paths often represent potential bottlenecks in supply networks and thus could be crucial to risk management. The mainstream solution to this task requires supply chain managers to manually review supply chain data to uncover critical paths, resulting in considerable human labor costs. To better study SCM, recent efforts have been made to construct supply chain knowledge graphs (KGs) that connect supply chain-related data from different sources, facilitating the identification of critical paths through KG reasoning. In this paper, we develop an automated approach for critical path identification (CPI) based on supply chain KGs. We encode supply chain KGs into text and use large language models (LLMs) for CPI. LLMs can not only analyze the topological KG information but also leverage their world knowledge for better path identification. We experiment with two popular LLMs, i.e., GPT-3.5 and GPT-4, and find that they are able to do CPI and meanwhile generate reasonable explanations.

1 Introduction

In today's interconnected global economy, effective supply chain management (SCM) plays a key role in entrepreneurial success. As a crucial task in SCM, critical path identification (CPI) in supply networks has recently gained increasing interest [1]. CPI aims to find the significant supply chain paths related to a certain user-interested company. Each supply chain of length $n-1$ follows the format of $(Company_1 \xrightarrow{supplies\ to} ... \xrightarrow{supplies\ to} Company_n)$, where $Company_n$ is the company of interest. Supply chain paths are considered critical when they

---

Y. Han and Z. Ding—Equal contribution.

© The Author(s), under exclusive license to Springer Nature Switzerland AG 2025
A. Meroño Peñuela et al. (Eds.): ESWC 2024, LNCS 15344, pp. 223–227, 2025.
https://doi.org/10.1007/978-3-031-78952-6_31

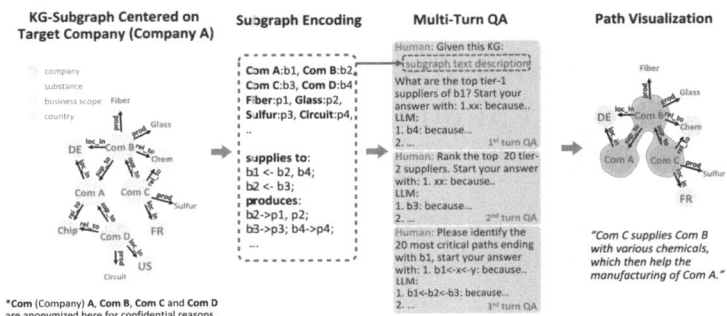

Fig. 1. Framework of approach. Best viewed in color.

constitute potential bottlenecks for specific products or other vital business operations. These critical paths are of strategic importance because they play crucial
roles in risk management. [4]. A major obstacle in solving CPI stems from the
lack of transparency in supply networks. Recently, Liu et al. [3] show that companies are usually limited to only knowing their direct (tier-1) suppliers without
complete knowledge of further tiers of suppliers. Consequently, they struggle to
identify longer critical paths in supply chains. To address this problem, Liu et al.
focus on developing transparent supply networks that provide visibility into suppliers up to the third tier while representing supply chains as knowledge graphs
(KGs). Despite the introduction of supply chain KGs, [3] has not explored automated approaches to address CPI within supply networks, which heavily rely on
manual labor by supply chain managers. Recently, there have been many efforts
to tackle KG reasoning with large language models (LLMs), e.g., [2], but little
attention has been put on the task of CPI. In this study, we present an automated solution for CPI utilizing LLMs. Given their robust emergent capabilities
in diverse downstream tasks without the need for fine-tuning, LLMs serve as a
promising tool for this task. Our approach can identify the critical paths given
the supply chain KG and any target company. To the best of our knowledge,
this is the first method to use LLMs to address CPI in large supply networks.

2   Approach

The framework of our approach is depicted in Fig. 1. Taking the supply chain
KG[1] $\mathcal{G}$ and a target company δ as input, we first extract the relevant subgraph
of δ from $\mathcal{G}$ by picking all the KG facts containing δ and all its tier-1 to tier-3
suppliers. Then, the subgraph is encoded into a text description. Based on the
description, we initiate a multi-turn question answering (QA) process with an
LLM, e.g., GPT-4, in order to step-by-step guide the LLM to provide critical
supply chain paths[2] along with corresponding explanations. The criticality of
these paths, as well as the consistency between the explanations and the supply

---

[1] The KG used here is proposed in [3]. Please refer to [3] for the ontology and statistics.

[2] In our use case, we only pay attention to the paths of length 2, among 3 entities.

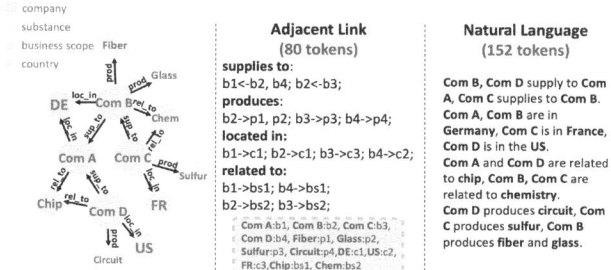

Fig. 2. Two encoding methods. For AL encoding, the contents in the yellow box are not passed to LLMs but serve as a reference for entity ID mapping. The names of the companies are anonymized for confidential reasons. (Color figure online)

chain KG, will then be evaluated by domain experts. Finally, a visualization will be generated for each path for better user understanding. Note that although the LLM-identified paths will be verified by humans, it is much easier than manually identifying critical paths from scratch.

How to encode a KG subgraph as LLM input? We design two encoding schemes: adjacent link (AL) encoding and natural language (NL) encoding. AL encoding (1) maps the names of all entities to distinct IDs, (2) groups the relationships by their types, and (3) translates the relationships into lists of adjacent links. For example, a link $b01 \longleftarrow b03, b05, b11$ under the group **supplies to** indicates that $b03$, $b05$, and $b11$ all supply to $b01$. On the other hand, NL does not anonymize the elements in the supply network but directly outputs a natural language description of it. While NL encoding is more interpretable by both humans and LLMs, it requires more tokens to convey the same information compared with AL. Figure 2 shows the outcomes of these two schemes, from which we can see this trade-off of token length and interpretability.

Why and how to use multi-turn QA? CPI on a large supply chain KG is a non-trivial task, hence we decompose it into several sub-tasks. A supply chain path of length 3 consists of the target company, one tier-1 supplier, and one tier-2 supplier. Hence, we start by asking the LLM to give the top 20 significant tier-1 suppliers of the target company, then proceed to ask about the top 20 significant tier-2 suppliers, which are direct suppliers from the LLM-generated tier-1 suppliers. We finally ask LLM to find the 20 most critical paths. We show in experiments that employing task decomposition promotes the LLM's performance in finding more reasonable critical paths.

3   Experiments

To evaluate the effectiveness of our approach, we select three target companies coupled with various sizes of supply chain subgraphs, i.e., **BASF**, **Siemens**

Table 1. Subgraph statistics (left) and experimental results (right). **multi** and **direct** mean with and without multi-turn QA (task decomposition), respectively.

	BASF	Siemens	Henkel	Model	GPT-3.5				GPT-4			
					NL		AL		NL		AL	
					multi	direct	multi	direct	multi	direct	multi	direct
# Entity	301	187	276	BASF	0.650	0.455	0.438	0.412	0.958	0.875	0.733	0.600
# Relation	5	5	5	Siemens	0.714	0.450	0.647	0.550	0.870	0.800	0.706	0.678
# KG Fact	1426	1336	903	Henkel	0.778	0.538	0.650	0.571	0.895	0.786	0.727	0.500

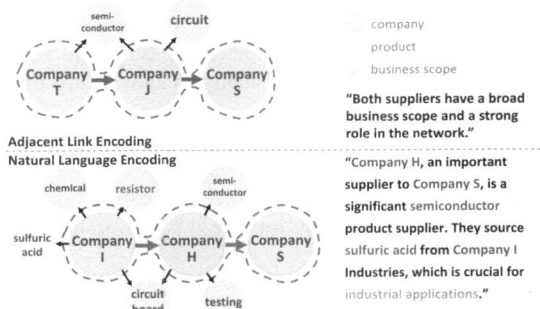

Fig. 3. Two identified critical paths from the subgraph of Company S. Natural language encoding helps the LLM to generate more informative explanations. Full names of the companies are hidden for confidential reasons.

and **Henkel** (statistics in Table 1 (left)). We run experiments for each target company with GPT-3.5 and GPT-4. We discard the paths returned by the LLMs that do not exist in the supply chain KG and take the rest as the identified critical paths. Some previous work [3] has proposed to assess the criticality of suppliers or paths by considering the node properties, often by assigning weighted scores to suppliers based on node centralities. However, solely relying on graph properties for evaluation is inadequate as real-world critical paths will be overlooked. Thus, in our approach, rather than relying on graph analysis, paths are evaluated by domain experts, who would check whether (1) the paths are indeed critical for SCM and (2) the generated explanations are consistent with the supply chain KG. If any of the two requirements is not met, we take the path as incorrect. We let the LLMs return the 20 most critical paths and calculate their accuracy. We show the results in Table 1 (right) and demonstrate two correctly identified paths with GPT-4 using different KG encoding strategies in Fig. 3. We observe that (1) LLMs have the ability to automatically do CPI; (2) NL serves as a better encoding strategy since it leverages background knowledge of companies stored in LLMs, making the explanations more reasonable; (3) decomposing CPI greatly helps LLMs to return more accurate critical paths with reasonable explanations since it forces LLMs to pay attention to the critical suppliers that are more likely to exist in critical paths.

Discussion on the Advantages of Using LLMs in CPI. Employing LLMs to address CPI is motivated by the following advantages: First, LLMs are prompted to consider the graph characteristics of KGs through multi-turn QA, which forces them to prioritize the critical suppliers of different tiers. In doing so, they not only focus on the centralities of these suppliers but also on the diversity of the relations they are associated with. Furthermore, LLMs leverage their world knowledge to identify critical paths. During the training phase, LLMs are exposed to information on various companies, including their crucial suppliers and the major business scopes. Therefore, LLMs are prone to include the suppliers with the most related business scopes to the target companies in the identified paths, even when such information is absent in the encoded KG. While a rule-based approach could potentially address the task of CPI, designing such rules typically demands considerable effort from domain experts, and these methods lack versatility and may not be readily adapted to different domains.

4   Conclusion

We propose an automatic approach to encode supply chain KGs and identify critical paths in them with LLMs. Our approach achieves strong performance under the evaluation of domain experts, serving as a new tool that greatly saves human labor in supply chain management. Nonetheless, a challenge persists in CPI, as discussed earlier. The evaluation of identified critical paths requires the help of domain experts due to the absence of "golden labels" for CPI. There is no trivial way to determine the number of critical paths in large-scale KGs and it is impossible for domain experts to assign binary labels to each path in a KG. Therefore, exploring methods to estimate and identify all critical paths in KGs remains an interesting direction for future research.

Acknowledgment. This work has been supported by the German Federal Ministry for Economic Affairs and Climate Action (BMWK) as part of the project CoyPu under grant number 01MK21007K.

References

1. Chen, I.J., Paulraj, A.: Understanding supply chain management: critical research and a theoretical framework. Int. J. Prod. Res. **42**(1), 131–163 (2004)
2. Ding, Z., Cai, H., Wu, J., Ma, Y., Liao, R., Xiong, B., Tresp, V.: Zero-shot relational learning on temporal knowledge graphs with large language models. CoRR abs/ arXiv: 2311.10112 (2023)
3. Liu, Y., He, B., Hildebrandt, M., Buchner, M., Inzko, D., Wernert, R., Weigel, E., Beyer, D., Berbalk, M., Tresp, V.: A knowledge graph perspective on supply chain resilience. In: D2R2. CEUR Workshop Proceedings, vol. 3401. CEUR-WS.org (2023)
4. Sharma, S.K., Bhat, A.K., Kumar, V., Agarwal, A.: Path analysis model for supply chain risk management. Int. J. Inf. Syst. Supply Chain Manag. **10**(2), 21–41 (2017)

Observations on Bloom Filters for Traversal-Based Query Execution over Solid Pods

Jonni Hanski[(⊠)], Ruben Taelman, and Ruben Verborgh

IDLab, Department of Electronics and Information Systems,
Ghent University – imec, Ghent, Belgium
jonni.hanski@ugent.be

Abstract. Traversal-based query execution enables the resolving of queries over Linked Data documents, using a follow-your-nose approach to locating query-relevant data by following series of links through documents. This traversal, however, incurs an unavoidable overhead in the form of data access costs. Through only following links known to be relevant for answering a given query, this overhead could be minimized. Prior work exists in the form of reachability conditions to determine the links to dereference, however this does not take into consideration the contents behind a given link. Within this work, we have explored the possibility of using Bloom filters to prune query-irrelevant links based on the triple patterns contained within a given query, when performing traversal-based query execution over Solid pods containing simulated social network data as an example use case. Our discoveries show that, with relatively uniform data across an entire benchmark dataset, this approach fails to effectively filter links, especially when the queries contain triple patterns with low selectivity. Thus, future work should consider the query plan beyond individual patterns, or the structure of the data beyond individual triples, to allow for more effective pruning of links.

1 Introduction

the traversal-based approach to query execution [7] builds upon the Linked Data principles [2] by offering a formally defined foundation for executing queries over such data [7]. This approach to query execution essentially functions by following directed *data links* between documents, integrating data discovery with query execution. Within a given *reachable subweb* of Linked Data documents and the data contained therein, bounded by the chosen *reachability-based query semantics*, this approach provides a computationally feasible means of executing queries while guaranteeing termination and completeness [6]. However, while this reachable subweb does provide bounds for the set of documents to consider via the *reachability conditions* set forth by the reachability-based query semantics, depending on the chosen conditions, not all of these documents may contain

A. Meroño Peñuela et al. (Eds.): ESWC 2024, LNCS 15344, pp. 228–233, 2025.
https://doi.org/10.1007/978-3-031-78952-6_32

data relevant for answering a given query or even links to other documents that would satisfy the conditions. Therefore, potential to further restrict these reachability conditions may exist, by requiring the linked documents to contain either query-relevant data or further links satisfying the original conditions, provided sufficient knowledge of the data contained behind a given link is available, which is the direction we have chosen to pursue within this work.

2 Methodology

Within this work, we have chosen to explore the extension of *reachability conditions* to filter data links based on the contents of the documents they link to. Essentially, the *reachability-based semantics* [6] restrict the scope of queries to a reachable subweb of Linked Data documents, where reachable documents are those that can be discovered by following chains of links that meet the reachability conditions, starting from the initial set of URIs either provided explicitly or extracted from the query itself. This restriction facilitates computability not attainable under full-Web semantics, without having to introduce purpose-built termination mechanisms that might result in nondeterministic execution [6]. the original authors present three reachability criteria: c_{All}, c_{None} and c_{Match} [6]. Essentially, c_{All} follows all data links, c_{None} follows no links at all, and c_{Match} follows links conditionally. With c_{None} having no further room for restrictions in traversal, we focused on c_{Match}, though c_{All} would also have worked.

We have conceptually extended this criterion to further restrict the data links considered for traversal, by including the use of Bloom filters to check whether the document identified by a given URI contains potentially query-relevant data or further links matching the criterion. Bloom filter is a probabilistic data structure, that may produce false positives but never false negatives [3], making it suitable for this purpose by not facilitating the accidental pruning of links that could point to query-relevant data. the filter is essentially an array of bits with a specified length, and entries to it are added by hashing the input into another array of bits of the same length and taking a bitwise `OR`. Testing whether a filter contains a specific value works by hashing the input and doing a bitwise `AND`.

Following the RDF schema [4], an RDF statement – a triple – consists of resources, properties and literals. Resources may appear as the subject or object of a statement, properties as the predicate, and literals as the object. Within this work, we ignored literals due to their versatility with regards to languages and datatypes, as well as blank node identifiers of resources due to potentially different means of generating or skolemizing them. This left us with globally unique URI identifiers for resources and properties, for which we will generate our Bloom filters. Through the reuse of an existing membership filter vocabulary[1], we can define a Bloom filter as a combination of a dataset URI, a *projected property* or *projected resource*, and the filter itself, where a property or resource is a globally unique URI identifier of either.

---

[1] http://semweb.mmlab.be/ns/membership.

Essentially, a Bloom filter defined this way offers the means to check whether a given property or resource URI occurs within the same triples together with another property or resource URI. Inspired by c_{Match}, for each data link u, if there exist Bloom filters generated for the dataset it is part of based on URI prefixes, we check whether any combination of property or resource URIs in the triple patterns in the query could be found in the dataset. Only if applicable filters exist, and only if all such filters reject every triple pattern in the query, can we reject the data link u. Otherwise, this link is accepted.

3   Experiments

Following the example set by prior evaluations of traversal-based query execution [9], we have chosen to evaluate our approach to Bloom filters using Solid-Bench[2], an adaptation of the LDBC social network benchmark [5] for the Solid initiative [10]. Within the scope of this work, we have integrated the generation of Bloom filters into the benchmark dataset preprocessing tool[3], and implemented the discovery and use of these filters in Comunica [8], a query engine framework also used in prior work on traversal-based query execution, as a set of additional components. Both the query engine components[4] and the experiments themselves[5] are available online for reproducibility.

For the purposes of evaluating the impact of Bloom filters, the following test cases were considered: i) *no filters* as the baseline for comparison, ii) *per-pod filters* generated for the full contents of a given Solid pod, iii) *per-subdirectory* filters generated for each subdirectory within a pod, and iv) *per-document* filters generated for each document. Within all the test cases, the filters were placed at the pod root for discovery prior to dereferencing individual subdirectories or documents. the experiments were executed by having both the Solid server to serve the data and the query engine to query it on the same machine. the main purpose of the experiments was to measure the differences in network request counts when using Bloom filters.

4   Observations

Initial results in Table 1 show the Bloom filters fail to prune any links, and their inclusion appears to unintentionally cause more links to be dereferenced, likely due to the URIs in filter metadata triples being picked by c_{Match} to the link queue. the average time taken to produce the first and the last result, as well as the combined dieefficiency [1] value are also not significantly different.

Upon further analysis of the benchmark dataset and the queries, detailed in Table 2, this ineffective filtering appears to be caused by a handful of triple

---

[2] https://github.com/SolidBench/SolidBench.js.
[3] https://github.com/SolidBench/rcf-dataset-fragmenter.js.
[4] https://github.com/surilindur/comunica-components.
[5] https://github.com/surilindur/comunica-experiments.

patterns matching most of the pods and documents, simply by virtue of the data being relatively uniform and merely distributed across a number of similarly structured documents and pods. For example, the worst offender in the form of `?s ldbc:hasCreator ?o` is found in 100% of the pods, and in 96% of all the documents, causing all queries with this pattern to not exclude any links in

Table 1. Overview of initial benchmark results for different Bloom filter configurations. the combined total HTTP request count and diefficiency values to produce all results ($dieff@full$), as well as the average time to produce the first (t_{first}) and last (t_{last}) result, are taken only for the common 10 queries that succeeded for all configurations.

Filter scope	Queries	Requests	$\overline{t_{first}}$ (s)	$\Delta \overline{t_{first}}$	$\overline{t_{last}}$ (s)	$\Delta \overline{t_{last}}$	Δ dieff@full
1. no filters	25 / 75	1,047	2.69	0.00 %	3.06	0.00 %	0.00 %
2. per-pod	27 / 75	1,062	2.73	+1.49 %	3.02	-1.31 %	-10.18 %
3. per-subdir	26 / 75	1,062	2.75	+2.23 %	3.03	-0.98 %	-4.02 %
4. per-document	26 / 75	1,062	2.87	+6.69 %	3.13	+2.29 %	-4.10 %

Table 2. When looking at the data stored in Solid pods in the SolidBench benchmark, and comparing it against individual triple patterns in instantiated queries without taking traversal or query planning into consideration, 16 patterns out of 141 match most of the pods, while the remaining patterns match $\leq 0.20\%$ of all pods each. These 16 patterns are also found in a considerable share of the queries.

#	Pattern	Queries	Pods	Documents	Triples
1.	`?s ldbc:hasCreator ?o`	20.00 %	100.00 %	96.22 %	2.49 %
2.	`?s ldbc:creationDate ?o`	33.33 %	100.00 %	84.71 %	3.39 %
3.	`?s ldbc:id ?o`	60.00 %	100.00 %	84.71 %	2.37 %
4.	`?s ldbc:isLocatedIn ?o`	6.67 %	100.00 %	84.71 %	2.37 %
5.	`?s ldbc:locationIP ?o`	6.67 %	100.00 %	84.71 %	2.37 %
6.	`?s ldbc:firstName ?o`	40.00 %	100.00 %	1.28 %	0.01 %
7.	`?s ldbc:lastName ?o`	40.00 %	100.00 %	1.28 %	0.01 %
8.	`?s (ldbc:content|ldbc:imageFile) ?o`	6.67 %	95.62 %	83.43 %	2.36 %
9.	`?s (ldbc:hasPost|ldbc:hasComment) ?o`	6.67 %	94.24 %	1.21 %	0.90 %
10.	`?s ldbc:content ?o`	26.67 %	92.15 %	54.44 %	1.37 %
11.	`?s ldbc:replyOf* ?o`	6.67 %	91.62 %	48.48 %	1.24 %
12.	`?s rdf:type ldbc:Comment`	20.00 %	91.62 %	48.48 %	1.24 %
13.	`?s ldbc:hasTag ?o`	6.67 %	88.68 %	24.58 %	2.00 %
14.	`?s rdf:type ldbc:Post`	26.67 %	88.15 %	34.95 %	1.12 %
15.	`?s ldbc:hasPerson ?o`	6.67 %	78.47 %	1.00 %	0.12 %
16.	`?s ldbc:knows ?o`	6.67 %	78.47 %	1.00 %	0.12 %
17.	`?s ldbc:hasPerson <http://.../pods/00000006597069767117/profile/card#me>`	1.33 %	0.20 %	0.00 %	0.00 %
18.	`?s ldbc:hasCreator <http://.../pods/00000004398046512167/profile/card#me>`	10.67 %	0.07 %	0.18 %	0.00 %
19.	`?s ldbc:hasCreator <http://.../pods/00000006597069767117/profile/card#me>`	10.67 %	0.07 %	0.07 %	0.00 %
20.	`?s ldbc:hasCreator <http://.../pods/00000000000000000933/profile/card#me>`	10.67 %	0.07 %	0.07 %	0.00 %
21.	`?s ldbc:hasCreator <http://.../pods/00000000000000001129/profile/card#me>`	10.67 %	0.07 %	0.01 %	0.00 %
22.	`?s ldbc:hasCreator <http://.../pods/00000002199023256684/profile/card#me>`	10.67 %	0.07 %	0.01 %	0.00 %
23.	`<http://.../pods/00000004398046512167/profile/card#me> ldbc:likes ?o`	1.33 %	0.07 %	0.00 %	0.00 %
24.	`<http://.../pods/00000006597069767117/profile/card#me> ldbc:likes ?o`	1.33 %	0.07 %	0.00 %	0.00 %
25.	`<http://.../pods/00000000000000001129/profile/card#me> ldbc:likes ?o`	1.33 %	0.07 %	0.00 %	0.00 %
26.	`<http://.../pods/00000000000000000933/profile/card#me> ldbc:likes ?o`	1.33 %	0.07 %	0.00 %	0.00 %
27.	`<http://.../pods/00000002199023256684/profile/card#me> ldbc:likes ?o`	1.33 %	0.07 %	0.00 %	0.00 %
	...	...	...	...	...
141.	`<http://.../pods/00000015393162789111/posts#893353506423> ldbc:replyOf* ?o`	1.33 %	0.00 %	0.00 %	0.00 %

practice, even though a mere 2.5% of all triples match this pattern. Even if this were somehow addressed, additional manual tests using c_{All} instead of c_{Match} revealed no difference with a number of example queries, as the benchmark dataset mostly links to itself and is relatively uniform.

5   Conclusions

Within this work, we have explored the use of Bloom filters for pruning query-irrelevant data links during traversal-based query execution over the SolidBench benchmarking dataset. Unfortunately, due to the relatively uniform nature of data contained within the benchmark and the type of triple patterns found in the associated queries, the chosen method of generating Bloom filters at triple level appears ineffective in pruning links. This leads us to conclude that the triple-level information on the co-occurrence of specific URIs, contained within Bloom filters as implemented within this work, is insufficient for pruning links when combined with triple patterns that have too many variables or when the data behind the majority of links partially matches the sought-after data. Thus, we believe triple patterns with fewer variables should be looked into for filtering, perhaps by taking into consideration the patterns' positions in the query plan, or by testing links against intermediate results rather than raw triple patterns, to the extent possible without unintentionally excluding query-relevant data. Additionally, approaches that capture both the data shape beyond individual triples and query structure beyond individual triple patterns should likely be investigated for more efficient filtering.

Acknowledgements. The described research activities were supported by SolidLab Vlaanderen (Flemish Government, EWI and RRF project VV023/10). Ruben Taelman is a postdoctoral fellow of the Research Foundation – Flanders (FWO) (1202124N).

References

1. Acosta, M., Vidal, M.-E., Sure-Vetter, Y.: Diefficiency metrics: measuring the continuous efficiency of query processing approaches. In: d'Amato, C., et al. (eds.) ISWC 2017. LNCS, vol. 10588, pp. 3–19. Springer, Cham (2017). https://doi.org/10.1007/978-3-319-68204-4_1
2. Berners-Lee, T.: Linked data - design issues (2006). http://www.w3.org/DesignIssues/LinkedData.html
3. Bloom, B.H.: Space/time trade-offs in hash coding with allowable errors. Commun. ACM **13**(7), 422–426 (1970)
4. Brickley, D., Guha, R.: Rdf schema 1.1. W3C recommendation, W3C (2014). https://www.w3.org/TR/2014/REC-rdf-schema-20140225/
5. Erling, O., et al.: The LDBC social network benchmark: Interactive workload. In: Proceedings of the 2015 ACM SIGMOD International Conference on Management of Data, pp. 619–630 (2015)
6. Hartig, O.: Sparql for a web of linked data: semantics and computability. In: Extended Semantic Web Conference, pp. 8–23. Springer (2012)

7. Hartig, O., Freytag, J.C.: Foundations of traversal based query execution over linked data. In: Proceedings of the 23rd ACM conference on Hypertext and social media, pp. 43–52 (2012)

8. Taelman, R., Van Herwegen, J., Vander Sande, M., Verborgh, R.: Comunica: a modular SPARQL query engine for the web. In: Proceedings of the 17th International Semantic Web Conference, pp. 239–255. Springer International Publishing (2018). https://doi.org/10.1007/978-3-030-00668-6_15

9. Taelman, R., Verborgh, R.: Link traversal query processing over decentralized environments with structural assumptions. In: International Semantic Web Conference, pp. 3–22. Springer (2023)

10. Verborgh, R.: Re-decentralizing the web, for good this time. In: Linking the World's Information: Essays on Tim Berners-Lee's Invention of the World Wide Web, pp. 215–230 (2023)

Datatypes for Lists and Maps in RDF Literals

Olaf Hartig[1,2]([⊠]) [iD], Gregory Todd Williams[1], Michael Schmidt[1], Ora Lassila[1],
Carlos Manuel Lopez Enriquez[1], and Bryan Thompson[1]

[1] Amazon Neptune Team, Amazon Web Services, Seattle, WA, USA
[2] Linköping University, Linköping, Sweden
`olaf.hartig@liu.se`

Abstract. We present an approach to represent composite values (lists
and maps, in particular) as literals in RDF data, and to extend SPARQL
with features related to such literals. These extensions include an aggregation function to produce these composite values, functions to operate
on these composite values in expressions, and a new operator to unfold
such composite values into their individual components. As resources
related to the approach, we provide two complete open source implementations, a formal specification, and a comprehensive test suite.

Keywords: Composite Datatypes · SPARQL Extension · JSON in
RDF

1 Introduction

Composite datatypes (CDTs) enable the representation of complex, possibly
nested data structures such as lists, maps, and sets. A popular mechanism to
represent such complex values is JSON, which nowadays is commonly supported
as a built-in datatype in database systems, including in relational systems such
as MySQL and PostgreSQL. Similarly, in the graph database world, Property
Graph query languages such as Gremlin and openCypher include support for
CDTs such as lists, maps, and paths. Novel Web-related query languages such
as GraphQL also focus on composite JSON-like structures.

In all these cases, CDTs are included as first-class citizens within the (storage
or runtime) data model, and query languages offer built-in support for constructing, accessing, and manipulating composite values. Based on these observations,
we argue that CDT support in RDF (and its query language, SPARQL) lags
behind the state of the art: instead of supporting them as built-in types, RDF
introduces so-called containers and collections [1], which allow users to model
composite values through dedicated vocabulary *on top* of the core data model.

O. Hartig–Appointed both as an Amazon Scholar and as a Senior Associate Professor
at Linköping University. This paper describes work performed at Amazon.

Figures 1(a) and 1(b) illustrate these options using an example with a list of three keynote speakers, Amy, Bob, and Cal, for some conference that is identified by the IRI `:CTConf`. Figure 1(a) utilizes an `rdf:List` collection, which models the list using two pointers, one to the first element (the triples with predicate `rdf:first`) and one to the tail of the list (predicate `rdf:rest`). The alternative in Fig. 1(b) uses an `rdf:Seq` container, in which the list members are enumerated using a sequence of so-called membership predicates `rdf:_1`, `rdf:_2`, `rdf:_3`.

```
:CTConf  :keynoteSpeakers  :List0 .
:List0 rdf:type rdf:List .
:List0 rdf:first <http://ex.com/Amy> .       :CTConf  :keynoteSpeakers  :Seq0 .
:List0 rdf:rest :List1 .                     :Seq0 rdf:type rdf:Seq .
:List1 rdf:first <http://ex.com/Bob> .       :Seq0 rdf:_1 <http://ex.com/Amy> .
:List1 rdf:rest :List2 .                     :Seq0 rdf:_2 <http://ex.com/Bob> .
:List2 rdf:first <http://ex.com/Cal> .       :Seq0 rdf:_3 <http://ex.com/Cal> .
:List2 rdf:rest rdf:nil .
```

(a) Representation as `rdf:List`   *(b) Representation as* `rdf:Seq`

```
:CTConf  :keynoteSpeakers
  "[<http://ex.com/Amy>, <http://ex.com/Bob>, <http://ex.com/Cal>]"^^cdt:List .
```

(c) Our proposal: representation as compact, self-contained RDF literal

Fig. 1. Example of different options to represent a list in RDF.

Modeling composite values as structures within the data itself— instead of representing them as compact, self-contained objects as proposed in this paper —comes with several drawbacks. First, representing composite values becomes verbose and bloats up the storage footprint, especially when it comes to large containers and collections. Second, extracting information from such composite values using SPARQL is tricky; for instance, in the (common) case where the size of an `rdf:List` is not known upfront, returning an ordered enumeration of elements using SPARQL requires a complex query containing a mix of property paths, grouping, and counting [2]. Third, the manipulation of composite values using SPARQL is complex; for instance, writing a query that inserts an element into (a given position) of an `rdf:List` or an `rdf:Seq` is hard to achieve using SPARQL update statements, if possible at all. Ultimately, all these aspects impact the usability and performance of handling composite values in RDF [2].

Our proposal is to introduce composite type literals in RDF—as illustrated in Fig. 1(c) for the running example—and to support them in SPARQL as first-class citizens. To facilitate the latter we propose language extensions for SPARQL to construct, access, and manipulate composite values at query and update time. By building upon the RDF literal mechanism, this approach is fully compatible with RDF, which means that it enables storage and retrieval of composite values as "black box" entities in existing triple stores, without modifications. Of course, systems that support the approach may leverage dedicated data structures to efficiently implement our proposed language extensions for SPARQL. The remainder of this short paper outlines the approach in more detail and describes the resources that we provide for the approach, which include a formal specification, tests suites, and two open source implementations.

2   Approach

The basis of the approach is to capture lists and maps as RDF literals with the datatype IRIs cdt:List and cdt:Map, respectively. The components of such a composite value may be RDF terms, including literals representing other composite values. The lexical form (i.e., the string representation) of such a cdt:List or cdt:Map literal contains the components of the composite value serialized in a format that is based on the RDF Turtle format [3]. For instance, the literal in the object position of the triple in Fig. 1(c) represents a list of three IRIs.

An example of two lists that contain literals are given in the following triples. This example illustrates that the Turtle shorthand notation for specific types of literals can be used inside the lexical forms of cdt:List (and cdt:Map) literals.

```
:s :p1 "[1, 2, 'hello', <http://example.org/>, [1,2,3], 2.5]"^^cdt:List .
:s :p2 "['1999-08-16'^^<http://www.w3.org/2001/XMLSchema#date>,4]"^^cdt:List .
```

Maps (i.e., collections of key-value pairs) are represented by cdt:Map literals as in the object position of the following triple.

```
:s :p "{ 'name': 'Warsaw'@en, 1: <http://example.org/>, 9: [1,2] }"^^cdt:Map .
```

By adopting the Turtle shorthand notation, the syntax of our approach is designed such that the lexical form of cdt:Map literals encompasses the grammar of JSON objects, including the possibility of nested structures.

Given such literals, we extend SPARQL in the following three ways with functionality related to the types of composite values that these literals capture.

First, we introduce various functions for such literals that can be used in expressions (as used in BIND clauses, FILTER clauses, ORDER BY clauses, HAVING clauses, and SELECT clauses). As an example, consider the following SPARQL query (prefix declarations omitted) that uses two such functions in a BIND clause; the function denoted by the IRI cdt:concat concatenates two lists, returning the resulting list as a cdt:List literal again, and the other function (cdt:size) returns the cardinality of the resulting list. When executing this query over the first example data above (the example with the two lists), the value produced for the ?combinedLength variable would be 8.

```
SELECT * WHERE {   :s :p1 ?l1 .
                   :s :p2 ?l2 .
                   BIND( cdt:size(cdt:concat(?l1,?l2)) AS ?combinedLength )   }
```

Further functions for cdt:List literals that we introduce are cdt:contains, cdt:get cdt:head, cdt:reverse, cdt:subseq, and cdt:tail ; where cdt:get and cdt:size are also defined for cdt:Map literals, in addition to cdt:containsKey, cdt:get, cdt:keys, cdt:merge, cdt:put, cdt:remove. and cdt:size. Additionally, we introduce constructor functions for these literals and define corresponding extensions to the SPARQL comparison operators such as = and <.

As our second extension to SPARQL, we introduce a new operator called UNFOLD that splits composite values into their individual components and, then, assigns these components separately to a new query variable. The following query illustrates how this operator can be used to extract all elements from all lists represented by the objects of triples that match a given triple pattern. When executing this query over the first example data above (again, the one with the two lists), the query result consists of eight solutions: six for the six elements of the list in the first triple of the example data and another two for the two elements of the list in the second triple.

```
SELECT ?element ?list WHERE {   :s ?p ?list .
                              UNFOLD( ?list AS ?element )  }
```

In addition to the one-variable version of UNFOLD as demonstrated above, we also define a two-variables version, which can be used for extracting the key-value pairs from cdt:Map literals.

Our third extension to SPARQL is an aggregation function called FOLD that produces composite values (as cdt:List or cdt:Map literals) for groups of solution mappings. The following query illustrates how this function can be used to create lists of persons that have the same name.

```
SELECT ?name (FOLD(?person) AS ?list) WHERE { ?person rdf:type foaf:Person .
                                              ?person foaf:name ?name . }
GROUP BY ?name
```

3   Resources

We have defined our approach in a specification[1] that we aim to submit to the SPARQL-DEV Community Group[2] at the W3C to be considered for standardization. Currently, our specification is maintained in a public Github repository.[3]

The specification defines the two datatypes in terms of their respective value space, lexical space, and lexical-to-value mapping, as required by the standard mechanism to extend RDF with custom datatypes. Additionally, the specification defines the corresponding extensions to SPARQL, including:

– extensions to existing SPARQL comparison operators such as = and < that define these operators for pairs of cdt:List and pairs of cdt:Map literals,
– new functions to construct and to access such literals in expressions,
– ordering behavior for such literals in ORDER BY clauses, and
– new operators to fold and unfold the represented lists and maps in queries.

---

[1] https://w3id.org/awslabs/neptune/SPARQL-CDTs/spec/latest.html.
[2] https://www.w3.org/community/sparql-dev/.
[3] https://github.com/awslabs/SPARQL-CDTs.

In addition to the specification document, we provide a comprehensive collection of test suites in the aforementioned Github repository . These tests cover all relevant aspects and special cases of all the extensions to SPARQL listed above and are specified in RDF using the framework [4] that was defined by the W3C RDF Data Access Working Group[5] and is now maintained by the RDF Test Curation Community Group[6] at the W3C. Since the test harnesses of many RDF and SPARQL systems are built on this framework, our test suites can readily be used when implementing support for our proposal in such systems.

Besides the specification and the tests, as resources to facilitate implementations, we have also already created *two complete, Open Source implementations* of the proposal. That is, we have integrated support for the approach directly into the RDF programming frameworks Apache Jena[7] (Java) and Attean[8] (Perl) .

4 Future Work

As our future work, in addition to the aforementioned plans to submit our proposal to the W3C (and also to other RDF triple store vendors), we are planning to study the performance that can be achieved with the proposed approach in our implementations. Moreover, we aim to extend the approach with options to explicitly capture typing constraints regarding elements of lists or maps, and we consider adopting the approach to also capture paths as a possible query result.

References

1. Brickley, D., Guha, R.: RDF Schema 1.1. W3C Recommendation. https://www.w3.org/TR/rdf11-schema/ (2014)
2. Daga, E., Meroño-Peñuela, A., Motta, E.: Sequential linked data: the state of affairs. Semantic Web **12**(6), 927–958 (2021)
3. Prud'hommeaux, E., Carothers, G.: RDF 1.1 Turtle. W3C Recommendation. https://www.w3.org/TR/turtle/ (2014)

---

[4] https://www.w3.org/2001/sw/DataAccess/tests/README.html.

[5] https://www.w3.org/2001/sw/DataAccess/homepage-20080115.

[6] https://www.w3.org/community/rdf-tests/.

[7] https://jena.apache.org/—Our implementation is currently in the following fork of the official Jena repository for which we are planning to request a merge. https://github.com/hartig/jena/tree/UnfoldAndFoldWithCompositeValues.

[8] https://github.com/kasei/attean—Our implementation is in the following branch of Attean, ready to be merged after discussion with the Attean community. https://github.com/kasei/attean/tree/mutli-value-exprs.

OAEI Machine Learning Dataset for Online Model Generation

Sven Hertling[1]([⊠])[iD], Ebrahim Norouzi[1][iD], and Harald Sack[1,2][iD]

[1] FIZ Karlsruhe – Leibniz Institute for Information Infrastructure,
Hermann-von-Helmholtz-Platz 1, 76344 Eggenstein-Leopoldshafen, Germany
{sven.hertling,ebrahim.norouzi}@fiz-karlsruhe.de
[2] Karlsruhe Institute of Technology (AIFB), Kaiserstr. 89, 76133 Karlsruhe, Germany
harald.sack@partner.kit.edu

Abstract. Ontology and knowledge graph matching systems are evaluated annually by the Ontology Alignment Evaluation Initiative (OAEI). More and more systems use machine learning-based approaches, including large language models. The training and validation datasets are usually determined by the system developer and often a subset of the reference alignments are used. This sampling is against the OAEI rules and makes a fair comparison impossible. Furthermore, those models are trained offline (a trained and optimized model is packaged into the matcher) and therefore the systems are specifically trained for those tasks. In this paper, we introduce a dataset that contains training, validation, and test sets for most of the OAEI tracks. Thus, online model learning (the systems must adapt to the given input alignment without human intervention) is made possible to enable a fair comparison for ML-based systems. We showcase the usefulness of the dataset by fine-tuning the confidence thresholds of popular systems.

Keywords: Ontology Matching · Machine Learning · Online Model Generation

1 Introduction

If applications want to use two or more knowledge graphs (KGs) simultaneously, the corresponding ontologies and instances must be aligned. This process is called ontology alignment (more generally, KG alignment). The inputs are two KGs (KG_1 and KG_2) as well as an input alignment A_{in}. The produced result is an improved alignment A_{out}. Each alignment consists of (possibly) multiple correspondences in the form $< e_1, e_2, r, c >$ where $e_1 \in KG_1$ and $e_2 \in KG_2$. r represents the relation between the entities, such as equivalence or subsumption relation (in case of class correspondences), and $c \in [0, 1]$ is a confidence value given by the matching process.

Starting from 2004, the Ontology Alignment Evaluation Initiative (OAEI) evaluates matching systems each year and allows for a fair comparison between

A. Meroño Peñuela et al. (Eds.): ESWC 2024, LNCS 15344, pp. 239–243, 2025.
https://doi.org/10.1007/978-3-031-78952-6_34

them. Over the years, more and more systems required correspondences for training and validating their machine learning-based approaches. Especially in 2023, systems for the conference track heavily relied on some form of training data[1] (due to the low number of correspondences in the reference alignment, this makes a huge difference in the final result metrics) but also in other tracks those systems would like to adapt their matching behavior to the task at hand.

In this paper, we introduce train, validation, and test splits for common OAEI datasets and argue that the models need to adapt to the given input alignment during the execution of the systems (online model generation) instead of downloading and generating a model by hand and package it into a matching system (offline model generation). With the latter, the systems will hardly be applicable to new datasets, which is one huge advantage of all matching systems participating at OAEI.

2   Related Work

Many systems submitted to OAEI require training data, and in the following, we list those systems together with their setup for generating training examples. In 2023, *GraphMatcher* [1] used the reference alignment in its 5-fold cross-validation and *TOMATO* [11] splitted the created dataset into 60% for training and 40% for testing. SEBMatcher [3] in 2022 generated a training dataset by reference and string alignments and sampled 20 % of the reference alignment to create positive cases. Fine-TOM [10] (participating in OAEI 2021) used a transformer architecture that needed fine-tuning. Their dataset included 20% of each reference alignment from the Anatomy, Conference, and Knowledge Graph track.

One first direction in creating a machine learning dataset for OAEI is done by He et al. [4]. They provide a train, validation, and test split for a new track called Bio-ML. In their evaluation, they used systems that are trained offline, which means the developers download the training alignments, tune the model, and upload a matcher including that model.

3   Generation of the Dataset

We use the defined tracks of OAEI and split the reference alignment into 20% for training, 10% for validation, and 70% for testing to align with He et al. [4] and most other systems that generate training data. The reason why the training and validation fraction is so low is the extreme imbalance between correct and incorrect correspondences. Furthermore, in the real-world setting, only a few positive correspondences will be provided as a training signal due to the high effort of creating those correspondences.

To have a good segmentation of the reference alignment, we stratify it by the following criteria: (1) entity type (class, property, instance) of the source and target entity, (2) relation type, and (3) difficulty of the mapping. For the

---

[1] https://oaei.ontologymatching.org/2023/results/conference/index.html.

latter, we further differentiate between easy, medium, and hard matches. Easy matches can be found by simple label matching with a bit of string processing like lowercasing and camel case splitting. Medium matches share at least one token among the labels, and the rest are considered hard matches.

The stratification for all criteria is achieved by creating subgroups for each combination, e.g., the group class-class-equivalence-easy and instance-instance-equivalence-medium are two subgroups that we use for stratification, such that in training, validation, and test, we ensure the same distribution as in the original reference alignment. We include the easy matches in the training and validation alignment because, in the real-world use case, the provided matches will also contain those simple correspondences (especially if the mapping is created by finding matching entities for a random sample of entities). The input to a matching system is only one alignment. To differentiate between the training and validation set, we added an additional correspondence extension to indicate to which set it belongs. If a system ignores this distinction, it can use the whole input as training data.

Only positive training examples are provided as input. For a machine learning model, negative examples are often required. Unlike [4], we do not provide negatives (they need it for easily evaluating a ranking-based method) but let the system create them on the fly. This can be achieved by assuming that, for an entity in the source, at most one entity exists in the target graph (or vice versa), and both graphs are duplicate-free. Then, given a correspondence $< A, B >$ in the training alignment, the system can use its own distance function to search for hard negatives of A and B. The advantage is that those correspondences are hard negatives for the matching system at hand and reflects the amount and distribution during the matching of the whole input KGs.

We used only OAEI test cases with at least 350 correspondences in the reference alignment, such that the combined training and validation sets have at least 100 correspondences. This results in the following tracks: Anatomy, BioDiv, Knowledge Graph, and Bio-ML.

All datasets are well integrated with MELT [7] and can be downloaded via the track repository[2] (there is a separated section for it). Code for the generation and evaluation can be found on GitHub[3].

4   Use Case

We analyze the usefulness of the presented dataset by using three matching systems from OAEI 2023, which return correspondences with a wide range of confidence values (not only 1.0). This results in the following systems: Matcha [2], LogMap [8,9], and OLaLa [5,6]. We use the training and validation data to adapt the confidence threshold to the task at hand and remove correspondences below the threshold, which could improve precision and eventually lower recall. Two automated approaches for finding the right threshold are implemented under the

---

[2] https://dwslab.github.io/melt/track-repository#ml-based-tracks.
[3] https://github.com/dwslab/melt/tree/master/examples/mlDataset.

assumption that the input alignment is partial (supervised partial - SPart) or complete (supervised complete - SComp). It computes the optimal threshold by using the training and validation data as a ground truth and finds the value that gives the highest F_1-Measure.

Table 1. Results of unsupervised (U) and two supervised approaches (SPart, SComp) for tuning the confidence threshold.

	Precision			Recall			F_1-Measure		
	U	SPart	SComp	U	SPart	SComp	U	SPart	SComp
Anatomy									
Matcha	93.09	93.42	**94.72**	**92.65**	92.37	91.23	92.87	92.89	**92.94**
LogMap	88.34	89.86	**96.85**	**85.01**	84.35	69.46	86.65	**87.02**	80.90
OLaLa	89.04	89.27	**95.93**	**89.63**	89.35	82.09	**89.34**	89.31	88.47
BioDiv									
Matcha	62.30	63.32	**63.69**	**99.12**	99.07	99.05	76.51	77.26	**77.53**
LogMap	61.02	61.86	**62.72**	**99.25**	98.30	93.84	75.58	**75.93**	75.19
OLaLa	63.37	63.69	**90.37**	**99.27**	99.18	90.63	77.36	77.57	**90.50**
KnowledgeGraph									
Matcha	7.01	13.35	**33.09**	**80.64**	74.88	56.63	12.90	22.66	**41.78**
LogMap	45.86	45.90	**46.31**	**72.65**	**72.65**	72.56	56.23	56.26	**56.54**
Bio-ML									
Matcha	61.37	61.45	**63.78**	**60.29**	60.18	57.31	60.80	**60.81**	60.37
LogMap	58.22	58.46	**64.51**	**58.43**	58.27	53.46	58.33	58.36	**58.47**
OLaLa	36.42	37.31	**51.11**	**42.30**	42.04	34.33	39.14	39.53	**41.07**

Table 1 shows the micro-averaged results for all tracks and matchers. The numbers represent the class matches except for the Knowledge Graph track, where the instance matches are shown (OLaLa is not capable of matching instances). The unsupervised case is evaluated on the same test set so that all numbers are comparable.

In most cases, there is only a slight improvement because the systems are highly tuned, and the alignment filtering relies solely on the confidence values. Nevertheless, in some cases, huge improvements can be observed. For example, when setting the right confidence threshold for OLaLa in the BioDiv dataset, there is a huge improvement of over 13% in terms of F_1-Measure. We hope to see larger improvements if systems use it to train their whole approach using more features to differentiate between correct and incorrect mappings.

5 Conclusion

In this paper, we introduced a new dataset for machine learning systems based on existing OAEI tracks. With the presented dataset, we hope to encourage matching system developers to use a given input alignment to tune and optimize their parameters online and only fall back to default/pre-trained parameters if no input alignment is given.

In the future, we plan to create datasets for the conference track that do not have many correspondences. Thus, one complete test case can be used as training data and another one as a test (in-domain transfer learning).

References

1. Efeoglu, S.: Graphmatcher system presentation. In: International Workshop on Ontology Matching (OM). vol. 3591, pp. 154–156. CEUR-WS.org (2023)
2. Faria, D., Silva, M.C., Cotovio, P., Ferraz, L., Balbi, L., Pesquita, C.: Results for matcha and matcha-dl in OAEI 2023. In: International Workshop on Ontology Matching (OM). vol. 3591, pp. 164–169. CEUR-WS.org (2023)
3. Gosselin, F., Zouaq, A.: Sebmatcher results for OAEI 2022. In: International Workshop on Ontology Matching (OM). vol. 3324, pp. 202–209. CEUR-WS.org (2022)
4. He, Y., Chen, J., Dong, H., Jiménez-Ruiz, E., Hadian, A., Horrocks, I.: Machine learning-friendly biomedical datasets for equivalence and subsumption ontology matching. In: International Semantic Web Conference, pp. 575–591. Springer (2022)
5. Hertling, S., Paulheim, H.: Olala: Ontology matching with large language models. In: Knowledge Capture Conference (K-CAP), pp. 131–139. ACM (2023). https://doi.org/10.1145/3587259.3627571
6. Hertling, S., Paulheim, H.: Olala results for OAEI 2023. In: International Workshop on Ontology Matching (OM). vol. 3591, pp. 170–177. CEUR-WS.org (2023)
7. Hertling, S., Portisch, J., Paulheim, H.: Melt-matching evaluation toolkit. In: International Conference on Semantic Systems, pp. 231–245 (2019)
8. Jiménez-Ruiz, E.: Logmap family participation in the OAEI 2023. In: International Workshop on Ontology Matching (OM). vol. 3591, pp. 157–158. CEUR-WS.org (2023)
9. Jiménez-Ruiz, E., Cuenca Grau, B.: Logmap: logic-based and scalable ontology matching. In: International Semantic Web Conference (ISWC), pp. 273–288 (2011)
10. Knorr, L., Portisch, J.: Fine-tom matcher results for OAEI 2021. In: International Workshop on Ontology Matching (OM). vol. 3063, pp. 144–151. CEUR-WS.org (2021)
11. Roussille, P., Teste, O.: TOMATO: results of the 2023 OAEI evaluation campaign. In: International Workshop on Ontology Matching (OM). vol. 3591, pp. 191–199. CEUR-WS.org (2023)

Searching and Analyzing Cross-Border Multilingual Legislation on the Semantic Web

Eero Hyvönen[1,2]([✉]) [iD], Hien Cao[1] [iD], Rafael Leal[1] [iD], Heikki Rantala[1] [iD], and Aki Hietanen[3]

[1] Semantic Computing Research Group (SeCo), Aalto University, Espoo, Finland
[2] Helsinki Centre for Digital Humanities (HELDIG), University of Helsinki, Helsinki, Finland
eero.hyvonen@aalto.fi
[3] Ministry of Justice, Helsinki, Finland

Abstract. This paper demonstrates how Linked Open Data (LOD) can be used for publishing, searching, and analyzing legislative documents in an international cross-broader multilingual setting. Cross-border services are needed, e.g., when one is moving from one country to another and looking for regulations for immigration, heath care, education, etc. in one's own language. The main novelty of the FinEstLawSampo demonstrator presented, based on legislation from Finland, Estonia, and the EU, is the provision of heterogeneous cross-country, multilingual, distributed legal data through multiple application perspectives for faceted searching, browsing, and for data analysis in legal informatics.

Keywords: Linked data · Law · Multilingual · Semantic portal · Data service

1 Introduction

Cross-border access to legislation published in different countries is often needed in international settings, such as the EU. Although legislation is often available openly, it is not necessarily Findable, Accessible, Interoperable, and Reusable (FAIR[1]). A specific problem is that the data and User Interfaces (UI) are typically available only in local languages that the end-user does not understand. In addition, different local keyword vocabularies for subject matter indexing and classification systems are used in different countries, which sets challenges for querying the data semantically and for precision and recall of information retrieval. Furthermore, legal documents are often available only as texts for the humans to read and not as data for machines, which makes them hard to use in applications of legal informatics[2] [3], e.g., in computational law[3].

---

[1] https://www.go-fair.org/fair-principles/.
[2] https://en.wikipedia.org/wiki/Legal_informatics.
[3] https://law.stanford.edu/2021/03/10/what-is-computational-law/.

A. Meroño Peñuela et al. (Eds.): ESWC 2024, LNCS 15344, pp. 244–248, 2025.
https://doi.org/10.1007/978-3-031-78952-6_35

There are two basic approaches for querying data on the Web. The *federated strategy* is to send the query to distributed local data services, collect the answers, and present them to the user. In the *centralized approach* the distributed heterogeneous datasets are first aggregated and harmonized into a global database for querying. Our demonstrator is based on the centralized approach. It is shown how legislation can be published, translated, and used as LOD, based on language-agnostic indexing schemes and/or by aligning local schemes onto each other. The data used is available as a LOD SPARQL endpoint[4] on top of which the portal FINESTLAWSAMPO was created[5]. The software is available in Github[6].

Our data model reuses that of LAWSAMPO[7] [6]. It is reused also for the Estonian statutes that were available in custom XML format[8], in Estonian and in English, and were transformed into RDF. The original Finnish and Estonian statutes were linked internally and externally to EU directives. NLP techniques were used for enriching the data further: 1) Legal keywords were extracted using EuroVoc[9] due to its cross-border nature (labels in 24 EU languages). 2) The documents were classified automatically using official life event classifications in use in Finland[10](9 event types) and in Estonia[11] (12 event types). The KG, published on the Linked Data Finland platform[12], contains nearly 13000 Finnish and Estonian statutes, and 5000 EU directives from the EU Cellar[13].

2 Using the FINESTLAWSAMPO Portal

The FINESTLAWSAMPO portal was implemented using the Sampo-UI framework [8,10] on top of a LOD service available[14] at the Linked Data Finland platform [7]. In the Sampo-UI model the user first comes on the *landing page* with *application perspectives* to the data, based on classes of the underlying KG. By selecting a perspective, the user can filter the instances of the perspective class by using faceted semantic search. After this it is possible to analyze the result set by seamlessly integrated data-analytic tools available as tabs, or alternatively investigate and browse individual results. The facets are based on the property values of the perspective class. In our case two perspectives are provided: *Statutes* (Finnish and Estonian) and *EU directives*.

Eight facets can be used in the Statutes perspective. Figure 1 depicts the faceted search interface for statutes with the eight facets on the left: 1) Traditional text search facet (of statute content), 2) Statute type (there are eight types

---

[4] LOD data service online: https://ldf.fi/datasets/finestlaw.

[5] Portal online: https://finestlaw.demo.seco.cs.aalto.fi/en.

[6] https://github.com/SemanticComputing/finestlaw-web-app.

[7] Documented at the namespace URI http://ldf.fi/schema/lawsampo/.

[8] Consolidated texts of of Estonian legislation: https://www.riigiteataja.ee/en/.

[9] https://data.europa.eu/data/datasets/eurovoc.

[10] Finnish classification of life events: https://www.suomi.fi/citizen.

[11] Estonian classification of life events: https://www.eesti.ee/en.

[12] http://ldf.fi.

[13] https://op.europa.eu/fi/web/eu-vocabularies/cellar.

[14] THe data service can be found at: https://www.ldf.fi/dataset/finestlaw.

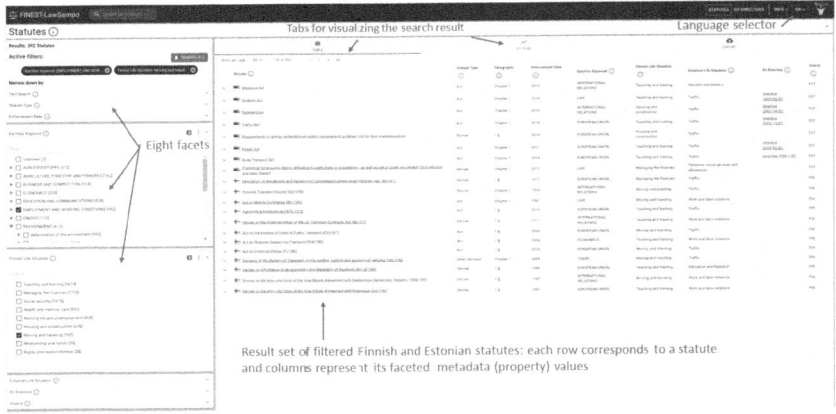

Fig. 1. Faceted search for Finnish and Estonian statutes

in use), 3) Enforcement date, 4) EuroVoc keyword, 5) Finnish life situation (nine options), 6) Estonian life situation (eleven options), 7) EU directive (mentioned in the statute), and 8) Source of legislation (Finland or Estonia). The user in the figure in considering moving from Finland to Estonia for working and has therefore selected from the EuroVoc keyword facet **EMPLOYMENT AND WORKING CONDITIONS** and from the Finnish life situation facet **Moving and traveling**. The results are shown on the **TABLE** tab on the right with country flags showing the source country of the statutes. By selecting the language on the menu on the upper right corner the language for providing the statutes can be selected: English, Finnish, or Estonian can be selected. In the figure, English is selected and the Estonian statutes are provided in English (and not in their original language Estonian). By selecting Finnish the statutes are automatically translated into Finnish. Also the language of the UI is changed accordingly.

In some cases, human made official translations of the statutes are available, but if not automatic machine translation is used. For example, Estonian statutes have been published officially in English, too, but not in Finnish. When machine translations are provided the end-user is explicitly warned that the content has been translated by AI and may not be fully correct. This is important especially in the legal domain in order to avoid misunderstandings. Based on informal testing, machine translations seem pretty good and useful.

In Sampo-UI-based interfaces the faceted search results can be analyzed on the tabs. For example, if the tab **BY YEAR** in Fig. 2 is selected, the search results are projected on a timeline based on the enforcement date. This visualization shows how the number of enforced statutes have evolved in time. The tab EXPORT opens a Yasgui SPARQL editor [11] window with the query used for filtering the current results. The idea of this tab is to give a user who knows SPARQL an easy way to use the underlying LOD service directly.

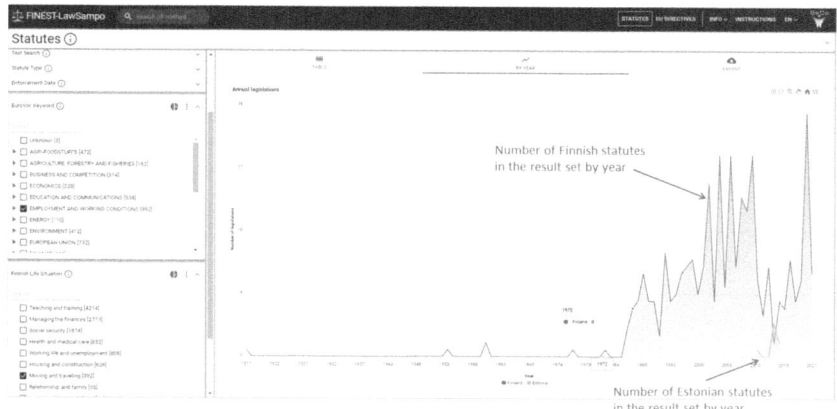

Fig. 2. Visualizing the number of statutes on a timeline by their enforcement day

The EU directives perspective makes it possible to search some 5000 EU directives based on EuroVoc keyword annotations. For each directive, links to Finnish and Estonian statutes related to the directive are provided.

3   Related Works and Discussion

Legislation is widely published online [9] as portals, such as legislation.gov.uk for the legislation for the UK, Scotland, Wales, and Northern Ireland[15], and EU level systems, such as HUDOC[16], EUR Lex[17], the EU Cellar[18], and the ECLI Search Engine[19] for the case law. Our work was influenced by the MetaLex Document Server[20] [4], the EU Cellar, LawSampo [6], and national legal online services in Greece, Luxemburg[21], France, Norway[22], and the U.S. [2].

A major point of comparison of our work is the cross-border N-Lex system[23], based on federated text search using local national legal web services. In Fin-EstLawSampo the challenges of the federated text search are addressed by harmonizing and aggregating all data, including available man-made translations, into a global KG on top of which the portal was developed. The contents were made semantically interoperable using ontologies. In this way arguably better search results are obtained but the price is more complex implementation.

---

[15] https://www.legislation.gov.uk.
[16] https://hudoc.echr.coe.int/.
[17] https://eur-lex.europa.eu/.
[18] https://data.europa.eu/euodp/en/data/dataset/sparql-cellar-of-the %2Dpublications-office.
[19] https://e-justice.europa.eu/content_ecli_search_engine-430-en.do.
[20] http://doc.metalex.eu.
[21] http://legilux.public.lu/editorial/eli.
[22] http://lovdata.no/eli.
[23] https://n-lex.europa.eu/n-lex/.

Usability of the Sampo model has been evaluated in some other Sampo portals [1] suggesting feasibility of the model in general. However, formal end user testing of FINESTLAWSAMPO remains a topic of further research. The scalability of the Sampo-UI framework depends on the complexity of the data model used. The number of instances to be searched for in largest Sampo systems [5] has been around one million.

Acknowledgments. This research was funded by the Nordic Council of Ministers and the Cross-border Digital Services (CDBS) programme. CSC – IT Center for Science provided computational resources for the project.

References

1. Burrows, T., Pinto, N.B., Cazals, M., Gaudin, A., Wijsman, H.: Evaluating a semantic portal for the mapping manuscript migrations project. DigItalia **2**, 178–185 (2020). http://digitalia.sbn.it/article/view/2643
2. Casellas, N., et al.: Linked legal data: improving access to regulations. In: Proc. of the 13th Annual International Conference on Digital Government Research (dg.o 2012), pp. 280–281. Assoc. for Comp. Machinery (2012)
3. Erdelez, S., O'Hare, S.: Legal informatics: application of information technology in law. Ann. Rev. Inf. Sci. Technol. **32** (1997)
4. Hoekstra, R.: The MetaLex document server. In: Aroyo, L., Welty, C., Alani, H., Taylor, J., Bernstein, A., Kagal, L., Noy, N., Blomqvist, E. (eds.) ISWC 2011. LNCS, vol. 7032, pp. 128–143. Springer, Heidelberg (2011). https://doi.org/10.1007/978-3-642-25093-4_9
5. Hyvönen, E.: Digital humanities on the semantic web: sampo model and portal series. Seman. Web Interoperability Usability Applicability **14**(4), 729–744 (2022). https://doi.org/10.3233/SW-190386
6. Hyvönen, E., et al.: LawSampo: a semantic portal on a linked open data service for finnish legislation and case law. In: The Semantic Web: ESWC 2020 Satellite Events. Revised Selected Papers, pp. 110–114. Springer (2019)
7. Hyvönen, E., Tuominen, J., Alonen, M., Mäkelä, E.: Linked data Finland: a 7-star model and platform for publishing and re-using linked datasets. In: ESWC 2014 Satellite Events, pp. 226–230. Springer (2014). https://doi.org/10.1007/978-3-319-11955-7_24
8. Ikkala, E., Hyvönen, E., Rantala, H., Koho, M.: Sampo-UI: A full stack JavaScript framework for developing semantic portal user interfaces. Semant. Web - Interoperability Usability Applicability **13**(1), 69–84 (2022). https://doi.org/10.3233/SW-210428
9. van Opijnen, M., Peruginelli, G., Kefali, E., Palmirani, M.: Online publication of court decisions in Europe. Leg. Inf. Manag. **17**, 136–145 (2017). https://doi.org/10.1017/S1472669617000299
10. Rantala, H., Ahola, A., Ikkala, E., Hyvönen, E.: How to create easily a data analytic semantic portal on top of a SPARQL endpoint: introducing the configurable Sampo-UI framework. In: VOILA! 2023 Visualization and Interaction for Ontologies, Linked Data and Knowledge Graphs 2023. CEUR Workshop Proceedings, Vol. 3508 (2023). https://ceur-ws.org/Vol-3508/paper3.pdf
11. Rietveld, L., Hoekstra, R.: The YASGUI family of SPARQL clients. Semantic Web - Interoperability Usability Applicability **8**(3), 373–383 (2017). https://doi.org/10.3233/SW-150197

CLARA Search Engine: Linking Licensed Educational Resources

Manoé Kieffer, Hugo Chabane, Matthéo Lécrivain,
and Patricia Serrano-Alvarado$^{(\boxtimes)}$

Nantes University, LS2N, CNRS, UMR6004, 44000 Nantes, France
{manoe.kieffer,patricia.Serrano-Alvarado}@univ-nantes.fr,
{hugo.chabane,mattheo.lecrivain}@etu.univ-nantes.fr

Abstract. A basic keyword search is the most frequent technique used by teachers looking for reusable Educational Resources (ER). Despite the abundance of ERs on the Web, many remain undiscovered because they are not well connected. In addition, usage rights issues arising from incompatible licences of ERs are a barrier for teachers. In this demonstration, we introduce the CLARA search engine, a web application based on a knowledge graph designed to help teachers in discovering relevant and license-compatible ERs. Based on a set of subjects given by a teacher, the CLARA search engine provides a ranked set of ERs that can be bookmarked to be reused in a new course. The licenses of bookmarked ERs are organised within a compatibility graph, which suggests the licenses that could protect the new course based on the compatibility of the licenses of the bookmarked ERs.

1 Introduction and Motivation

In the CLARA project[1], we aim to help teachers create content reusing relevant Educational Resources (ER) without having to delve into licensing aspects. Despite the abundance of valuable resources available on the Web, ranging from slides, videos, figures, text, and code, many remain undiscovered because they are not well connected [1]. In addition, there are usage rights problems since it is not legal to combine resources in a teacher's course if their licenses are not compatible with the course's license. These legal issues represent a barrier for the teacher himself and the institution that is hosting his course. Ideally, analysing available resources to match a course plan and the license verification should not be time-consuming.

There are platforms to help learners construct personalized learning paths[2], to allow teachers to share their ERs[3], or even platforms to help teachers

---

[1] https://project.inria.fr/clara/.
[2] https://labs.tib.eu/edoer/.
[3] https://www.merlot.org/.

© The Author(s), under exclusive license to Springer Nature Switzerland AG 2025
A. Meroño Peñuela et al. (Eds.): ESWC 2024, LNCS 15344, pp. 249–253, 2025.
https://doi.org/10.1007/978-3-031-78952-6_36

create new ERs[4],[5]. However, a solution to help teachers find relevant and license-compatible ERs is missing. CC Search Portal[6], finds images licensed under a Creative Commons license. Similarly, the Google search engine can filter images by access rights according to licenses (Creative Commons licenses and other commercial licenses). However, if a user wants to reuse multiple images protected by different licenses, these search engines do not suggest the license that might protect the image mashup. Moreover, there are tens of open and free licenses[7] and they are not considered in these solutions.

An effective way to enhance the discoverability and reusability of ERs is by using Linked Data principles. Thus, we have developed a search engine based on a knowledge graph (KG) to help teachers find ERs. Its functionalities are the following: (1) It returns an ordered set of the most relevant ERs to a subject search. (2) Each ER indicates its accessible URL, authors, license, year of publication and most relevant subjects. (3) The search can be filtered by language, format, and license. (4) A visual graph with the resulting ERs linked with their most relevant subjects is provided. (5) ERs that are interesting for a new course can be bookmarked and the compatibility graph of their licenses is provided [4]. The goal is to highlight licenses capable of protecting new content based on the licenses of the bookmarked ERs. If a suitable license cannot be found, our tool provides explanations regarding incompatible licenses. This strategic feature gives teachers the means to design new resources that integrate ERs without the hassle of incompatible licensing issues.

In this paper, we describe the design of the CLARA search engine.

2   CLARA Search Engine

ERs can be described with several properties such as title, authors, language, license, etc., as well as the subjects they cover. While ERs may cover multiple subjects, not all subjects are equally significant to the resource. Some subjects serve as primary focal points, while others are briefly mentioned. Consequently, it is essential to assess the relevance of each subject and weigh their relationship with each ER accordingly. Statement-level reification[8], allows us to annotate with scores the relation between ERs and the subjects they treat. As an example, the following triple (in RDF-star[9]) states that an ER focuses, with a score of 0.4, on a subject : « :ER1 dct:subject :Query_Language » uno:pageRank "0.4".

---

[4] https://www.oercommons.org.

[5] See this metasearch engine of OERs https://oer.deepwebaccess.com/.

[6] https://search.creativecommons.org/.

[7] https://en.wikipedia.org/wiki/Free_license/.

[8] Reification allows to write RDF statements about RDF statements. We focus on statement-level reification which allows to write RDF statements about a single RDF statement.

[9] https://w3c.github.io/rdf-star/cg-spec/2021-12-17.html.

Various reification models exist, each with distinct syntax and performance implications for storage and query processing. In [2], we compare four statement-based reification models (including standard reification, singleton properties, named graphs, and RDF-star) on four triplestores (Virtuoso, Jena, Oxigraph, and GraphDB) to determine the most pertinent choice for our use case. The four versions of the analyzed knowledge graphs (KG) are available in [3]. Our experiments indicate that both, standard reification and named graphs, when used with a Virtuoso triplestore, exhibit the best performance with our KG. While RDF-star presents an elegant and concise model for statement-based annotations, the efficiency of its implementations should be improved if *quoted triples* are included in RDF 1.2.

Currently, the CLARA KG links 45,000 ERs (licenced under twelve different open licences) with 135,000 subjects, collected in the European project X5GON[10]. Statement-level reification is used to annotate the `dct:subject` relation with a PageRank score, ranging from 0 to 1, obtained through a wikification process[11]. On average, each ER is linked to 184 subjects (with a median of 171 subjects per ER). In contrast, subjects are more sparsely distributed, with an average of 61 ERs linked to each subject (with a median of 2 ERs per subject). Therefore, linking ERs through their relevant subjects enables the discovery of relevant and related ERs that can be reused in a course given a list of subjects.

Normalization of PageRank scores. The PageRank score of a subject is local to an ER, as it depends on the number of subjects associated with this ER. The sum of the PageRank scores of all subjects linked to an ER is 1. Consequently, the more subjects linked to an ER, the lower their individual PageRank scores. This local nature of the metric complicates the comparison of resources by subject. For example, an ER highly relevant to a particular subject but linked to multiple other subjects may have a lower PageRank for that subject compared to a less relevant ER linked to fewer subjects. This issue makes necessary a ranking function that uses normalized PageRank scores to account for a proportional distribution of these values by subject.

The normalized PageRank score of a subject linked to an ER uses the magnitude of the vector which is composed of all the PageRank scores of the ER. We define the magnitude of the vector of an ER as:

Definition 1. $magnitude_{ER_i} = \sqrt{PageRank_{s1}^2 + PageRank_{s2}^2 + ... + PageRank_{sn}^2}$

where s_i are the subjects linked to the ER. This magnitude allows the definition of normalized vectors as:

Definition 2. $normVector_{ER_i} = \left[\frac{PageRank_{s1}}{magnitude_{ER_i}}, \frac{PageRank_{s2}}{magnitude_{ER_i}}, ..., \frac{PageRank_{sn}}{magnitude_{ER_i}} \right].$

The normalized vectors are then used to compare ERs by subject in a manner that is not influenced by the length of the vectors, as the magnitude of a normalized vector is always 1.

---

[10] https://www.x5gon.org.
[11] Wikifier tool https://wikifier.org.

Ranking function. From a set of subjects provided by the user, the ranking function creates a hypothetical ER (a goal) which serves as the ideal response to the query. Currently, this hypothetical ER does not distinguish the relevance of subjects. In other words, all subjects are considered equally relevant, with identical PageRank scores, and their sum equals 1. The search engine then ranks the existing ERs based on their distance (cosine similarity) from this hypothetical goal. The cosine similarity function is used to calculate the pairwise similarity between the ER representing the goal and all other ERs. Cosine similarity is defined as the dot product of the vectors divided by the product of their magnitudes. Since the magnitude of normalized vectors is always 1, the similarity is simplified to just the dot product of the vectors.

The web application. The web application of the CLARA search engine is implemented with the framework Vue.js[12] in TypeScript.

- The backend calculates the similarity measures using Elasticsearch[13] to index the subjects, the related ERs and the corresponding normalized PageRank scores. The produced ranking is used to request the ERs to our Virtuoso endpoint with SPARQL queries. Results contain several properties of each ER as their title, authors, license, language, abstract, etc. The backend is accessible from a public API and can be used independently.
- The frontend displays results in pages of twenty ERs each. Additionally, a graph tab provides a visualization containing the same twenty ERs along with their three best-linked subjects. To ensure continuity of teacher activities, bookmarked ERs are saved between sessions using the browser's local storage, facilitating continued selection of ERs over time.

3   Demonstration

Fig. 1 shows a screenshot of the CLARA search engine. In this example, four ERs are bookmarked to be reused in a new course. On the right, the compatibility graph of licenses shows in green the license that is compliant to the licenses of the bookmarked resources. If all the licenses are red, a problem of license compatibility exists. During the demonstration, attendes will be able to use the CLARA search engine.

All our resources are publicly available under open licenses.

- The CLARA search engine: https://clara.univ-nantes.fr/.
- The associated API: https://clara.univ-nantes.fr/api-docs.
- The source code: https://gitlab.univ-nantes.fr/clara/CLARA-Backend and https://gitlab.univ-nantes.fr/clara/CLARA-front
- A SPARQL endpoint to access the knowledge graph (in standard reification): https://clara.univ-nantes.fr/sparql.

---

[12] https://vuejs.org.

[13] https://github.com/elastic/elasticsearch.

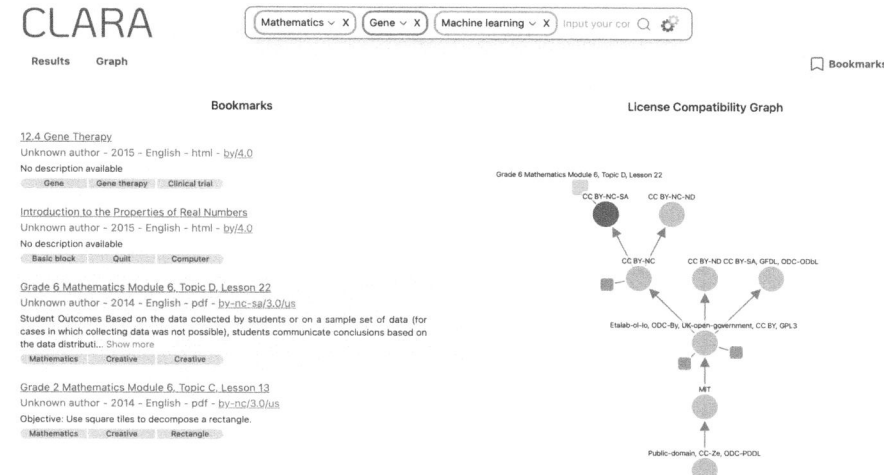

Fig. 1. Screenshot of the **CLARA** search engine. It shows the compatibility graph of licences of some bookmarked ERs. The license in green can protect a new course mixing-up the bookmarked ERs. (Color figure online)

- The CLARA knowledge graph is available at https://doi.org/10.5281/zenodo.8403142
- A video of the **CLARA** search engine: https://youtu.be/2MEZd5Wr-IE.

Acknowledgment. This work has received a French government support granted to the Labex Cominlabs excellence laboratory and managed by the French National Research Agency in the "Investing for the Future" program under reference ANR-10-LABX-07–01. The authors acknowledge, Matthieu Perrin for his help in defining the ranking function, as well as Ginwa Fakih, and Master's students in Computer Science at Nantes University for their involvement in this project.

References

1. Cortinovis, R., Mikroyannidis, A., Domingue, J., Mulholland, P., Farrow, R.: Supporting the discoverability of open educational resources. Educ. Inf. Technol. **24**, 3129–3161 (2019)
2. Kieffer, M., Fakih, G., Serrano-Alvarado, P.: Evaluating reification with multi-valued properties in a knowledge graph of licensed educational resources. In: 19th International Conference on Semantic Systems (SEMANTiCS). Leipzig, Germany (2023). https://doi.org/10.3233/SSW230008
3. Kieffer, M., Fakih, G., Serrano Alvarado, P.: CLARA knowledge graph of licensed educational resources (2023). https://doi.org/10.5281/zenodo.8403142
4. Moreau, B., Serrano-Alvarado, P., Perrin, M., Emmanuel, D.: Modelling the compatibility of licenses. In: 16th Extended Semantic Web Conference (ESWC). Springer, Portoroz, Slovenia (2019). https://doi.org/10.1007/978-3-030-21348-0_17, https://hal.archives-ouvertes.fr/hal-02069076

A Method and a Library for Visual Data Schemas

Lelde Lāce📧, Aiga Romāne📧, Jana Fedotova📧, Mikus Grasmanis📧,
and Kārlis Čerāns(✉)📧

Institute of Mathematics and Computer Science, University of Latvia, Riga, Latvia
karlis.cerans@lumii.lv

Abstract. We describe a method for computing and visualizing data schemas for existing Linked data endpoints, combined with creation of visual query environments over these endpoints. We evaluate the method on a set of externally available small-to-medium size data sets and present the obtained visualization results in a form of interactive library.

Keywords: Linked data · Knowledge graph schema · Visual schema diagram

1 Introduction

A data schema of a knowledge graph or a Linked data endpoint can be seen as a high-level presentation of the data set, involving the used class and property vocabularies and their connections. Visual presentation of a data schema can be expected to help a user to comprehend the graph/endpoint structure and, therefore, use more efficiently the data contained therein.

There are tools allowing visualization of existing Linked data endpoint schemas, such as LD-VOWL [1] and LODSight [2], allowing to obtain on-the-fly visualizations of the class-to-property relations present in the suitably sized data sets. We propose a schema visualization pipeline that separates the schema extraction, and the schema visualization steps since that allow working with schemas of larger size and heterogeneity, as well as allows for user interaction with the schema visualization process.

The RDF data shape languages SHACL [3] and ShEx [4] provide also rich means for knowledge graph schema description. The concepts used in the data schema can also be described by means of OWL ontologies [5], with a wealth of tools available for visual ontology structure presentation (cf. [7–11]). Our schemas differ both from the *a priori* built OWL ontology and ShEx/SHACL shape presentations in that it concerns the actual data structure, as it is present in the data endpoint, and it involves a focus on important nuances (as the relevance of a class as a property source or target) that are not present or are present partially in the existing visualization tools.

The idea of extracting the schema from the data set automatically has been explored already in [12], where the schema presentation in the form of a UML style diagram is considered. More recently, [13] demonstrates the possibility of extracting validating SHACL shapes from a given SPARQL endpoint (the shapes can be further visualized in

A. Meroño Peñuela et al. (Eds.): ESWC 2024, LNCS 15344, pp. 254–258, 2025.
https://doi.org/10.1007/978-3-031-78952-6_37

UML form). The uniqueness of our approach is in selecting means for practical diagram structuring (as e.g., subclassing, and characteristic property placement), and applying them in the context of numerous already existing data sets.

The described visualization method was presented earlier in [14], where the used data schema structure has been outlined. The work presented here involves new diagram structuring options (e.g., class contraction and property link splitting), and it analyzes the method applicability on more than 45 externally available data sets.

2 Visual Schema Diagram Principles

We propose creation of visual diagrams of the data schemas for existing data endpoints, based on the following principles and options:

a) Represent the classes as the schema graph nodes, and the properties as edges connecting their source and target class nodes, or as node attributes.
b) Ascribe the properties to their most characteristic places in the class hierarchy (e.g., to avoid the property ascription to both a subclass and a superclass).
c) Introduce anonymous super-classes to reduce edge and attribute repetitions in the diagram (no-loss and possibly lossy options are available).
d) Provide contraction of class nodes with equal or similar attribute and edge sets (no-loss and possibly lossy options available here, as well).
e) Possibility to split overloaded property links (by recording the other end information at both the edge source and target vertices).

The strength of (c), (d) and (e) parameters can be tuned within the user interface, where a no-loss mode can be applied for smaller-scale visualizations and a merging possibility can be increased gradually to obtain legible and informative diagrams for larger schemas at the cost of moving the attributes and link ends to nodes corresponding to a higher abstraction level over the data. The split of overloaded links (multiple links with the same property in the diagram) can be tuned independently.

Figure 1 contains a simple example of a schema for Nobel Prizes endpoint[1] with automated no-loss anonymous superclass *dbo:City or dbo:Country*. Note the single appearance of *dct:hasPart* and *dct:isPartOf* links in the diagram, in their "most characteristic" place in the class hierarchy, whereas a naïve way of connecting classes by properties would have extra edges for them starting or ending at *dbo:Award*, as well.

3 Schema Extraction and Visualization Pipeline

The SPARQL endpoint schema visualization process is available as a part of a larger schema extraction and visualization process that also creates an environment for visual creation of queries in the *ViziQuer* notation [6] over the endpoint. The pipeline for the process is the following:

---

[1] Data from the original https://data.nobelprize.org/sparql endpoint have been copied locally to http://85.254.199.72:8890/sparql, Named graph: http://nobelprizes.local for the analysis.

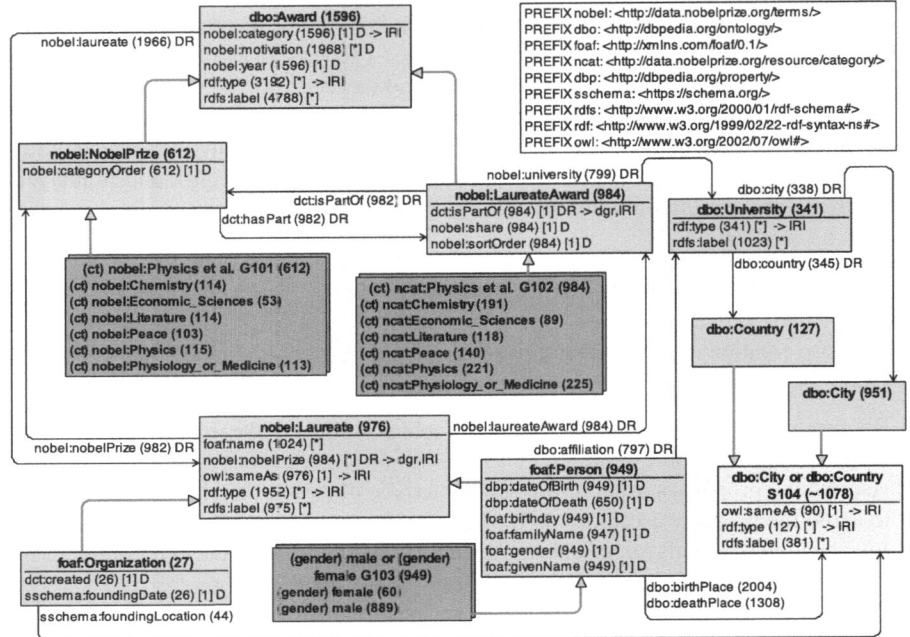

Fig. 1. Nobel Prizes Data Schema (with some classifiers)

1. Extract the schema of the SPARQL endpoint, using the *OBIS Schema Extractor* tool[2] (a schema file in a.JSON format is obtained, cf. [15] for the principles of the schema extraction description).
2. Store the schema in the database of *Data Shape server* (DSS),[3] ready to be served to *ViziQuer* visual query tool and to other potential clients (namespace prefix fine-tuning in the *ns* table of the data schema can be beneficial).
3. Create a visual query project with the respective schema in the *ViziQuer*[4] tool, enter the project and invoke the schema diagram creation, where the diagram creation parameters can be tuned, if desired. Export the schema diagram for use in the diagram visualization tool or visualize it directly within the *ViziQuer* environment (experimental functionality).
4. Open the created schema diagram in the diagram visualization tool (*DSS Schema explorer*[5]); one can manually fine-tune the positioning and the contents of the automatically created diagram. *DSS Schema Explorer* allows diagram export in.SVG format, as well.

Instructions for performing these steps are in the respective tool repositories.

---

[2] https://github.com/LUMII-Syslab/OBIS-SchemaExtractor.

[3] https://github.com/LUMII-Syslab/data-shape-server.

[4] https://github.com/LUMII-Syslab/viziquer, https://viziquer.lumii.lv/

[5] https://github.com/LUMII-Syslab/dss-schema-explorer, works on *Microsoft Windows* only.

4   Schema Library

We describe the schema extraction and visualization process and its result on a set of 58 small-to-medium schema size data sets (50 classes or less; 44 successful visualizations) from Linked Data repository, ISWC 2023 Proceedings and Inria Catalogue,[6] as well as provide visualizations of select schemas including Nobel Prizes, Academy Sampo, War Sampo[7] and Inria Catalogue itself.

The experiment setup, its process, and results, the DSS database dump with the data schemas and obtained schema visualizations in.SVG format are made available on GitHub,[8] where also a link to a running ViziQuer server instance is provided.[9] We also provide releases of DSS,[10] ViziQuer[11] and Schema Explorer[12] tools for producing the visual query and schema environments from the provided DSS database dump.

The results of the experiment show that the proposed schema visualization pipeline can handle the visualization of schemas of the considered small-to-medium size and that it has a potential of handling larger schema visualizations, as well. All 14 missing data schemas were due to the problems in the schema extraction step (9 interface issues and 5 process complexity (e.g., timeout) issues). We note that only two schemas from the bulk schema data set required a considerable (above 15 min) time for manual schema positioning to obtain a reasonable schema presentation. The presentation of two schemas involved resorting to displayable names based on entity labels (currently to be done by a SQL script on the DSS schema level).

5   Discussion and Conclusions

The performed experiments show that the provided method offers a promising approach for obtaining an environment where both a visual schema presentation and visual data queries are available.

Although the visual query environments for large and heterogenous data endpoints as *DBPedia* and *Wikidata* are available, their schema visualizations are currently not within the scope of the proposed method. We expect that reasonable visualization solutions for schemas with up to 300 – 500 essential data classes can be provided (using the schema fragment/slice visualization options, where appropriate, and employing more powerful abstraction mechanisms), however, this would require further experiments. Important future work avenues would also be the schema creation pipeline simplification and providing the visual query option right from the visual data schema.

Acknowledgments. This work has been partially supported by a Latvian Science Council Grant lzp-2021/1–0389 "Visual Queries in Distributed Knowledge Graphs".

---

[6] http://prod-dekalog.inria.fr/sparql.

[7] https://www.ldf.fi/datasets.html

[8] https://github.com/LUMII-Syslab/viziquer/tree/development/doc/demo/schemas24a.

[9] Currently https://schemas24a.viziquer.app/

[10] https://doi.org/10.5281/zenodo.11069027.

[11] https://doi.org/10.5281/zenodo.11072804.

[12] https://doi.org/10.5281/zenodo.11072854.

References

1. Weise, M., Lohmann, S., Haag, F.: Ld-vowl: Extracting and visualizing schema information for linked data. In Voila! 2016, pp. 120–127 (2016)
2. Dudáš, M., Svátek, V., Mynarz, J.: Dataset summary visualization with LODSight. In: The 12th Extented Semantic Web Conference (ESWC 2015). http://lod2-dev.vse.cz/lodsight/lod sight-eswc2015-demopaper.pdf
3. Shapes Constraint Language (SHACL). https://www.w3.org/TR/shacl/
4. ShEx - Shape Expressions. http://shex.io/
5. Web Ontology Language (OWL). https://www.w3.org/OWL/
6. Čerāns, K., et al.: ViziQuer: A web-based tool for visual diagrammatic queries over RDF Data, in Gangemi, A., et al. (ed.), Proceedings of The Semantic Web: ESWC 2018 Satellite Events. ESWC 2018. LNCS, Vol. 11155. Springer, Cham, pp. 158–163 (2018). https://doi.org/10.1007/978-3-319-98192-5_30
7. Lohmann, S., Negru, S., Haag F., Ertl, T.: Visualizing ontologies with VOWL. Semantic Web 7(4), 399–419 (2016)
8. Bārzdiņš, J., Čerāns, K., Liepiņš, R., Sproģis, A.: UML style graphical notation and editor for OWL 2. In: Proc. of BIR 2010. LNBIP, vol. 64, pp. 102–113. Springer (2010)
9. Mouromtsev, D., Pavlov, D., Emelyanov, Y., Morozov, A., Razdyakonov, D., Galkin, M.: The simple, web-based tool for visualization and sharing of semantic data and ontologies. In: ISWC P&D 2015, CEUR, vol. 1486 (2015). http://ceur-ws.org/Vol-1486/paper_77.pdf
10. Dudáš, M., Lohmann, S., Svátek, V., Pavlov, D.: Ontology visualization methods and tools: a survey of the state of the art. Knowl. Eng. Rev. 33 (2018)
11. Labra Gayo, E., Fernández Álvarez, D., García González, H.: RDFShape: an RDF Playground Based on Shapes. In: ISWC 2018 Posters & Demonstrations (2018)
12. Li, H., Zhang, X. Visualizing RDF data profile with UML diagram. In: Proceedings in Complexity, pp. 273–285. Springer (2013). https://doi.org/10.1007/978-1-4614-6880-6_24
13. Rabbani K., Lissandrini M., Hose K. Extraction of validating shapes from very large knowledge graphs. Proc. VLDB Endowment 16(5), 1023–1032 (2023). https://doi.org/10.14778/3579075.3579078
14. Lāce, L., Romāne, A., Grasmanis, M., Čerāns, K.: A method of visual presentation of data schemas. In: VOILA! 2023. CEUR Workshop Proceedings, vol. 3508, pp. 57–62 (2023). https://ceur-ws.org/Vol-3508/paper6.pdf
15. Čerāns, K., Ovčiņņikova, J., Bojārs, U., Grasmanis, M., Lāce, L., Romāne, A.: Schema-backed visual queries over europeana and other linked data resources. In: Verborgh, R., et al (ed.), Proceedings of The Semantic Web: ESWC 2021 Satellite Events. ESWC 2021. LNCS, vol. 12739. Springer, Cham, pp. 82–87 (2021b). https://doi.org/10.1007/978-3-030-80418-3_15

Ontogenia: Ontology Generation with Metacognitive Prompting in Large Language Models

Anna Sofia Lippolis[1,2(✉)], Miguel Ceriani[1], Sara Zuppiroli[1], and Andrea Giovanni Nuzzolese[1]

[1] CNR - Institute of Cognitive Sciences and Technologies, Rome, Bologna, Italy
{annasofia.lippolis,miguel.ceriani,sara.zuppiroli,
andrea.nuzzolese}@istc.cnr.it
[2] Department of Philosophy and Communication Studies, University of Bologna,
Bologna, Italy

Abstract. Recent advancements in Large Language Models (LLMs) have primarily focused on enhancing task-specific performances by experimenting with prompt design. Despite the proven effectiveness of Metacognitive Prompting (MP), its application in the field of ontology generation remains an uncharted territory. This study addresses this gap by exploring this prompting technique in supporting the ontology design process, particularly with GPT-4, where this strategy has demonstrated consistent superiority over conventional and more direct prompting methods in recent research. Our methodology, named Ontogenia, employs a gold-standard dataset of ontology competency questions translated into SPARQL-OWL queries. This approach allows us to explore various types and stages of knowledge refinement using MP, while adhering to the eXtreme Design methodology, a well-established protocol in ontology design. Finally, the quality and performance of the resulting ontologies are assessed using both standard ontology quality metrics and evaluation by an ontology expert. This research aims to enrich the discussion on methods of ontology generation driven by LLMs by presenting concrete results on the use of metacognitive prompting and ontology design patterns.

Keywords: Ontology Engineering · Competency Questions · Large Language Models · Metacognitive Prompting

1 Introduction and Related Work

Ontology design involves conceptualizing and formalizing knowledge networks for semantic technologies. Methodologies like eXtreme Design (XD) [2] offer structured frameworks for ontology engineers, yet their complexity demands substantial expertise and resources. Manual curation and validation of ontological elements are labor-intensive, suggesting a need for intelligent automation. Large

Language Models (LLMs), being able to effectively perform various natural language processing goals, present a compelling solution. More so, in the field of the so-called "Cognitive AI", which is now considered an essential prerequisite for the development of more advanced AI forms [7]. In particular, the Metacognitive Prompting (MP) technique [8], inspired by human introspective processes, encourages self-evaluation through the introduction of a series of steps, building and supposedly improving performance over other methods such as Chain of Thought. Derived from the field of cognitive psychology, metacognition concerns an individual's capacity to self-reflect and critically evaluate their cognitive processes [3,6]. While traditional prompting might direct the LLM to simply create an ontology based on a set of parameters or data, MP involves asking the LLM to consider its own reasoning process, evaluate the credibility and reliability of the information it uses, and adapt its strategies based on this self-assessment, as shown by [9]. This could lead to more accurate and robust outcomes with respect to classic prompting techniques, as the model not only generates outputs but also critically analyzes its methods and decisions, much like the self-reflection and self-inquiry methodologies employed in recent studies to mitigate hallucinations and improve data handling [1]. This approach could effectively reduce errors and enhance the logical consistency of outputs, bringing them closer to human cognitive processes where reflection is crucial in learning and decision-making. Furthermore, incorporating Ontology Design Patterns can guide the process by injecting structured knowledge patterns that lend structure to the knowledge itself as a top-down approach. Starting from these studies, in this paper we define the Ontogenia methodology to explore the usage of LLMs for one of the most crucial and creative steps in ontology design methodologies: the actual specification and formalisation of an ontology (or module thereof) based on a specific set of requirements[1]. The main aim of this work is to advance the discussion on automated ontology generation using LLMs. The main contributions are:

– A methodology to test the efficacy of MP and its application in automated ontology generation;
– A framework to assess the influence of Ontology Design Patterns (ODPs) on the ontology generation process, and, more broadly, to incorporate the eXtreme Design methodology in LLM-assisted ontology generation;
– A qualitative and quantitative evaluation of this framework, which identifies both advantages and specific deficiencies in LLMs' generation of ontology features.

2   The Ontogenia Methodology

The Ontogenia methodology outlines a concise yet comprehensive approach to ontology development through an iterative and incremental process.

---

[1] Data and code used for the work is available at this link: https://github.com/dersuchendee/Ontogenia.

Domain and CQ Definition. The dataset under consideration is derived from a recognized gold-standard used for testing and benchmarking in the field of competency questions research and ontology querying, detailed in [4]. For this study, a specific use case has been selected: the African Wildlife Ontology. This choice facilitates modeling a sufficiently broad domain with respect to the others in the dataset while simultaneously being able to use domain-specific ontology design patterns. The chosen subset comprises 14 distinct competency questions, providing a potentially comprehensive starting point for analysis.

Ontology Design Patterns Selection. Being readily available online, Ontology Design Patterns can be a valuable resource for facilitating transfer and analogy learning. In fact, they enable structured knowledge adaptation to new scenarios, a key component in MP where both shared commonsense knowledge and abstract reasoning are essential. This approach also helps maintain human involvement in the loop. The definition of the Ontology Design Patterns to reuse starts from the list of Content Ontology Design Patterns in the Ontology Design Patterns website[2]. From these, eight have been selected by ontology experts for their relevance to the domain and included in a dataset to be dynamically inputted to the prompt: *AgentRole, AquaticResources, Classification, Climatic Zone, Collection Entity, PartOf, Linnaean Taxonomy, SpeciesEat*. Collectively, these ODPs can provide a comprehensive foundation for answering the targeted competency questions, enabling a thorough exploration of animal-related topics in a systematic and informed manner.

Procedure and Prompt Design. The procedure design was crafted through an iterative process, with each phase incrementally tested to evaluate the outcomes. This design strategy aims to amalgamate the MP technique with the eXtreme Design methodology [2], which requires the use of pre-selected competency questions—a collaborative effort between the ontology design team and domain experts. Additionally, it involves the selection, reuse, and integration of specific Content Patterns. This iterative approach, coupled with constant testing and reassessment, has ensured the procedure's alignment with the initial requirements. To bridge any gaps in the LLM's understanding of specific ontology features, these elements were explicitly incorporated into the procedure, enhancing its comprehensiveness and effectiveness.

The prompt design is meant to incorporate information about the procedure, eventual previous output, competency questions and patterns to be also added dynamically to the prompt on the basis of specific needs. A specification to not repeat itself and not send comments was added in order to refine the output. The resulting procedure is mapped to the MP five steps as shown in Table 1.

Evaluation Measures Definition. The definition of the evaluation is twofold. On the one hand, it involves an ontology engineer expert that analyzes the

---

[2] http://ontologydesignpatterns.org/wiki/Submissions:ContentOPs.

Table 1. Mapping between the Ontogenia methodology and the MP procedure.

MP stages	Ontogenia stages	Description
Comprehension clarification	1. Competency question understanding.	The LLM interprets the CQs, contextualizing them.
Preliminary judgement	2. Preliminary identification of the context. 3. Divide the competency question into subject, predicate, object, and predicate nominative.	Logical analysis supports class and property identification from CQs.
Critical evaluation	5. Starting from your knowledge, extend the ontology with these restrictions.	Reflect on CQs to add rules and restrictions, enhancing the model.
Decision confirmation	8. Confirm the final answer and explain the reasoning.	Justify the decision-making process.
Confidence assessment	9. Make a confidence evaluation and explanation, testing the ontology on instances.	Evaluate the process and test the model's correctness with specific instances.

produced ontologies in terms of essential requirements such as required classes and object properties and usage of restrictions. On the other hand, in order to complement the expert analysis, it involves the Ontometrics service[3] and the OOPS! Ontology Pitfall Scanner [5].

Testing. We use GPT-4 Turbo API (gpt-4-1106-preview[4]) as our backbone model, with greedy decoding. Because GPT has a token limit in output, we came up with a division of competency questions to be given one group at a time, and each time the previous output is provided in order not to have a repeating of classes and properties.

We conducted four trials to evaluate the effect of different inputs on ontology generation. Trial 1 used competency questions with a generic prompt, Trial 2 added ontology design patterns, Trial 3 involved only competency questions and MP, and Trial 4 combined competency questions with the prompting procedure and patterns. We tested both the original and thematically grouped questions by GPT. The total computation cost was $2.10. Experiment details are documented in a Github repository[5].

---

[3] https://ontometrics.informatik.uni-rostock.de/ontologymetrics/.

[4] https://openai.com/blog/new-models-and-developer-products-announced-at-devday.

[5] https://github.com/dersuchendee/Ontogenia.

3   Results and Discussion

Table 2 shows the metrics obtained using the OntoMetrics service for each case considered in the experiment. It can be seen that in our experiment the adoption of MP favors a richer formalisation. This is also evident from Table 3 that shows usage of a set of different types of axiom types across the test cases. At the same time, it should be noted that there are important limitations common to all the cases, such as the absence of property hierarchical relationships.

The pitfalls found by OOPS! were also analysed. Some issues are common to all the cases, as the lack of annotations (P08) and inverse relationships (P13)[6]. All the cases except case 3 contain at least a property that is defined with more than one domain or range (P19). This happens when the LLM generates multiple times the definition of an object property, with somewhat different domain/range values. It seems that the "intent" of the LLM would be to define the property over the union of the referenced classes, mirroring a common beginner's error in RDFS modelling. In the cases using patterns (2 and 4) an "untyped class" (P34) and "different naming conventions" (P22) are found. These are both due to the erroneous of an object property (`hasPart`) imported from a pattern but used as it was a class. Furthermore, in Case 1, no disjoint axioms are used (P10) and there are a couple of properties missing explicit domain/range declaration (P11)[7]. The ontology obtained in Case 3 is the only one featuring an ontology element, the `Plant` class, unconnected from the rest of the ontology. Nevertheless, Case 3 is the one having less pitfalls.

For what concerns basic metrics, Ontometrics shows a larger number of axioms when a pattern is used, along with a higher number of classes and object properties. Data properties are instead a weaker point, despite their use having been specified in the procedure.

According to the qualitative analysis by the ontology expert, while the LLM successfully identifies necessary classes and relevant subclasses, the generated ontologies exhibit numerous intrinsic and domain-related issues. Particularly problematic is the pairing of classes and properties. Properties like `eats` often possess overly specific domains and ranges, leading to the creation of unrelated properties such as `eatsPlant`, `eatsAnimal`, and `eatsPlantPart`. While simple restrictions in class definitions are generally correct, the classification of animals by diet consistently falls short. This shortfall is partly due to the ambiguity of terms like "carnivore" in biological contexts, where strict logical constraints are challenging to establish. This highlights the necessity for further research into the collaboration between ontology design teams and LLMs, opening avenues for exploring new directions.

The findings of this work suggest that while the use of Metacognitive Prompting and Ontology Design Patterns in LLM-driven ontology generation shows

---

[6] The lack of license information (P41) is also common to all the cases, but this is not an information to be expected from the LLM.

[7] Domain and range of those two properties are actually in part inferable because, errors aside, they are meant to be defined in relationship to other properties.

Table 2. How Ontometrics base metrics vary between various test cases and the reference ontology. For each case, it is indicated whether the patterns or the MP have been used.

Ontometrics	Case1 No pattern No MP	Case2 Pattern No MP	Case3 No pattern MP	Case4 Pattern MP	Reference Ontology
Axioms count	49	119	64	118	108
Logical axioms count	26	74	36	76	56
Class count	14	17	14	21	31
Object property count	8	11	8	14	5
Data property count	0	2	3	2	0
Properties count	8	13	11	16	5
Individual count	1	19	0	11	0
DL expressivity	ALCROI	AL(D)	ALC(D)	ALCI(D)	SRI

Table 3. Use of types of OWL axioms in various test cases. For each case it is indicated whether the patterns or MP were used.

Axiom type	Case1 No pattern No MP	Case2 Pattern No MP	Case3 No pattern MP	Case4 Pattern MP
owl:Ontology	Yes	Yes	Yes	Yes
owl:Class	Yes	Yes	Yes	Yes
owl:ObjectProperty	Yes	Yes	Yes	Yes
owl:DatatypeProperty	No	No	Yes	Yes
rdfs:domain	Yes	Yes	Yes	Yes
rdfs:range	Yes	Yes	Yes	Yes
rdfs:subClassOf	Yes	Yes	Yes	Yes
rdfs:subPropertyOf	No	No	No	No
owl:disjointWith	No	No	Yes	Yes
owl:equivalentClass	Yes	No	Yes	No
owl:Restriction	Yes	No	Yes	Yes
owl:imports	No	Yes	No	Yes

promise for richer formalization and a higher complexity of generated structures, significant issues persist. These include the lack of proper property hierarchies, annotation errors, and incorrect domain/range assignments, indicating that the current state of LLM-driven ontology tools may not yet be ready for real-world applications. However, these results provide valuable insights that can stimulate further discussion and drive refinements in both the methodology and implementation of LLMs in ontology design, potentially leading to more robust and accurate systems in the future. The outcomes from this initial work have prompted new questions: Can automated tools replace ontology experts for ontology validation? Can we achieve higher levels of accuracy in self-generated models? In the future, we aim to extend our research to other models of LLMs and expand the set of instructions and patterns employed in the procedure design, possibly including an automatic selection step by the LLM.

Acknowledgements. This work was supported by (i) by FOSSR (Fostering Open Science in Social Science Research), funded by the European Union - NextGeneration-EU under NRRP Grant agreement n. MUR IR0000008; and (ii) the European Union's Horizon Europe research and innovation programme within the context of the project HACID (Hybrid Human Artificial Collective Intelligence in Open-Ended Domains, grant agreement No 101070588).

Disclaimer. The content of this article reflects only the authors' view. The European Commission and the Italian Ministry of University and Research are not responsible for any use that may be made of the information it contains.

References

1. Berberette, E., Hutchins, J., Sadovnik, A.: Redefining hallucination in LLMs: towards a psychology-informed framework for mitigating misinformation (2024)
2. Blomqvist, E., Presutti, V., Daga, E., Gangemi, A.: Experimenting with extreme design. In: Cimiano, P., Pinto, H.S. (eds.) Knowledge Engineering and Management by the Masses, pp. 120–134. Springer, Berlin Heidelberg, Berlin, Heidelberg (2010)
3. Lai, E.R.: Metacognition: a literature review. Always Learn. Pearson Res. Rep. **24**, 1–40 (2011)
4. Potoniec, J., Wiśniewski, D., Ławrynowicz, A., Keet, C.M.: Dataset of ontology competency questions to SPARQL-OWL queries translations. Data Brief **29**, 105098 (2020)
5. Poveda-Villalón, M., Gómez-Pérez, A., Suárez-Figueroa, M.C.: OOPS! (OntOlogy Pitfall Scanner!): an on-line tool for ontology evaluation. Int. J. Seman. Web Inf. Syst. (IJSWIS) **10**(2), 7–34 (2014)
6. Schraw, G., Moshman, D.: Metacognitive theories. Educ. Psychol. Rev. **7**, 351–371 (1995)
7. Spivack, N., Douglas, S., Crames, M., Connors, T.: Cognition is all you need – the next layer of AI above large language models (2024)
8. Wang, Y., Zhao, Y.: Metacognitive prompting improves understanding in large language models. arXiv preprint arXiv:2308.05342 (2023)
9. Zhou, Y., Liu, Z., Jin, J., Nie, J.Y., Dou, Z.: Metacognitive retrieval-augmented large language models. arXiv preprint arXiv:2402.11626 (February 2024), https://arxiv.org/abs/2402.11626

Optimizing Class Subsumption Through Controlled Dynamics of n-Balls in Vector Space

Aniket Mitra[(⊠)] and Vinu E. Venugopal[(⊠)]

International Institute of Information Technology, Bangalore, India
{aniket.mitra,vinu.ev}@iiitb.ac.in

Abstract. Representing entities from an ontology as geometric shapes (such as balls, boxes, etc.) in a low-dimensional vector space, known as *Region-based Geometric Knowledge Graph Embedding* or RKGE, has demonstrated the ability to outperform traditional knowledge graph embedding methods in reasoning tasks while preserving the structural properties and syntactic characteristics of ontological axioms. In this study, we introduce a novel approach to enhance the subsumption capability of geometric embeddings based on *n-balls*. Additionally, we propose techniques to enhance the quality of such embeddings by extracting meta-information from the information-rich lexicons or annotations within the domain ontology.

Keywords: $\mathcal{EL}^{++}$ DL · n-Ball Embedding · Knowledge Graph Embeddings

1 Introduction

Model theoretic languages like Description Logic (DL) are used to represent the semantics of OWL ontology axioms. $\mathcal{EL}$, a sub-language of DL, is widely used to represent large biomedical ontologies such as GO and SNOMED due to its fast reasoning (tractable) property and support of major symbolic logic constructs including concept intersection, existential relations between concepts, etc. Notably, the *general* TBox axioms of $\mathcal{EL}^{++}$ (an extension of $\mathcal{EL}$) can be reduced to one of the below normal forms (NF 1 to 4) in linear time maintaining resultant normalized TBox size linear to the original TBox thereby still guaranteeing tractable reasoning property [1].

– **NF 1-4 (Concept axioms):** $C \sqsubseteq D$, $C \sqcap D \sqsubseteq E$, $\exists R.C \sqsubseteq D$, $C \sqsubseteq \exists R.D$

The bottom concept axioms can be represented by assigning $\perp$ to the right-hand side of NF1-3. Role inclusion axioms can be normalized in linear time and represented as below. We named them as NF 5-7 for the ease of addressing.

– **NF 5 (Bottom concept axioms):** $C \sqcap D \sqsubseteq \perp$, $\exists R.C \sqsubseteq \perp$, $C \sqsubseteq \perp$

A. Meroño Peñuela et al. (Eds.): ESWC 2024, LNCS 15344, pp. 266–271, 2025.
https://doi.org/10.1007/978-3-031-78952-6_39

– NF 6-7 (Role inclusion axioms): $R \sqsubseteq S$, $R_1 \circ R_2 \sqsubseteq S$

where $\{C, D, E, \bot\} \in N_c$ & $\{R, R_1, R_2, S\} \in N_r$. Here N_c and N_r denote the set of classes and roles in the ontology respectively.

In EmEL^{++} model [5] (a.k.a. *n-ball* approach), an extension of *Region-based Geometric Knowledge Graph Embedding* (RKGE) model called ELEm model [4], the authors attempted geometric construction of each concept and role as *balls* and translation vectors respectively in vector space $\mathbb{R}^n$. They formulated specific loss functions preserving the semantic meaning of each of these $\mathcal{EL}^{++}$ NFs and optimized the balls via a Machine Learning (ML) model trained on these loss functions. Proper training will assign close vector representations to subsumption balls and bigger radius to the super-concept ball such that the sub-concept ball is totally engulfed by it's super-concept ball. Later, [6] introduced *box-shape* to represent concepts since balls do not satisfy intersectional closure property. An alternative technique for embedding ontological data utilizes the graph-walk approach, albeit it ignore the structural nuances and characteristics inherent in the underlying ontology. In this method, each concept is represented as a node, while the relationships are illustrated as edges within the graph. Multiple rounds of randomized walks are executed on this graph structure to generate embeddings. Among these methodologies, OWL2Vec* [2] stands out by harnessing the substantial meta-information inherent in ontologies, including labels, synonyms, definitions, and more. By integrating this information into the graph structure, OWL2Vec* achieves a more comprehensive representation of the ontology, thereby enhancing its reasoning capabilities.

The ball method conducts reasoning operations in linear time utilizing a straightforward ML model with minimal hyper-parameters, as opposed to complex graph-walk models that entail multiple path explorations, extensive pre-trained language models, and numerous parameters. Nevertheless, the accuracy of RKGE is significantly contingent upon the design of its loss functions. However, the meta-information present in the ontology is largely ignored while fine-tuning the model. We hypothesize that since a sub-ball is nothing but the more specific version of it's super-ball, they must have common metadata terms that can be utilized to push the sub-balls properly inside their correct super-balls by tailoring accurate loss functions as depicted in Fig. 2.

2   Proposed Approach: Meta-n-Ball Model

Figure 1 outlines the general workflow of our proposed approach, *Meta-n-ball Model*[1]. We gather meta-information from the ontology and feed it through a pre-trained NLP model to extract biomedical terms. These terms are then initialized as n-dimensional (n-D) vectors in the metadata vector space, also known as *meta-space*. Simultaneously, concepts are initialized in the Concept Vector Space, or *con-space*, as n-D balls. Our meta-n-ball module subsequently refines these balls to generate the final embeddings.

---

[1]https://github.com/bda-lab/meta-n-ball.

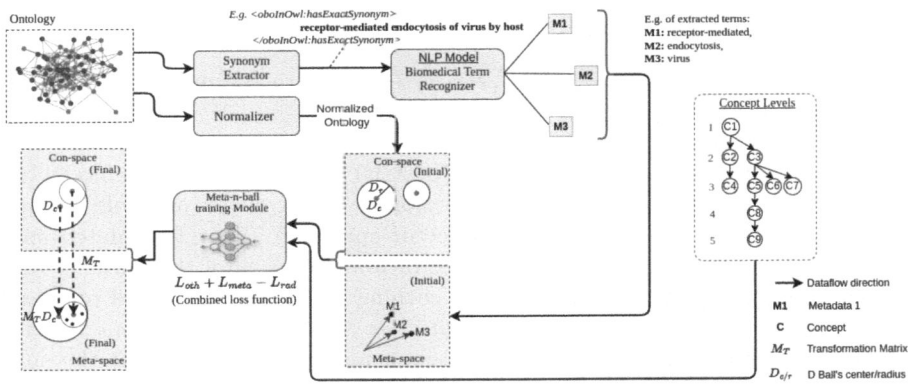

Fig. 1. Dataflow showing the generation of Meta-n-ball from domain ontology

In order to maintain the distinctiveness of the explicit concepts from both the ontology and the extracted meta-information, we have chosen to represent them in two separate vector spaces as mentioned above, drawing inspiration from [3]. The combined loss function for the con-space and the meta-space vectors contains three components as shown in Fig. 1. The loss functions of the seven NFs, as denoted collectively by L_{oth}, are designed for training the con-space entities based on [5]. Additionally, L_{rad} incorporates concept-level information. To enhance the quality of the ball's radius, the shortest distance to a specific concept from the root concept node in the concept hierarchy (a DAG) also called level is taken into consideration. This approach emphasizes the loss function more prominently for smaller balls. In Eq. 1, Le_i (0 if unavailable) denotes level of a concept with radius R_i and γ denotes margin loss parameter.

$$L_{rad} = \begin{cases} [R_i]_- + \gamma & \text{if } Le_i = 0 \\ \left[\sqrt{Le_i} * R_i\right]_- & \text{if } Le_i >= 1 \end{cases} \tag{1}$$

The loss function L_{meta}, representing the third type of loss function, is dedicated to learning meta-information. In Eq. 2, we use transformation matrix M_T which maps the concepts to meta-space and ensures that the metadata m resides inside it's correct concept C (center C_c & radius R_c) in meta-space.

$$L_{meta} = \left[\|M_T C_c - m\| - R_c - \gamma\right]_+ + \left|\|C_c\| - 1\right| + \left|\|m\| - 1\right| \tag{2}$$

In the Eqs. 1 and 2, $[x]_+$, $[x]_-$ symbolizes $max(0, x)$ and $min(0, x)$ respectively. During training, the concepts, relations, metadata embeddings and M_T are optimized at every iteration in mini-batches based on the aggregation of these loss functions to reach their final values.

3   Results and Conclusion

Evaluation Metrics. The existing evaluation metrics primarily focus on calculating the distance between the centers of subsumption balls, often overlooking the quality aspects of the generated balls. This includes whether the radii are positive, whether the super-ball has a greater radius, the quality of subsumption (either *total* or *partial*, where total is preferred more), etc. Keeping these in mind we design the following evaluation criteria: (1) *Valid Radius Proportion (VRP)* – The proportion of test cases where both radii are positive and the radius of the super-concept ball is larger than that of sub-concept. Naturally, the higher this proportion, the better the model is. (2) *Overall Distance between Centers (ODC)* – To assess whether the distance between the centers of sub and super balls has decreased across all test cases in our new model, we conducted a one-tailed t-test to determine which model exhibits greater distance values. We calculate the distance between the balls in meta-space in the case of the meta-n-ball model. The reporting format is as follows: if there is a significant reduction (p-val< 0.05) in distance for the meta-n-ball model than $EmEL^{++}$, it is denoted as $(T - statistic, emel > meta - nball)$, and vice versa. The subsumed ball pairs are expected to have lesser distance between them for the better model. (3) *Perfect Overlapping Proportion (TOP)* – The proportion of valid VRP test cases where the sub-concept ball is completely inside it's super-concept ball in meta-space. Higher proportion is expected for better model. Here the term "valid" denotes all the test cases where both the sub and super balls have radius greater than 0 and super-ball's radius is greater than it's sub-ball. The format for reporting VRP and TOP are: $< proportion(count\,of\,proportion) >$ Eg: *0.25 (500)*

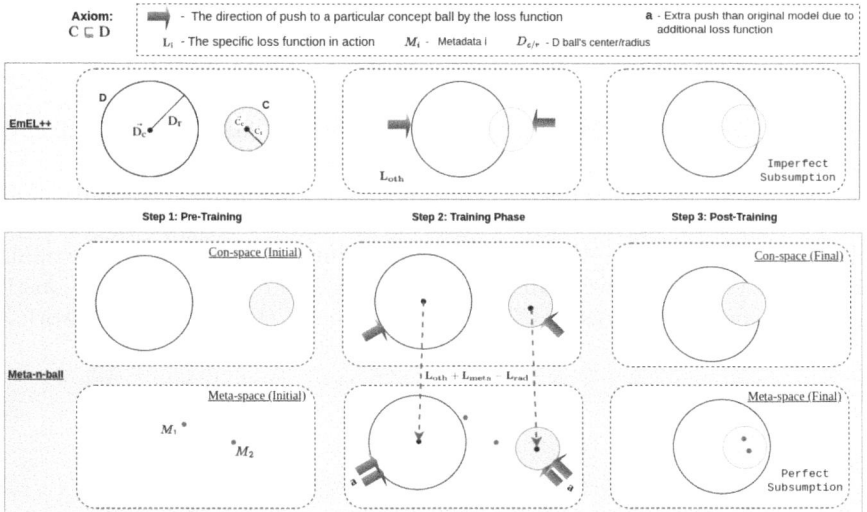

Fig. 2. Additional Loss Functions Improving Subsumption Quality

Table 1. Comparing n-ball (EmEL++) and Meta-n-ball approaches.

Dataset	Evaluation Metrics	EmEL++	Meta-n-ball	EmEL++	Meta-n-ball	EmEL++	Meta-n-ball
Test Splits		Split1		Split2		Split3	
GO	VRP	0.707 (8391)	**0.742 (8813)**	0.596 (7066)	**0.640 (7596)**	0.587 (6971)	**0.628 (7456)**
	ODC(T-test)	**14.88, emel>meta-nball**		**69.19, emel>meta-nball**		**64.09, emel>meta-nball**	
	TOP	0.241 (2862)	**0.424 (5029)**	0.242 (2872)	**0.385 (4573)**	0.234 (2782)	**0.344 (4088)**
HPO	VRP	0.621 (6584)	**0.683 (7239)**	0.381 (3994)	**0.430 (4502)**	0.402 (4243)	**0.442 (4661)**
	ODC(T-test)	3.156, meta-nball>emel		**14.62, emel>meta-nball**		**5.71, emel>meta-nball**	
	TOP	0.203 (2153)	**0.238 (2521)**	0.091 (956)	**0.121 (1267)**	0.089 (938)	**0.140 (1468)**

Experiments and Results. We utilized the Python package *Scispacy* with the *en_core_sci_md* NLP model, pretrained on $50K$ relevant biomedical entities. Metadata was extracted from synonym data (*hasExactSynonym, hasRelatedSynonym, hasBroadSynonym, hasNarrowSynonym*) found in the Gene Ontology[2] (GO) and Human Phenotype Ontology[3] (HPO). We set hyper-parameters for both models as follows: $n = 100$, $\gamma = -0.1$, *epoch*= 1000 where n denotes the number of dimensions, γ denotes the margin loss parameter and *epoch* is the number of iterations the algorithms will run for. Concept levels were extracted from the respective *.obo* files available on official websites[2,3] using the Python *goatools* package. Our model was tested on three separate valid-test splits, as shown in Table 1, with each test sample containing the true subsumption relation in the format ($< sub - ball >< super - ball >$). Our meta-n-ball approach consistently enhances the quality of ball radii and rectifies numerous imperfect subsumptions, as evidenced by improved VRP and TOP values across all test splits in Table 1. ODC performance is also commendable across almost all test splits indicating meta-n-ball model has successfully reduced the distance between the centers of subsumption ball pairs. But, upon closer examination of extracted biomedical terms, it is apparent that some metadata are overly generic (e.g., "activity", "positive") or near-duplicates (e.g., "ureteric reflux", "ureteral reflux"). Hence, implementing filtering criteria to include only relevant terms is essential.

Conclusions. The experimental studies substantiate our hypothesis that the integration of metadata alongside meticulously designed loss functions can effectively enhance subsumption quality, thereby stimulating further exploration. Filtering out imperfect metadata and exploring additional meta-information, such as definitions and labels, while ensuring performance, presents an intriguing research challenge. This work suggests promising future research directions for advancing knowledge representation and reasoning in the RKGE framework.

---

[2]https://geneontology.org/docs/download-ontology/.
[3]https://hpo.jax.org/app/data/annotations.

References

1. Baader, F., Brandt, S., Lutz, C.: Pushing the EL envelope. In: Proceedings of the IJCAI, pp. 364–369. Professional Book Center (2005)
2. Chen, J., Hu, P., Jiménez-Ruiz, E., Holter, O.M., Antonyrajah, D., Horrocks, I.: OWL2Vec*: embedding of OWL ontologies. Mach. Learn. **110**(7), 1813–1845 (2021)
3. Hao, J., Chen, M., Yu, W., Sun, Y., Wang, W.: Universal representation learning of knowledge bases by jointly embedding instances and ontological concepts. In: Proceedings of the 25th ACM SIGKDD, pp. 1709–1719. ACM (2019). https://doi.org/10.1145/3292500.3330838
4. Kulmanov, M., Liu-Wei, W., Yan, Y., Hoehndorf, R.: EL embeddings: Geometric construction of models for the description logic EL++. arXiv preprint arXiv:1902.10499 (2019)
5. Mondal, S., Bhatia, S., Mutharaju, R.: EmEL++: Embeddings for EL++ description logic. In: Proceedings of the AAAI-MAKE, vol. 2846. CEUR-WS.org (2021)
6. Peng, X., Tang, Z., Kulmanov, M., Niu, K., Hoehndorf, R.: Description logic EL++ embeddings with intersectional closure. arXiv preprint arXiv:2202.14018 (2022)

KGSnap!: query Knowledge Graphs by Snap!

Vincenzo Offertucci, Maria Angela Pellegrino$^{(\boxtimes)}$ ⓘ, and Vittorio Scarano ⓘ

Dipartimento di Informatica, Università degli Studi di Salerno, Salerno, Italy
v.offertucci@studenti.unisa.it, {mapellegrino,vitsca}@unisa.it

Abstract. As the block programming paradigm has been successfully used to teach programming skills, this demo proposes `KGSnap!`, an extension of the block-based programming environment `Snap!`, which allows lay users to build and run queries on a SPARQL endpoint. The proposed approach has the potential to enable lay users to access knowledge graphs without requiring technical skills in query languages.

Keywords: SPARQL · Block-based programming · Snap!

1 Introduction and Related Work

The Semantic Web technologies are increasingly used to model any field of interest, increasing the quantity and diversity of available data modeled by Knowledge Graphs (KGs). However, its usefulness risks to be left untapped due to the SPARQL complexity [6]. Lay users interested in consuming KGs require tools to mitigate the technical challenges SPARQL poses.

Block programming languages that guide users in dragging and connecting fragments shaped like jigsaw puzzle pieces have successfully introduced programming to non-experts [3]. Just think the vast exploitation of Blockly[1] as part of code.org's Hour of Code, Scratch [4] to create animations and games and MIT App Inventor [8] to build Android Apps. The proposal of letting lay users query data by block-based programming is not new. `SQheLper` [2], `DBLearn` [7], and `DBSnap++` [5] are block-based programming interfaces to query databases. In the Semantic Web community, Bottoni and Ceriani [1] proposed `SPARQL Playground`, introducing KGs querying in Blockly. This demo proposes `KGSnap!`, an extension of Snap! to query KGs that expose SPARQL endpoints.

2 KGSnap!: query Knowledge Graphs by Snap!

`Snap!`[2] (formerly Build Your Own Blocks) is a free, open-source, block-based educational graphical programming language and online community allowing learners to explore, create, and remix interactive animations, games, and stories while learning about mathematical and computational ideas.

---

[1] Blockly, https://developers.google.com/blockly.
[2] Snap! https://snap.berkeley.edu.

A. Meroño Peñuela et al. (Eds.): ESWC 2024, LNCS 15344, pp. 272–275, 2025.
https://doi.org/10.1007/978-3-031-78952-6_40

KGSnap! (visible in Fig. 1, freely accessible online[3] and available on GitHub with an Open Source license[4]) extends the Snap! architecture by introducing the possibility to perform SELECT queries on KGs provided with a working SPARQL endpoint. By default, KGSnap! is configured to query Wikidata. However, users can easily introduce any SPARQL endpoint of interest by a dedicated block, **define a new endpoint**, shown in Fig. 2 among others. KGSnap! mimics the structure of SPARQL queries to follow the philosophy of block programming to guide learners to experiment gradually with the underlying language and, in the end, to be able to switch to programming in that language. Hence, SPARQL queries are formulated by specifying triples (subject, predicate, object).

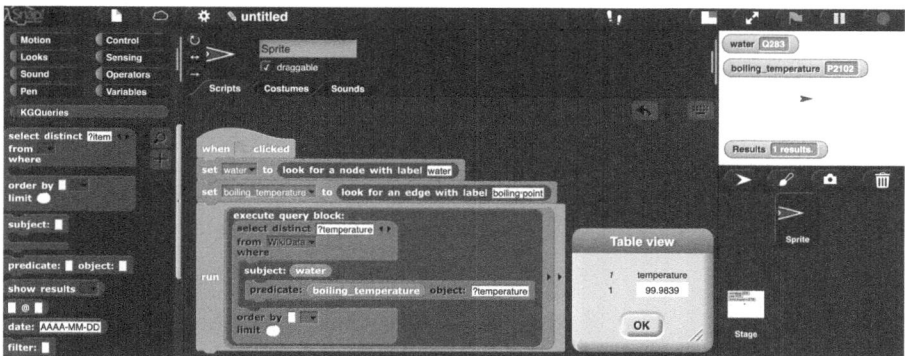

Fig. 1. KGSnap! interface.

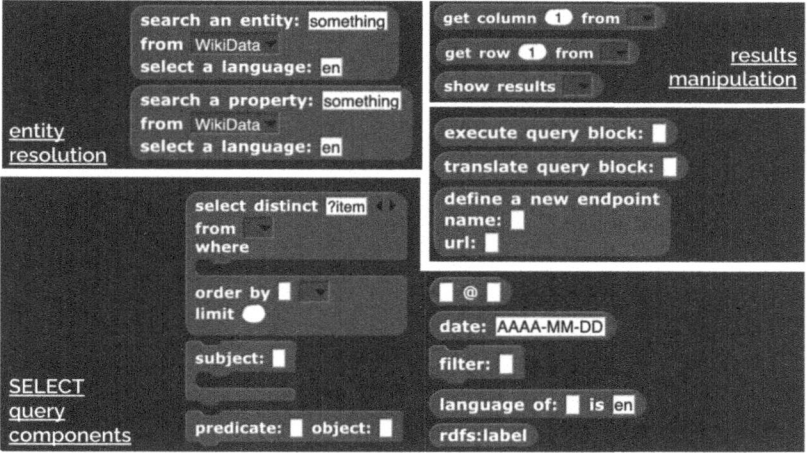

Fig. 2. Blocks implemented in KGSnap!.

---

[3] KGSnap!: https://isislab-unisa.github.io/Snap/snap.html.
[4] KGSnap! https://github.com/isislab-unisa/KnowledgeGraphsAndSnap.

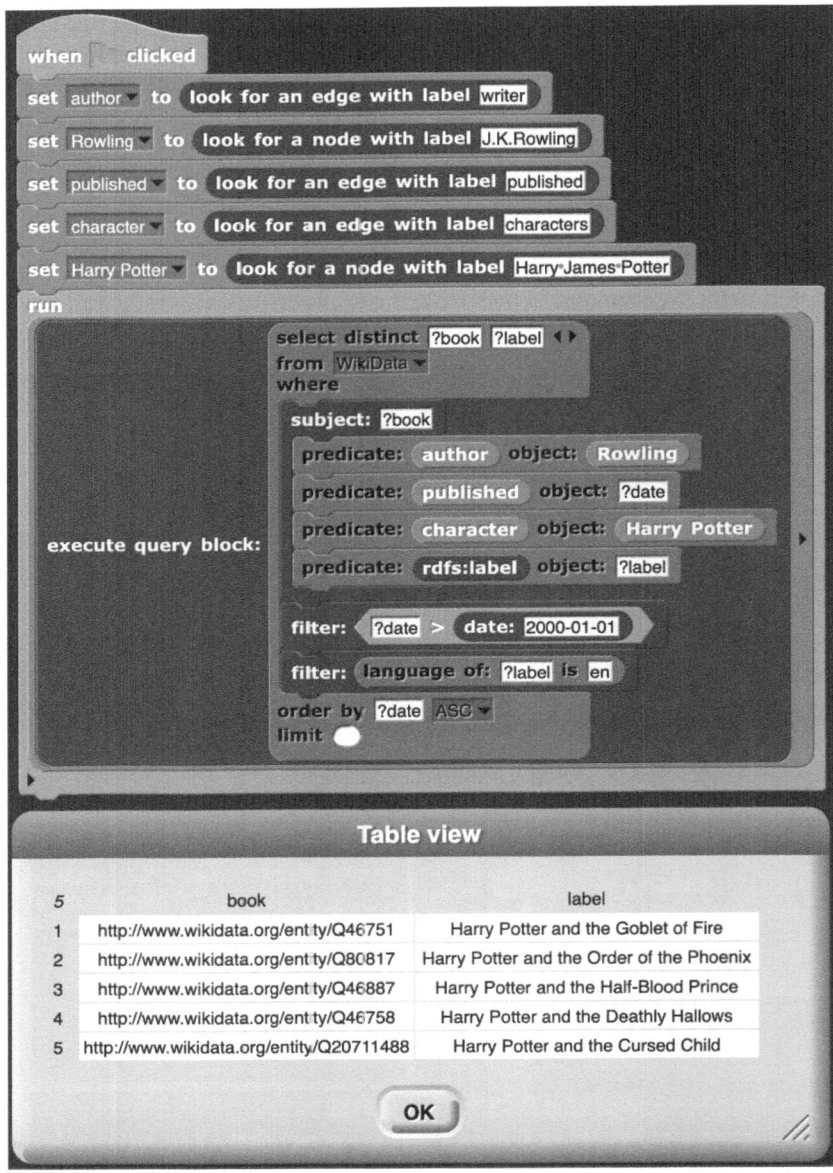

Fig. 3. Use case of `KGSnap!`. We query Wikidata to retrieve books authored by J.K.Rowling with Harry Potter as character.

The complete set of supported features is visible in Fig. 2 and concerns entity resolution from user-defined labels, components to assemble SELECT queries covering Basic Graph Patterns, such as path traversal, filters, sorting, and other

Fig. 4. Entity resolution performed by KGSnap! to solve user-defined labels.

supporting features to manipulate results and introducing new endpoints. Once the SPARQL query is completed, users can visualize them as data tables and store specific results in variables to refine queries iteratively. Query results can be downloaded as JSON or CSV files, while the query as a TXT file.

Demonstration. During the demo, we will show KGSnap! in practice. Supposing we are interested in retrieving all the books authored by J.K. Rowling, having Harry Potter as a character and published in this century. The resulting query is visible in Fig. 3, which relies on the definitions of custom functions, wrapping blocks for performing entity resolution visible in Fig. 4.

References

1. Bottoni, P., Ceriani, M.: Sparql playground: a block programming tool to experiment with sparql. In: VOILA@ISWC, pp. 103 (2015)
2. Jacobs, S., Jaschke, S.: Sqhelper: a block-based syntax support for SQL. In: Global Engineering Education Conference (EDUCON), pp. 478–481. IEEE (2021)
3. Moon, H., Cheon, J., Lee, J.: Teaching block-based programming: a systematic review of current approaches and outcomes. In: Society for Information Technology and Teacher Education International Conference, pp. 73–78. Association for the Advancement of Computing in Education (AACE) (2020)
4. Resnick, M., et al.: Scratch: programming for all. Communications **52**(11), 60–67 (2009)
5. Silva, Y.N., Nieuwenhuyse, A., Schenk, T.G., Symons, A.: Dbsnap++: creating data-driven programs by snapping blocks. In: the 23rd Annual Conference on Innovation and Technology in Computer Science Education, pp. 170–175. ACM (2018)
6. Vargas, H., Aranda, C.B., Hogan, A., López, C.: RDF explorer: A visual SPARQL query builder. In: ISWC, pp. 647–663. Springer (2019)
7. Vinayakumar, R., Soman, K., Menon, P.: DB-learn: studying relational algebra concepts by snapping blocks. In: 9th International Conference on Computing, Communication and Networking Technologies (ICCCNT), pp. 1–6. IEEE (2018)
8. Wolber, D., Abelson, H., Spertus, E., Looney, L.: App inventor. O'Reilly Media, Inc. (2011)

KGHeartBeat: A Knowledge Graph Quality Assessment Tool

Maria Angela Pellegrino[1]([✉])[ID], Anisa Rula[2][ID], and Gabriele Tuozzo[1]

[1] Dipartimento di Informatica, Unviersità degli Studi di Salerno, Fisciano, SA, Italy
mapellegrino@unisa.it, g.tuozzo4@studenti.unisa.it
[2] Department of Information Engineering, University of Brescia, Brescia, Italy
anisa.rula@unibs.it

Abstract. This demo proposes KGHeartBeat, a community-shared open-source knowledge graph quality assessment tool to periodically perform quality analysis on all the freely available knowledge graphs registered on the LOD cloud and DataHub. As a proof of concept, we discuss the comparison of different linguistic versions of DBpedia via KGHeartBeat.

Keywords: Quality assessment · Knowledge Graph · Framework

1 Background and Motivation

A considerable amount of data is published using the Semantic Web technologies [8], but they range from extensively curated to relatively low-quality Knowledge Graphs (KGs) [7]. Data quality assessment is a multidimensional problem encompassing heterogeneous and multiple quality dimensions including but not limited to accessibility, interlinking, performance, syntactic validity, and completeness [10]. Several quality assessment tools have been proposed over time, such as RDFUnit [7] (formerly DataBugger), Luzzu [3], SPARQLES [9], SemQuire [8], DYLDO [5], LODLaundromat [2], ABECTO [6]. However, there is no KG quality assessment tool as a reference in the Semantic Web community.

This demo presents KGHeartBeat, a community-shared open-source tool designed to facilitate the assessment and comparison of KGs based on several quality metrics. This tool represents a significant contribution to the field of KG, offering developers and lay users a comprehensive solution for assessing the quality of KGs. While developers are provided with APIs[1] to integrate quality metric computation in any data management workflow, lay users can utilize a user-friendly web-based interface to explore KG quality results visually. The demo primarily focuses on showcasing the KGHeartBeat web application interface[2], which allows users to compare linguistic versions of DBpedia. The interface offers intuitive features for exploring and comparing KG quality metrics.

---

[1] KGHeartBeat API: https://pypi.org/project/kgheartbeat/.

[2] KGHeartBeat web application: http://www.isislab.it:12280/kgheartbeat.

A. Meroño Peñuela et al. (Eds.): ESWC 2024, LNCS 15344, pp. 276–280, 2025.
https://doi.org/10.1007/978-3-031-78952-6_41

2   KGHeartBeat

KGHeartBeat is a fully automatic KG quality assessment community-shared framework, publicly available on GitHub[3]. KGHeartBeat weekly computes the quality assessment of all the KGs that can be automatically retrieved by widely used data and knowledge aggregation platforms, e.g., LOD Cloud[4] and DataHub[5]. The metrics computations rely on data retrieved by working SPARQL endpoints, metadata contained in the VoID file and those returned by platforms for data and knowledge aggregation. KGHeartBeat implements a large set of well-known quality metrics proposed by Zaveri et al. [10] belonging to different quality dimensions, focusing on those that can be automatically and objectively computed without requiring a gold standard. The implementation details of all the supported quality metrics are freely accessible online[6]. Results can be downloaded as CSV files or visually explored via a freely accessible web application(see footnote 4) visible in Fig. 1. Users are initially prompted to choose their desired KG(s), after which they can visually explore quality dimensions presented in graphical charts via the web interface. Quality dimensions can be selected from the left-side panel, as shown in Fig. 1 (2), with the corresponding chart displayed in the central panel, as seen in Fig. 1 (4). Quality scores are presented in a simple table format or a more complex chart. depending on the selected quality dimension. Data visualizations aim to enhance understanding for end-users, making assessment and comparison easier to grasp. Quality metric scores can be examined for a specific date, configurable through Fig. 1 (3), or analyzed over time.

Metrics' ratings are then linearly combined into an overall quality assessment score with a numeric value ranging from 0.0 to 100.0, with higher scores indicating better quality. In the KGs ranking tab, users can access the quality scores of all KGs automatically analyzed by KGHeartBeat. Moreover, in the View Score tab, users can view quality scores specific to the selected KGs. For example, Fig. 2(a) shows the ranking computed for the linguistic versions of DBpedia. In this tab, end-users can customize weights assigned to each metric, allowing them to tailor quality scores to match the use case of interest requirements. Both tabs are accessible via the top-level panel shown in Fig. 1(1).

3   Use Case Driven Metrics and Results

This section overviews metrics and results concerning the Information disorder and automatic fact-checking use case. The University of Salerno is involved in the SERICS project [1], which focuses on security and rights in cyberspace, with

---

[3] KGHeartBeat repository: https://github.com/isislab-unisa/KGHeartbeat
Permanent URL: https://zenodo.org/records/10275888.

[4] LOD Cloud: https://lod-cloud.net/.

[5] DataHub: https://datahub.io/.

[6] Metric details: https://isislab-unisa.github.io/KGHeartbeat.

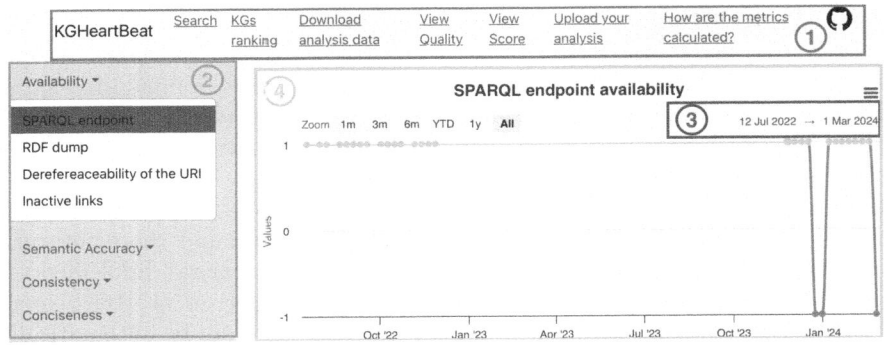

Fig. 1. KGHeartBeat interface. The top-level panel (1) shows the navigation bar, the left-side panel (2) lets users explore quality dimensions, the calendar (3) gives the possibility to customize the time frame of reported quality dimensions scores, and the central panel (4) overviews quality dimensions results graphically according to the end-users configuration.

Table 1. Top-5 KGs according to Trust and Data dynamicity dimensions. Scores range from 0 to 100. The higher, the better for all the dimensions. SPARQL stands for SPARQL endpoint.

Metric	Def	Input	Output
Verifiability	Provenance details	SPARQL & VoID	[0,1]
Reputation	Credit computed via the PageRank	Metadata	[0,1]
Believability	The provider is a trustful	Metadata	[0,1]
Currency	Freshness of data [10]	SPARQL & VoID	[0,1]
Timeliness	Presence of frequency of data validation [10]	SPARQL	{0,1}

KG	Verifiability	Reputation	Believability	Currency	Timeliness	Score
Italian Chamber of Deputies	0.66	$8.57e-7$	0.37	1.0	1.0	60.80
Bibliography of the Italian Parliament and electoral studies	0.66	$8.11e-3$	0.25	1.0	1.0	58.30
PGxLOD	0.49	$8.64e-3$	0.37	1.0	1.0	57.47
Corporate Body Named Authority List	0.49	$8.71e-3$	0.37	1.0	1.0	57.47
Country Name Authority List	0.49	$8.61e-4$	0.37	1.0	1.0	57.47

one of its key objectives being the detection and mitigation of information disorder, encompassing a wide range of misinformation. Among different perspectives that can be used to debunk misinformation, KGs play a crucial role when the information content must be explored and automatically compared with external sources [11]. It requires evaluating the trustworthiness and timeliness of information sources [4], emphasizing the credibility of the data and its dynamic nature. To do so, KGHeartBeat can be configured to prioritize the dimensions of trust and dataset dynamicity in computing the final score. The top-5 KGs are reported in Table 1. All of them are curated by (national) organizations, but PGxLOD that is part of the PractiKPharma project[7]. Scores are rather low. Hence, further effort should be invested in curating trust and dynamicity dimensions.

---

[7] https://practikpharma.mystrikingly.com.

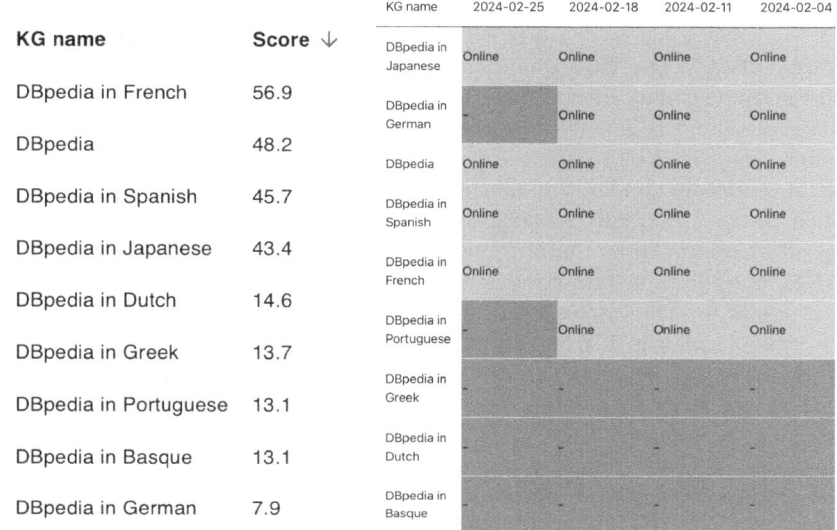

(a) Quality score table

(b) SPARQL endpoint availability

Fig. 2. KGHeartBeat charts to compare linguistic DBpedia versions.

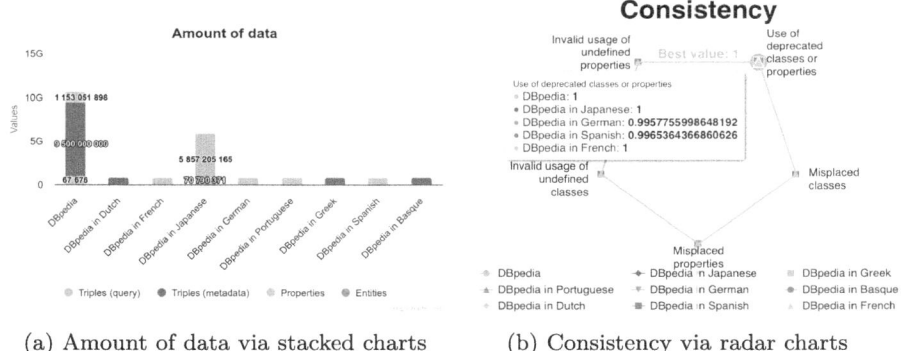

(a) Amount of data via stacked charts

(b) Consistency via radar charts

Fig. 3. (...continue) KGHeartBeat charts to compare linguistic DBpedia versions.

4   Demonstration

This section overviews how to use the KGHeartBeat web application(see foot-note 4) in practice. Demonstration videos are available in the GitHub repos-itory[8]. Supposing that we are interested in comparing the different linguistic versions of DBpedia as a proof-of-concept. We select all the available linguistic

---

[8] Demonstration videos: https://github.com/isislab-unisa/KGHeartbeat/tree/main/ examples/videos.

versions of DBpedia, resulting in nine different KGs, listed in Fig. 2(a). Figures 2 and 3 overview some of the quality dimensions scores as graphically rendered by `KGHeartBeat`. The KGs quality is extremely heterogeneous, spanning from 8/100 for the German version of DBpedia to 57/100 for its French version. The quality assessment is heavily impacted by the availability of a working SPARQL endpoint (see Fig. 2(b)). Linguistic versions of DBpedia attached to an offline SPARQL endpoint during the analysis (February 25th, 2024) are ranked as the worst in the overall quality score table visible in Fig. 2(a). `KGHeartBeat` adopts a best-effort approach to compute metrics. When a KG is attached to a working SPARQL endpoint, metric computations rely on current data. As an alternative, it looks for the corresponding value in metadata. The amount of data metric (visible in Fig. 3(a)) is an example in this direction. Figure 3(b) shows the *Consistency* dimension. As all the KGs reach almost the same score in this dimension, lines are in overlap, and exact values are visible by hovering chart points corresponding to KGs.

Acknowledgments. This work was partially supported by the SERICS (PE000 00014) under the MUR National Recovery and Resilience Plan funded by the European Union - NextGenerationEU.

References

1. The SERICS project. https://serics.eu. Accessed April 2024
2. Beek, W., Rietveld, L., Bazoobandi, H.R., Wielemaker, J., Schlobach, S.: LOD laundromat: a uniform way of publishing other people's dirty data. In: ISWC, pp. 213–228 (2014)
3. Debattista, J., Auer, S., Lange, C.: Luzzu-a methodology and framework for linked data quality assessment. J. Data Inf. Qual. **8**(1), 1–32 (2016)
4. Esteves, D., Rula, A., Reddy, A.J., Lehmann, J.: Toward veracity assessment in RDF knowledge bases: an exploratory analysis. ACM J. Data Inf. Qual. **9**(3), 16:1–16:26 (2018)
5. Käfer, T., Umbrich, J., Hogan, A., Polleres, A.: Towards a dynamic linked data observatory. In: Proceedings of the LDOW Workshop at WWW (2012)
6. Keil, J.M.: ABECTO: an ABox evaluation and comparison tool for ontologies. In: The Semantic Web: ESWC Satellite Events, pp. 140–145 (2020)
7. Kontokostas, D., Westphal, P., Auer, S., Hellmann, S., Lehmann, J., Cornelissen, R.: Databugger: a test-driven framework for debugging the web of data. In: 23rd International World Wide Web Conference, WWW, pp. 115–118 (2014)
8. Langer, A., Siegert, V., Göpfert, C., Gaedke, M.: SemQuire - assessing the data quality of linked open data sources based on DQV. In: Pautasso, C., Sánchez-Figueroa, F., Systä, K., Murillo Rodríguez, J.M. (eds.) ICWE 2018. LNCS, vol. 11153, pp. 163–175. Springer, Cham (2018). https://doi.org/10.1007/978-3-030-03056-8_14
9. Vandenbussche, P.Y., Umbrich, J., Matteis, L., Hogan, A., Buil-Aranda, C.: SPARQLES: monitoring public SPARQL endpoints. Semant. web **8**(6), 1049–1065 (2017)
10. Zaveri, A., Rula, A., Maurino, A., Pietrobon, R., Lehmann, J., Auer, S.: Quality assessment for linked data: a survey. Semant. Web **7**(1), 63–93 (2016)
11. Zhou, X., Zafarani, R.: A survey of fake news: fundamental theories, detection methods, and opportunities. ACM Comput. Surv. **53**(5), 109 (2020)

CLASS MATE: Cross-Lingual Semantic Search for Material Science Driven by Knowledge Graphs

Aleksandr Perevalov[1,2(✉)], Jiveshwari Chinchghare[1], Mouli Krishna[1], Shivam Sharma[1], Amal Nimmy Lal[1], Aryman Deshwal[1], Andreas Both[2,3], and Axel-Cyrille Ngonga-Ngomo[1]

[1] Paderborn University, Paderborn, Germany
`alpe@mail.uni-paderborn.de`
[2] Leipzig University of Applied Sciences, Leipzig, Germany
[3] DATEV eG, Nuremberg, Germany

Abstract. As diverse linguistic backgrounds contribute valuable insights to scientific research, effective Cross-Lingual Semantic Search (CLSS) mechanisms, which often remain overlooked, become crucial. This paper introduces CLASS MATE(https://lass-kg.demos.dice-research.org/)—a CLSS application working over material science knowledge graphs (KGs). Our work aims to bridge the digital language divide in the research community by employing advanced knowledge representation techniques. In particular, (1) we acquire our KG containing chemical substances with multilingual entity labels; (2) we implement a symbolic similarity-based named entity recognition algorithm; and (3) we develop a demo application employing the previous steps for retrieving information requested by a user from our KG and LOD sources in multiple languages. Our industry partner Springer Nature provided us with a KG as an information source to understand information needs. To the best of our knowledge, we made the first contribution to CLSS within material science.

Keywords: Cross-Lingual Semantic Search · Question Answering

1 Introduction

Many research fields, including the field of material science, are undergoing a paradigm shift towards cross-lingual information retrieval due to the increasing international collaboration of researchers. While established commercial (e.g., Springer Materials[1]) and research (see Sect. 3) solutions exist for information search within the field, they often overlook the information access in different languages. This gap hinders researchers from fully benefiting from the diverse knowledge of the international scientific community. We introduce a pioneering

---

[1] https://materials.springer.com/.

A. Meroño Peñuela et al. (Eds.): ESWC 2024, LNCS 15344, pp. 281–285, 2025.
https://doi.org/10.1007/978-3-031-78952-6_42

exploration into a cross-lingual semantic search over knowledge graphs tailored specifically for material science, focusing on multilingual functionality. First, we enrich our RDF-based knowledge graph (KG) with domain-specific information (chemical substances and properties) from public knowledge graphs like Wikidata. We focus on supporting the following *languages*: English, German, Chinese, Japanese, Arabic, Persian, Hindi, and Russian. Secondly, we develop a domain-specific algorithm for named entity recognition (NER) followed by fuzzy string matching for named entity linking (NEL) within our KG. Given the linked entities, a SPARQL query is executed on a KG to find the information requested by a user. Finally, the retrieved information is presented to a user in the language of their input query by injecting named entity labels of the respective language into a Large Language Model (LLM) through a translation prompt.

This work is a collaboration with Springer Nature, which provided us with their internal data for better domain understanding. The accessibility of our research is ensured by releasing the demo and open-source data[2], accompanied by a video tutorial[3]. To the best of our knowledge, this is the first contribution to tackle cross-lingual semantic search within the material science domain.

2   Class Mate

We define the *objective of semantic search* as to identify answers $\mathcal{A}$ that fulfill an informational need of a NL query q, utilizing a knowledge graph $\mathcal{KG}$. In its turn, cross-lingual semantic search systems *provide a possibility of searching for information in several languages* $l \in \mathcal{L}$, $|\mathcal{L}| > 1$. Hence, a user may pose a query in different languages: $q_{l_1}, \ldots, q_{l_n}$, where $n = |\mathcal{L}|$. At the same time, a system may search for answers in KGs in different languages: $\mathcal{KG}_{l_1}, \ldots, \mathcal{KG}_{l_n}$ (if multilingual information is not merged into one KG instance). For example, a user writes the question q_{l_i} (written in language l_i) and a system finds an answer $\mathcal{A}$ in the $\mathcal{KG}_{l_j}$ (instantiated for language l_j) [4].

For instance, when asking "What is the density of Propane?" one expects to see a particular density *value* or a *phase diagram* of propane. While the values or the phase diagrams are provided by our project partner within their data, our task here is to correctly navigate a user to the right point where this data is available (independently from the question's language).

Knowledge Graph Enrichment. As the initial *Springer Materials KG* (SM KG) from our industry partner contains only English entity representations, we enriched the graph with multilingual representations taken from Wikidata—an open collaborative KG. First, we narrowed down our search space to the only relevant entities using the entity types (e.g., Chemical Property (Q764285[4])). Second, we used English entity labels from the SM KG as an identifier for matching the respective entities in Wikidata. If there was a match, we connected it to

---

[2] https://doi.org/10.6084/m9.figshare.24592428.v1.
[3] https://youtu.be/2-YwbFWMW7Q.
[4] https://www.wikidata.org/wiki/Q764285.

the matched Wikidata entity via an `owl:sameAs` property. After that, the now integrated multilingual representations can be simply retrieved using SPARQL.

The Demo Engine. The *user interface* is a Web application written using the React framework[5]. We designed it as a chat window with an input field, auto-completions, and auto-suggestions. Figure 1 demonstrates the user interface in detail. The *entity-linking algorithm* has a straightforward implementation. For each entity type (`SUBSTANCE` (e.g., Propane), `PROPERTY` (e.g., density)) we use a separate entity-label index. Given a user's input query, we iterate through all the items of the label index and measure the ratio of the most similar sub-string. Finally, the algorithm returns the linked entity (ID, language, label, similarity), which label has the highest similarity within a user's search term (unless the similarity is lower than a pre-defined threshold). The *query engine* deals with the following cases: (1) Both `SUBSTANCE` and `PROPERTY` were recognized; (2) Either `SUBSTANCE` or `PROPERTY` was recognized; (3) No entities were recognized. In the first case, based on the entity ID obtained from the entity-linking step, we query the SM KG to identify whether (a) data on `SUBSTANCE` is available; (b) data on `PROPERTY` is available; (c) combined data on and `PROPERTY` is available. In the second case, we query either (a) or (b), In the last case, we do not perform any queries on the SM KG.

Finally, we verbalize the answer in a user-friendly form. We use HTML to include hyperlinks if the queries (a), (b), and (c) were successfully executed. We translate the HTML into the language of a user's initial input, which is detected upon the language tag of the identified entities, by using OpenAI's `gpt-3.5-turbo`[6] with the following prompt template: "`Translate to {lang} (ISO-639-1) while keeping HTML consistent: {HTML}`" (the entity labels are injected in the original language). Figure 2 demonstrates the overall "big picture" of the workflow within this paper.

3   Related Work

Text2Mol [3] uses a combined model to link natural language and molecular structures, enhancing performance significantly. SynKB [1] introduces an open-source knowledge base that extracts chemical synthesis procedures from patents, providing accessible information for chemists. Unlike commercial databases, it is freely available and excels in query performance. MolT5 [2] is a framework addressing tasks like generating captions for molecules or creating molecules from text descriptions, displaying promising results in advancing molecule-language understanding. However, a critical gap exists in applying these techniques to semantic search within material science. We were not able to find any scientific publications on cross-lingual semantic search applied to material science. This emphasizes the need for domain-specific semantic search functionalities tailored to its unique characteristics and complexities.

---

[5] https://react.dev/.

[6] https://platform.openai.com/docs/models/gpt-3-5.

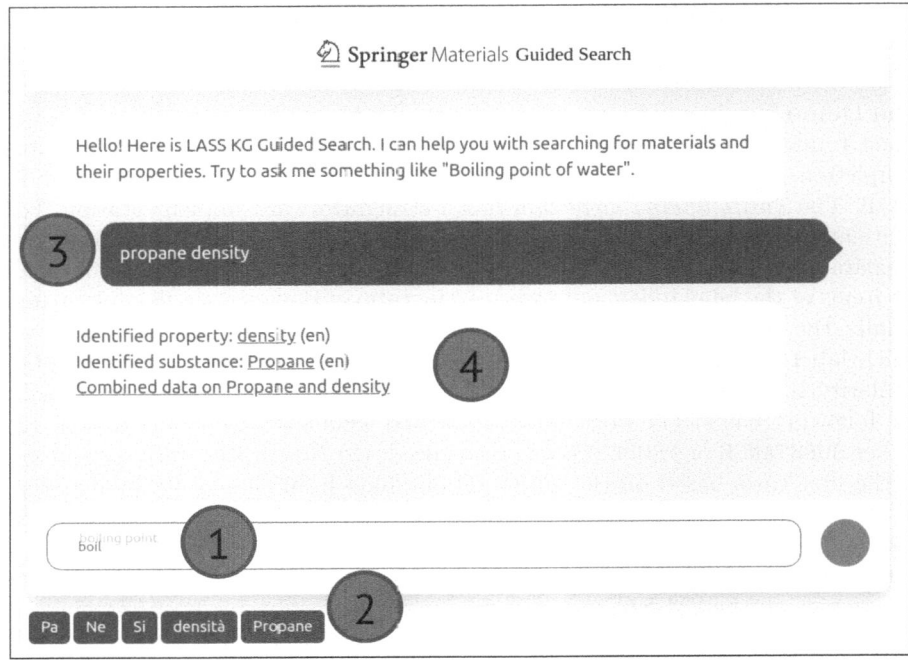

Fig. 1. User Interface: (1) the input field with auto-completions, (2) the auto-suggestions section, (3) the user's message, (4) the system's answer.

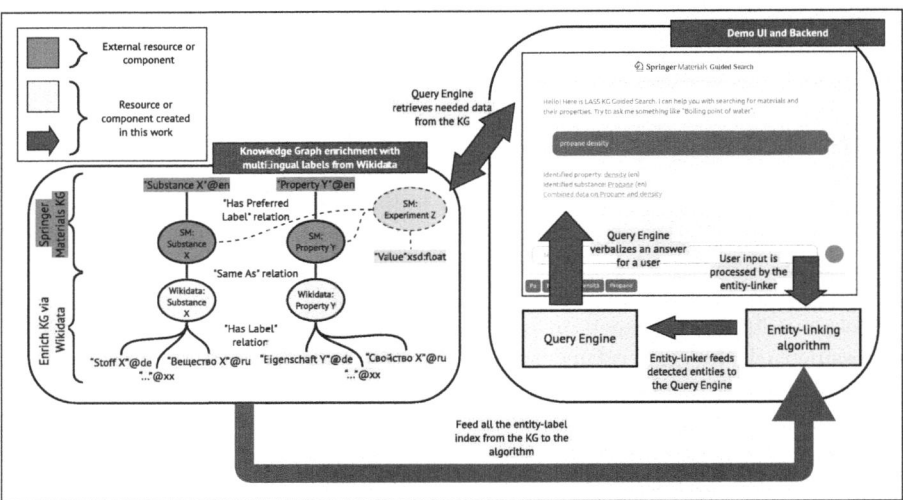

Fig. 2. Big picture of the workflow in our paper. First, we enriched our KG via connecting it to Wikidata. Secondly, we build a demo UI and backend that recognizes and links entities as well as retrieves them from our KG.

4 Conclusion

CLASS MATE introduces a significant step towards bridging linguistic barriers within the material science domain. However, certain limitations persist, such as reliance solely on preferred labels from a KG, and neglecting synonyms, typos, and other fluctuations in language when doing NEL. In addition, this approach requires proper and trustworthy evaluation. Despite these constraints, our demo application marks a crucial advancement, fostering collaboration and exploration in the complex landscape of material science. Moreover, considering synonyms, typos, and linguistic fluctuations in the NEL process and exploring the pre-training of domain-specific multilingual LMs and the fine-tuning of LLMs could significantly improve the effectiveness of our approach.

Acknowledgements. We would like to thank Springer Nature for supporting this work, in particular, we would like to say thank you to Stefan Scherer, Alexander Eckl, Volha Bryl, Marcel Karnstedt-Hulpus, and Harald Wirsching. This research has been funded by the Federal Ministry of Education and Research (BMBF) under grant 01IS17046. as part of the Software Campus project "LASS KG: Language Agnostic Semantic Search driven by Knowledge Graphs".

References

1. Bai, F., Ritter, A., Madrid, P., Freitag, D., Niekrasz, J.: SynKB: semantic search for synthetic procedures. In: Proceedings of the 2022 Conference on Empirical Methods in Natural Language Processing: System Demonstrations, pp. 311–318. Association for Computational Linguistics, Abu Dhabi, UAE (2022). https://doi.org/10.18653/v1/2022.emnlp-demos.31
2. Edwards, C., Lai, T., Ros, K., Honke, G., Cho, K., Ji, H.: Translation between molecules and natural language. In: Proceedings of the 2022 Conference on Empirical Methods in Natural Language Processing, pp. 375–413. Association for Computational Linguistics (2022). https://doi.org/10.18653/v1/2022.emnlp-main.26
3. Edwards, C., Zhai, C., Ji, H.: Text2Mol: cross-modal molecule retrieval with natural language queries. In: Proceedings of the 2021 Conference on Empirical Methods in Natural Language Processing, pp. 595–607. Association for Computational Linguistics (2021). https://doi.org/10.18653/v1/2021.emnlp-main.47
4. Perevalov, A., Both, A., Ngomo, A.C.N.: Multilingual question answering systems for knowledge graphs—a survey (2024). https://www.semantic-web-journal.net/system/files/swj3633.pdf, under review

When Ontologies Met Knowledge Graphs: Tale of a Methodology

Romana Pernisch[1,2]([✉]), María Poveda-Villalón[3], Diego Conde-Herreros[3],
David Chaves-Fraga[4], and Lise Stork[1]

[1] Department of Computer Science, Vrije Universiteit Amsterdam, Amsterdam,
The Netherlands
{r.pernisch,l.stork}@vu.nl
[2] Discovery Lab, Elsevier, Amsterdam, The Netherlands
[3] Ontology Engineering Group, Universidad Politécnica de Madrid, Madrid, Spain
{diego.conde.herreros,m.poveda}@upm.es
[4] Grupo de Sistemas Inte_ixentes, Universidade de Santiago de Compostela, Santiago,
Spain
david.chaves@usc.es

Abstract. The current state of the art of knowledge engineering lacks
proper methodologies to deal with the ever-changing nature of knowledge. In this short paper, we present LOT4KG: a first step towards
including the changing nature of knowledge in the knowledge graph lifecycle. We extend the LOT ontology engineering methodology to include
activities associated with knowledge graph construction, better reflecting how they are engineered in the real world. Further, we analyse how
these lifecycles compare to ontology evolution frameworks and what work
is there to be done in the future to step from engineering towards full
knowledge graph evolution.

Keywords: KG construction · KG lifecycle · methodology

1 Introduction

The constantly evolving nature of knowledge has become a major problem in
the way we engineer and publish data on the Web in the form of knowledge
graphs (KGs)[1] [5]. We lack methodologies that accurately capture the problem of
evolving KGs and at the same time propose how to deal with changing KGs over
time. This problem is aggravated by the fact that today we have methodologies
for the engineering of ontologies [2,4,6], and KGs [1,8] separately.

Although Ontology 101 [4] specifically includes the activity "creation of
individuals", it does not consider today's technologies such as RML, SHACL,
ShEx, which are involved in the engineering of KGs. Even LOT [6], one of the
newest ontology engineering methodologies, focuses only on the engineering of

---

[1] We consider a KG to consist of a Tbox (terminology, schema) and Abox (assertions).

A. Meroño Peñuela et al. (Eds.): ESWC 2024, LNCS 15344, pp. 286–290, 2025.
https://doi.org/10.1007/978-3-031-78952-6_43

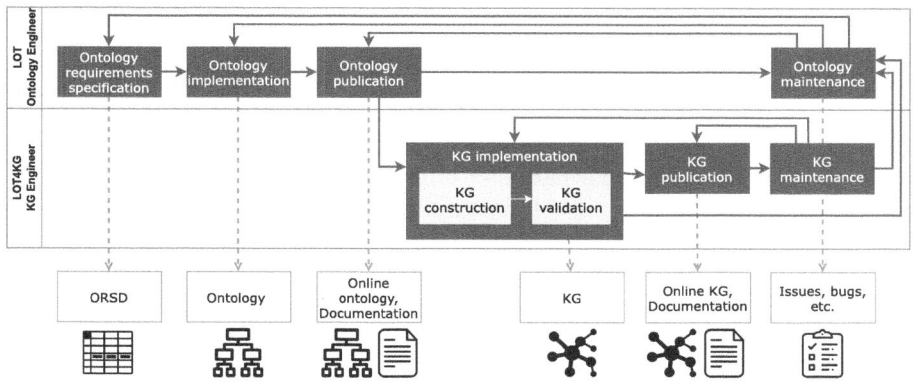

Fig. 1. High-level methodology overview with the LOT methodology [6] (top), and knowledge graph (KG) lifecycle (bottom).

the schema, or what we refer to as ontology, and does not consider the population with large amounts of data. Works such as those by Radulovic et al. [7], Chaves-Fraga et al. [1] and Simsek et al. [8] have abstracted the process to different levels and varying focus. Radulovic et al. [7] provide guidelines on what steps to take, and Chaves-Fraga et al. [1] describe the process they used when engineering a KG for research-performing organisations. Simsek et al. [8] abstract the process, which is where we take our inspiration for the proposed methodology.

Therefore, in this short work, we propose to extend LOT into a new methodology, which integrates the engineering of the schema as captured by LOT [6] and adds the engineering of KG into a joint methodology. Then, we discuss our proposal in the context of knowledge evolution and propose future research on integrating it into LOT4KG.

2 Proposed Methodology

The original LOT methodology [6] details the process of *ontology requirements specification*, *ontology implementation*, *ontology publication* and *ontology maintenance*, shown in the upper lane of Fig. 1. Our extensions, the KG lifecycle (bottom lane), is described in detail further below.

We identify three high-level activities: *KG implementation*, *KG publication*, and *KG maintenance*, mirroring the LOT ontology lifecycle. The KG lifecycle starts after the publication of the ontology, so there is an activity flow from *ontology publication* to *KG implementation*. Unlike the ontology engineering process, no requirement specification activity is required: the ontology imposes requirements on the KG. *KG implementation* is analogous to the ontology implementation activity and describes the steps taken to construct the KG. We also distinguish lower-level activities: KG construction and KG validation, similar to [8]. During KG construction, we generate relationships between heterogeneous data sources and ontology terms using mapping languages (e.g., RML or SPARQL-Anything). In a separate step, SHACL shapes are generated, which impose constraints on the shape of the KG and are thus used for KG validation. The output of the validation activity may generate a refined version of the KG. These two activities may be divided into more fine-grained activities such as the generation of mapping rules, the transformation of input sources into RDF and debugging. *KG publication* includes the publication of the KG and its corresponding documentation in human-readable format. The publication also includes not only documentation of the actual KG but also of the associated assets (e.g. documentation of RML mappings or SHACL) Lastly, *KG maintenance* is analogous to that of ontology maintenance. Issues and bugs are collected during a certain period of time, which, in turn, can trigger the implementation and publication of KG.

3   Context of Knowledge Evolution

In ontology and, consequently, in KG evolution, the need for change can come from different sources [11] other than from the process of fixing issues and bugs. These needs for change can be divided into two categories: (i) changes in business requirements, therefore, changes to ontology requirements, and (ii) changes to the underlying application domain, which needs to be represented by the ontology/KG [9]. Further discussion and deliberation are needed, as changes can also come from input sources, affecting the KG construction, depending on the changes and possibly the ontology. Such changes and update activities are not captured with LOT and its presented extension at this point, although the methodologies are circular. Once integrate, we propose to refer to it as LOT4KG. Additionally, KG maintenance faces more challenges in comparison to ontology maintenance because of the technologies involved in KG construction and their less mature tool support. With ontology editors, changing an ontology has been relatively easy for many years, but we do not edit a large KG which was created using RML but rather recreate it. Further, the SHACL validation also requires an update and depending on the changes this can become a costly endeavour.

Therefore, as a research community, we need to evaluate how KG maintenance is done today and how it compares with known ontology evolution frameworks [10,11]. The activities that need to be discussed are distinct from ontology and KG implementation activities to the extent that the engineers are updating the already existing artefact rather than creating a new one. Hence, at the ontology level, we should be able to produce a list of changes [3,11] according to which the KG can be updated. In a KG update, not all mapping rules and validation shapes need to be regenerated. Those that are affected by the ontology change need to be adjusted, either automatically or with some expert input, and then the KG does not need to be regenerated from scratch, potentially saving resources and, in turn, being more sustainable.

A further challenge that needs to be addressed is the distributed nature of the Semantic Web. Changes which need incorporating in the KG can come from the ontology or from the source data from which the KG is constructed. Both of these can be considered to be internal or external. Internal sources of change are easier to handle because of an existing direct communication channel. However, in real-world scenarios, the ontology or data used in a KG can be provided by different organisations with their own processes. With the separation between ontology engineering and KG construction, we enable organisations to adapt either one or both parts of the methodology. Further investigations are necessary in the future to identify pitfalls and challenges in such scenarios.

4   Conclusions and Future Work

In this short article, we give a high-level overview of the LOT4KG methodology. We present a first-of-its-kind theoretical methodology, which is based on previous work for dealing with the KG lifecycle as a whole. LOT4KG presents an extension to the LOT framework [6]: the inclusion of the KG lifecycle, describing the general steps that are followed when creating a KG from a given ontology or schema. In the future, we plan to make a lower-level definition of activities available, similar to what is already published for LOT. Furthermore, we discussed how ontology and KG evolution compare to the proposed methodology and how we plan to continue to extend it to make the lifecycle firmly encompass the maintenance of the artefacts as well, calling it LOT4KG in the future. This will lead to the definition of evolution activities on both levels, the ontology and KG. Implementations of the KG lifecycle are also of interest; however, these can be highly dependent on the available infrastructure. More interesting is the investigation into the evolution activities, as tool support is, to the best of our knowledge, still scarce.

This methodology is the first of its kind to combine the lifecycles of ontology and KG. The methodology can be beneficial in different real-world scenarios, especially when considering the sometimes vague separation between ontology/schema and KG. It would, therefore, enforce a clearer separation and would urge KG engineers to look at the ontology as an artifact by itself which requires its own evolution, separate from the KG. Further, with a clear separation between ontology KG, the methodology is also applicable in cases where the ontology and KG are not in the hands of the same person or team. The ontology can be engineered and maintained completely disconnected from the KG and vice versa. Once extended to include the evolution, LOT4KG will be helpful by providing tangible actions that need to be taken to keep the KG up to date when the ontology evolves. With the formalisation of such a methodology, we open up discussion on how ontologies and KGs are engineered today. The methodology also fosters further methodological research, as the Semantic Web community has to some extent mastered the engineering of ontologies and KGs but still needs to work on maintaining them over time.

Acknowledgments. María Poveda-Villalón is funded by the European Union's Horizon 2020 research and innovation programme under the grant agreement no. 101016854

(AURORAL). David Chaves-Fraga is funded by the Galician Ministry of Education, University and Professional Training and the European Regional Development Fund (ERDF/FEDER program) through grants ED431C2018/29 and ED431G2019/04. This work is partially supported by the project *Knowledge Spaces* (Grant PID2020-118274RB-I00 funded by MCIN/AEI/10.13039/50110 0011033) & partially funded by Spanish Statistical Office (INE).

References

1. Chaves-Fraga, D., Corcho, O., et al.: Systematic construction of knowledge graphs for research-performing organizations. Information **13**(12) (2022). https://doi.org/10.3390/info13120562
2. Fernández-López, M., Gómez-Pérez, A., Juristo, N.: METHONTOLOGY: From ontological art towards ontological engineering. In: Proceedings of the Ontological Engineering AAAI-97 Spring Symposium Series (1997)
3. Khattak, A.M., Latif, K., Lee, S.Y., Lee, Y.K., Rasheed, T.: Building an integrated framework for ontology evolution management. In: 12 th International Conference on International Business Information Management Association, Malaysia (2009)
4. Noy, N.F., McGuinness, D.L.: Ontology development 101: a guide to creating your first ontology (2001)
5. Polleres, A., Pernisch, R., et al.: How does knowledge evolve in open knowledge graphs? Trans. Graph Data Knowl. **1**(1), 11:1–11:59 (2023). https://doi.org/10.4230/TGDK.1.1.11
6. Poveda-Villalón, M., Fernández-Izquierdo, A., Fernández-López, M., García-Castro, R.: LOT: an industrial oriented ontology engineering framework. Eng. Appl. Artif. Intell. **111**, 104755 (2022). https://doi.org/10.1016/j.engappai.2022.104755
7. Radulovic, F., Poveda-Villalón, M., Vila-Suero, D., Rodríguez-Doncel, V., García-Castro, R., Gómez-Pérez, A.: Guidelines for linked data generation and publication: an example in building energy consumption. Autom. Constr. **57**, 178–187 (2015). https://doi.org/10.1016/j.autcon.2015.04.002
8. Simsek, U., et al.: Knowledge graph lifecycle: Building and maintaining knowledge graphs. In: Second International Workshop on Knowledge Graph Construction, vol. 2873. CEUR-ws.org (2021)
9. Stojanovic, L.: Methods and tools for ontology evolution. PhD Thesis, Karlsruhe Institute of Technology, Germany (2004)
10. Wardhana, H., Ashari, A., Kartika, A.: Review of ontology evolution process. Int. J. Comput. Appl. **179**(25), 26–33 (2018). https://doi.org/10.5120/ijca2018916537
11. Zablith, F., et al.: Ontology evolution: a process-centric survey. Knowl. Eng. Rev. **30**(1), 45–75 (2015). https://doi.org/10.1017/S0269888913000349

From Liberating to Questioning Tabular Data in Documents Using Knowledge Graphs

Kautuk Raj[1,2,3]([✉]) and Pierre Maret[1]

[1] Université de Lyon, CNRS UMR 5516 Laboratoire Hubert Curien,
Saint Étienne, France
{kautuk.raj,pierre.maret}@univ-st-etienne.fr
[2] York University, Toronto, Canada
[3] IIIT Bangalore, Bangalore, India

Abstract. Tables, a primary modality for organizing and presenting information for human comprehension, are ubiquitously found in documents. Their design poses significant challenges for systems, including large language models, when it comes to processing and understanding tabular data. We propose a novel method to free the tabular data encumbered inside documents (PDFs, HTML pages, Word documents, etc.) and perform question-answer (QA) on this data via natural language interaction. Our method stresses on its domain-agnostic and "open"-QA-oriented abilities, that exceed the performance of current LLMs in certain situations. We achieve this using a combination of table extraction tools, followed by the creation of a knowledge graph using the tabular data sources and employing QAnswer (https://www.qanswer.eu/), a QA system generator. A video demonstration showcases our tool's capabilities on United Nations (UN) disability documents and webpages.

Keywords: Question Answering · Knowledge Graph · Semantic Web

1 Introduction

Tables efficiently summarize information in a visually organized framework to facilitate comprehension and comparison across dimensions. They are commonly incorporated in scientific, business, and financial documents to present data.

Interpreting tabular information using standard language representations becomes challenging as table complexity increases [11]. PDF documents prioritize layout for human readers, which results in poor machine readability, requiring complex algorithms to recognize text, tables, and retrieve tabular structure [7].

Extensive research exists to extract and leverage valuable tabular data for natural language processing (NLP) tasks, including table QA which comprehends and reasons with tables to provide accurate answers to user questions.

© The Author(s), under exclusive license to Springer Nature Switzerland AG 2025
A. Meroño Peñuela et al. (Eds.): ESWC 2024, LNCS 15344, pp. 291–295, 2025.
https://doi.org/10.1007/978-3-031-78952-6_44

Our approach involves extracting tables contained in a document using several open-source table extraction tools to convert them to comma-separated values (CSV) format. This CSV is then transformed into a resource description format (RDF) file to create knowledge graphs corresponding to all tables in the document. We further enrich these knowledge graphs and leverage them as an additional, complementary data source to the original document text. The two data sources are integrated with QAnswer, a QA system generator, which is tuned to simultaneously query documents and knowledge graphs.

The main contributions of this work are:

- A domain-independent approach, unlike pre-trained transformers, enabling application to specialized and unobserved domain data.
- Capable of handling complex table layouts and hierarchies while preserving structure; not flattening tables thus retaining contextual information.
- Performs "open"-QA which retrieves relevant documents and extracts answers, essential for real-world user queries across extensive documents, unlike impractical "closed"-QA which unrealistically provides documents alongside questions.
- Advances over LLM-based methods by addressing challenges of inadequate table interpretation, token limits on large tables, hallucination and erroneous symbolic operations.

2   Related Work

Transformer-based methods such as [1,5] excel and set benchmarks on open-domain datasets like WikiTableQuestions[1] and Natural Questions[2]. Tables appearing in such datasets exhibit simpler structures, lacking row headers and having a single, non-hierarchical column header [9]. Experiments [6] show that even advanced pre-trained transformers struggle with domain-specific table layouts.

Works like [1,9] reduce tables to text, however, text-focused representations are sub-optimal for tables as they neglect special cell relationships [11].

Closest to our work, [8] utilizes knowledge graphs for table QA, but unlike ours, it demands table URIs for "closed"-QA and flattens tables to text strings post Wikipedia pre-training.

[2] evaluates LLMs on table QA datasets, noting their failures with "huge" tables due to token limits and doubts their ability to supplant symbolic methods. Evaluation of 14 LLMs in [10] reveals their imperfect factual knowledge grasp, particularly for non-popular entities.

3   Methodology

Table extraction is challenging since tables lack semantics, have varied layouts and span pages with repeating headers/footers requiring analysis of context and

---

[1] https://ppasupat.github.io/WikiTableQuestions/.
[2] https://ai.google.com/research/NaturalQuestions/.

format for accurate association. Real-life tables appear embedded in text, necessitating abilities to handle multi-content QA.

The first step in our methodology extracts tables from documents using both deterministic and non-deterministic methods via open-source tools like Tabula, Camelot, and pdfplumber. Discernible cell boundaries are parsed with OpenCV-based transformations while tables with whitespace separators are processed by detecting tabular areas, guessing column structure, and geometrically matching words to cells. Our method integrates the strengths of each tool, optimizing for context-specific performance. In the QA phase, it leverages the best-extracted output to formulate answers (Fig. 1).

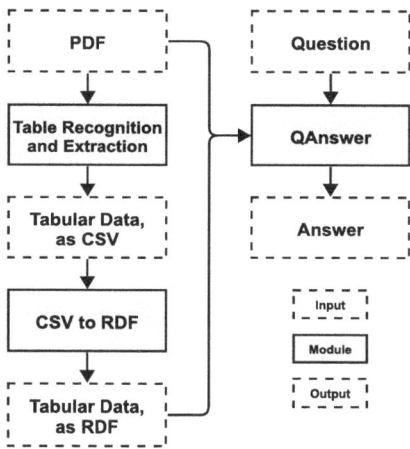

Fig. 1. Flow for the Proposed Methodology

The second step saves the tool outputs as a CSV file, enabling FAIR data principles compliance through openness and interoperability via a non-proprietary format.

The third step converts CSV data to RDF, the backbone for knowledge graphs, using the CSV on the Web (CSVW)[3] vocabulary which enables uniform semantic representation of tabular structures through RDF triples, streamlining alignment of diverse domain and format tables while avoiding elaborate ontology construction, rather maintaining a simplified set of mapping guidelines. The RDF format facilitates knowledge graph creation and increases data openness.

The final step enables combining QA systems over text (like PDFs) [4] and over knowledge graphs (RDF) [3] on the QAnswer platform. User queries are sent to both QA systems, which have been made combinable, so they execute the queries and compare results based on calculated confidence levels to determine the best answer to render to the user. Thus, we created one QA system with RDF

---

[3] https://www.w3.org/TR/tabular-data-primer/.

data extracted from tables and another QA system with the original document texts from which tables were extracted. These systems have been integrated into a combined QA system that leverages both structured and unstructured data sources to execute queries and get better results.

4 Demonstration

A demonstration is presented to exemplify the capabilities of our tool on a corpus comprising publicly accessible United Nations (UN) documents and webpages sourced from the disability domain. An end-to-end presentation of the method along with test runs and comparisons can be found in a video accessible at https://youtu.be/ve6xCwP1LHs.

5 Conclusions and Future Work

We present a pioneering approach to liberate tabular data within documents and perform QA via NLP interaction. We intend to evaluate the approach on a popular benchmark dataset to further assess its capabilities in comparison to existing methods, including large language models. Future plans include incorporating numerical and symbolic reasoning, multilingual table querying, and user interface (UI) enhancements for combined QA systems.

Acknowledgements. This research occurs in the context of the Disability Wiki project (https://www.christoelmorr.ca/ai-disability-advocacy.html), a collaboration between Laboratoire Hubert Curien, York University (Canada) and The QA Company (https://the-qa-company.com/) .

References

1. Alberti, C., Lee, K., Collins, M.: A BERT baseline for the natural questions (2019). http://arxiv.org/abs/1901.08634
2. Chen, W.: Large Language Models are few(1)-shot Table Reasoners. In: Findings of the Association for Computational Linguistics: EACL 2023 (2023). https://doi.org/10.18653/v1/2023.findings-eacl.83
3. Diefenbach, D., Giménez-García, J., Both, A., Singh, K., Maret, P.: QAnswer KG: designing a portable question answering system over RDF Data. In: European Semantic Web Conference 2020 (2020). http://dx.doi.org/10.1007/978-3-030-49461-2_25
4. Guo, K., Defretiere, C., Diefenbach, D., Gravier, C., Gourru, A.: QAnswer: towards question answering search over websites. In: Companion Proceedings of the Web Conference 2022. ACM. http://dx.doi.org/10.1145/3487553.3524250
5. Herzig, J., Nowak, P.K., Müller, T., Piccinno, F., Eisenschlos, J.: TaPas: weakly supervised table parsing via pre-training. In: Proceedings of the 58th Annual Meeting of the Association for Computational Linguistics (2020). https://doi.org/10.18653/v1/2020.acl-main.398

6. Katsis, Y., et al.: AIT-QA: question answering dataset over complex tables in the airline industry. In: Proceedings of the 2022 Conference of the North American Chapter of the Association for Computational Linguistics. AChttps://doi.org/10.18653/v1/2022.naacl-industry.34

7. Khusro, S., Latif, A., Ullah, I.: On methods and tools of table detection, extraction and annotation in PDF documents. J. Inf. Sci. (2014). https://doi.org/10.1177/0165551514551903

8. Knoblach, J., Acharya, N., Koranemkattil, B., Both, A., Collarana, D.: Combining knowledge graphs and language models to answer questions over tables. In: 18th International Conference on Semantic Systems (2022). https://ceur-ws.org/Vol-3235/paper15.pdf

9. Oğuz, B., et al.: UNIK-QA: unified representations of structured and unstructured knowledge for open-domain question answering. Findings of the association for computational linguistics: NAACL (2022). https://doi.org/10.18653/v1/2022.findings-naacl.115

10. Sun, K., Xu, Y.E., Zha, H., Liu, Y., Dong, X.L.: Head-to-tail: how Knowledgeable are large language models (LLM)? A.K.A. Will LLMs Replace Knowledge Graphs? (2023). https://arxiv.org/abs/2308.10168

11. Zayats, V., Toutanova, K., Ostendorf, M.: Representations for question answering from documents with tables and text. In: Proceedings of the 16th Conference of the European Chapter of the Association for Computational Linguistics (2021). https://doi.org/10.18653/v1/2021.eacl-main.253

Searching and Analyzing Coin Finds with a Linked Data Based Web Application

Heikki Rantala[1]([✉]) [ID], Eljas Oksanen[1,2] [ID], Frida Ehrnsten[2,3] [ID], and Eero Hyvönen[1,2] [ID]

[1] Semantic Computing Research Group (SeCo) Aalto University, Aalto, Finland
{heikki.rantala,eljas.oksanen,eero.hyvonen}@aalto.fi
[2] University of Helsinki, Helsinki, Finland
{eljas.oksanen,frida.ehrnsten,eero.hyvonen}@helsinki.fi
[3] The National Museum of Finland, Helsinki, Finland
https://seco.cs.aalto.fi

Abstract. This paper presents the CoinSampo demonstrator, a web application and data service created to open data on numismatic citizen finds reported in Finland between 2013 and 2023. The data has been converted to Linked Open Data (LOD) using light weight ontologies that were based on the data. The CoinSampo web application queries a knowledge graph with SPARQL, and offers users faceted search and various visualization options for data analysis. The application is aimed at researchers, heritage professionals, citizen scientists, amateur archaeologists, educators and the general public. We will also show how the underlying user interface framework can be applied to other similar data such as the finds data of the British Museum.

1 Introduction and Related Work

The amount of reported metal-detected objects in Finland has considerably increased in the recent years [7,13]. Coin finds are usually the most numerous of the object type reported by the public and can be identified more precisely than other common finds, producing higher quality data and making them specially suitable for describing semantically. Coin movement has also been historically international, and therefore creating Linked Open Data LOD resources that enable transnational comparison and data harmonization has wide relevance in numismatics and in digital Cultural Heritage (CH) more generally [5].

CoinSampo was created as part of the *DigiNUMA – Digital Solutions for European Numismatic Heritage* [5,6,10,11][1] research project, in response to the new needs in Finnish and international CH data management, research, and dissemination. The CoinSampo web application[2] and data service[3] were opened

---

[1] This paper has been partially extended in [10].

[2] https://coinsampo.ldf.fi.

[3] https://www.ldf.fi/dataset/coinsampo.

A. Meroño Peñuela et al. (Eds.): ESWC 2024, LNCS 15344, pp. 296–300, 2025.
https://doi.org/10.1007/978-3-031-78952-6_45

to public on February 28th, 2024. The underlying data was collected in the National Museum of Finland between 2013 and 2023 based on the reports made by the objects' finders, mostly recreational metal-detectorists, and includes data of some 18000 objects.

CoinSampo builds upon the Sampo model[4] [2] and the FindSampo framework [3] and web service [9]. FindSampo opens data about archaeological citizen finds of all types that have been catalogued and redeemed in to the national collections of the Finnish Heritage Agency (FHA). However, only prehistoric and medieval finds are consistently redeemed and recorded by the FHA. In contrast CoinSampo opens data about all reported numismatic finds, including thousands of Early Modern coins.

Our work was influenced by Nomisma.org[5] [1], a collaborative international project that aims to provide necessary ontologies for representing numismatic concepts as Linked Data. CoinSampo is also inspired by the ARIADNEplus[6] [12] project. ARIADNEplus is a pan-European research infrastructure and aggregation project of archaeological data including coin finds.

In addition to the demonstrator for Finnish data, we are also developing a more generic version of the CoinSampo web application, one that could be used to search and visualize any data that uses the Nomisma.org ontology. We have also applied the user interface framework to analyzing the citizen finds data of the Portable Antiquities Scheme (PAS)[7] of the British Museum, which includes around 500 000[8] coin finds.

2   CoinSampo Web Application

The CoinSampo KG was created using existing tabular CSV data collected by the National Museum of Finland. The data was converted to RDF format using light weight ontologies created from the data. The ontologies are linked to external resources, mainly to Wikidata[9], where possible. The conversion process was done largely by reusing as much as possible the existing Python script for converting FindSampo data. However, there was only limited opportunity to reuse FindSampo ontologies because the main ontological work there concerned object types, which wasn't relevant in data consisting completely of coins. The data[10] is served openly from a SPAQRL endpoint and data service hosted by the Linked Data Finland platform.

The CoinSampo web application[11] is based on the Sampo-UIframework [4,8]. The application works by querying the data using SPARQL queries created based

---

[4] Cf. Sampo series of systems: https://seco.cs.aalto.fi/applications/sampo/.
[5] http://Nomisma.org.
[6] https://ariadne-infrastructure.eu.
[7] https://finds.org.uk/.
[8] Data export obtained in early 2023.
[9] https://www.wikidata.org/.
[10] https://www.ldf.fi/dataset/coinsampo.
[11] See source code at https://github.com/SemanticComputing/coinsampo-web-app.

on selections made by the user and then presenting the data to the user using various JavaScript libraries. The user can refine the search using various facets, view and browse coin finds individually or as a table, or analyze the data by selecting one of the available visualization tabs. For example in Fig. 1 a user has limited the search to coins from the Viking Age (here defined as AD 800–1150) that were found in the municipality of Nousiainen. The visualization shows arcs on a map[12] starting from the minting place of the coin and ending at the findsite municipality. It is easy to see that coins found in Finland were minted in many places around Europe, and also arrived from further afield such as from modern Uzbekistan. The mint concepts have been mapped to Wikidata and their coordinates have been extracted from there. Similarly, find municipalities are mapped to the place ontology YSO (General Finnish Ontology) Places. The CoinSampo web application also offers perspectives for searching and visualizing authorities (such as rulers) and mints.

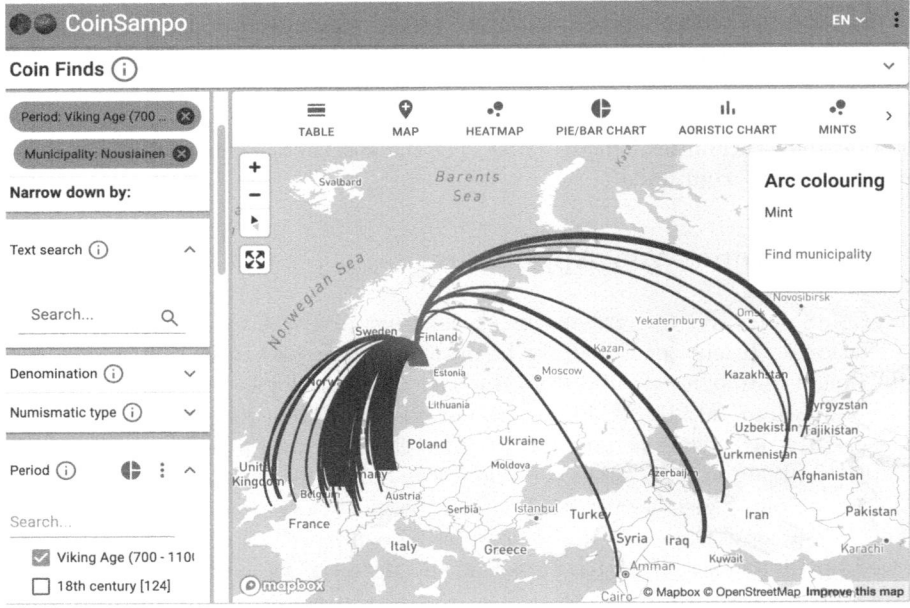

Fig. 1. An example of a visualization created with CoinSampo application showing the identified mint sites of Viking Age coins found in municipality of Nousiainen.

We have also applied the user interface framework to PAS finds data from England. The data was first converted to simple RDF using a CSV export from PAS data, and then a simple portal was created for it. We call this new application PASampo. As of 2024, it is still a work in progress and unavailable online,

---

[12] The map is rendered using Mapbox (https://www.mapbox.com/about/maps/) service which is based on OpenStreetMap (http://www.openstreetmap.org/copyright.

but it can already be used to analyze the PAS data and to make comparisons with the Finnish data. For example, in Fig. 2 a statistical Sampo tool has been used to create pie charts comparing the relative proportions of various materials of manufacture among PAS and Finnish coin finds. At over 80% (Finland) and 60% (PAS) copper is clearly the most common material in both cases, but there are significant differences among other materials (e.g., silver and gold), indicating very different numismatic histories between these two regions.

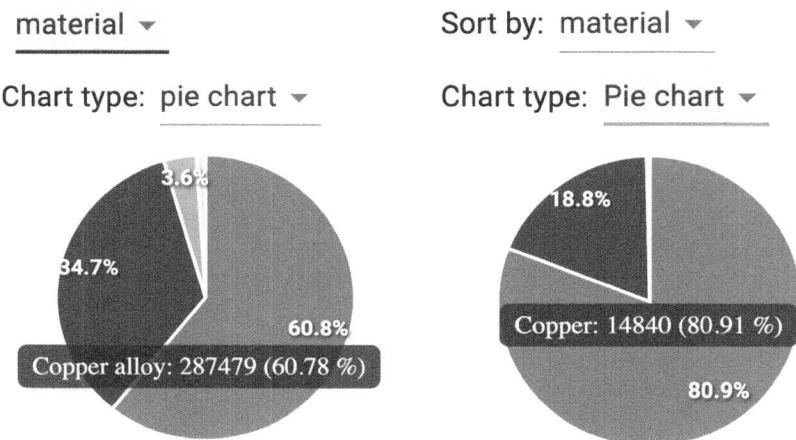

Fig. 2. Comparing relative numbers of different materials in coin finds from England (chart on the left) and Finland (on the right) with pie charts generated using Sampo portals.

3 Conclusion

The CoinSampo demonstrator is an example of how practical applications can be build on top of SPARQL endpoints, and how ontologies mapped to external resources can be used to enrich the data and make it easier to search and analyze. The web application framework is easy to modify so that it can be applied to other similar data as show by the PAS example. However, some of the visualizations would require specific semantic information such as coordinates for mints. Comparing different sets of data meaningfully in more complex cases would also require harmonizing the data which may require significant effort.

Acknowledgements. Our work has been funded by the Jenny and Antti Wihuri Foundation and the European Union's Horizon 2020 research and innovation programme under the Marie Sklodowska-Curie grant agreement No 896044. CSC – IT Center for Science has provided computational resources.

References

1. Gruber, E., Meadows. A.: Numismatics and linked open data. ISAW Papers **20.6** (2021). http://hdl.handle.net/2333.1/q83bkdqf
2. Hyvönen, E.: Digital humanities on the semantic web: Sampo model and portal series. Semantic Web - Interoperability, Usability, Applicability **14**(4), 729–744 (2022). https://doi.org/10.3233/SW-190386
3. Hyvönen, E., et al.: Citizen science archaeological finds on the semantic web: the FindSampo framework. Antiquity Rev. World Archaeol. **95**(382), e24 (2021). https://doi.org/10.15184/aqy.2021.87
4. Ikkala, E., Hyvönen, E., Rantala, H., Koho, M.: Sampo-UI: a full stack JavaScript framework for developing semantic portal user interfaces. Semantic Web - Interoperability, Usability, Applicability **13**(1), 69–84 (2022). https://doi.org/10.3233/SW-210428
5. Oksanen, E., Ehrnsten, F.. Rantala, H., Hyvönen, E.: Semantic solutions for democratising archaeological and numismatic data analysis. ACM J. Comput. Cult. Heritage **16**(4) (2024). https://doi.org/10.1145/3625302
6. Oksanen, E., et al.: Digital humanities solutions for pan-european numismatic and archaeological heritage based on linked open data. In: DHNB 2022 The 6th Digital Humanities in Nordic and Baltic Countries Conference, pp. 352–360. CEUR Worksahop Proceedings, vol. 3232 (2022). https://ceur-ws.org/Vol-3232/paper34.pdf
7. Oksanen, E., Wessman, A.: New horizons in understanding finnish iron age material culture through metal-detected finds. Internet Archaeology (forthcoming). https://www.helsinki.fi/en/disciplines/archaeology/research/deepfin
8. Rantala, H., Ahola, A., Ikkala, E., Hyvönen, E.: How to create easily a data analytic semantic portal on top of a SPARQL endpoint: introducing the configurable Sampo-UI framework. In: VOILA! 2023 Visualization and Interaction for Ontologies, Linked Data and Knowledge Graphs 2023. CEUR Workshop Proceedings, vol. 3508 (2023). https://ceur-ws.org/Vol-3508/paper3.pdf
9. Rantala, H., et al.: FindSampo: A linked data based portal and data service for analyzing and disseminating archaeological object finds. In: The Semantic Web: ESWC 2022. LNCS, vol. 13261, pp. 478–494. Springer (2022). https://doi.org/10.1007/978-3-031-06981-9_28
10. Rantala, H., Oksanen, E., Ehrnsten, F., Hyvönen, E.: Publishing numismatic public finds on the semantic web for digital humanities research – coinsampo linked open data service and semantic portal. In: First International Workshop of Semantic Digital Humanities (2024). accepted
11. Rantala, H., Oksanen. E., Hyvönen, E.: Harmonizing and using numismatic linked data in digital humanities research and application development: case diginuma. In: The Semantic Web: ESWC 2022 Satellite Events. Lecture Notes in Computer Science, vol. 13384, pp. 26–30. Springer (2022). https://doi.org/10.1007/978-3-031-11609-4_5
12. Richards, J., Niccolucci, F. (eds.): The Ariadne Impact. Archaeolingua, Budapest (2019). https://doi.org/10.5281/zenodo.3476712
13. Wessman, A., Thomas, S., Rohiola, V.: Digital archaeology and citizen science: introducing the goals of FindSampo and the SuALT project. SKAS **1**, 2–17 (2019)

PySPARQL Anything Showcase

Marco Ratta[1]([✉])[iD], Enrico Daga[1]([✉])[iD], and Luigi Asprino[2][iD]

[1] The Open University, Walton Hall, Milton Keynes, UK
{marco.ratta,enrico.daga}@open.ac.uk
[2] University of Bologna, Bologna, Italy
luigi.asprino@unibo.it

Abstract. In this demo paper we present *PySPARQL Anything*, the Python library of *SPARQL Anything*, an open source project for supporting semantic web technologists in building RDF graphs from heterogeneous sources. *PySPARQL Anything* enables developers to inject RDF graphs into their Python *RDFlib*, *NetworkX* or *pandas*-powered data science processes, opening new opportunities for developing complex, data-intensive pipelines for generating and manipulating RDF data. In addition, the library exposes a Python-based Command Line Interface (CLI) allowing easier installation and use.

Keywords: Knowledge Graph Construction · Façade-X · SPARQL Anything · Python

1 Introduction

Knowledge Graphs are nowadays first-class citizens in data science as they allow the seamless integration of diverse data [6]. Therefore, there has been increasing effort in supporting Python developers to work with RDF Knowledge Graphs [3,4]. In this demo, we aim to present and disseminate to the Semantic Web community *PySPARQL Anything*[1], the Python library of *SPARQL Anything*[2], an open source project that supports semantic web technologists in building RDF graphs from heterogeneous sources. *SPARQL Anything* is a data integration system that implements the *Façade-X* meta-model [2], resolving the heterogeneity of sources by structurally mapping them onto a set of RDF components upon which semantic mappings can be constructed. A technical report illustrating the overall architecture and functionalities of *SPARQL Anything* can be found in [1].

The research leading to this publication has received funding from the European Union's Horizon 2020 research and innovation programme under grant agreement "Polifonia: a digital harmoniser of musical cultural heritage" (Grant Agreement N. 101004746), https://polifonia-project.eu. The publication reflects the author's views. The Research Executive Agency (REA) is not liable for any use that may be made of the information contained therein.

[1] https://github.com/SPARQL-Anything/PySPARQL-Anything.
[2] https://github.com/SPARQL-Anything/sparql.anything.

Using the JSON data hosted at https://sparql-anything.cc/example1.json for example, one can select the TV series starring "Courteney Cox" with the SPARQL query:

```
PREFIX xyz: <http://sparql.xyz/facade-x/data/>
PREFIX rdf: <http://www.w3.org/1999/02/22-rdf-syntax-ns#>
PREFIX fx: <http://sparql.xyz/facade-x/ns/>
SELECT ?seriesName
WHERE {
    SERVICE <x-sparql-anything:https://sparql-anything.cc
        /example1.json> {
        ?tvSeries xyz:name ?seriesName .
        ?tvSeries xyz:stars ?star .
        ?star fx:anySlct "Courteney Cox" .
    }
}
```

to directly obtain the results:

```
seriesName
"Cougar Town"
"Friends
```

The accumulated experience and feedback from the community of *SPARQL Anything* users, has lead to the decision of developing a Python integration. This is because of the emergent need to support the increasing community of Python users of Semantic Web technologies and the wide spread adoption of Python based tools for downstream tasks. *PySPARQL Anything* enables developers to inject RDF graphs into their Python *RDFlib*[3], *NetworkX*[4] or *pandas*[5]-powered data science processes, opening new opportunities for developing complex, data-intensive pipelines for generating and manipulating RDF data. Additionally the library exposes a Python-based Command Line Interface (CLI) allowing for easier installation and use. We demonstrate the usage of *PySPARQL Anything* via a "pythonic" re-interpretation of the *showcase-musicxml*[6] showcase, available at the *SPARQL Anything Github* repository for comparison.

2   PySPARQL Anything

PySPARQL Anything has been designed by borrowing some concepts of the Command behavioural pattern. The `pysparql_anything.SparqlAnything` class, with its `run`, `ask`, `select` and `construct` methods, defines the frontend interface of the system. The user specifies the parameters of their *SPARQL*

---

[3] https://github.com/RDFLib/rdflib.

[4] https://github.com/networkx/networkx.

[5] https://github.com/pandas-dev/pandas.

[6] https://github.com/SPARQL-Anything/showcase-musicxml.

request as Python keyword arguments. "Under the hood", these are automatically encapsulated by the language as a `dict` object that is passed, together with a receiver instance, to a specific execution method.

This receiver is a `pysparql_anything.SparqlAnythingReflection` object, which is a Python "reflection" of the `SPARQLAnything` class, the entry point of *SPARQL Anything*. This has been implemented using the *PyJNIus*[7] library.

The output of the user's request is either printed to the terminal, saved to a file (when using the `run` method), or returned as a Python object. Specifically, the tool supports returning the results of `SELECT` queries as `dict` or `pandas.DataFrame` objects and the results of `CONSTRUCT` queries as `rdflib.Graph` or `networkx.MultiDiGraph` objects. These can be achieved via the `select` and `construct` methods respectively. The results of `ASK` queries are returned as Python booleans when calling the `ask` method.

PySPARQL Anything also offers a CLI which processes the optional query arguments and passes them directly to the receiver object. This is accessed via the terminal using the `sparql-anything` command.

PySPARQL Anything is distributed on the *Python Package Index* (PyPI)[8] and is installed by typing the following in your machine's terminal.

```
$ pip install pysparql-anything
```

The code is also available at the corresponding *Github* repository[9].

3 Demo

In the demo, we will first illustrate the interface of *PySPARQL Anything* and then look at how *SPARQL* queries may be integrated into Python code.

As an example, the query showed in the introduction section above can be executed via either the command line interface as

```
!sparql-anything --query queries/select/testSelect.sparql
```

where one would obtain the same output as before, printed on the terminal,

```
seriesName
Friends
Cougar Town
```

or within a Python script or shell as

```
engine.select(
    query="queries/select/testSelect.sparql", output_type=pd.DataFrame
)
```

where one could (optionally) have the result returned as the `pandas.DataFrame` object:

---

[7] https://github.com/kivy/pyjnius.
[8] https://pypi.org/project/pysparql-anything/.
[9] https://github.com/SPARQL-Anything/PySPARQL-Anything.

```
<class 'pandas.core.frame.DataFrame'>

     seriesName
0        Friends
1   Cougar Town
```

Furthermore, we will present an end-to-end scenario, based on a case study in computational musicology [5]. A music score in MusicXML is processed with *PySPARQL Anything* to generate a Knowledge Graph. Such graph is then analysed with Python libraries to derive interesting metrics such as statistics on note trigrams and derive a probability mass function of the data.

The demo can be accessed and executed via a live Google Colab notebook at the following address: https://bit.ly/pysa-demo

Step 1. In the first step, we setup the library and load the MusicXML files:

```
import pysparql_anything as sa
# Construct the SparqlAnything object
engine = sa.SparqlAnything()
# Assign the root directory of the files to a variable
root_dir = "showcase-musicxml/musicXMLFiles/AltDeu10/"
# Create a list of the names and paths to the xml files
xmls= [(name, os.path.join(root_dir, name)) for name in os.listdir(root_dir)]
```

Step 2. Next, we proceed with extracting melodic information, specifically, we show how one can use *PySPARQL Anything* to integrate SPARQL queries into a downstream task:

```
melody_dfs = [engine.select(
        query="showcase-musicxml/queries/getMelodyParam.sparql",
        values={"filePath": xml[1]},
        output_type=pd.DataFrame
    ) for xml in xmls]
```

Step 3. In the following code, we build trigrams from the data and count them:

```
# helper function to build and count the trigrams from a melody DataFrame
def count_trigrams(notes: list, trigrams_dict=dict()) -> dict[str, int]:
  for i in range(len(notes) - 2):
    trigram = notes[i] + "-" + notes[i + 1] + "-" + notes[i + 2]
    if trigram in trigrams_dict:
      trigrams_dict[trigram] += 1
    else:
      trigrams_dict[trigram] = 1
  return trigrams_dict
# Construct the trigrams and count their frequencies.
# Store the results in a dictionary
trigrams = dict()
for melody_df in melody_dfs:
  notes = list(melody_df["pitch"])
  count_trigrams(notes, trigrams)
```

Step 4. Finally, we produce the probability mass function of the data:

```
# Calculate the total number of trigrams in the dataset
total = sum(list(trigrams.values()))
# Construct the probability mass function of the trigrams in the dataset
pmf = {k: v / total for k, v in trigrams.items()}
# (Optional) Convert the pmf to a pd.DataFrame
```

```
pmf_df = pd.DataFrame(
    data=[[k, v] for k, v in pmf.items()],
    columns=["trigram", "P(trigram)"]
)
```

As a result we obtain

```
index , trigram ,P( trigram )
0 ,A4–C5–D5 ,0.0011237357972281184
1 ,C5–D5–E5 ,0.0032463478586590086
2 ,D5–E5–E5 ,0.0011237357972281184
3 ,E5–E5–A4 ,6.242976651267325 e −05
...
```

which can be compared to the result file *trigramAnalysis.csv* of the showcase.

4   Conclusion

In this demo paper we have proceeded to introduce *PySPARQL Anything* to the Semantic Web community. This is the Python library of the *SPARQL Anything* open source project that supports semantic web technologists in building RDF graphs from heterogeneous sources. We have also provided a description of the basic architecture underlying the backend of the system and have provided examples of how a *SPARQL* query can be executed with *PySPARQL Anything*. Further, a scenario from computational musicology illustrating how *SPARQL* queries can be integrated into a Python workflow has also been described.

The full live demo is available at https://bit.ly/pysa-demo.

References

1. Asprino, L., Daga, E., Dowdy, J., Mulholland, P., Gangemi, A., Ratta, M.: Streamlining knowledge graph construction with a fa\c {c} ade: the sparql anything project. arXiv preprint arXiv:2310.16700 (2023)
2. Asprino, L., Daga, E., Gangemi, A., Mulholland, P.: Knowledge graph construction with a façade: a unified method to access heterogeneous data sources on the web. ACM Trans. Internet Technol. **23**(1), 1–31 (2023)
3. Dasoulas, I., Chaves-Fraga, D., Garijo, D., Dimou, A.: Declarative RDF construction from in-memory data structures with RML (2023)
4. Liang, L., Li, Y., Wen, M., Liu, Y.: KG4Py: a toolkit for generating python knowledge graph and code semantic search. Connect. Sci. **34**(1), 1384–1400 (2022)
5. Ratta, M., Daga, E.: Knowledge graph construction from MusicXML: an empirical investigation with SPARQL anything (2022)
6. Wilcke, X., Bloem, P., De Boer, V.: The knowledge graph as the default data model for learning on heterogeneous knowledge. Data Sci. **1**(1–2), 39–57 (2017)

Integrating Action Robot Ontology for Enhanced Human-Robot Interaction: A NAO Robot Case Study

Diego Reforgiato Recupero(✉)⬤ and Lorenzo Boi

Department of Mathematics and Computer Science, University of Cagliari, Via Ospedale 72, 09124 Cagliari, Italy
diego.reforgiato@unica.it

Abstract. This paper presents an approach that allows the NAO humanoid robot to respond to a question from a user and gesticulate depending on the text that it is saying. The question might also be an action command spoken by the user that the robot recognizes and executes. A Large Language Model is integrated within the approach to provide the question-answering capabilities. For the action commands, we have used an action robot ontology that we have defined in past work. We have extracted the pertinent classes and individuals and generated a three-word string for each action that is matched semantically with the user's text. Moreover, as far as the action commands are concerned, the system can work in two modes: STATELESS and STATEFUL. When in STATEFUL mode, the robot knows its current posture and performs the command only if it is compatible with its current state.

Keywords: Action Robot Ontology · Human-Robot Interaction · Natural Language Processing · Large Language Models

In the realm of robotics and Artificial Intelligence (AI), recent advancements have given rise to a multitude of robot-centric applications. There is a growing conviction that there is a 50% probability of AI surpassing human capabilities across all tasks within 45 years, eventually leading to the automation of all human jobs in 120 years, as noted by authors in [6]. Social robots are rapidly gaining prominence and are now being deployed in various countries, serving diverse purposes. The overarching objective of social robots is to enhance interaction with humans, aiming for more effective and efficient engagements.

On the one hand, Large language models (LLMs) have emerged as transformative tools within the realm of robotics applications, playing a pivotal role in augmenting the capabilities of robotic systems [12]. The integration of LLMs, such as OpenAI's GPT-4, into robotics research and development has opened new avenues for enhanced human-robot interaction, cognitive processing, and autonomous decision-making. One notable application of LLMs in robotics involves natural language understanding, enabling robots to interpret

A. Meroño Peñuela et al. (Eds.): ESWC 2024, LNCS 15344, pp. 306–310, 2025.
https://doi.org/10.1007/978-3-031-78952-6_47

and respond to human commands with unprecedented accuracy [10,11]. This linguistic proficiency facilitates more intuitive and user-friendly interfaces, allowing users to communicate with robots using everyday language. This not only simplifies the user experience but also broadens the accessibility of robotic technologies to individuals with varying levels of technical expertise.

On the other hand, the advent of humanoid robots, exemplified by models like NAO, has sparked a rapid proliferation across various domains. Robots are increasingly being leveraged for a multitude of tasks, catalyzing a surge in interdisciplinary research aimed at exploring their integration into diverse applications [1–5,7,8]. From the controlled environments of research laboratories to the dynamic landscapes of real-world scenarios, humanoid robots are making their presence felt. Their adaptability and versatility make them invaluable assets in fields as varied as healthcare, education, entertainment, and beyond. Researchers and practitioners alike are actively exploring the potential of these robots to augment human capabilities and improve efficiency across a wide spectrum of tasks.

In this paper, we propose an innovative approach that leverages the question-answering capabilities of LLMs to facilitate dynamic conversations between users and a NAO humanoid robot. The user's response is intelligently parsed into sub-sentences, which are then articulated by the robot. If a given sub-sentence implies an action corresponding to the robot's ontology, the robot seamlessly executes the action. Otherwise, the robot engages in the standard *Animated Say* animation. Additionally, users have the option to issue action commands directly. In such cases, by leveraging the semantic similarity between the sentence embeddings and three-word strings created from the action robot ontology introduced in [9], the robot determines the appropriate action to perform. This results in a fluid and natural interaction between the user and the robot. The scripts developed for the Action Recognition Engine and the Choregraphe script are freely available in a public repository[1]. Additionally, a video showcasing an example of the interaction can be accessed publicly[2].

1   How it Works

The architecture of the approach proposed in this paper is illustrated in Fig. 1. The NAO robot is situated within the same local area network as a server hosting an Action Recognition engine that we have developed and that queries the elements from the action robot ontology. Efficient communication between the NAO and the server is facilitated through a router. The NAO executes a Choregraphe[3] program that we have designed to perform the following actions. The robot initiates interaction by asking the user to speak. Subsequently, it waits for

---

[1] https://github.com/loriboi/zoraProject.

[2] https://www.youtube.com/watch?v=hEC9EHhjVe4&feature=youtu.be. We have edited the video to remove the instances when the robot was waiting for responses from the network. We can provide a link to the unedited video, which contains all the original footage.

[3] https://www.robotlab.com/choregraphe-download-resources.

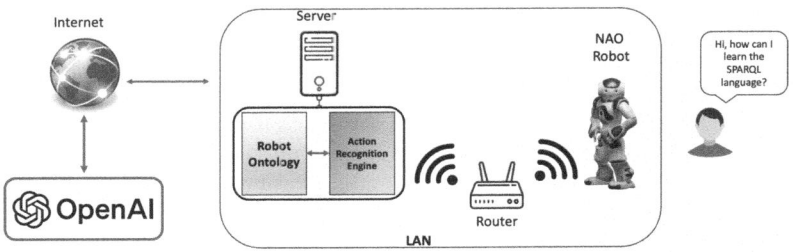

Fig. 1. Architecture of the proposed approach.

the user to articulate a response. Once the user speaks, the robot records everything he/she says. The recorded audio is then transmitted to OpenAI Speech-to-text capability[4] for speech-to-text conversion. OpenAI Speech-to-text promptly returns the corresponding text to the robot based on the recorded audio. Following this, the robot sends the obtained text to the Action Recognition engine on the server. The robot then waits for the output from the Action Recognition engine. If the output from the engine is identified as a command action, then the robot proceeds to execute it. However, if the text is not recognized as an action command, the robot forwards it to OpenAI ChatGPT to generate an appropriate response through its question-answering capabilities. The robot retrieves the response from OpenAI ChatGPT and promptly forwards it back to the Action Recognition engine for further processing. Subsequently, the robot receives a dictionary from the Action Recognition engine. Each entry in the dictionary contains a pair: each sub-sentence extracted from the response generated by ChatGPT and the associated action to be performed.

The Action Recognition engine, operating on the server, undertakes the following tasks. Initially, it awaits a text sent from the robot. Upon receipt, it computes the semantic similarity between the received text and all possible actions defined in the action command ontology we have defined[5]. Specifically, the **text representing each action** is transformed into embeddings using the *bert-base-nli-mean-tokens* Sentence Transformer[6]. Subsequently, the semantic similarities between the text and all actions are sorted in decreasing order. If the first element in the list is higher than an empirically determined fixed threshold of 0.8, the engine communicates the identified action (corresponding to the first element in the list) back to the robot for execution. However, if no match is found with any action of the ontology, the engine returns a specific code, signaling the absence of a match, and awaits further text from the robot. Following this, the Action Recognition engine retrieves the text from the robot, which will return a response to the user's input obtained from ChatGPT, and divides the response into sub-sentences. Constructing a dictionary, each entry corresponds to a sub-

---

[4] https://platform.openai.com/docs/guides/speech-to-text.

[5] https://github.com/Fspiga13/Humanoid-Robot-Obeys-Human-Action-Commands-through-a-Robot-Action-Ontology.

[6] https://huggingface.co/sentence-transformers/bert-base-nli-mean-tokens.

sentence and is associated with the closest action based on semantic similarity. If, for a certain entry, the semantic similarity falls below the threshold, the action linked to the underlying sub-sentence will be the *Animated Say* of NAO. This process highlights the engine's intricate semantic analysis, action determination, and response generation capabilities within the proposed framework.

To define the **text representing each action** previously mentioned, we analyzed the action command ontology referenced earlier. Initially, we identified the `BodyPartWord` individuals along with their corresponding `keywords` and `synonyms`. For instance, `arm` is a `BodyPartWord` individual with `keywords` and `synonyms` such as *arm, appendage, bicep, forearm, fore-limb*. Next, we retrieved all classes that are subclasses of `BaseAction` and `SimpleAction`, including `ArmAction`, `HandAction`, `HeadAction`, `LegAction`, `Walk` and `Posture`. Subsequently, we extracted individuals from these classes, such as `LegDown`, `LegUp`, `HeadDown`, `HeadForward`, `HeadLeft`, `HeadRight`, `HeadUp`, `ArmDown`, `ArmForward`, `ArmSide`, `ArmUp`, `Crouch`, `LyingBack`, `LyingBelly`, `WalkBackward`, etc. Let this set be denoted as S. To collect the objects of the action and formulate a string representation, for each $s \in S$, we extracted elements $w \in W$ and $b \in B$ such that $\{s,$ `involves`, $t\}$ and $\{t,$ `uses`, $w\}$ and $\{t,$ `bodySide`, $b\}$ and $\{w,$ `is_a`, `BodyPartWord`$\}$. Also, to gather other elements of the action, for each $s \in S$, we collected all $a \in A$ such that $\{s,$ `uses`, $a\}$ and $\{a,$ `is_a`, `ActionWord`$\}$. Finally, we obtained the `keyword` and `synonym` values of each element from W, B and A. This process allowed us to formulate all possible combinations for each potential action recognized by the ontology, using the body parts W, the side of the body B, and the remaining action words A.

For instance, considering the `ArmDown` instance, we would derive the sets $W = \{arm, bicep, forearm, hand, claw, paw, etc.\}$, $B = \{left, right\}$, and $A = \{down, drop, lower, etc.\}$ Each combination of values extracted from these three sets would generate a three-word string corresponding to the `ArmDown` instance. The combination with the highest similarity to the user's text is then retrieved: it represents the robot's action corresponding to the user's input.

Additionally, concerning the action commands, the system operates in two modes: STATELESS and STATEFUL. In STATELESS mode, the robot executes each human expression correctly interpreted as an action command, and then reverts to its default posture. In STATEFUL mode, the robot is aware of its current posture and executes a command only if it is compatible with its existing state. In this mode, the robot does not return to its default posture. A sequence of action commands can be given to the robot. For instance, in STATEFUL mode, the user might instruct the robot to stand on its left leg, then ask a question that the robot responds to using ChatGPT and then give one more action to walk. However, the last action will not be performed due to its incompatibility with the current state (left leg raised). The list of incompatibilities has been taken from the defined robot action ontology.

References

1. Alonso, R., Bonini, A., Recupero, D.R., Spano, L.D.: Exploiting virtual reality and the robot operating system to remote-control a humanoid robot. Multim. Tools Appl. **81**(11), 15565–15592 (2022)

2. Alonso, R., Concas, E., Recupero, D.R.: A flexible and scalable social robot architecture employing voice assistant technologies. In: Carolis, B.N.D., Gena, C., Lieto, A., Rossi, S., Sciutti, A. (eds.) Proceedings of the Workshop on Adapted intEraction with SociAl Robots, cAESAR 2020, Cagliari, Italy, 17 March 2020. CEUR Workshop Proceedings, vol. 2724, pp. 36–40. CEUR-WS.org (2020). https://ceur-ws.org/Vol-2724/paper10.pdf

3. Atzeni, M., Recupero, D.R.: Multi-domain sentiment analysis with mimicked and polarized word embeddings for human-robot interaction. Future Gener. Comput. Syst. **110**, 984–999 (2020). https://doi.org/10.1016/J.FUTURE.2019.10.012, https://doi.org/10.1016/j.future.2019.10.012

4. Cauli, N., Recupero, D.R.: Video action recognition and prediction architecture for a robotic coach (short paper). In: Consoli, S., Recupero, D.R., Riboni, D. (eds.) Proceedings of the First Workshop on Smart Personal Health Interfaces co-located with 25th International Conference on Intelligent User Interfaces, SmartPhil@IUI 2020, Cagliari, Italy, 17 March 2020. CEUR Workshop Proceedings, vol. 2596, pp. 69–77. CEUR-WS.org (2020). https://ceur-ws.org/Vol-2596/paper6.pdf

5. Gerina, F., Massa, S.M., Moi, F., Recupero, D.R., Riboni, D.: Recognition of cooking activities through air quality sensor data for supporting food journaling. Hum. centric Comput. Inf. Sci. **10**, 27 (2020)

6. Grace, K., Salvatier, J., Dafoe, A., Zhang, B., Evans, O.: Viewpoint: when will AI exceed human performance? evidence from AI experts. J. Artif. Intell. Res. **62**, 729–754 (2018)

7. Recupero, D.R.: Technology enhanced learning using humanoid robots. Future Internet **13**(2), 32 (2021)

8. Recupero, D.R., Dessì, D., Concas, E.: A flexible and scalable architecture for human-robot interaction. In: Chatzigiannakis, I., de Ruyter, B.E.R., Mavrommati, I. (eds.) Ambient Intelligence - 15th European Conference, AmI 2019, Rome, Italy, 13-15 November 2019, Proceedings. LNCS, vol. 11912, pp. 311–317. Springer (2019). https://doi.org/10.1007/978-3-030-34255-5_21, https://doi.org/10.1007/978-3-030-34255-5_21

9. Recupero, D.R., Spiga, F.: Knowledge acquisition from parsing natural language expressions for humanoid robot action commands. Inf. Process. Manag. **57**(6), 102094 (2020). https://doi.org/10.1016/J.IPM.2019.102094

10. Yoshikawa, N., et al.: Large language models for chemistry robotics. Auton. Robot. **47**(8), 1057–1086 (2023). https://doi.org/10.1007/s10514-023-10136-2

11. Zeng, A., Ichter, B., Xia, F., Xiao, T., Sindhwani, V.: Demonstrating large language models on robots. In: Bekris, K.E., Hauser, K., Herbert, S.L., Yu, J. (eds.) Robotics: Science and Systems XIX, Daegu, Republic of Korea, 10-14 July 2023 (2023). https://doi.org/10.15607/RSS.2023.XIX.024

12. Zhang, C., Chen, J., Li, J., Peng, Y., Mao, Z.: Large language models for human-robot interaction: a review. Biomimetic Intell. Robot. **3**(4), 100131 (2023). https://doi.org/10.1016/j.birob.2023.100131

Semantic Tool Hub: Towards a Sustainable Community-Driven Documentation of Semantic Web Tools

Achim Reiz[1]([✉]) [ID], Fajar J. Ekaputra[2] [ID], and Nandana Mihindukulasooriya[3] [ID]

[1] Universität Rostock, Rostock, Germany
achim.reiz@uni-rostock.de
[2] WU Vienna, Vienna, Austria
[3] IBM Research AI, New York, USA

Abstract. The semantic web community has developed and still is developing a tremendous number of tools and software. While the activity underlines the continuous importance of the field and the commitment of its members, it also poses a challenge, especially for people entering the field. Identifying the right tools for one's use case is increasingly difficult. A lot of software is no longer actively maintained, and going through all publications and source repositories to find the software with the proper set of functions is tedious. In this demo, we propose a workflow and an initial Wikidata-based toolkit to support knowledge engineers and developers in documenting and finding the right tools. We categorized existing tools into a pre-defined taxonomy and integrated them with GitHub metadata about their recent developments when applicable. The condensed information with the new taxonomy is integrated into Wikidata, ready for further use.

Keywords: Semantic Web · Knowledge Graph · Software · Tools

1 Introduction

From 2010 to 2023, more than 2,400 papers were presented and published alone at the Extended and International Semantic Web Conferences (e.g., ESWC and ISWC). Moreover, there are many more additional journals, conferences, and workshops (e.g., SWJ, KEOD, LDAC). We develop countless knowledge graph construction, querying, and storing approaches, often supported by or implemented in software. While that is, in some respect, a sign of a healthy research community, it also poses a challenge, especially for people entering the field.

Currently, documenting and searching for the right Semantic Web (SW) software for a given practical problem is tedious: (1.) There is no common repository for documenting SW software (for example, similar to LOV for vocabularies), and relevant information is scattered throughout the various research outlets. (2.) There is no standardized semantics and taxonomy to describe the SW tools. Additionally, many tools and frameworks cover more than one element of the

© The Author(s), under exclusive license to Springer Nature Switzerland AG 2025
A. Meroño Peñuela et al. (Eds.): ESWC 2024, LNCS 15344, pp. 311–315, 2025.
https://doi.org/10.1007/978-3-031-78952-6_48

knowledge graph (KG) development toolchain. For example, Apache Jena is mainly regarded as a Java framework. However, it also integrates a triple store with a reasoning engine and allows the validation of incoming data for conformance based on SHACL shapes.

Many SW researchers and practitioners acknowledge these challenges and try to address them in many forms. The Awesome Semantic Web initiative[1] provides a GitHub repository to collect and report SW tools. The page contains more than 100 software tools related to SW. However, it contains many outdated software and does not provide information beyond categories and descriptions. A recent technical report from the OntoCommons [1] collects a collection of tools metadata, including description, homepage, code repository, documentation page, and related publications from more than 60 tools based on a survey. The report, however, is only available as a PDF and not as a machine-readable resource. Existing Knowledge Graphs, such as Wikidata and DBPedia, contain information about traditional and popular software, such as Protégé[2]. However, these pages typically are missing for newer or less popular software –albeit potentially of similar or higher importance – such as Chowlk [2] for ontology creation or Widoco [3] for ontology documentation. Furthermore, there is currently no dedicated visualization page to render their sub-graphs on SW software.

The Semantic Tool Hub targets to ease these challenges: it aims to bring the scattered knowledge on the SW software tools into Wikidata –an open and community-driven Knowledge Graph– according to a predefined taxonomy representing the semantic artifact development process.

The data is further enriched with metadata from their GitHub repositories (if applicable) to identify recent activity. The Semantic Tool Hub is meant to strengthen the application of FAIR principles [4] for semantic web research by making the tools findable, accessible at a centralized, open location, interoperable through standardized semantic web protocols and the Wikidata vocabulary and reusable by stating the license and source code, if applicable.

In the rest of the paper, we will describe the proposed methodology and our initial toolkit to support the documentation and retrieval process of the SW software centered around Wikidata.

2   The Semantic Tool Hub

The main idea behind the Semantic Tool Hub is to develop a Wikidata-based solution for sustainable community-driven documentation and retrieval of SW tools. In this work, we defined our scope only to include tools targeting RDF-based technologies. To this end, we propose a workflow (cf. Fig. 1) consisting of the following steps:

---

[1] https://github.com/semantalytics/awesome-semantic-web.

[2] https://dbpedia.org/page/Protege_(software);   https://www.wikidata.org/wiki/Q2066865.

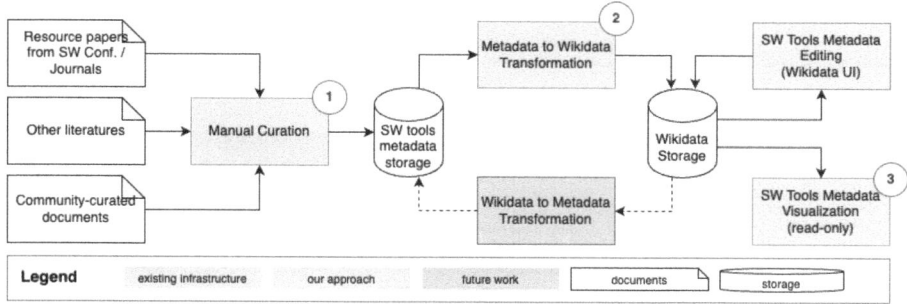

Fig. 1. The Semantic Tool Hub Workflow

Taxonomy Development. At the beginning of our research, we realized a strong need for a solid categorization of the tool. To this end, we combine the existing categorization tool from OntoCommons report [1] and the semantic web lifecycle [5] to develop our SW software taxonomy, shown in Fig. 2. The taxonomy is modeled in Wikidata and available to the full extent in GitHub[3].

Step 1. Manual Data Curation. Next, we collected and manually curated existing literature, both from scientific communities (e.g., SW conferences and journals) and other sources (e.g., awesome SW initiative), to gather metadata about tools. This step aimed to ensure the distributed information about software tools currently scattered among different sources can be collected and structured according to the taxonomy developed previously.

Our initial prototype collects data from three primary sources: (i) recent ISWC/ESWC conferences, (ii) awesome SW initiative, and (iii) OntoCommons report. In total, we have collected almost 150 tools annotated with metadata, including their categorizations. The original annotation information is available as a spreadsheet file (see footnote 3).

Step 2. Metadata to Wikidata Transformation. We decided to use Wikidata as part of our solution approach due to the flexibility, machine-readability, and nature of crowdsourcing of the Wikidata content development. We believe that our decision will allow for a broader involvement of the community in documenting the available SW tools. Furthermore, it facilitates users with easy access to retrieving and searching for suitable SW tools.

We are currently utilising Open Refine[4] and Wikipedia Quickstatements[5] to transform our spreadsheet data into RDF triples suitable for Wikidata.

Step 3. SW Tools Metadata Visualization. Wikidata contains an extensive collection of knowledge on various topics and granularity, which makes it hard for

---

[3] https://github.com/semantic-tool-hub/SW-Tool-Hub-data/releases/tag/0.1.

[4] https://openrefine.org/.

[5] https://github.com/magnusmanske/quickstatements.

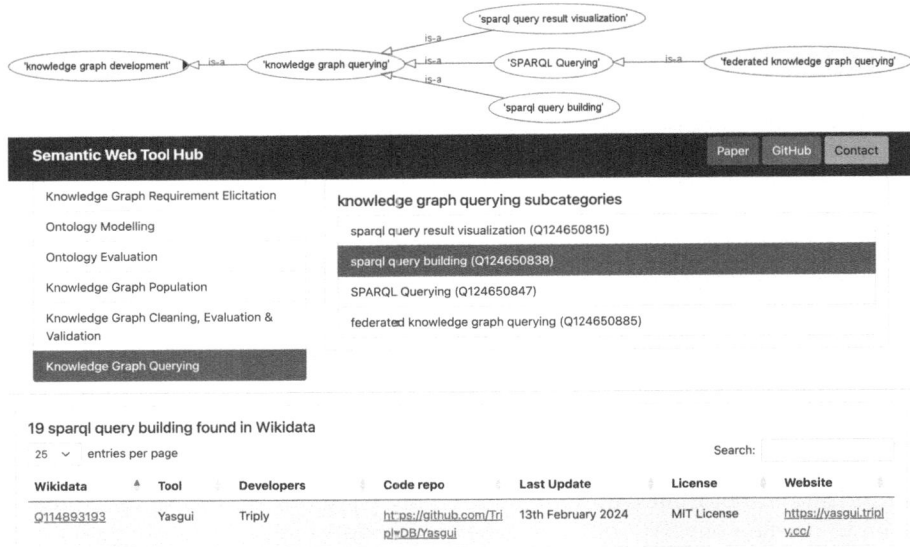

Fig. 2. An excerpt of the Semantic Tool Hub taxonomy (top) & the Semantic Tool Visualization and Search Interface (bottom)

users to browse for relevant information on specific topics quickly. Therefore, a specific interface is needed to help users quickly search for information about specific tools.

In the context of this paper, we have developed a webpage[6] to visualize and search/retrieve the knowledge that we have developed to help users in searching and finding information about SW tools (cf. Fig. 2 bottom).

Step 4. Adding New Data Over Time. At the time of publication, the Semantic Tool Hub contains manually curated data collected by the author of this demo. In the future, we hope the semantic web community picks up the idea, and the crowd updates the data collaboratively. Data ingestions and updates can be done directly through the Wikidata interface or using GitHub issues. The GitHub repository contains further information on how to participate[7].

3   Conclusion and Future Work

This paper describes our approach to support a sustainable community-driven documentation and search of SW tools based on Wikidata. We hope the Semantic Tool Hub gets picked up by the semantic web community and establishes itself

---

[6] https://semantic-tool-hub.github.io/.

[7] https://github.com/semantic-tool-hub/SW-Tool-Hub-data.

as an entry point for finding potential software for knowledge graph development efforts.

In the future, we plan to increase the ease of use and means for contributions through a two-way synchronization between Wikidata and the git-based metadata storage. That includes a phase-out of the Excel sheet towards a JSON-based flat-file architecture for managing the various tools, in addition to the existing Wikidata editor UI and GitHub Issues.

References

1. Skjæveland, M.G., Slaughter, L.A., Kindermann, C.: OntoCommons D4.3 - report on landscape analysis of ontology engineering tools, April (2022). https://doi.org/10.5281/zenodo.6504670
2. Chávez-Feria, S., García-Castro, R., Poveda-Villalón, M.: Chowlk: from UML-based ontology conceptualizations to owl. In: Groth, P., et al. (eds.) European Semantic Web Conference, pp. 338–352. Springer, Cham (2022). https://doi.org/10.1007/978-3-031-06981-9_20
3. Garijo, D.: WIDOCO: A Wizard for Documenting Ontologies. In: d'Amato, C., et al. (eds.) ISWC 2017. LNCS, vol. 10588, pp. 94–102. Springer, Cham (2017). https://doi.org/10.1007/978-3-319-68204-4_9
4. Barker, M., et al.: Introducing the FAIR principles for research software. Sci. Data, **9**(1), 622 (2022). ISSN 2052-4463. https://doi.org/10.1038/s41597-022-01710-x, https://www.nature.com/articles/s41597-022-01710-x
5. Breit, A., Waltersdorfer, L., Ekaputra, F.J., Miksa, T., Sabou, M.: A lifecycle framework for semantic web machine learning systems. In: Kotsis, G., et al. (eds.) International Conference on Database and Expert Systems Applications, pp. 359–368. Springer, Cham (2022). https://doi.org/10.1007/978-3-031-14343-4_33

German Tourism Knowledge Graph

Umutcan Serles[1,2](✉) , Elias Kärle[2] , Richard Hunkel[3], and Dieter Fensel[1]

[1] STI Innsbruck, Department of Computer Science, University of Innsbruck,
Innsbruck, Austria
{umutcan.serles,dieter.fensel}@sti2.at
[2] Onlim GmbH,Vienna, Austria
elias.karle@onlim.com
[3] German National Tourist Board, Frankfurt, Germany
richard.hunkel@germany.travel

Abstract. Tourism is one of the most critical sectors of the global economy. Due to its heterogeneous and fragmented nature, it provides one of the most suitable use cases for knowledge graphs. In this poster, we introduce the German Tourism Knowledge Graph that integrates tourism-related data from 16 federal states of Germany and various other sources to provide a curated knowledge source for various applications. It is publicly available through GUIs and an API.

Keywords: tourism · knowledge graphs · data integration

1 Introduction

Tourism is one of the most fragmented sectors, bringing many different services together, such as accommodation, transportation, events, and many more. From a data management perspective, such fragmentation and abundance of service providers bring a large size and heterogeneity in data sources. Most of the data are isolated behind closed systems, preventing digitalization in tourism from reaching its full potential. Using the power of integrated data and benefiting from the synergies between regional touristic offers can help overcome these obstacles.

With that motivation, the German National Tourist Board (GNTB)[1] commissioned the construction of German Tourism Knowledge Graph (GTKG) that integrates data from the regional marketing organizations[2] of 16 states in Germany. It was launched in May 2023 and being updated daily by the regional marketing organizations of German states. To the best of our knowledge, GTKG is the first tourism knowledge graph driven by stakeholders in the tourism industry that is continuously updated and maintained at a large scale.

In the remainder of this paper, we will first briefly describe different tasks for building the GTKG in Sect. 2. Then, we provide a literature review and

---

[1] In German, Deutsche Zentrale für Tourismus. https://germany.travel.
[2] These are agencies that promote tourism in their regions.

A. Meroño Peñuela et al. (Eds.): ESWC 2024, LNCS 15344, pp. 316–320, 2025.
https://doi.org/10.1007/978-3-031-78952-6_49

comparison with similar knowledge graphs in Sect. 3. We conclude the paper by summarizing the key points and indications for future work in Sect. 4.

2   Building the German Tourism Knowledge Graph

We will present the building process of GTKG in three steps, namely knowledge creation, enrichment and deployment. The necessary tooling is provided by GNTB through its technical provider Onlim GmbH[3]. Onlim provides the technical infrastructure for each step of building the knowledge graph as well as support and training for the data providers.

2.1   Knowledge Creation

The knowledge creation task can be split in two: the creation of the schema (TBox) and the instantiation of the schema (ABox). The schema used in the GTKG is created by the Open Data Tourism Alliance[4]. Open Data Tourism Alliance (ODTA) is an initiative consisting of tourism domain experts representing the DACH region (Germany, Austria and Switzerland). The main goal of the initiative is to create *domain specifications* [4] for tourism-related data. Domain specifications are extended subsets of schema.org. ODTA selects the relevant subsets of types and properties from schema.org and extends them with new types and properties when schema.org is not enough for more detailed description of touristic items. Furthermore, constraints (e.g. cardinality) on the properties can be defined. The domain specifications are encoded as SHACL shapes[5].

The regional marketing organizations of German states create instances of the types in the TBox and import it to GTKG on a daily basis. Each instance is verified against its corresponding SHACL shape (based on target declarations and explicit shape references on instances) to ensure that they satisfy all constraints provided by the domain specifications made by ODTA. The regional marketing organizations typically use RML [2] mappings between the ODTA schemas and the metadata of their internal systems.

The major types[6] represented in GTKG (on 07/03/2024) are schema:Event (239K instances), odta:PointOfInterest (118K instances), odta:Trail (23K instances), schema:LodgingBusiness (25K instances), schema:LocalBusiness (70K instances) and schema:FoodEstablishment (20K instances)[7].

---

[3] https://onlim.com.

[4] https://open-data-germany.org/en/open-data-germany/.

[5] The list of domain specifications currently used by GTKG can be found here: https://semantify.it/list/LRVOilZZ6. There was a new release of ODTA domain specifications in February 2024 (https://odta.sti2.org/) and the migration process is still ongoing.

[6] See https://semantify.it/list/LRVOilZZ6 for the domain specifications based on these types.

[7] *schema* is the prefix for schema.org namespace. *odta* is the prefix for https://odta.io/voc/ namespace that represents newly created types and properties. Instance counts are result of the query here: https://purl.archive.org/gtkg/queries.

2.2   Knowledge Enrichment

The knowledge graph created based on the data provided by 16 regional marketing organizations is further enriched with data from other sources. The enrichment is conceptually a standalone step, and can be initiated outside of the knowledge creation process. However, it is also possible to configure it to run during knowledge creation.

A prominent example of enrichment is geo-linking of e-charging stations[8] and public transportation stops[9] with other points of interest. The enrichment process can be configured via the API by the data providers. The configuration mainly contains the SPARQL queries that select the sets of candidate instances that can be linked and the distance threshold for two POIs to be considered *close enough* to each other. If the distance between two POIs is below the configured threshold, these POIs are linked. The details of the configuration is presented in the API documentation (Sect. 2.3) under "Guides".

2.3   Knowledge Deployment

The GTKG API[10] enables programmatical access to the GTKG. It allows SPARQL queries against the graph but also many other ways of accessing the knowledge graph (e.g., search by name). The API needs an authentication key, which can be obtained from GNTB free of charge[11]. Listing 1 shows an example request to the API to run the SPARQL query in https://purl.archive.org/gtkg/queries.

```
curl --request POST \
    --url https://proxy.opendatagermany.io/api/ts/v1/kg/sparql \
    --header 'Accept: application/sparql-results+json' \
    --header 'X-API-KEY: fb0758867a9a01fce51546b0e537bb56' \
    --header 'content-type: text/plain' \
    --data 'PREFIX schema: <https://schema.org/>   PREFIX odta:
↪   <https://odta.io/voc/> SELECT ?s ?name ?poi (xsd:decimal(?dist) as
↪   ?distance) ?unit WHERE  { ?s a odta:PointOfInterest. ?s schema:name
↪   ?name. ?s odta:geoLink [odta:linkSource/schema:name ?poi;
↪   odta:walkingDistance/schema:value ?dist;
↪   odta:walkingDistance/schema:unitCode ?unit] } LIMIT 10'
```

Listing 1: A SPARQL query to return 10 results about POIs and the walking distances to the entities linked via geo-linking to them

---

[8] https://ladestationen.api.bund.dev/.
[9] https://www.opendata-oepnv.de/.
[10] See https://purl.archive.org/gtkg/api-doc for a comprehensive documentation.
[11] https://purl.archive.org/gtkg/access.

Additional to the API, the GTKG provides a graphical user interface. The Search Widget[12] allows text-based search of instances and filtering by type. Different visualization modalities can be accessed for an instance from the search results.

GTKG allows the regional marketing organizations to use their own instance identifiers, which may not be always dereferencable. To mitigate this drawback, GTKG provides a a *wrapper URI* that takes the instance identifier as query parameter and creates an HTML depiction as well as provides a way of downloading an RDF serialization of the instance. See https://purl.archive.org/gtkg/example for an example.

3 Related Work

The survey from Abu-Salih [1] covers domain-specific knowledge graphs, including tourism-related knowledge graphs. These graphs typically target specific regions and may focus on specific kinds of tourism-related data. For example, Tyrol region in Austria [3], London in England, Madeira in Portugal and Cote d'Azur in France [5].

Although many other knowledge graphs exist in the tourism domain, the German Tourism Knowledge Graph stands out. It is not a purely academic project, but driven and funded by stakeholders in the tourism sector. It contains data about various tourism-related topics and has a national coverage instead of focusing a single region. It also provides various access modalities that can serve different purposes (e.g., machine or human consumption).

4 Conclusion and Future Work

We presented the German Tourism Knowledge Graph. The knowledge graph is a publicly accessible resource and uses a schema.org-based schema to describe the integrated data. It is important to note that the GTKG is built around standard semantic technologies like RDF(S), SPARQL, SHACL and widespread technologies like RML. Each instance in the knowledge graph has its own license, which is typically a Creative Common license like CC-BY-SA.

The German National Tourism Board is currently internally testing a chatbot powered by the GTKG, which will be available for public soon. Many other applications have been developed at a hackathon in November 2023[13]. Currently, individual instances can be downloaded in an RDF serialization. However, periodic releases of the entire knowledge graph are also considered in the future work.

---

[12] Currently being tested on a subset of GTKG https://purl.archive.org/gtkg/search.
[13] https://de.linkedin.com/posts/german-national-tourist-board_kollaboration-innovation-dzt-activity-7132391151659016192-k5hW.

References

1. Abu-Salih, B.: Domain-specific knowledge graphs: a survey. J. Netw. Comput. Appl. **185**, 103076 (2021). https://doi.org/10.1016/j.jnca.2021.103076
2. Dimou, A., Sande, M.V., Colpaert, P.: RML: a generic language for integrated rdf mappings of heterogeneous data. In: Proceedings of the Workshop on Linked Data on the Web @WWW 2014, Seoul, South Korea (2014)
3. Kärle, E., Şimşek, U., Panasiuk, O., Fensel, D.: Building an ecosystem for the tyrolean tourism knowledge graph. In: Pautasso, C., Sánchez-Figueroa, F., Systä, K., Murillo Rodríguez, J.M. (eds.) ICWE 2018. LNCS, vol. 11153, pp. 260–267. Springer, Cham (2018). https://doi.org/10.1007/978-3-030-03056-8_25
4. Şimşek, U., Angele, K., Kärle, E., Panasiuk, O., Fensel, D.: Domain-specific customization of schema.org based on SHACL. In: Pan, J.Z., et al. (eds.) ISWC 2020. LNCS, vol. 12507, pp. 585–600. Springer, Cham (2020). https://doi.org/10.1007/978-3-030-62466-8_36
5. Troncy, R., Rizzo, G., Jameson, A., et al.: 3cixty: building comprehensive knowledge bases for city exploration. J. Web Semant. **46–47**, 2–13 (2017). https://doi.org/10.1016/j.websem.2017.07.002

Finding Root Causes for Outliers
in Semantically Annotated Sensor Data

Tim Strobel[1,2]([⊠]) [ID], Tim Pychynski[1], and Andreas Harth[2] [ID]

[1] Bosch Center for Artificial Intelligence, Sunnyvale, USA
{Tim.Strobel,Tim.Pychynski}@bosch.com
[2] Friedrich-Alexander-Universität Erlangen-Nrnberg,
Erlangen and Nuremberg, Germany
Andreas.Harth@fau.de

Abstract. Causal inference creates insights into observational data. Such insights could explain an outlying value to perform Root Cause Analysis. But how can causal inference be used with semantically annotated observations? The following demo showcases how to use semantically annotated sensor data for causal inference. The method's implementation uses an agent pattern interacting with a knowledge graph.

Keywords: Sensor Data · Root Cause Analysis · Causal Inference

1 Introduction

Causal inference explains events in observations (e.g. an outlying value) in more detail than standard statistical analysis [4]. Therefore, it is a helpful tool for performing Root Cause Analysis (RCA) to understand the cause of an undesired event. Our demo shows how to use semantically annotated data to create causal insights into observations. Our contribution includes annotating a causal model based on observations described with the Semantic Sensor Network Ontology (SOSA) [2]. In addition, we show a localized, recursive causal model evaluation using a knowledge graph in the Resource Description Framework (RDF).

2 Causality

According to Pearl [4], a causal graph encodes the dependencies of a system's variables and the direction of their influences on each other. A causal graph represents variables with nodes and dependencies with directed edges [4]. We can define causal mechanisms for each node based on the encoded structure. A causal mechanism describes the behavior of the associated variable with respect to its parent variables in the graph. Based on a causal model, causal inference infers explanations about observed data. A ground truth causal model encodes the physical mechanisms used to generate an observation, but nature hides this ground truth causal model from us [4]. To uncover parts of the ground truth causal model, we use the knowledge of a system's domain expert or algorithms from causal discovery.

© The Author(s), under exclusive license to Springer Nature Switzerland AG 2025
A. Meroño Peñuela et al. (Eds.): ESWC 2024, LNCS 15344, pp. 321–325, 2025.
https://doi.org/10.1007/978-3-031-78952-6_50

3   Approach

Our approach demonstrates how to add causal dependencies and mechanisms to SOSA observations in an RDF graph. Based on the built RDF graph, we demonstrate causal inference in a recursive, localized manner to find root causes for outliers. The implementation follows a *Simple Reflex Agent* [5] pattern. The agents retrieve data from an RDF graph via SPARQL queries, process the data with pre-set rules, and save inferred conclusions into the graph.

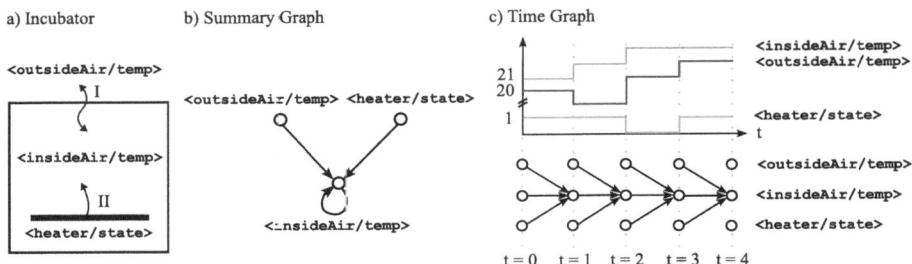

Fig. 1. Simplified incubator example of Feng et al. [1] with `sosa:ObservableProperty` `<insideAir/temperature>`, `<outsideAir/temperature>`, and `<heater/state>`

We use the running example *Incubator* described by Feng et al. [1] in a simplified version displayed in Fig. 1a. The *Incubator* has three `sosa:Observable Property`, which are `<insideAir/temperature>`, `<outsideAir/temperature>`, and `<heater/state>`. To add the causal knowledge to the RDF graph containing the SOSA annotated observations, instances of `sosa:ObservableProperty` are also assigned to the class `:CausalNode`. We can describe a causal dependency in the RDF graph by linking two causal nodes via a `:CausalEdge`. A causal mechanism can be added using the class `:CausalMechanism`. We can explain outliers through causal inference by adding causal nodes, edges, and mechanisms to the observations in the RDF graph (see Fig. 2 for an example).

RCA uses a set of observations for each time-step for every `sosa:Observable Property` (as displayed in the time-dependent graph in Fig. 1c). We sample observations using a simulated ground truth causal model for the *Incubator*. To build this ground truth, we use the assumptions by Feng et al. [1]. This model defines heat exchange between `<insideAir>` and `<outsideAir>` (see Fig. 1a/I). In addition, heat is exchanged between `<heater>` and `<insideAir>` (see Fig. 1a/II). To distinguish the direction of influences, we assume the following: Changing `<insideAir/temperature>` will not affect `<outsideAir/temper-ature>` as well as changing `<insideAir/temperature>` will not affect `<heater/-state>`. Also, we add a self-cycle on `<insideAir/temperature>` since this observable depends on earlier observations in the time series. The resulting summary causal graph is referenced in Fig. 1b. The according rolled-up, time-dependent causal graph is shown in Fig. 1c.

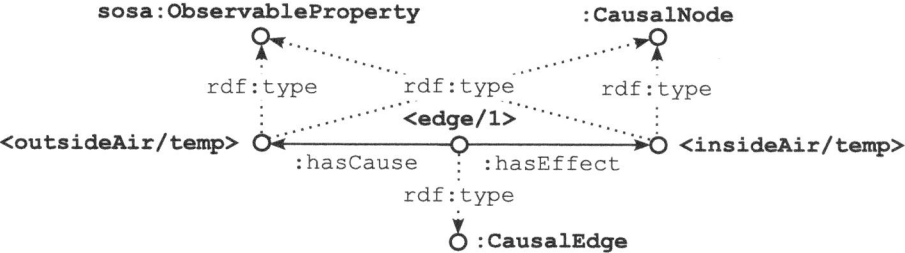

Fig. 2. The RDF representation of the causal edge connecting `<:CausalNode>` `<outsideAir/temperature>` and `<insideAir/temperature>`.

3.1 Regression Agent

The *Regression Agent* retrieves the causal dependencies and the observations from the RDF graph to fit regression models as causal mechanisms for each `:CausalNode`. The regression model's inputs are the parent `:CausalNode` instances. The temperature measurement within the *Incubator* is a time-series observation. Therefore, the agent fits a linear auto-regressive model for the `:CausalNode` `<insideAir/temperature>` with inputs `<outsideAir/temperature>` and `<heater/state>`. The linear auto-regressive model contains one learnable coefficient per input. The auto-regressive approach will assume a time lag of 1. In the future also more sophisticated methods could be used to determine the time lag automatically. The time lag considers that a new value is predicted based on the value one time instance before the prediction value in the time series (see time t in Fig. 1c). The agent compresses and adds the regression model with a specific URI into the RDF graph.

3.2 Outlier Explanation Agent

The *Outlier Explanation Agent* uses a method described by Janzing et al. [3]. This approach utilizes an Additive Noise Model (ANM) and Shapley values [6]. ANMs take into account that each observation contains an amount of noise. To calculate the amount of noise of one observation, we compute the difference between the observation we made and the estimation of our causal mechanism – the prediction of the regression model. High noise, therefore, means that a high amount of the observation is not explainable by the parent nodes, which are influencing the observed value. With the *Incubator* example, we use the regression model of `<insideAir/temperature>` with the parent variable's observations as input and compute an estimation. With the computed estimation, we calculate the noise as the difference between the estimation and the actual observation for `<insideAir/temperature>`. For all variables with no parent variables and therefore no known causal mechanism to explain the observation, we use the observation's value as the noise feature (e.g., for `<outsideAir/temperature>`).

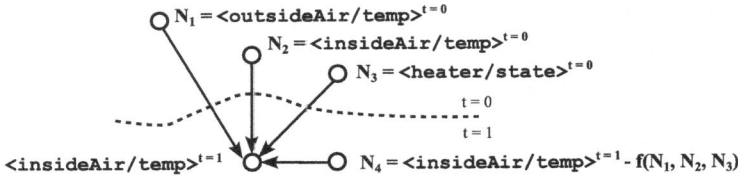

Fig. 3. Computing noise terms using the causal mechanism f

To compute the contribution of each noise feature to our outlying value, Janzing et al. [3] use Shapley values. To do so, we need to describe our outlying observation of `<insideAir/temperature>` as a function of all associated noise features. We implemented the noise-dependent function in a recursive and localized manner using the RDF graph (see Algorithm 1). For the *Incubator* this function is `<insideAir/temp>`$^{t=1} = f(N_{parents}) + N_4$ (see Fig. 3) with causal mechanism f. Noise terms with high contributions are assumed to be the root causes of the outlier. As visualized in Fig. 3, four noise terms are potential root causes for the outlier on `<insideAir/temperature>` at the investigated time $t = 1$.

Algorithm 1: Localized, Recursive Noise-dependent Function

Data: Target Node T, Noise Samples N, RDF Graph G
Result: Prediction d for Target Node T based on Noise Samples
Function NoiseDependentFunction(T):

    $parents = G.queryParents(T)$;
    if $len(parents) == 0$ **then**
        return $N[T]$;
    else
        $model = G.queryModel(T)$;
        $input = [\text{NoiseDependentFunction}(p) \text{ for } p \text{ in } parents]$;
        return $N[T] + model.estimate(input)$;
    end

---

4   Conclusion

We showed causal inference on causal annotated SOSA observations with a localized and recursive noise-dependent function. The limitations of this approach include the fact that the causal structure needs to be known. A wrongful causal structure could lead to wrong conclusions. Another limitation is that the computational effort for Shapley values increases drastically with an increased amount of causal nodes. In future research, we will continue working on the knowledge representation of causal functional dependencies and investigate the scalability to use cases with many causal nodes.

Acknowledgements. The authors would like to thank Daniel Henselmann for his helpful feedback.

References

1. Feng, H., Gomes, C., Thule, C., Lausdahl, K., Sandberg, M., Larsen, P.G.: The incubator case study for digital twin engineering. arXiv preprint arXiv:2102.10390 (2021)
2. Janowicz, K., Haller, A., Cox, S.J., Le Phuoc, D., Lefrançois, M.: SOSA: a lightweight ontology for sensors, observations, samples, and actuators. J. Web Semant. **56**, 1–10 (2019)
3. Janzing, D., Budhathoki, K., Minorics, L., Blöbaum, P.: Causal structure based root cause analysis of outliers. arXiv preprint arXiv:1912.02724 (2019)
4. Pearl, J., Verma, T.S.: A theory of inferred causation. In: Studies in Logic and the Foundations of Mathematics, vol. 134, pp. 789–811. Elsevier (1995)
5. Russell, S.J., Norvig, P.: Artificial Intelligence a Modern Approach. London (2010)
6. Shapley, L.S., et al.: A value for n-person games (1953)

RMLdoc: Documenting Mapping Rules for Knowledge Graph Construction

Jhon Toledo[1] , Ana Iglesias-Molina[1(✉)] , David Chaves-Fraga[2] ,
and Daniel Garijo[1]

[1] Ontology Engineering Group, Universidad Politécnica de Madrid, Madrid, Spain
{ja.toledo,ana.iglesiasm,daniel.garijo}@upm.es
[2] Grupo de Sistemas Intelixentes, Universidade de Santiago de Compostela,
Santiago, Spain
david.chaves@usc.es

Abstract. In this demo we present RMLdoc, a Python package designed
to generate documentation for RML mappings when constructing knowledge graphs from heterogeneous sources. Given an input mapping file
written in R2RML, RML, or YARRRML, RMLdoc will generate a
detailed Markdown documentation explaining each mapping with corresponding diagrams, in a human readable manner. Thanks to RMLdoc,
we aim to shed light in the knowledge graph construction process, making mappings easier to maintain and understand by knowledge engineers.
Code repository: https://github.com/oeg-upm/rmldoc/
Demo: https://w3id.org/rmldoc/example

Keywords: Documentation · Knowledge Graph Construction · RML

1 Introduction

Knowledge Graphs (KGs) are commonly constructed by transforming a set of
heterogeneous data sources (e.g., CSV, JSON files) into RDF graphs. These
transformations are performed by relating all input sources with the target ontology terms, and can be described using declarative mapping languages such as
the W3C recommendation R2RML[1] or its widely adopted extension RML [7].
Institutions such as the European Railway Agency[2] or the European Commission
(e.g., in the EU Public Procurement Data Space[3]) describe their transformations
using these languages in some of their projects.

Knowledge engineers are usually responsible for developing the mapping rules
needed to construct KGs. In many cases, these engineers rely on graphical interfaces (e.g., RMLEditor [5]) and human-friendly serializations like YARRRML [4]
or Mapeathor [6] to aid them in the creation of mapping rules. However, the mapping documents resultant from these efforts are, in many cases, complex and

---

[1] https://www.w3.org/TR/r2rml/.
[2] https://data-interop.era.europa.eu/.
[3] https://europa.eu/!qx9WxQ.

A. Meroño Peñuela et al. (Eds.): ESWC 2024, LNCS 15344, pp. 326–330, 2025.
https://doi.org/10.1007/978-3-031-78952-6_51

hard to interpret, which reduces their reusability by other engineers. Furthermore, there is a lack of tools to generate a comprehensive and human-readable documentation of mapping rules. This situation delegates mappings as second-class resources in the KG development process, without documentation (scattered comments in the mapping document at most) or essential metadata (e.g., version, creators, license).

In this paper, we present RMLdoc [8],[4] an open source Python package designed to create a human-readable documentation of the mapping rules used to construct a Knowledge Graph. RMLdoc supports mapping rules described in R2RML, RML, and YARRRML, helping practitioners better understand the relationships between the original data sources and the ontology terms. To the best of our knowledge, this is the first approach that proposes the generation of human-readable mapping documentation. RMLdoc takes one step closer towards completing technological support for KG-driven ecosystems.

2 Mapping Documentation with RMLdoc

RMLdoc processes R2RML, RML and YARRRML mappings to generate a human-readable documentation as follows:

Mapping Upload and Processing. The tool takes as input an existing mapping written in R2RML, RML or YARRRML. The mappings documents are processed as RDF graphs. In the case of receiving YARRRML, these mappings are first translated into RML using Yatter.[5] Then, mappings are validated to check for grammar errors, and next they are loaded internally as a graph. RMLdoc supports both the original proposal of RML [3] and the specification lately developed by the Knowledge Graph Construction W3C Community Group [7].

Querying and Information Extraction. The mapping graph is then queried to extract the relevant information for its documentation: (i) metadata, (ii) namespaces and (iii) mapping rule sets. First, the *metadata* of the mapping document is queried. This information is optional in the mapping, but recommended for improving its documentation (e.g., description, authors, creation date, license). We retrieve this information taking a mapping document as a `dcat:Dataset` or `schema:Dataset` [2]. Next, the *namespaces* and prefixes declared in the document are extracted, followed by the elements that compose the *mapping rule sets* (in RML, *Triples Map*). From each rule set, RMLdoc extracts the data source, subject and predicate-object description, and the joins performed to create triples with references between different rule sets (in RML, *Join Conditions*).

Serialization and Writing. The information retrieved in the previous step is structured and written using Jinja templates[6] in a Markdown document to

---

[4] https://pypi.org/project/rmldoc/.
[5] https://pypi.org/project/yatter/.
[6] https://jinja.palletsprojects.com/en/2.10.x/templates/.

generate the human-readable documentation. Additionally, the triples and joins documented in each rule set are accompanied with a diagram, automatically generated with the Mermaid library.[7]

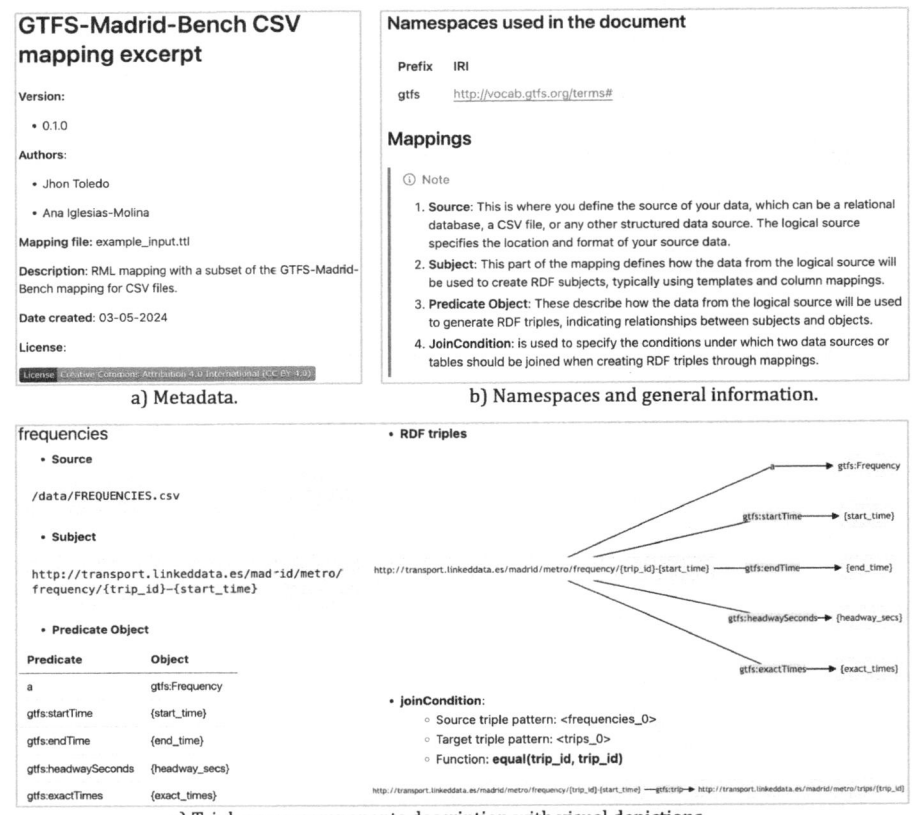

a) Metadata.

b) Namespaces and general information.

c) Triples map components description with visual depictions.

Fig. 1. Demo example from https://w3id.org/rmldoc/example.

Figure 1 shows a **demo** example documentation for a mapping subset of the GTFS-Madrid-Bench [1], showing how the mapping information is structured in the Markdown file: the mapping metadata (1a) including title, version, authors, file name, description, creation date, and license; the prefixes used and a brief conceptual description of the mapping components (1b); and a exemplary rule set (`frequencies`, 1c). The diagram shows the essential mapping elements in a human-friendly manner, adding a visual aid while avoiding introducing constructs from the languages that are not necessary for the comprehension of the transformation rules.

---

[7] https://mermaid.js.org/.

The source code of RMLdoc is openly available under Apache 2.0 license.[8] Following open science best practices, each release automatically generates a dedicated DOI [8]. Additionally, the tool is available in PyPi as a package.4

3   Conclusions and Future Steps

In this paper we present RMLdoc, a Python library designed to generate human-readable documentation for mappings used in declarative knowledge graph construction. This tool processes mapping documents written in either RML, R2RML or YARRRML and produces a Markdown file with the essential information for understanding the transformation rules, also depicting them in visual diagrams. As future steps, we plan to extend the tool further to consider named graphs, and be fully compliant with all modules of the new RML specification [7], as well as to allow metadata annotation on the *Triples Map* level. We also plan on supporting HTML export and launching the tool as a GitHub action, with the aim of facilitating an effortless documentation during the KG development process. This is the first approach developed for documenting mapping rules for knowledge graph construction, which we believe that it is a necessary step towards the governance of the artifacts involved in KG-driven ecosystems.

Acknowledgments. David Chaves-Fraga is funded by the Galician Ministry of Education, University and Professional Training and the European Regional Development Fund (ERDF/FEDER program) through grants ED431C2018/29 and ED431G2019/04.

References

1. Chaves-Fraga, D., Priyatna, F., Cimmino, A., Toledo, J., Ruckhaus, E., Corcho, O.: GTFS-Madrid-bench: a benchmark for virtual knowledge graph access in the transport domain. J. Web Semant. **65**, 100596 (2020)
2. Dimou, A., De Nies, T., Verborgh, R., Mannens, E., Mechant, P., Van de Walle, R.: Automated metadata generation for linked data generation and publishing workflows. In: Workshop on Linked Data on the Web (LDOW@WWW 2016). CEUR Workshop Proceedings, vol. 1593 (2016)
3. Dimou, A., Sande, M.V., Colpaert, P., Verborgh, R., Mannens, E., Van De Walle, R.: RML: a generic language for integrated RDF mappings of heterogeneous data. In: Workshop on Linked Data on the Web (LDOW@WWW 2014). CEUR Workshop Proceedings, vol. 1184 (2014)
4. Heyvaert, P., De Meester, B., Dimou, A., Verborgh, R.: Declarative rules for linked data generation at your fingertips! In: Gangemi, A., Gentile, A.L., Nuzzolese, A.G., Rudolph, S., Maleshkova, M., Paulheim, H., Pan, J.Z., Alam, M. (eds.) ESWC 2018. LNCS, vol. 11155, pp. 213–217. Springer, Cham (2018). https://doi.org/10.1007/978-3-319-98192-5_40
5. Heyvaert, P., et al.: RMLEditor: A graph-based mapping editor for linked data mappings. In: Sack, H., Blomqvist, E., d'Aquin, M., Ghidini, C., Ponzetto, S.P., Lange, C. (eds.) ESWC 2016. LNCS, vol. 9678, pp. 709–723. Springer, Cham (2016). https://doi.org/10.1007/978-3-319-34129-3_43

---

[8] https://github.com/oeg-upm/rmldoc.

6. Iglesias-Molina, A., Pozo-Gilo, L., Doña, D., Ruckhaus, E., Chaves-Fraga, D., Corcho, O.: Mapeathor: simplifying the specification of declarative rules for knowledge graph construction. In: ISWC 2020 Demos and Industry Tracks. CEUR Workshop Proceedings, vol. 2721 (2020)
7. Iglesias-Molina, A. et al.: The RML Ontology: A community-driven modular redesign after a decade of experience in mapping heterogeneous data to RDF. In: Payne, T.R., et al. (eds.)The Semantic Web – ISWC 2023. ISWC 2023. LNCS, vol. 14266. Springer, Cham (2023). https://doi.org/10.1007/978-3-031-47243-5_9
8. Toledo, J., Chaves, D., Iglesias-Molina, A., Garijo, D.: OEG-UPM/RMLDOC: RMLDOC 0.1.5 (2024). https://doi.org/10.5281/zenodo.10797980

Granular Access to Policy-Governed Linked Data via Partial Server-Side Query

Joachim Van Herwegen$^{(\boxtimes)}$ ⓘ and Ruben Verborgh ⓘ

IDLab, Ghent University – imec, Deprtment of Electronics and Information Systems, Ghent, Belgium
{Joachim.VanHerwegen,ruben.verborgh}@ugent.be

Abstract. The Solid Protocol defines a document-oriented interface to access Linked Data subject to usage control policies that define who can read or write it. Common use cases with different read and write granularities cannot easily be supported with a one-to-one mapping from HTTP interface to a document-based storage system. We propose an interpretation of the Solid Protocol with Derived Data Resources, which are a server-side selection of data from different underlying resources. This demo covers our implementation in the Community Solid Server, detailing its more granular data control. Our implementation can guide other proposals, and the evolution of the specification to support the growing demand of Solid use cases with divergent read/write patterns.

Keywords: Solid · RDF · policies

1 Introduction

The Solid ecosystem is a standards-based initiative to extend the application range of RDF from Linked Open Data to the entire private–public data spectrum. The current Solid Protocol [1] presents the latest draft for an HTTP interface to RDF data under access control. At present, this interface—mirroring general Web architecture—defines a document-based view into the RDF-based knowledge graph hosted by a single server instance, also known as "pod". Most implementations conceptually implement this specification as a one-to-one mapping of HTTP resources to documents in an underlying storage. For example, the resources /a and /b would, under the hood, correspond to independent RDF documents in a database or filesystem.

However, earlier research revealed that such a straightforward correspondence incorrectly assumes use cases to exhibit a symmetry in read and write access granularity [2]. For example, just because one application has *write* access to a resource /bank-statements/2024/03/15/, this does not imply that the *read* access is also organized by date; one app might only be allowed to read leisure transactions across all bank statements. Such cases are highly common, but hard to support in an exclusive one-to-one document mapping.

ⓒ The Author(s), under exclusive license to Springer Nature Switzerland AG 2025
A. Meroño Peñuela et al. (Eds.): ESWC 2024, LNCS 15344, pp. 331–335, 2025.
https://doi.org/10.1007/978-3-031-78952-6_52

To this end, we propose an extended interpretation of the existing Solid Protocol to support a virtual kind of resource, analogously to how the HTTP specification transparently supports the interpretation of resources as static files on a server or as dynamically generated resources by server-side technologies such as PHP or Node.js. A *Derived Data Resource* can be defined as a selection of data from other underlying resources, thereby allowing more granular server-side permissioning beyond the document level.

2   Derived Data Resources

As support for use cases with read/write granularity mismatches [2], we extend a Solid server to support *Derived Data Resources*. These are resources whose contents are not written directly to the server by a client. Instead, their contents are based by performing a query on one or more other resources on the server, enabling an asymmetry in defining usage control policies. The query needs to happen server-side for confidentiality reasons, as the client might have read access to the query result, but not to the sources contributing to that result.

In this demo we showcase one way derived resources could be defined and interpreted on a Solid server. To do this we have extended the Community Solid Server [4], which is a Solid server designed specifically to be easily extensible to support research such as this. The new component can be found at https:// github.com/SolidLabResearch/derived-resources-component.

2.1   Defining a Derived Resource

To define a derived resource, our implementation requires 3 parameters:

- A *template*, defining the URL template that needs to be matched.
- One or more *selectors*, which are the input resources.
- A *filter*, to pick the necessary parts from the input.

When a request is made to a derived resource, it goes through those three steps to generate a response. The component has been designed so that any of these parts can easily be replaced with a different implementation, so you could define a new way to filter without having to change how selectors work, for example.

Templates. As template, the component expects a URL. When this URL is dereferenced, the result of the derived resource is returned.

Besides standard URLs, there is also support for URI templates as defined in RFC 6570 [3], such as `http://localhost:3000/foo/{bar}`, where a value will be assigned to `bar` based on the contents of the actual URL. These variable mappings are then passed to the selectors and filter for reuse there.

Selectors. Selectors are the URLs of one or more RDF resources that already exist on the server. The contents of all these resources will then be merged into a single RDF store and passed to the filter.

Instead of an exact URL location of a selector, the selector can also contain a pattern defined using * and ** wildcards, which follow a common path expansion pattern[1]. All resources on the server that match this pattern will be used.

Filters. To filter the selected data we make use of SPARQL CONSTRUCT queries, executed over the RDF store generated in the previous step. The result of this query is what is returned when a derived resource is being accessed.

To support the variables generated by matching a URI template, values can be injected into the SPARQL query. To do this, the variable names should be surrounded with two $. Using the example above, `$bar$` would be replaced with the actual value of the URL.

2.2 Where to Define a Derived Resource

Solid resources can have a description resource, also commonly called the metadata of a resource. We make use of this metadata to store the necessary information that defines a derived resource, using a custom ontology.

3 Demonstration

The README[2] details the instructions on how to run the demonstration. It includes a script to start a server with several pre-defined example resources.

```
@prefix derived: <urn:npm:solid:derived-resources:> .
<> derived:derivedResource [
    derived:template "template/{var}";
    derived:selector </selectors/data>;
    derived:filter </filters/var>
  ].
```

Listing 1. Metadata defining a derived resource

Listing 1 shows a sample of the example metadata that defines such a derived resource, which can be found at `http://localhost:3000/.meta` after starting the demo server. There we can see all the fields that were discussed in 2.1. The template is a string as the full URL is determined by concatenating its value to the URL of the resource this metadata belongs to. The other fields reference existing resources, where the selector contains the input data, and the filter contains a SPARQL query to execute on that data. Combining all of the above, after starting the server, we can access a derived resource by going to

---

[1] https://git-scm.com/docs/gitignore.
[2] https://github.com/SolidLabResearch/derived-resources-component/blob/main/README.md.

`http://localhost:3000/foaf:knows`, which will result in an RDF dataset only returning the `foaf:knows` triple. This is just one of the examples found in the repository.

4   Conclusion

Our new components can help Solid specification writers and implementers by showing how support for different read/write granularities could be implemented without changes to the protocol. By allowing users to create resources that depend on others, they can update their data in one place and still share different parts of it in multiple different places. This way, they no longer have to duplicate data to achieve the same goal.

Derived resources are defined through three different parts: the pattern determines where to find the derived resource the selector determines the input data, and the filter determines the query to perform on the input data.

While the component is an extension of the Community Solid Server, its design allows for this component itself to be further extended for purposes of research of specification design. For example, future work could examine the impact of using reasoning as a filter instead of the current SPARQL proposal.

This demo exemplifies a solution direction within the current document-based entry point of a Solid server. Other solutions include building different entry points into the Protocol, such as query-based mechanisms to make data selections of varying granularities [5]. Should the Solid Protocol evolve to have such functionality built-in, this solution can thus serve as a comparison point for evidence-based research into how the Solid protocol can best be modified to support this functionality.

Acknowledgements. The research in this paper was supported by SolidLab Vlaanderen (Flemish Government, EWI and RRF project VV023/10).

References

1. Capadisli, S., Berners-Lee, T., Verborgh, R., Kjernsmo, K.: Solid protocol. Editor's draft, W3C Solid Community Group (2022). https://solidproject.org/TR/2022/protocol-20221231
2. Dedecker, R., Slabbinck, W., Wright, J., Hochstenbach, P., Colpaert, P., Verborgh, R.: What's in a pod? – A knowledge graph interpretation for the Solid ecosystem. In: Proceedings of the 6th Workshop on Storing, Querying and Benchmarking Knowledge Graphs. CEUR Workshop Proceedings, vol. 3279, pp. 81–96 (2022). https://solidlabresearch.github.io/WhatsInAPod/
3. Fielding, R.T., Nottingham, M., Orchard, D., Gregorio, J., Hadley, M.: URI Template. RFC 6570 (2012). https://doi.org/10.17487/RFC6570, https://www.rfc-editor.org/info/rfc6570

4. Van Herwegen, J., Verborgh, R.: The community solid server: supporting research & development in an evolving ecosystem. Semant. Web J. https://doi.org/10.5281/zenodo.7595116, under submission
5. Verborgh, R., et al.: Triple pattern fragments: a low-cost knowledge graph interface for the Web. J. Web Semant. **37–38**, 184–206 (2016). https://doi.org/10.1016/j.websem.2016.03.003

Taking Control of Your Health Data: A Solid-Based Mobile App for Wearable Data Collection and RDF Visualization

Thomas Wehr[1]([✉])[iD], Michael Freund[2][iD], and Andreas Harth[1,2][iD]

[1] Friedrich-Alexander-Universität Erlangen-Nürnberg, Nürnberg, Germany
{thomas.wehr,andreas.harth}@fau.de
[2] Fraunhofer Institute for Integrated Circuits IIS, Nürnberg, Germany

Abstract. While wearables generate valuable health data, proprietary ecosystems limit interoperability and user control. We address this challenge with a user-friendly Android application that seamlessly collects data from diverse wearables via the Web of Things (WoT), converts the collected data into interoperable RDF using the SOSA/SSN ontology, and stores RDF in user-controlled Solid servers. Unlike existing solutions, our approach includes mapping the data to established ontologies and provides a user interface, empowering everyday users to explore their health data through interactive visualizations. We showcase the application's functionalities through live demonstrations - code, demo videos, and an installable apk are publicly available at https://github.com/derwehr/WoT-Solid/.

Keywords: RDF · Solid · Web of Things

1 Introduction

Wearables have become a common tool for tracking daily activities such as running, biking, or simply counting steps. Wearable manufacturers try to bind users to their ecosystem by not adopting a unified interface. As a result, users face two challenges: interacting with devices from different manufacturers requires multiple applications, and the applications store collected data in varying data formats on manufacturer-controlled storage systems.

Research providing parts of the solution to the interoperability and data storage challenges already exists. On the one hand, the W3C recommendation Web of Things (WoT) addresses accessing arbitrary devices using a semantic interface description called Thing Description (TD) [6]. On the other hand, the Social Linked Data (Solid) project focuses on breaking up silos by using the Resource Description Framework (RDF) and giving users back ownership of personal data [7]. However, the two components must be combined to provide a comprehensive end-to-end solution for collecting data from different devices, converting the collected data into an open human- and machine-readable format, and storing it in user-owned storage systems.

A. Meroño Peñuela et al. (Eds.): ESWC 2024, LNCS 15344, pp. 336–339, 2025.
https://doi.org/10.1007/978-3-031-78952-6_53

Previous authors have implemented the WoT standards to gather measurements from wearables [2], or store health data in Solid servers [1,3]. Research connecting the WoT standard with Solid exists, but it does not map the data gathered via WoT technologies to existing ontologies [5] or lacks a user interface enabling everyday users to use the developed approaches [4].

Our demo paper presents a user-friendly Android application that can seamlessly interact with Bluetooth Low Energy (BLE) wearables described by TDs. The application collects data from wearables converts the collected data into RDF using the Sensor, Observation, Sample, and Actuator (SOSA/SSN) ontology[1], annotates the resulting SOSA observations with additional information such as location and time, and stores the RDF data in the users' Solid server. In addition, the application visualizes measurement data retrieved from Solid servers.

2 Architecture

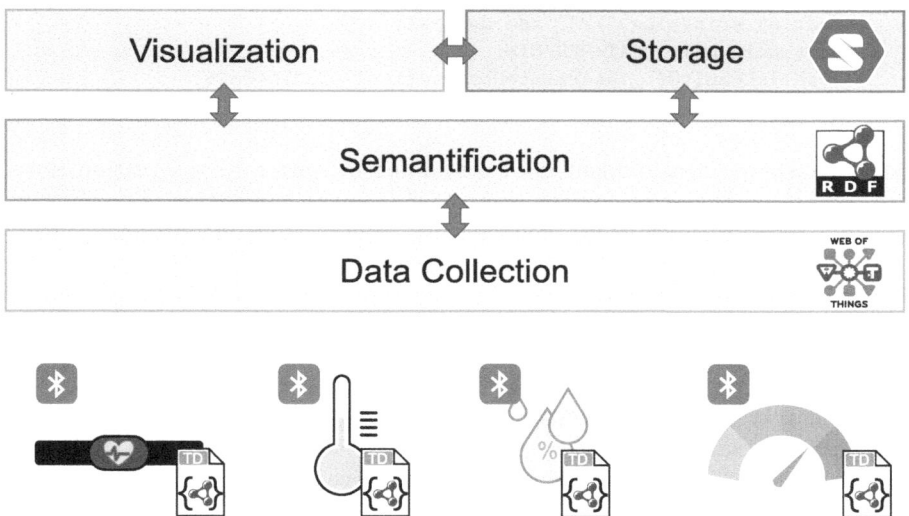

Fig. 1. Layers of the application

Figure 1 shows an overview of the application's layers. The lowest layer, the Data Collection Layer, is responsible for discovering and interacting with BLE devices to collect data. To enable out-of-the-box compatibility for varying devices, the Data Collection layer implements the WoT recommendations. All gathered data passes the Semantification layer, our connection of the WoT with Solid. The

---

[1] https://www.w3.org/TR/vocab-ssn/.

Semantification layer converts the measurement data to RDF and adds semantic annotations using the vocabulary of established ontologies by the W3C and the QUDT.org organization. An example of gathered data annotated with these ontologies is shown in Listing 1.1.

```
1  @prefix qudt: <http://qudt.org/2.1/schema/qudt#>.
2  @prefix unit: <http://qudt.org/2.1/vocab/unit#>.
3  @prefix geo: <http://www.w3.org/2003/01/geo/wgs84_pos#>.
4  @prefix sosa: <http://www.w3.org/ns/sosa/>.
5  @prefix xsd: <http://www.w3.org/2001/XMLSchema#>.
6  @prefix s4wear: <https://saref.etsi.org/saref4wear/> .
7
8  _:heartrateObservation1702382040625 a sosa:Observation;
9     sosa:hasFeatureOfInterest <https://ex.solidpod/profile/card#me>;
10    sosa:resultTime "2023-12-12T11:54:00.625Z"^^xsd:dateTime;
11    sosa:observedProperty s4wear:HeartRate;
12    geo:lat "49.594672"^^unit:DEG;
13    geo:long "11.0033571"^^unit:DEG;
14    sosa:hasResult _:heartrateResult1702382040625.
15 _:heartrateResult1702382040625 a sosa:Result;
16    qudt:numericValue "72"^^xsd:decimal;
17    qudt:unit unit:BEAT-PER-MIN;
18    sosa:isResultOf _:heartrateObservation1702382040625.
```

Listing 1.1. Heart rate measurement data annotated with semantic information

Listing 1.1 shows measurement data containing a heart rate observation (lines 8–14) and the observation's result (lines 15–18) in turtle notation. The observation is modelled with the SOSA vocabulary to describe the observation's feature of interest, result time, and the observed property (lines 9–11). The geographic location of the measurement is added to the observation using the W3C's Basic Geo (WGS84 lat/long) vocabulary[2] (lines 12–13), and the SOSA result of the observation is semantically enhanced with the vocabulary of the QUDT ontology to describe the unit of measurement (lines 16–17). To generate annotations, the application retrieves the result time and geographic location each time the Semantification layer creates an observation, i.e., every time the Data Collection layer receives data from a device. The Storage layer provides the Solid WebId, and all other annotations are parsed from the device's TD. Two layers communicate with the Semantification layer: The Visualization and the Storage layers. The Storage layer provides a Solid interface to persist the annotated RDF graphs, and the Visualization layer generates representations for live data and persisted RDF data from Solid servers.

---

[2] https://www.w3.org/2003/01/geo/.

3   Demonstration

To demonstrate our approach, we connect the Polar H9[3] and the Magene heart rate sensors[4] to the application by providing their respective TDs enriched with semantic information. After connecting the devices, we present annotated RDF data of the device measurements and live plotting of the RDF data. Additionally, we demonstrate our application's ability to browse and visualize historical measurement data stored in Solid servers.

The application and videos showcasing the above functionalities are publicly available at https://github.com/derwehr/WoT-Solid/.

4   Conclusion

Our demonstration presents an end-to-end solution for collecting and storing heterogeneous data from wearable fitness devices implemented in a user-friendly Android application. The application implements the WoT standards to enable out-of-the-box interoperability with diverse devices and maps the devices' data to RDF annotated with established ontologies to improve data interoperability. The annotated RDF data is stored in Solid servers, providing decentralized storage solutions with fine-grained access control. Moreover, the application generates visualizations for live- and historical data to enable comprehensive analysis.

References

1. Ammar, N., Bailey, J.E., Davis, R.L., Shaban-Nejad, A., et al.: Using a personal health library-enabled mHealth recommender system for self-management of diabetes among underserved populations: use case for knowledge graphs and linked data. JMIR Form. Res. **5**(3), e24738 (2021)
2. Bedogni, L., Manfredini, S., Poggi, F., Rossi, D.: WISE: a semantic and interoperable web of things architecture for smart environments. In: 8th World Forum on Internet of Things (WF-IoT). IEEE (2022)
3. Calbimonte, J.P., Aidonopoulos, O., Dubosson, F., et al.: Decentralized semantic provision of personal health streams. J. Web Semant. **76**, 100774 (2023)
4. Freund, M., Fries, J., Dorsch, R., Schiller, P., Harth, A.: WoT2Pod: an architecture enabling an edge-to-cloud continuum. In: IoT 2023 (2023)
5. Fries, J., Freund, M., Harth, A.: A solid architecture for machine data exchange with access control. In: SWoCoT'23: 1st International Workshop on Semantic Web on Constrained Things (2023)
6. Lagally, M., McCool, M.: IoT interoperability with W3C web of things. In: 2022 IEEE 19th Annual Consumer Communications and Networking Conference (CCNC), pp. 1–5. IEEE (2022)
7. Sambra, A.V., Mansour, E., Hawke, S., et al.: Solid: a platform for decentralized social applications based on linked data. Technical report, MIT CSAIL & Qatar Computing Research Institute (2016)

---

[3] https://www.polar.com/en/sensors/h9-heart-rate-sensor.

[4] https://www.magene.com/sensors/52-h303-heart-rate-monitor.html.

Compatibility Challenges of the Current State-of-the-Art Provenance Tools

Rudolf Wittner[1,2](✉) and Matúš Formánek[1]

[1] Masaryk University, Žerotínovo nám. 617/9, 601 77 Brno, Czech Republic
{wittner,formanekmato}@mail.muni.cz
[2] BBMRI-ERIC, Neue Stiftingtalstrasse 2/B/6, 8010 Graz, Austria
rudolf.wittner@bbmri-eric.eu

Abstract. Provenance is information about the history of a described object. The current standard for provenance representation, W3C PROV, results from several years of efforts in the semantic web, linked data, computational workflows, databases, and other computer science-related communities. The standard is currently used as a groundwork for developing the ISO 23494 provenance standard series. During the development of the ISO standard, the PROV model's two major implementations – Prov Python and ProvToolbox – were used and found not fully compatible. This paper introduces the current standardization effort and related projects, describes issues encountered during the usage of the implementations, and discusses the potential causes and conclusions.

Keywords: provenance · standardization · Common Provenance Model · W3C PROV · ISO 23494

1 Introduction

Provenance is a record that describes people, institutions, entities, and activities involved in producing, influencing, or delivering a piece of data or a thing [1]. Depending on the actual content of provenance, it can be used for various purposes, such as to assess the trustworthiness or quality of a described object [10].

Provenance information has been investigated by various computer science communities since the eighties [7]. Database provenance [2] aimed to explain the results of a database query. Workflows provenance [4] aimed to support reproducibility of computational workflows. Semantic web, linked data, and librarian communities developed multiple ontologies for provenance for various purposes (e.g., [3,9]). The plethora of available provenance representations and ontologies motivated the researchers to understand the different representations used for provenance, the common aspects, and the reasons for differences. Consequently,

This work has been supported by EU's Horizon Europe research and innovation programme under grant agreement No 101046203 (BY-COVID project), and under grant agreement No 101131701 (EvolveBBMRI project).

a consensus on the need for a common provenance standard emerged [7]. As a result, the W3C PROV standard [5] was developed.

W3C PROV is the current major standard that supports interoperable interchange of provenance information in heterogeneous environments such as the Web [5]. The standard's core is a conceptual data model, PROV-DM [1], representing provenance as a graph, where graph nodes represent entities, activities, or agents, and edges represent their relations. The data model is expressed in PROV Ontology (PROV-O [6]) using the OWL2 Web Ontology Language (OWL2).

One of the current research focuses in the provenance domain is to enable a unified traversal, processing, and analysis of distributed provenance chains [12] – sets of mutually interconnected provenance graphs, where each of the graphs is possibly stored and managed by a different organization. Such a provenance chain documents an object that traverses multiple organizations during its life cycle, so each can provide only a part of the documentation of the object's history.

The Common Provenance Model[1] (CPM) is a current extension of the PROV-DM that supports the creation of such distributed multi-organizational provenance chains. The CPM was developed as part of the EOSC-Life project[2] and is currently being adopted and refined in other European projects, namely BY-COVID[3], BIOINDUSTRY 4.0[4], or EvolveBBMRI[5]. The CPM serves as an open conceptual foundation for the *ISO 23494 Provenance information model for biological material and data* [11] provenance standard series, which is currently under development. However, despite more than ten years of presence of the accepted W3C PROV standard, the two major implementations of the PROV-DM – Prov library[6] for Python and ProvToolbox library[7] for Java – were found not fully compatible[8] during their adoption in the aforementioned projects.

2   Results

The ProvToolbox and Prov Python libraries enable Java/Python representation of PROV-DM and support conversions between various formats, such as PROV-O (RDF) or PROV-JSON. As the libraries implement the same standard for provenance representation, they are naturally expected to be compatible, meaning that we can serialize provenance using one library and deserialize it with the other. Despite the presence of proper compatibility tests of the libraries[9],

---

[1] https://commonprovenancemodel.org/.
[2] https://www.eosc-life.eu/.
[3] https://by-covid.org/.
[4] https://bioindustry4.hub.inrae.fr/.
[5] https://www.bbmri-eric.eu/scientific-collaboration/evolvebbmri/.
[6] https://pypi.org/project/prov/.
[7] https://lucmoreau.github.io/ProvToolbox/.
[8] The term compatibility is used in the sense that one library can generate a provenance representation that can not be parsed or is misinterpreted by the other.
[9] https://github.com/openprov/interop-test-harness.

several compatibility issues were found during the current standardization and adoption efforts, for instance:

1. Identifiers in PROV are qualified names (IRIs) that consist of a namespace and a local part. Both libraries enable serialization of provenance containing an identifier with a space in the local part of the identifier, but ProvTool-box can not deserialize such a document when it is serialized in PROV-N notation [8].
2. ProvToolbox expects that the "prov" and "xsd" namespaces are explicitly defined in the PROV-JSON serialization. However, according to PROV-JSON specification, the namespaces are implicit, which causes deserialization issues when a PROV-JSON file is serialized using the Prov Python library, which does not explicitly define the namespaces.
3. There is a difference in how the ProvToolbox and the Prov Python represent microseconds in timestamps. During deserialization between the implementations, both libraries can experience some loss of information.
4. If a PROV-JSON document contains "prefix.default" node, the ProvToolbox does not consider it as a default namespace but adds it to *regular* names-paces and adds an implicit default namespace, which negatively affects the interpretation of identifiers with the original default namespace.

A demonstration and descriptions of the complete list of the issues experienced are available at Github repository[10]. The issues were found between Prov-Toolbox version 2.0.2 and Prov Python version 2.0.0. The issues were reported to the authors of the libraries and have been fixed already.

3   Discussion and Conclusions

The presence of SW bugs is common, and fixing bugs is a standard part of a SW development process. Additionally, the PROV standard is relatively extensive, and it may be very difficult to capture all bugs and potential compatibility issues during the development of libraries, so it can be expected that some bugs emerge during the proper adoption of the tools. This is to say that we do not consider the issues encountered to be the fault of the libraries' authors. Based on these presumptions, we deduce that the implemented tools were probably used **in an isolated way**, so adopters of the libraries had no chance to encounter the aforementioned issues during their adoption. However, isolated usage of tools in heterogeneous environments, such as the Web, for which the underlying PROV standard is intended, can hardly be feasible.

In addition, as the provenance-related research in the last decade was mostly focused on prototyping new technologies, adoption of the PROV-DM in various domains, or demonstrating new research outcomes, minor bugs, which are oth-erwise critically important from the compatibility perspective, could have been ignored (e.g., the issue 4. in the list above). As a result, we encourage everyone

---

[10] https://github.com/mf-16/bakalarka.

to report any bugs they encounter despite not preventing the usage of a particular tool for intended usage. Continuous responsible reporting of bugs could have accelerated the adoption of the tools and the PROV standard in the ongoing research and standardization efforts.

Acknowledgements. We want to acknowledge the authors of the provenance libraries, namely Luc Moreau and Trung Dong Huynh, who rapidly fixed reported bugs and provided insights into how the libraries are meant to be used.

References

1. Belhajjame, K., et al.: PROV-DM: the PROV data model. W3C Recommendation (2013)
2. Buneman, P., Khanna, S., Wang-Chiew, T.: Why and where: a characterization of data provenance. In: Van den Bussche, J., Vianu, V. (eds.) ICDT 2001. LNCS, vol. 1973, pp. 316–330. Springer, Heidelberg (2001). https://doi.org/10.1007/3-540-44503-X_20
3. da Silva, P.P., McGuinness, D.L., Fikes, R.: A proof markup language for semantic web services. Inf. Syst. **31**(4), 381–395 (2006). https://doi.org/10.1016/j.is.2005.02.003, the Semantic Web and Web Services
4. Davidson, S.B., Freire, J.: Provenance and scientific workflows: challenges and opportunities. In: Proceedings of the 2008 ACM SIGMOD International Conference on Management of Data. SIGMOD '08, pp. 1345–1350. Association for Computing Machinery, New York, NY, USA (2008). https://doi.org/10.1145/1376616.1376772
5. Groth, P., Moreau, L.: PROV-overview. W3C Working Group Note (2013)
6. Lebo, T., et al.: Prov-o: the prov ontology. W3C Recommendation (2013)
7. Moreau, L., Groth, P., Cheney, J., Lebo, T., Miles, S.: The rationale of prov. J. Web Semant. **35**, 235–257 (2015). https://doi.org/10.1016/j.websem.2015.04.001
8. Moreau, L., Missier, P., Cheney, J., Soiland-Reyes, S.: Prov-n: the provenance notation. W3C Recommendation (2013)
9. Sahoo, S.S., Sheth, A.P.: Provenir ontology: towards a framework for eScience provenance management (2009)
10. Simmhan, Y.L., Plale, B., Gannon, D.: A survey of data provenance in e-science. SIGMOD Rec. **34**(3), 31–36 (2005). https://doi.org/10.1145/1084805.1084812
11. Wittner, R., et al.: Toward a common standard for data and specimen provenance in life sciences. Learn. Health Syst. **8**(1), e10365 (2024). https://doi.org/10.1002/lrh2.10365
12. Wittner, R., et al.: Lightweight distributed provenance model for complex real-world environments. Sci. Data **9**(1), 503 (2022). https://doi.org/10.1038/s41597-022-01537-6

Author Index

© The Editor(s) (if applicable) and The Author(s), under exclusive license
to Springer Nature Switzerland AG 2025
A. Meroño Peñuela et al. (Eds.): ESWC 2024, LNCS 15344, pp. 345–348, 2025.
https://doi.org/10.1007/978-3-031-78952-6

The manufacturer's authorised representative in the EU is Springer
Nature Customer Service Centre GmbH, Europaplatz 3, 69115 Heidelberg,
Germany. If you have any concerns regarding our products, please
contact ProductSafety@springernature.ccm

Printed and bound by CPI Group (UK) Ltd, Croydon, CR0 4YY

27/04/2026

02097586-0011